D1029277

Problem-Finding in
Educational Administration

Problem-Finding in Educational Administration

Trends in Research and Theory

Edited by
Glenn L. Immegart
William Lowe Boyd
University of Rochester

LexingtonBooks
D.C. Heath and Company
Lexington, Massachusetts
Toronto

Library of Congress Cataloging in Publication Data

Main entry under title:

Problem-finding in educational administration.

    Proceedings of a seminar held in Rochester, N.Y. in May 1977.
    Includes index.
    1. School management and organization—Congresses. 2. School manage-
ment and organization—Research—Congresses. 3. Problem solving—Congresses. I. Immegart, Glenn L. II. Boyd, William L.
LB 2806.P76   371.2   78-19912
ISBN 0-669-02438-4

Published simultaneously in Canada.

Printed in the United States of America.

International Standard Book Number: 0-669-02438-4

Library of Congress Catalog Card Number: 78-19912

For our wives—Mary Lou and Emily—and our children—Mary Sue and Heidi, and Stephen, Katherine, and Anne.

Contents

Preface and Acknowledgments

Educational administration as a field of practice and a context for research is vibrant and changing. Although it is not a new field, educational administration has seen much expansion and considerable redirection since the mid-1950s, when leaders in the field substantially upgraded graduate level preparation and shifted to a concern for theory, research, and a more scholarly perspective. These developments have been detailed elsewhere but are not unrelated to this book, which presents the proceedings of a Career Development Seminar on research in educational administration, cosponsored by the University of Rochester and the University Council on Educational Administration (UCEA) and held in Rochester, New York in May 1977.

Largely as a result of the numerous challenges to public education from its turbulent environment of recent years, there has been considerable reassessment and soul-searching in educational administration. Questions about the quality and utility of research on educational administration have been one of the persistent themes in much of the critical analysis, but typically these questions have been subordinated to other considerations in most journal articles and conferences. Indeed, despite widespread professed emphasis on inquiry in departments of educational administration, this book reports the first systematic collective assessment of research in the field as a whole since 1959, when UCEA and the U.S. Office of Education sponsored a series of three regional seminars on research in educational administration, leading to the publication in 1963 of *Educational Research: New Perspectives.*

In a complex venture such as the University of Rochester-UCEA Seminar and this book, we naturally are indebted to many for their assistance and contributions. Most particularly we are appreciative of the scholarship and work of the contributing authors. Dean James I. Doi, of the Graduate School of Education and Human Development at the University of Rochester, provided the critical financial support and intellectual climate for the seminar and the encouragement and facilitation necessary for publication of the proceedings. Our national planning committee was invaluable in providing direction for the seminar. We also appreciate the contributions of UCEA and Dr. Jack Culbertson, UCEA's executive director, to the overall project. UCEA provided encouragement and specific assistance as well as the seminar model or framework—the Career Development Seminar—within which this assessment took place. Dr. Culbertson was actively involved in the seminar planning and implementation, and he and the UCEA staff supported and promoted our efforts in many ways.

Our colleagues on the faculty of the Center for the Study of Educational Administration at the University of Rochester also were very helpful in the planning and implementation of the seminar as well as in the editing of this book. We appreciate the assistance of two Center graduate students, Mr. William Faucette and Mr. David Ragusa. Mr. Faucette assisted ably in the implementation and operation of the seminar, and Mr. Ragusa competently assisted in the editing and production of this book. As usual, our Center's secretaries, Miss Muriel Parkin and Mrs. Emma Drysdale, contributed in countless ways to the seminar and the book. In particular, Miss Parkin carried major responsibility for the seminar arrangements and the preparation of the final manuscript. She also shouldered the brunt of the work in obtaining permission to reprint material. The willing and able assistance of Mrs. Mildred Heffer, of the Graduate School, in typing the manuscript is likewise appreciated. To the many others who assisted, in small or large measure, we are also grateful.

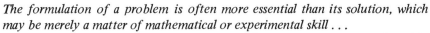

The formulation of a problem is often more essential than its solution, which may be merely a matter of mathematical or experimental skill . . .
—Albert Einstein and Leopold Infeld

Introduction: Problem-Finding in a Turbulent Professional Field

Glenn L. Immegart and
William Lowe Boyd

Robert Lynd observed that "the controlling factor in any science is the way it views and states its problems."[1] In the field of educational administration, there is evidence that this "controlling factor" is in a state of significant transition. Indeed, the views developed by the contributors to this book suggest that the field may be in the midst of a paradigm shift. Thus, the theme of this book, the importance of problem-finding and problem formulation in both research and practice, is a peculiarly appropriate one for educational administration at this time.

Presently, educational administration is a field characterized by turbulence from both without and within. Changes in the environment of public education and concomitant changes within the profession of educational administration have created a number of significant tensions and confusions. Since the external turbulence, associated with such problems as unrest among minority groups and taxpayers, has been the subject of many penetrating commentaries,[2] we shall pass over it here to focus on the more neglected matter of internal turbulence in the field.

With the barrage of criticisms and new problems generated by the turbulent environment of public education since the mid-sixties, and the frequent inability of either practitioners or researchers in educational administration to respond adequately to these developments, there came an increasing disenchantment with much of the research and theory that supposedly informed the field. Largely as a result of this, the degree of unity existing among scholars of educational administration—focused mainly around theories of administrative behavior—began to decline sharply. In the search for new models and theories better suited to the new challenges the field faced, new specializations and subfields blossomed rapidly. The result was increasing fragmentation of the field. This tendency toward balkanization exacerbated communication problems within the field and added internal cacophony to external discord.

The growing disarray of the field naturally prompted a number of scholars to attempt to assess what was happening and where the field was going. These personalized assessments, although useful, were usually limited to a few segments of the fragmented field and seldom resulted in any productive, sustained dialogue among scholars or practitioners. Two very general, but hardly very helpful, conclusions were that the research emphasis within the field was more professed than practiced and that the quality of the research needed much improvement. Surprisingly, as noted in the preface, despite the obvious need for some kind of collective assessment to place these individual assessments into perspective, prior to 1977 the only conference on research in the field as a whole occurred in 1959.

Thus, because of the clear need for a systematic collective assessment of the status of research in educational administration, and because of the appearance of some signs of promising themes and patterns within the segmentation of efforts in the area, the faculty of the Center for the Study of Educational Administration at the University of Rochester initiated conversations in 1975 with the University Council for Educational Administration (UCEA). This ultimately led to a jointly sponsored Career Development Seminar on the subject in May 1977. There was agreement that the time was ripe for such a venture, both because of the long lapse since the first such conference and because of the unusual ferment within the field.

A single seminar in an expanding and changing field cannot attend to everything. It was decided, therefore, to focus the seminar in the hope that others, in turn, would go beyond this initial step. In the planning for the seminar, the national committee convened for this purpose was much taken with Jacob Getzel's persuasive argument for a theme emphasizing the importance of problem-finding in research. The committee felt that this theme would provide a fruitful unifying framework for approaching the categories and perspectives of research deriving from the practice of educational administration and from disciplinary perspectives.[3] It was also clear that the problem-finding theme provided a linkage to other matters the committee felt should be emphasized, namely, directions for future inquiry and selected methodological issues and variables affecting research in educational administration.

As a number of scholars have observed, care in the formulation of research problems has been neglected all too often in favor of concerns about methodology, the kinds of data available or needed, and the like.[4] The result frequently is the opportunistic application of "increasingly sophisticated techniques on increasingly sterile ideas."[5] Moreover, in an applied field of study, such as educational administration, the importance of the quality of problem-finding and formulation skills is not limited just to researchers; decision- and policy-making, which are at the heart of the practice of administration, are also contingent on these skills.

Or so we have been given to understand. In the present ferment in theory about the behavior of educational organizations, it is significant that Michael Cohen and James March challenge this line of thinking.[6] However, they do so in a way that may sharpen our sense of how the complex and little-understood process of problem formulation occurs, particularly in educational organizations. Cohen and March argue that decision opportunities are basically ambiguous stimuli in organizations, such as schools and colleges, where the organizational ends and means are unclear, and participation and membership within the organization fluctuates rapidly. With such organizations in mind, they propose, possibly with some exaggeration, that

> Although organizations can often be viewed as vehicles for solving well-defined problems and as structures within which conflict is resolved through bargaining, they are also sets of procedures through which organizational participants arrive at an interpretation of what they are doing and what they have done while doing it. From this point of view, an organization is a collection of choices looking for problems, issues and feelings looking for decision situations in which they might be aired, solutions looking for issues to which they might be the answer, and decision makers looking for work.[7]

In what they view, from this perspective, as organizations utilizing a "garbage can" rather than a "rational" model of organizational choice, they conclude that "Despite the dictum that you cannot find the answer until you have formulated the question well, you often do not know what the question is in organizational problem solving until you know the answer."[8]

Many practitioners and scholars in educational administration will appreciate the "messiness" of the process of organizational choice that Cohen and March emphasize. Indeed, if they are right—and we shall consider this question in the final chapter—problem formulation in educational organizations, and consequently to some extent in the study of educational administration, may be more difficult than in many other domains of activity. In any event, their analysis calls attention to the fact that problem formulation in research and practice—and perhaps particularly in organizations with the characteristics of those in the educational realm—generally occurs through a process of successive approximations in which—it is hoped—the questions will become more intelligent as time goes on. Yet, in research, especially in a time of ferment and disagreement, there also frequently is a dialectical process going on in which competing problem formulations ultimately elicit a synthesis that restates the problem in a fresh and novel way, often opening up new vistas. Part of the reason for holding the University of Rochester-UCEA seminar was the hope of gaining glimpses of such vistas. Although it is clear that much cacophony remains within the field, we believe that this hope has been realized to a surprising degree.

In editing the proceedings of a conference, the common approach is to provide commentaries at the outset, and at the beginning of sections of the book, that will help to place the contents into perspective and highlight important themes. Instead of pursuing this approach, we have elected to try to let the data "speak for themselves," as Thomas B. Greenfield might say. Although we believe that there are important unifying themes running through the book, and, moreover, even believe that these themes suggest that the controlling factor in the field is changing, we recognize that there is sure to be disagreement about what the contents add up to. Rather than interject interpretive material that might color the thinking of readers, we have decided to present our conclusions in the final chapter. Thus, readers who work their way straight through the book can compare their assessment of the contents with ours. On the other hand, if they wish, they can read the last chapter first and then compare the conclusions there with those they form in reading the book. (A third alternative, of course—which we hope few readers will choose—is to skip the final chapter altogether.)

In the light of the theme and purposes of the seminar, one set of the invited papers was focused on research problems or questions and the productivity of inquiry in well-defined areas reflecting research from the orientations of practice and disciplines. The authors were asked to develop their papers with the following questions in mind: Have we been asking the right questions? How productive have our research problems been? What are promising research questions and lines of inquiry? What factors affect the quality of research in educational administration? A second set of invited papers focused on selected methodological issues (for example, "hard" versus "soft" approaches and field-based inquiry) and on variables affecting inquiry in the professional field of educational administration (that is, the state of knowledge in educational administration, institutional factors, and characteristics of the researchers themselves).

By drawing on the talents of respected authorities and experienced researchers in the field, the papers represent the continuing analysis and thought of the authors about their areas of expertise. At the same time, and crucial to the purposes of the seminar, mechanisms were built in to provide for the collective assessment of the proceedings. Thus, although none of the seminar discussions appear in this book, they were used as sounding boards for the authors in subsequent revisions or refinement of their chapters. Equally as important, the seminar discussions also are reflected implicitly in the remarks of the seminar critics in chapter 13 as well as the concluding chapter. Together, these chapters attempt to both capture and enhance the collective assessment running through the deliberations of the seminar.

In part I, the theme of problem-finding is introduced in the remarks of University of Rochester President Robert L. Sproull as he opened the seminar. The theme is then developed in rich detail in Professor Jacob W. Getzels' keynote presentation for the seminar (chapter 1). Both Sproull and Getzels address the critical nature of the formulation of the research question or problem and the need to attend to the quality of problems in improving research. Their statements also underscore the value of dialogue and reflection in assessing inquiry. In developing the theme of problem-finding and formulation, Getzels specifically discusses the implications for graduate education and research and for practice in educational administration. Chapter 2, by Professor R. Oliver Gibson, analyzes the historical development of thought and the state of knowledge in the field of educational administration. Gibson documents paradigm shift in the field and suggests that the field has just entered a new stage, which he calls "critical consciousness."

The chapters in part II critically assess research activity in well-defined areas of inquiry deriving from the realm of practice in educational administration. In chapter 3, Dean Daniel E. Griffiths appraises the large body of research on administration and administrative behavior. He focuses on problems related to what is researched, the transferability of findings, and the quality of theory. In chapter 4, Professor Donald J. Willower assesses inquiry related to school operations and organization. He examines issues in the three areas of the methodology of research, the relation of theory and research, and the linkage of research and practice. In chapter 5, Professor James W. Guthrie analyzes research from the areas of educational finance, law, and policy. He frames his assessment in terms of progress relative to the values of equality, efficiency, and liberty. In each of the chapters in this section, the authors make suggestions for the improvement of research and theory.

Part III presents critical assessments of research on educational administration emanating from two disciplinary domains. Professor Charles E. Bidwell discusses research based on theory and concepts from sociology in chapter 6. He focuses on inquiry on the school as a formal organization and on what has been overlooked by researchers in this area. On the basis of recent research, he provides numerous examples and suggestions for the directions such inquiry should take. In chapter 7, Professor Frederick M. Wirt assesses studies of educational administration deriving from the perspectives of political science. He covers inquiry on educational politics and the political context of education and sets forth a research agenda from the vantage point of political science.

In part IV, the authors address their analysis to methodological issues and other factors affecting research in educational administration. In chapter 8, Dean William H. Meckling underscores the need for scientific rigor in administrative research and notes the uniqueness of administration in the public educational sector and the implications of this for inquiry. In chapter 9, Professor Thomas B. Greenfield analyzes the effects of ideas or theoretical concepts on methodology and develops the notion that ideas bias both inquiry procedures and what is seen in data. Professor James F. McNamara is concerned, in chapter 10, with the credibility of research in educational administration. He also addresses the importance of field inquiry (research in schools) and quantitative approaches in research. In chapter 11, Professors Emil J. Haller and Kenneth A. Strike view educational policy as an important realm of choice and an area where inquiry can contribute to practice. They develop a model for policy research in an applied field and provide a range of research leads and methodological insights.

Chapter 12 analyzes variables affecting research in the professional field of educational administration. In the first part of the chapter, Professor Glenn L. Immegart looks at researchers in departments of educational administration and the effect of developments in relation to these researchers on the study of educational administration. In the second part of the chapter, Dean Howard S. Bretsch discusses organizational or institutional variables in higher education settings that condition the quantity and quality of the research efforts of professors.

The two concluding chapters in part V attempt to place the seminar into critical perspective. Chapter 13 presents the summary remarks of three seminar participants who were asked to serve as critics and synthesizers: Daniel E. Griffiths, Charles E. Bidwell, and Dean Arthur S. Goldberg. Their commentaries reflect the tenor of the seminar discussions and present their own critical reactions to the seminar papers as well as suggestions for inquiry based on the collective assessment. In the final chapter, the editors focus on the lines of convergence that emerge from the chapters of this book. The synthesis they arrive at provides some clear directions for future research and raises some potentially controversial issues about the forces that have shaped the character of research and practice in educational administration.

The rich diversity of views in the following chapters makes it clear that there is no shortage of problems for productive research in educational administration. Some of these problems are clearly identified, especially in the converging views of a number of the authors. But still other problems, and perhaps some of the most fruitful ones, will have to be discovered by those with minds that can grasp, in the richness and tension of the diverging views and models, the hidden promise of a new problem formulation. The essence of such a quest was captured long ago in the words of Shakespeare:

> And thus do we of wisdom and of reach
> With windlasses and with assays of bias,
> By indirections find directions out.

Notes

1. Robert Lynd, as quoted in Ira Katznelson, "The Crisis of the Capitalist City," in Willis D. Hawley et al., *Theoretical Perspectives on Urban Politics* (Englewood Cliffs, N.J.: Prentice-Hall, 1976), p. 216.

2. For a perceptive synthesis concerning the external turbulence affecting educational administration, see Frederick M. Wirt, "Political Turbulence and Administrative Authority in the Schools," in Louis H. Masotti and Robert L. Lineberry, eds., *The New Urban Politics* (Cambridge, Mass.: Ballinger, 1976), pp. 61-89.

3. In light of the fact that Professor Getzels takes as his text, in his

seminar keynote address (chapter 1), Albert Einstein's famous statement on the importance of problem formulation, it is quite fitting that this book is being published in 1979, the year of the hundredth anniversary of Einstein's birth.

4. See, for example, Robert K. Merton, "Notes on Problem-Finding in Sociology," in Robert K. Merton et al., *Sociology Today* (New York: Basic Books, 1959), pp. ix-xxxiv.

5. Personal communication from Donald Erickson, January 15, 1979.

6. Michael D. Cohen and James G. March, *Leadership and Ambiguity* (New York: McGraw-Hill, 1974).

7. Ibid., p. 81.

8. Ibid., p. 82.

Part I
Problem-Finding and Paradigm Shift in Educational Administration

Looking back, I think it was more difficult to see what the problems were than to solve them . . .

—Charles Darwin

Text of Opening Remarks to the Seminar on Research in Educational Administration

Robert L. Sproull

It is a distinct pleasure to open this seminar on research in educational administration. Part of the pleasure comes from welcoming you colleagues from other institutions to a conference where we will be stimulated by your imagination and accomplishments. Part comes from the circumstance that during the last half dozen years our own College of Education (now Graduate School of Education and Human Development) has been transformed by its faculty and its Dean to a research orientation.

There is, of course, nothing wrong with the orientation toward practitioners, but the nation has many such institutions. Almost all of them vastly exceed us in size, and most have large tax revenues and substantial constituencies behind them. We will necessarily remain small and must therefore choose our areas of concentration; we have chosen to emphasize research and the kind of graduate education that comes naturally in a research-oriented institution.

We hope to contribute in a courageous way. For example, state-supported institutions may have some diffidence about research on financing education. Such research can hardly be value-free or implication-free. We hope to serve best by undertaking research that could have unpopular consequences. I personally hope that this work on finance eventually includes the financing of higher education, an area that cries out for fresh attention.

The emphasis of this seminar on the formulation of problems is also something I cordially welcome. There can be no doubt of its importance. When we face crucial decisions of attracting or promoting faculty, a key element is always the taste of the individual in selecting problems and the questions he asks in undertaking his research. The taste of one who selects only easy problems or works in areas not likely to have consequences can hardly be applauded. His work can be pure but can hardly be basic, either to applications or to continued development of the structure of his field of knowledge. As to questions, only the very young think that every question has an answer. A student of calculus who reduces his understanding to the level of asking, "What is zero divided by zero?" or "What is infinity divided by infinity?" is never going to learn calculus. A student of physics who asks, "Is the electron a wave or a particle?" just cannot get there from here. A person who asks, "What is the color of a mirror?" does not understand what a mirror is. Formulation of problems, asking the rewarding and pregnant question—that is the essence of the research that others will rely on and use.

Another theme of this seminar is the counterpoint between research arising from the disciplines and research suggested by real problems in the field. Both kinds are promising, but I celebrate especially the latter. The key feat of imagination is to distill the generalizable from the specific. If this element is lacking, the research is sterile and only "explains" (or, less, only describes) a situation localized in space and time; others cannot stand on its shoulders.

One corollary of research stimulated from the field is that it helps to give graduate students (in Harvey Brooks' phrase) *"respect for applied problems."* It is a constant need in graduate education to encourage students to reach out, to apply, to do anything other than to emulate their professors. Stimulation from the problems of people in the field can be a big help to generate respect for those who have to wrestle with field problems.

My only unhappiness with this seminar is that it does not extend into the administration of higher education. Research in this area is very thin indeed. There are a small number of seminal papers and books, but a large bulk of publications are by "high priests" who rewrite their theses over and over.

At the other extreme of the higher education axis are we practitioners. We are all really amateurs. We try to add to our (I hope) competence in our own fields enough accounting, law, personnel management, finance, and public relations skills to get by. We have to add the acquisition of a great deal of patience, often used to learn things (usually about people) we would rather not know. Some of us make quick trips to seminars or short courses in educational administration, but we are still just amateurs.

Thus, when you get K through 12 in better shape, please come help us poor devils.

1

Problem-Finding and Research in Educational Administration

Jacob W. Getzels

I take as my text the statement by Albert Einstein: "The formulation of a problem is often more essential than its solution, which may be merely a matter of mathematical or experimental skill. To raise new questions, new possibilities, to regard old questions from a new angle, requires creative imagination and marks real advance in science."[1]

This, I shall argue, is true not only in science but in all inquiry and thought, including research in educational administration. Max Wertheimer generalized Einstein's point in the classic treatise, *Productive Thinking:*

> The function of thinking is not just solving an actual problem but discovering, envisaging, going into deeper questions. Often in great discoveries the most important thing is that a certain question is found. Envisaging, putting the productive question is often more important, often a greater achievement than solution of a set question.[2]

Need problems be *found*?[3] Is not the world already teeming with problems and dilemmas at home and in business, in economics and in education, in art and in science—and surely in the administration of our schools? The world is of course teeming with dilemmas. But the dilemmas do not present themselves automatically as *problems* capable of resolution or even sensible contemplation. They must be posed and formulated in fruitful and often radical ways if they are to be moved toward solution. The way the problem is posed is the way the dilemma will be resolved.

Let me contrive a simple example to illustrate the distinction I shall be making throughout between *dilemma* and *problem.*[4] An automobile is traveling on a deserted country road and blows a tire. The occupants of the automobile go to the trunk and discover there is no jack. They define the dilemma by posing the problem: Where can we get a jack? They recall that they had not seen any habitation nearby but that several miles back they had passed a service station, and they decide to walk to the station for a jack. While they are gone, another automobile coming from the other direction also blows a tire. The occupants of this automobile go to the trunk and, by the happy coincidence needed for our example, they too discover that there is no jack. They define the dilemma by posing the problem: How can we raise the automobile? They look about and see that adjacent to the road is a barn with a pulley for lifting bales of hay to the loft. They move the automobile to the barn, raise it on the pulley, change the tire, and drive off, while the occupants of the first car are still trudging toward the service station.

I exclaim, "What a clever solution!" Einstein's ghost, who happens to be hovering about, hears me and says, "No, what a clever question!" For the quality of the solution that was attained was a function of the quality of the question that was formulated. The same dilemma faced the occupants of both cars. But those in the first car transformed the dilemma into the problem: How can we get a jack, which pointed to one policy and course of action. Those in the second car transformed the same dilemma into a different problem: "How can we raise the car," which pointed to another policy and course of action. And this—finding and formulating the problem—made all the difference in the quality of the solutions reached by the two groups to the identical dilemma. Precisely the same issue—as we shall see—is crucial in research in educational administration: How shall a problem—the productive problem—be posed?

What is extraordinary and fascinating is that despite the self-evident effect of the quality of problems on the quality of solutions, and despite the manifest function of new problems in guiding thought toward new solutions, very little is known about how problems are found and formulated. Although there are dozens of theoretical treatises and literally thousands of empirical studies of problem-solving, there are hardly any systematic theoretical or empirical studies of problem-finding itself. Indeed, with the exception of our own studies that I shall be reporting here, I do not know of any previous extended empirical work on the subject.

On the Meaning and Variety of Problems

Let me begin, then, by asking you to think seriously about what is meant by a problem. Of course, you say, we know what is meant by a problem; it is hardly worth thinking about. And, in fact, in the large literature on problem-solving—whether in its own right or in educational administration and elsewhere—it is taken for granted that everyone knows what is meant by a problem.

But consider several attempts at definition.[5] Norman R.F. Maier says, "A problem exists when a response to a given situation is blocked."[6] Karl Duncker similarly says, "A problem arises when a living creature has a goal but does not know how the goal is to be reached."[7] This seems reasonable enough; a problem is an obstacle, a block toward a goal. But hear John Dewey on the same topic: "A problem represents the partial transformation of a problematic situation into a determinate situation."[8] Here a problem is no longer a block but a step toward a goal. And read Webster: A problem is "a question raised or to be raised for inquiry, consideration, discussion, decision, or solution."[9] Here, as in the case of a scientist voluntarily seeking a problem on which to work or the artist voluntarily creating a still-life problem (and even more so in recent so-called conceptual art) the problem is in a very real sense the goal itself.

One need compare only the definitions by Maier that "a problem exists when a response to a given situation is blocked" and the one by Webster that a problem is "a question raised or to be raised for inquiry" to realize at once the different—indeed, the contradictory—phenomena subsumed under the single term problem. At one extreme, a problem may refer to an undesirable situation the individual wishes to avoid or vitiate; at the other, it may refer to a desirable situation the individual strives to find or create.

From this point of view, the ordinary conception of problems as simply obstacles or blocks to a goal is misleading and by no means covers the variety of problematic situations. It is in fact this simple-minded view of the problematic, with the consequent confusion between dilemma and problem, that leads to the oft-reported perplexity of the graduate student when he is confronted with the problem of finding a problem for his dissertation research. Is he to find an obstacle? Or is the task of finding the problem the obstacle? Or put more broadly, is the problem he is given—to find a problem—the same kind of phenomenon as the problem he is supposed to find?

I have presented elsewhere a classification of some dozen types of problems, the details of which will take us too far afield here.[10] It will suffice for our present purposes to distinguish only three classes of problems or problem situations: (1) *presented problem situations,* (2) *discovered problem situations,* and (3) *created problem situations,* depending on whether the problem already exists, who propounds it, and whether it has a known formulation, known method of solution, or known solution.

In a *presented problem situation,* or to be precise in one form of it, the problem exists, it is propounded to the problem-solver, and it has a known formulation, a known method of solution, and a known solution. For example, a teacher teaches that the area of a rectangle is side a multiplied by side b, and the pupil is required to solve the problem: What is the area of a rectangle when a = 3, b = 4? Here the problem is given—it is presented—to the problem-solver, and in the particular instance, it has a known formulation, known method of solution, and known solution. This is the problem situation most prevalent by far in the school setting.

Consider now what we have called the *discovered problem situation,* or one form of it as an instance. Here the problem also exists but it is envisaged by oneself rather than propounded by another, and it may or may not have a known formulation, known method of solution, or known solution. For example, a four year old asks spontaneously, "Why does it get lighter outside when you put the light out?"[11] Or Roentgen sees a fogged photographic plate as others had before him and asks, "Why is the plate fogged?"—a self-initiated problem that led not only to the X-ray but to a revolution in atomic science. Here the problems were not presented to the individual by another; they discovered the problems themselves, and in fact took some joy in doing so. This is clearly a different order of problem situation from the presented problem situation.

Consider finally the *created problem situation*. Here the problem does not exist at all until someone invents or creates it. For example, Norman R.F. Maier invents a series of puzzles or problems to test the problem-solving abilities of his subjects; the scientist conceives of the problem: What is the nature and speed of light? The artist creates a still-life problem where no such problem existed before. Surely it makes no sense to think of these situations as merely obstacles one meets up with through ill-fortune, ignorance, or ineptitude. Quite the contrary; these problems are situations that one strives to find and formulate.

The Human Being as Problem-Finder

The view of problems as situations one must have and strives to find or create is so against the grain of common sense that I must cite a classic experiment and then several concrete instances to illustrate the point. Bexton, Heron, and Scott[12] paid subjects more than they earned by working, "just to do nothing." The subjects were well fed and comfortably housed. But there was one experimental condition: stimulation and the opportunity to deal with the problematic were minimized. The subjects could not see, hear, touch, or communicate with anyone. At first nothing happened; the subjects merely rested or slept. Soon, however, they became restless, could not sleep, and exhibited random behavior as if looking for something to do, problems to work on. The situation became so unbearable that it was impossible to keep the subjects in the experiment for more than two or three days despite the satisfaction of all their bodily needs and the high pay for presumably doing nothing. On leaving, they reported feelings of intellectual disorganization, nausea, and fatigue. As the investigators pointed out, normal behavior seems to require sensory input and, what is more important in the present context, an opportunity to seek out problems to cope with. If I may put it this way, the human being is constitutionally not only a stimulus-reducing or problem-solving organism; he is also a stimulus-seeking or problem-finding organism. He is not only a problem-solver; he is a problem-finder.

Indeed, the portion of human activity that is held in highest esteem as uniquely human—activity that can be described only as pure science, fine art, basic research—is devoted as much to finding or creating as to solving problems.[13] This behavior is not undertaken to overcome obstacles that must be overcome because they are a threat to personal well-being; on the contrary, the problems are sought out often at the risk of personal well-being and sometimes of life itself. Galileo raised questions about the accepted cosmology despite the threat of being burnt at the stake for it; Matisse gave himself the problem of painting grass red and roses green despite the derision of the established artists, who called him a "wild beast"; right now, a number of geneticists persist in asking the question, what would happen if they combined one genetic stuff with another as in recombinant DNA, despite the possibility of catastrophic outcomes.

This engagement of human beings with the problematic almost for its own sake is characteristic not only of art, science, or research, where it reaches the highest level, but of more mundane activities like working at puzzles, reading mystery stories, traveling to strange places, climbing high mountains, exploring deep caves. In all these activities, the human being is not reacting to problems as obstacles that threaten his pleasure or well-being; rather he is finding problems because they—the problems themselves—give him pleasure and serve his well-being.

All animals have a capacity for taking notice of problems as obstacles to a goal. Even machines can be programmed to sense problems. But the human being alone not only senses problems as obstacles standing in his way but goes out of his way to discover and create new problems. He is, as he has been called, a problemizing being—a being who feels the need for and a pleasure in posing problems in addition to those posed by the natural and social environment.[14]

This capacity for discovering and inventing problems and not only for solving problems (which other organisms also do), makes human thought uniquely human, and the deeper the problems found and posed (and in due course solved) the greater the human achievement. If I may refer to our taxonomy of problems, the production of discovered and created problems is often a more significant accomplishment than the production of solutions to presented problems. It is in fact the discovery and creation of problems that often sets the extraordinary scientist apart from other scientists. Such a scientist need not solve all the problems he finds and formulates; he may just feed—directly or indirectly—other scientists with problems, the solutions to which are likely to constitute advances in knowledge. The thirty-one "Queries" propounded by Newton in his *Opticks,* to cite one instance, supplied research problems for generations of investigators;[15] the creation of the problems was surely as important a scientific achievement as the solutions that were ultimately obtained. No, they were more important, for the researchers might have had nothing to do had they not been presented with the discovered or created problems.

This, at least in part, is what Einstein meant when he said that the formulation—the finding—of a problem is often a more essential achievement in science, as in research more generally, than is the solution of the problem once it has been found and formulated. It is this circumstance—its essential role in dealing with scientific, artistic, and practical dilemmas—that makes problem-finding so important a problem for inquiry in its own right.

The Empirical Study of Problem-Finding

Over a period of some years my students and I have been attempting to investigate just this: the nature of problems and the process of finding and formulating them. The results are, I think, pertinent to educational administration. We began with problem-finding in art partly by accident and partly because the problems an artist works on are visible, we assumed. We proceeded to problem-finding in more ordinary thought, then to interpersonal relations and student behavior in school, and we are just now moving gingerly into educational administration.

If the origin and form of these investigations are to be understood, a word about my research interests is needed. One interest is administrative behavior, another creative thinking, and I seem to have alternated at about six-year intervals from one to the other, at least as marked by major publications. In 1955 there was the monograph with Coladarci, *The Uses of Theory in Educational Administration;* in 1962 there was the book with Jackson, *Creativity and Intelligence: Explorations with Gifted Students;* and in 1968 there was *Educational Administration as a Social Process* with Lipham and Campbell. After completing this and almost without intending, I returned to where I had left off in the book *Creativity and Intelligence.* The outcome was the recently published volume with Csikszentmihalyi, *The Creative Vision: A Longitudinal Study of Problem Finding in Art.*[16] And now I am back to educational administration. but with insights or at least observations gained from the work in creative thinking.

The earlier investigation of creativity had been with children, and through the years one of the criticisms raised against the work had been that if one is to study creativity, why study it with children, why not with people known to be creative or at least people undertaking creative endeavor? Accordingly, in the new work we selected for investigation a group of art students at one of the world's leading art schools. We gave them the usual group of nomothetically oriented tests of personality and intellect, and in fact found highly significant relations between several of these measures and artistic achievement. For example, the correlation between low economic values as measured by the Allport-Vernon-Lindzey *Study of Values* and the grade point average in studio courses was .47—a relation almost as high as usually found between IQ and academic achievement. We were exhilarated by the results, and published them with some pride in a number of basic research journals in psychology, sociology, education, and aesthetics.[17]

But when our initial exhilaration was over, and we stepped back and surveyed the results, we were struck with the thought that they had not gotten us much closer to understanding, or even describing, creative production any more than the ubiquitous correlational studies in educational administration have gotten us very much closer to understanding or describing the process of administrative behavior. We knew something more about the *correlates* of creative performance than when we started, but we did not know much more about the *process* of creative performance. There was of course the statistically significant .47 correlation between values and creative achievement as an instance. Yet what did this say about the way in which the creative achievement was attained?

We realized that our work had been focused on only group or nomothetic observations, and we had neglected individual or idiographic observations. We were chagrined that we should have done this, since over the years we had been dismayed when the same thing had so often been perpetrated by others in educational administration when using the so-called nomothetic-idiographic model. That is, only the nomothetic aspects of the formulation were noted; the explicitly stated idiographic aspects were disregarded. They, and certainly we, should have been sensitive to the equal importance of the two types of observations; indeed, the index of *Educational Administration as a Social Process* gives a twelve-page reference for the entry *idiographic* and only a nine-page reference for *nomothetic.*[18]

In any case, we recognized that if we wished to come to grips with understanding the process of creativity, we had to find a way to observe idiographically the process through which a work of art was produced from its inception to its conclusion.

We began by watching each artist as he worked at his easel. The observations were bewildering. Everyone had his own way of working. Some proceeded rapidly, some slowly, some daubed flecks of color on the canvas with a brush, and others seemed to smear heavy smudges of paint on the canvas with a trowel. The phenomena seemed to make no sense. Yet clearly some artists were consistently more successful than others. What was it about the way they proceeded that eventuated in more original and more valuable products?

Two events converged at this point to alter our thinking about research not only into the artistic process but also into the administrative process, to which we shall come in due course. We found ourselves wondering about the difference between an advertising artist and a fine artist. We believed the difference lay in their technical skill; the fine artist was a more skillful draftsman. This was simply not so. The difference lay rather in this: When an advertising artist enters his studio, he has already been given a problem—draw an illustration for a corn-flake box, for example; when a fine artist enters his studio, he has only a blank canvas before him—he must find a problem to work on himself. That is, advertising artists worked predominantly with presented problems, and fine artists with discovered and created problems. This line of thought called attention to what Einstein had said about the critical role of problem-finding in creative science, which, it occurred to us, might be true also of creative art. And, as we shall see, it may be true more generally wherever there are dilemmas, including educational administration.

We finally recognized the obvious. We had arrived at problem-finding as a crucial phase of the creative process, and we had to observe in some way, directly or indirectly, not only how the artistic problem is solved, which we had been doing, but also how the artistic problem is found.

The methods for studying problem-solving are clear enough. If I want to observe how one goes about solving a problem, I present him or her with one of the numerous instruments devised for this purpose—say, the Kohs Blocks or the Goldstein-Scheerer Sorting Task, or for that matter the Binet or Wechsler Intelligence Tests. I watch the performance and draw inferences about the problem-solving ability and style from what was done, supplemented by what he or she reports that he or she did.

But suppose I want to observe how one finds a problem—how one discovers, creates, and formulates a problem. Now what do I do? We were surprised that despite our diligent search we were unable to locate any existing methods. There simply was no precedent for this kind of observation. We ourselves had to devise a way to observe the phenomena of problem-finding—just as ways had been devised to observe the phenomena of problem-solving.

This, without any apologies, is what we did, although on the basis of hindsight we might do many things differently now. We rented a studio at the Art School, put in it two tables, a drawing board, and a variety of drawing materials. On one table we placed a collection of some thirty objects that were used at the school to construct still-life problems. We then asked each of thirty-one fine art students to use one or more of the objects on the first table to create a still-life problem on the second table and to produce any drawing they wished of the still-life problem they had created.

We observed what they did in creating the still-life problem and in producing the drawing, and we interviewed them regarding what they had done and how they felt in the situation. In this way we were able to differentiate the quality of problem-finding behavior among the thirty-one artists along a number of dimensions—for example, the quantity of objects examined, the depth of exploration of the objects, and the uniqueness of the objects used. We ranked the thirty-one artists on the quality of their problem-finding, and then arranged an exhibition of the drawings and asked five recognized artist-critics to rank the drawings on their quality as original work. The relation between the rankings by us on the quality of the problem-finding before the drawing was begun and the ranking by the artist-critics of the originality of the finished drawings was positive; to be precise, the correlation was .54, significant at the .01 level.

The full details of the investigation are given in *The Creative Vision: A Longitudinal Study of Problem Finding in Art;*[19] I shall say no more about it except to add a word about the longitudinal phase. We waited six years after the students had graduated from art school, which was about eight years after the problem-finding observations were made, and related the problem-finding rankings to the relative success of the former students as professional artists. The relation was positive and statistically significant.

Four conclusions may be suggested from this inquiry. Problem-finding can be studied objectively; there are individual differences in problem-finding just as there are in problem-solving; there is a positive relation between the quality of a problem that is found and the quality of the solution that is reached; problem-finding ability seems to be an enduring characteristic.

Let me run quickly through the relevant results of three dissertation studies following the model and then turn at some greater length to the issue of problem-finding in educational administration.

Patricia Arlin undertook a dissertation study of the quality of problem-finding as an aspect of the thought processes of college students—a study that was to win her the biennial national Pi Lamda Theta award for the best dissertation.[20] She showed that problem-finding is not an aberrant variable but is systematically related to other aspects of human thought.

The second dissertation on this model was undertaken by Donald Schwartz, who moved the inquiry from the artistic and cognitive realms to the social domain.[21] He showed that the same interpersonal dilemma is posed by some individuals as one problem and by other individuals as another problem, and that there seems to be a hierarchy of styles of social problem-posing, producing at one extreme low-level egocentric problems and at the other extreme high-level socially sensitive problems.

The third dissertation, by Jonathan Smilansky, brought the issue of problem-finding directly into the school setting.[22] He raised the questions: If secondary school students were given complete freedom to pose any problems they wished regarding their school, what would be the content and form of the problems, and what would be the relation of the quality of problems to the personal characteristics of the students? The results were quite straightforward. The content of the problems fell into a number of well-defined categories; surprisingly, by far the most frequently mentioned problem was not "too much homework" or "low grades" but "unfair teachers"—almost 50 percent of the students gave this as a problem. The form in which the problems were posed—even when the content was the same—varied widely among students and could be categorized according to Schwartz's problem-posing styles: from egocentric to socially sensitive. There were systematic relations between both the content and form of the problems and certain characteristics of the students; for example, there was a highly significant relation between the creativity of students and their mentioning "boring teachers" as a problem. In addition, there was a significant tendency for measures of the quality of problem-posing to be positively related to measures of problem-solving.

Encouraged by these observations in art, cognition, interpersonal relations, and school behavior, I have been attempting to study administrative behavior along the same lines. More specifically, I have been studying how administrative dilemmas are posed as problems through examining actual cases provided by principals and superintendents of schools.

Although one must beware of analogies, it turns out that the processes are often very close to those of the studies just cited and to the dilemma of the flat tire, from which different problems were formulated, leading to very different policies and courses of action.

The case I shall present here as an instance was given to me by Bruce McPherson, now the director of the University of Chicago Laboratory Schools and a former superintendent of schools.[23] He related the following occurrence, edited slightly to highlight my point.

The Markham School had become increasingly overcrowded, and the larger building to replace it would not be completed for two years. In the meantime, seventeen mobile classrooms already filled Markham's playground and parking lot. But this was not sufficient to meet the influx of even more pupils the coming autumn.

The dilemma was obvious—overcrowding. Discussions among the superintendent, the principal, and the president of the board of education led to the following formulation: should more mobile classrooms be obtained, or should the excess children be sent to other schools? Note, if you will, how the dilemma had been transformed into the two problems of whether to get more mobile classrooms or whether to get rid of children. The principal pointed out that getting more mobile classrooms would mean using up the last bit of open space around his school; the superintendent pointed out that getting rid of children from Markham would mean overcrowding other schools in his district.

There the matter rested until the superintendent realized that the problem was not really getting more mobile classrooms nor getting rid of children. The problem was really how to get more space. Here then was the same dilemma transformed into yet another problem. The superintendent talked to an architect, who suggested the possibility of erecting a new temporary building on a nearby empty lot which would meet school code requirements but could also be converted easily to a facility for business or industry.

The temporary school building was constructed in several months, and the overflow pupils were transferred to it when the school year began. When the new permanent school was finished, the temporary school was vacated and sold at no loss to a local manufacturer. Observe, if you will, the similarity of this actual situation to the paridigmatic instance—getting a jack or raising the car, more mobile classrooms or more space?

Although this process of going from a dilemma to a problem seems quite typical, I have also come across instances where the administrator goes in the opposite direction. That is, he moves from the already formulated problem that is brought to him and goes back to the dilemma before accepting at face value the problem as given to him. In effect, to refer to my model of problem situations, he alters the presented problem situation into a discovered problem situation. This, say a number of administrators, may in fact be the more frequent case and the more difficult administrative condition; once someone has transformed a dilemma into a particular problem, it is hard to see the dilemma as any other problem.

Here is an account of such a case, also given to me by McPherson, again, edited slightly. Joe Daniels, the new English teacher, had been hired just before the opening of the school year. He had the reputation of being a superb teacher but also rather abrasive in his relationships with administrators. On the first day of school, one-half hour before the bell for the first period, Joe walked into the principal's office and made a request: "I like to sit on a high stool when I am teaching. Could you get one for me?" In our terms, this was the presented problem.

The principal thought quickly. Joe did not have a permanent classroom; his four classes would be taught in different rooms on various floors and corners of the building. Did Joe really want one stool? Would he carry it up and down the stairs with him? Joe seemed serious enough in his request, but the principal wondered what Joe was really asking. What was the dilemma behind the problem? The principal decided that either consciously or unconsciously Joe was testing the teacher-administrator relationship at the school. Would the new administrator be like all the others, or would a teacher really receive assistance, even when his requests seem somewhat eccentric?

If the discovered rather than the presented problem was the real issue, then the principal felt he had to respond quickly and decisively. He hurriedly located the custodian; together they found four stools and placed one in each of the four rooms before the first period began, explaining to the homeroom teachers that Mr. Daniels would be using the high chair the rest of the year. In McPherson's words, "At the end of the day Daniels came into the principal's office with outstretched hand and a warm smile of admiration; for his entire tenure at the school he was the principal's staunchest advocate."

Looking at administrative behavior from the standpoint of problem-finding has so far been as illuminating for us as looking at artistic behavior from the same standpoint. I do not know whether six years hence I shall have a volume titled, *The Administrative Vision: A Longitudinal Study of Problem-Finding in Educational Leadership,* as a parallel to *The Creative Vision: A Longitudinal Study of Problem-Finding in Art.* But I do believe this: in both the study and practice of educational administration, as of art, attention must be directed not only to the ultimate product or solution but also, since the quality of solutions is a function of the quality of the problems, to how problems are found.

Problem-Finding and Graduate Training and
Research in Educational Administration

In view of the importance of problem-finding, it is curious that so little attention is given to it in education. It is even more curious that in view of the centrality of problem-finding in the practice and study of administration, so little attention has been given to it in graduate programs purporting to prepare students for research in educational administration.

The result of this neglect has been that so many students who enroll for the Ph.D. end up with only the A.B.D. ("All But Dissertation")! Even for those who manage to get the Ph.D., the dissertation becomes the first and last piece of research they will do. Graduate study, which should open up a research career, either stops it before the Ph.D. is obtained or ends it immediately after. And the point at which the damage is so often done is at the dissertation proposal stage, when the student is suddenly required to switch from solving problems already formulated by teachers to finding a problem he himself formulates.

Consider the educational career of the usual Ph.D. student. He has had eight years of elementary school, where he dealt almost exclusively with presented problems in the form of textbook exercises, classroom recitations, examination questions. He has had four years of secondary school, where again he was primarily required to find answers to questions posed by others. He has had four years of undergraduate work with more of the same. He comes to graduate school for several years of courses for yet more in the same vein. As his entree to doing research, he is given the Ph.D. Preliminary Examination, usually the quintessence of a presented problem situation. And now after eighteen or more years of preparation in finding answers to presented problems, he is told he is ready to find and formulate on his own a problem or, as we say, a dissertation topic—a task that goes against the grain of virtually all his training.

Many graduate students—in some departments and schools the majority—are not able to make the shift from problem-solving to problem-finding. The result is the A.B.D. with consequent sense of nonfulfillment if not tragedy for the student and failure for the university. For many of the other students who persist and do manage the task, the experience is so painful they never return to it.

It is ironic that faculty members in the very departments and schools where the A.B.D. is the predominant terminal degree and whose students, even when they manage the Ph.D., rarely do another bit of research, insist there is no dearth of what they call "interesting" problems lying about. One does not have to work at finding or formulating them, they say, nor is it necessary to provide students with such learning experiences.

It may be that so-called interesting problems are lying around for the picking. But interesting problems are not necessarily the same as significant or fruitful problems any more than interesting information is the same as significant knowledge. Ripley's *Believe It or Not* is full of interesting information; it is not thereby full of significant knowledge. If indeed there is no dearth of fruitful research problems, if important research problems are just lying around as is claimed, why do so many graduate students have so much trouble picking one up? And if I may say so, not only graduate students but some of us older folk as well have such trouble.

The conditions of graduate education for research cannot be fully altered without altering the conditions throughout education. And, to be sure, one cannot teach a set number of foolproof rules for finding and formulating productive research problems any more than one can prescribe rules for finding artistic problems. Nonetheless, it might not be amiss to call attention to some possible sources of research problems and to say a word or two regarding some possible criteria for identifying a fruitful problem.

Ignorance plays a part in problems, for a problem points to a gap in knowledge.[24] But so too does knowledge play a part in problems. A well-formulated problem is at once a result of knowledge and a stimulus to more knowledge, and it is itself knowledge and therefore worth teaching. Listen carefully to Michael Polanyi on problems as knowledge: "To see a problem is a definite addition to knowledge, as much as it is to see a tree, or to see a mathematical proof—or a joke. . . . To recognize a problem which can be solved and is worth solving is in fact a discovery in its own right."[25] Can we then characterize more specifically the situations in which problems are likely to be found? I follow here Mary Henle's formulations.[26]

First, contradictions and dilemmas in phenomena of all kinds provide fruitful sources of research questions. Conflicting results, unpredicted observations, negative cases, contrary theories are all occasions for posing new problems. Here are two examples from educational administration.[27] One observer states unequivocally that major impetus for change in organizations is from the outside. But another observer states that change forced on an organization from the outside may lead only to expedient change or tokenism; essential change must be generated from within the organization itself. Or to take another instance, there are those who argue that the predominant characteristic of the American school is its rigidity; it is too little prone to change. But there are those who insist that the predominant characteristic of the American school is its faddism; it is too much prone to change. Contradictions of this sort are a fruitful source of research problems.

Second, just as contradictions lead to problems, so too can unexpected similarities. An investigator sees similarities, not previously noticed, between phenomena and may seek to determine whether the unknown events can be explained in the same manner as the phenomena already understood. Recall the rich source of research problems in educational administration deriving from the similarities in behavior of children in clubs, students in classrooms, and workers in industry under certain types of leadership. Or recall how the observed similarity in emotional and in intellectual inflexibility gave rise to a series of research problems on the possibility of the so-called authoritarian personality syndrome. In physics, the same basic ideas that account for the motions of microscopic colloidal particles in solution also account for the motions of stars in clusters.

Third, questions arise when we encounter strange, striking, or new phenomena. Unusual events compel our attention, and we wonder how the strange phenomenon can come about. For example, the rainbow was a conspicuous phenomenon that demanded attention, and there were a number of theories about it from Aristotle, Newton, and Descartes right down to a recent *Scientific American*. In psychology, the singularity of the achievement of the idiot savant, or of the creative imagination of the artistic genius, or of the bizarre hallucination of the psychotic have led to productive research problems. In educational administration, it would seem to me the relatively new phenomena of decreasing school enrollments, the loss of confidence by Americans in education, the encroachment of union influence on customary managerial prerogatives, the requirements of affirmative action, the growing role of the courts in educational decisions, and the increasing threat to tenure as a result of no-growth in higher education are all sources of research problems.

Fourth, as a corollary to this, new instruments and techniques of observation and analysis play a role not only in the solving of problems but also in raising questions which might otherwise never even have been thought of. The microscope opened to view the strange world of microscopic life, which then became a source of research problems that could otherwise not have been possible to raise. The telescope of course did the same thing for outer space. Were the microscope and telescope more notable for the answers they gave or the problems they permitted us to pose? We do not have instruments of such power and precision in the social sciences. Yet think of the research problems having their source in data provided by such instruments as the Binet, or such observational methods as the Sociometric, or by such analytic techniques as path analysis. Although educational administration is not rich in such means, recall the research problems that had their source in Halpin's application of the Leadership Behavior Description Questionnaire—problems that became so commonplace we ungratefully forget their source.

Fifth, among the most fruitful sources of research problems is, of course, theory. For the most common form of a scientific question is the hypothesis derived from a theory. In this respect, a theory must be seen at least as much a tool for asking questions—a source of research problems—as for providing solutions. When we say a theory has lost vitality, it is not that it no longer explains that which it set out to explain but that it has been exhausted of new hypotheses that can be drawn from it—it has ceased to be a source of research problems.

Indeed, the formulation of certain problems cannot be understood outside the context of the theory used as a tool for raising the problem. To take an extreme instance, the question of whether a horse might evolve into a tree-climbing animal cannot even be posed outside evolutionary theory.[28] As a less extreme and more familiar instance, the current problem of the possible stages through which a child's intellect develops—a problem to which several hundred studies are devoted annually—would not have arisen except for Piaget's theory. Intelligent behavior as a phenomenon existed all along, but the research problem of whether it develops linearly or through stages did not exist until the theory was formulated. The current preeminence of Piaget, like that of Freud before him, is not that he provided unalterable answers—clearly all theoretical answers are alterable—but that his formulation provided tools for asking questions we might otherwise never have thought of asking. In fact, his formulation directed our attention to phenomena we would not even have noticed.

More pertinently, in educational administration the theoretical formulations of Bakke, Barnard, Homans, Katz, Simon, and Parsons, and of the group dynamicists and the so-called idiographic-nomothetic model-makers at the Midwest Administration Center, served as the source of research problems for a generation of graduate students and investigators.[29] More recently, if I read the numerous commentaries on the "theory movement" rightly, theories have come to be looked upon almost exclusively in the manner of dogmas supposed to give inviolable practical answers instead of at least in part as directions for posing possibly fruitful research problems. The current excoriation of organizational theory by some people for not telling them exactly what they ought to do (or have done) as practicing administrators strikes me as an example of this kind of misapprehension of the function of theory. And, may I say in passing, the production of commentaries on the theory movement (whatever that is) seems to have become an industry; I wonder whether it is not time to call a moratorium.

Sixth, we have discussed a number—surely not all—the conditions that are conducive to finding and formulating research problems. I shall mention only one other condition without which many questions are lost—a condition that brings us back to our original conception of the human being as a stimulus-seeking and problem-finding organism. This is an attitudinal condition of the creative or research-oriented person who has retained this stimulus-seeking and problem-finding attitude. As Professor Henle says, "Questions occur to the welcoming mind." She cites Bronowski on so-called chance discoveries—discoveries that seem made by accident but are really a result of the discoverer's having found the productive problem:

> Why does chance enter this way? The answer is simply that the mind is roving in a highly charged, active way and is looking for connections, for unseen likenesses in these circumstances. It is the highly inquiring mind which at the moment seizes the chance and turns what was an accident into something providential. The world is full of people who are always claiming that they really made the discovery, only they missed it. There were many people whose photographic plates had been fogged before Roentgen in fact asked himself: "Why is the plate fogged?" . . . It was chance; but it was the chance that was offered to the highly active and inquiring mind in this creative state . . .[30]

Whether the source is in perceived contradictions, dilemmas, or unexpected similarities, in strange or familiar phenomena or in new instruments, in systematic theories or in apparently accidental observations, fruitful problems do not just arise automatically. The problems must be formulated and posed in productive ways. I know of no single set of criteria guaranteeing that a research problem will be productive. But the following are some qualities worth keeping at least tentatively in mind.[31] There is a body of knowledge (concepts, data, techniques) within which the problem may be placed; stray problems (how many Ph.D.'s are there in Timbuktu?) are not likely to be productive. The problem must be well-conceived in the sense that its background and presuppositions—and every problem has presuppositions—are neither false nor undecided. The problem must be circumscribed; the question "what is Being?" is not likely to be a fruitful formulation. Conditions necessary to solving the problem must be available; that is, the ability and opportunity to obtain the needed observations and perform the pertinent analyses are assured. Consideration should be given before settling on the problem to the possible kinds and forms of solution that might be forthcoming, although of course such consideration should not predetermine the actual solution that is attained.

But one should not apply these criteria too stringently, for they may confine the research effort only to cut-and-dried issues, or to what we have called presented problems, and turn the imagination away from what we have called discovered and created problems, which may ultimately be more productive even if as yet not so well formulated. And perhaps most important of all in productive problem-finding is a condition of a psychological order: The problem must catch the passion of the problem-finder, for research no less than art requires passionate devotion if it is to be fruitful.

Conclusion

Let me summarize what I have attempted to do and add a final word.

1. I argued that finding and formulating a productive research problem is often as great an intellectual and creative achievement as is providing a solution to a problem once it has been found and formulated.

2. I suggested that there are several types of problems, and described a model of problem situations eventuating in systematic distinctions between presented, discovered, and created problems.

3. I reported several empirical studies of the process of finding and formulating problems in terms of this model, including possible applications to research and practice in educational administration.

4. I set forth some consequences of neglecting the "problem of the problem" for graduate education as well as research, suggesting a number of sources of productive research problems and several tentative criteria for assessing the possible productivity of a research problem.

Finally, let me end by citing two comments about problems and questions, one by Einstein, with whom we began, and the other by Gertrude Stein.

In describing what impels the productive scientist, Einstein made this distinction between the scientist and the detective, although both investigate problems: "For the detective, the crime is given, the problem posed: Who killed Cock Robin? The scientist must at least in part, commit his own crime [pose his own problem] . . ."

This may be apocryphal, but it is reported that when Gertrude Stein lay dying, her life-long companion Alice Toklas came to her bedside and asked, "Well, Miss Stein, what is the answer?" Gertrude Stein is reputed to have replied, "No, Alice, what is the question?"

Notes

1. Albert Einstein and Leopold Infeld, *The Evolution of Physics* (New York: Simon and Schuster, 1938), p. 92.

2. Max Wertheimer, *Productive Thinking* (New York: Harper and Row, 1945), p. 123.

3. Jacob W. Getzels, "Problem Finding," (The 343rd Convocation Address, The University of Chicago) *The University of Chicago Record* 7, no. 9 (November 21, 1973):281-283.

4. See Jacob W. Getzels, "Problem Finding and the Inventiveness of Solutions," *Journal of Creative Behavior* 9 (1975):12-18.

5. J. Smilansky, "Problem Posing: What Students Perceive as Problems in School" (Ph.D. diss., University of Chicago, 1977).

6. Norman R.F. Maier, *Problem Solving and Creativity in Individuals and Groups* (Belmont, Calif.: Brooks-Cole, 1970), p. 203.

7. Karl Duncker, "On Problem Solving," *Psychological Monographs* 58, no. 5 (1945):1.

8. John Dewey, *Logic: The Structure of Inquiry* (New York: Putman, 1938), p. 108.

9. *Webster's New International Dictionary*, 3d ed. s.v. "problem."

10. Jacob W. Getzels, "Creative Thinking, Problem-solving, and Instruction," in E.R. Hilgard, ed., *Theories of Learning and Instruction*, 63d Yearbook of the National Society for the Study of Education, Pt. 1 (Chicago: University of Chicago Press, 1964), pp. 240-267.

11. Mary Henle, "The Snail beneath the Shell," *Abraxas* 1 (1971):123.

12. W.H. Bexton, W. Heron, and T.H. Scott, "Effects of Decreased Variation in Sensory Environment," *Canadian Journal of Psychology* 8 (1954):70-76.

13. See Getzels, "Creative Thinking."

14. Mario Bunge, *Scientific Research I: The Search for System* (New York: Springer-Verlag, 1967), p. 165.

15. Ibid., p. 166.

16. Jacob W. Getzels and Mihaly Csikszentmihalyi, *The Creative Vision: A Longitudinal Study of Problem Finding in Art* (New York: John Wiley and Sons, 1976).

17. Ibid., see bibliography therein.

18. Jacob W. Getzels, James M. Lipham, and Roald F. Campbell, *Educational Administration as a Social Process: Theory, Research, Practice* (New York: Harper and Row, 1968), pp. 415-416.

19. See Getzels and Csikszentmihalyi, *The Creative Vision.*

20. Patricia K. Arlin, "Problem Finding: The Relation between Cognitive Process Variables and Problem-finding Performance" (Ph.D. diss., University of Chicago, 1974).

21. D.M. Schwartz, "A Study of Interpersonal Problem-Posing" (Ph.D. diss., University of Chicago, 1977).

22. See Smilansky, "Problem Posing."

23. I am grateful to Dr. McPherson, whose cooperation was, as usual, beyond the call of duty.

24. See Duncker, "On Problem Solving."

25. Michael Polanyi, *Personal Knowledge* (Chicago: University of Chicago Press, 1958), p. 120.

26. See Henle, "The Snail beneath the Shell," pp. 122-127. This is a superb article, which I recommend to anyone interested in the "problem of problems."

27. See Jacob W. Getzels, "Creative Administration and Organizational Change: An Essay in Theory," in L.J. Rubin, ed., *Frontiers in School Leadership* (Chicago: Rand McNally, 1970), pp. 69-85.

28. Bunge, *Scientific Research I,* p. 187.

29. See Getzels, Lipham, and Campbell, *Educational Administration as Social Process,* pp. 39-51, and the numerous references to dissertation and other research studies throughout the volume.

30. Henle, "The Snail beneath the Shell," p. 127. Reprinted with permission.

31. See Bunge, *Scientific Research I,* p. 189, on which this is based.

2 An Approach to Paradigm Shift in Educational Administration

R. Oliver Gibson

To some the title of this chapter may appear to be a too parochial way of viewing how ideas about educational administration come to change over time. For others it will suggest the work of Kuhn[1] and bring to mind the charge that he used the word *paradigm* in a number of ways, making the concept so low in intellectual rigor and in operational reliability that it is of questionable utility. For still others, particularly those of strictly empirical bent of mind, it will appear as idle efforts at broad speculation, the outcome of which is at best dubious. If there be such agnostics, my first response must be one that recalls to mind the fact that fantasy, both individual and collective, and intellectual myth-making have proved, on occasion, very heuristic. Copernicus, it appears, as a young man of twenty-three, attended the lectures on astronomy by the neoplatonist Novara at Bologna. The paradigm probably was the Platonic myth of the cave, which gave central importance to the light of the sun, thus providing the nonempirical, highly speculative intellectual base for the heliocentric hypothesis. The law of acceleration of falling bodies is predicated on the fictitious mental construct "vacuum." It is my suggestion that we relax for a time our empirical bias, if we have it, and engage in some speculation about approaches to the ways in which our ideas about educational administration, and consequently its study, have been changing during the present century.

General Approach

One need not be restricted to one approach, as the title may suggest. Educational administration, it may fairly be said, is still an intellectual upstart that has advanced scarcely beyond childhood and certainly not to maturity. If such an assumption possesses some validity, any approach, in aeronautical terms, is something like an airplane seeking to land on a foggy airstrip. My efforts, then, may be seen as taking the form of making some "passes" at landing. And the outcome will be to conclude that another takeoff is in order.

My purpose is to focus on some of the ideas that appear to have guided practice and research in educational administration during this century and to speculate briefly about where our ideas may be leading us. The analysis makes the assumption that runs through the field of the sociology of knowledge, namely, that ideas involve some sort of interaction between and among individuals and groups. The metaphor is something like that of contagion; ideas may be seen as being "in the air," taken up by certain individuals and transmitted by intellectual institutions such as journals, universities, and conferences.

To approach this task, it seems necessary to take an overview of the intellectual context within which the study of educational administration has emerged as an area of intellectual concern in the latter half of the twentieth century, to seek to gauge what are the present currents of thought, and to speculate briefly about whither they may be tending. To undertake such a broad task in the brief space available may strike some as the height of arrogance. My thoughts have been formulated, and are now advanced as some tentative hypotheses that have occurred to me in the course of reading, experience, and reflection. Certainly, alternative frameworks and logically derived hypotheses may be advanced by others. I shall hypothesize however, that paradigm shift is a function of modernization, related especially to the tendency to move from particularism toward universalism.

Method

A few words on how this hypothesis was arrived at and how it was handled are in order. *Method* is used in the sense of the procedure used in the pursuit of an inquiry.[2] There are differences of point of view about how method is to be reported.[3] Method, here, will tell roughly how I got from being asked to prepare this chapter to its production.

The request came because of my interest in how thought patterns or paradigms behind inquiry shift over time. This inquiry began with a review of recent trends in research in educational administration in the United States[4] and was extended to an analysis of articles that appeared in the *Educational Administration Quarterly* between 1965 and 1974.[5] Another question that had come to mind was: How have ideas changed over the current century? (The request came just when this question was being pondered.

The inquiry had to be undertaken along with many other demands upon time and without any research assistant staff. It was assumed that what people write (text) is indicative of what they think. The historical text available was that in the library at the State University of New York at Buffalo. Professor L.O. Cummings, first dean of the School of Education at Buffalo, had been a student of Professor Paul Hanus, first dean of the Graduate School of Education at Harvard, who was active nationally, along with such professors as Cubberly of Stanford and Strayer of Columbia, in the school survey movement during the early part of the century. Many of those surveys are in the Buffalo library in memory of Paul Henry Hanus, (The Gift of a Former Student). The text used in this analysis was that in the Hanus collection and some others in the library holdings; the status of the sample rests on how the collection was put together. Time did not permit a detailed content analysis of the several analyses of school administration that appeared in those reports.

It was assumed that the survey analyses were based on paradigms then current among professors concerned about the study of educational administration. (An alternative approach could have been through the reports of proceedings of national meetings of school administrators. This was not done, in part because of limits of time, effort, and availability of proceedings.) Yearbooks of the National Society for the Study of Education were another source. Later in the century the American Educational Research Association reviews of research in educational administration appeared and were seen as reasonably indicative of the field.

All the above were surveyed and mulled over for some time. The theme that came to mind was a pervasive shift from attention to people and procedure to general ideas and social process. In the course of struggling to make sense of it all, Marion Levy's analysis of modernization came to mind, including his use of the shift from particularism toward universalism as an indicator of modernization. It was only when writing of this chapter was under way that the central hypothesis became relatively clear as a way of making sense out of much that had been read. (The method section was the last written.) In this sense it is a retrospective hypothesis that is advanced as a first approximation to understanding the social text of our field. There is much yet to be done on the odyssey of application of hermeneutic method to text analysis in this field.

Macroscopic Context

Even a cursory view of the history of science makes one aware of the complexity of the events and their interrelationships. Thus, one has to be on guard against too easy generalizations. But, to look at the general contour or current in those events need not imply insensitivity to the fact that there are many details. One can speak of the Gulf Stream, mobility, and modernization as general concepts and still recognize the great deal of complexity in the associated phenomena. Whitehead somewhere advised a search for generalization combined with distrust. That is the orientation at this point.

First we need to remind ourselves that the paradigm, metaphor, or symbolic image by which we represent the world-out-there to ourselves is mankind-made, that is, cultural. And that invention took place here on this planet within recorded history. Whitehead contends in his *Science and the Modern World*:

> This new tinge to modern minds is a vehement and passionate interest
> in the relation of general principles to irreducible and stubborn

facts. . . . It is this union of passionate interest in detailed facts with
equal devotion to abstract generalization which forms the novelty in
our present society.[6]

He saw modern scientific interest as a confluence of two major currents, the
one stemming from Greek thought and the other from Mediaeval aesthetic
interest in natural objects. He saw the paradigm (used here in the more general
usage of Kuhn) of an ordered world from which dependable principles could be
derived as descended from the Greek conception of tragedy. "Their vision of
fate, remorseless and indifferent, urging a tragic incident, to its inevitable issue,
is the vision possessed by science. Fate in Greek tragedy becomes the order of
nature in modern thought."[7] The Justinian Code was seen as an extension of
this lawfulness in events to the sociocultural area in which lawful and law-
enforcing authority was institutionalized.

Machievelli provides an example of one of the early efforts to organize
general principles on the basis of observation of experience. Elsewhere I have
referred to these two major dimensions of the scientific mind as the Apollinian
and the Dionysian.[8] Their mix has been different in various times and places.
Many observers, for example Duhem,[9] have commented on the relatively strong
bent of the Anglo-Saxon mind for empirical observation, while the continental
European mind, notably in Germany and France, has tended toward theoretical
formulation.

An unduly severe separation of abstract thought and concrete observation
(roughly equivalent to thinking and doing) emerged quite early and has persisted
in the issue of theory versus practice. Despite Kant's emphatic answer to the
issue in 1793,[10] it continues to be treated as a binary rather than a dialectical
question.

If Marion Levy, Jr.[11] is correct in his formulation of the process of
modernization, one of the characteristics of the process is a shift from a
relatively particularistic orientation to one that is relatively universalistic. His
conception of movement from the particular to the general in social affairs
includes a shift from emphasis on who a person is to what a person can do,
roughly equivalent to transition from personality to competence. An illustration
of such a change can be found in the literature on leadership. During the
nineteenth and early twentieth century a key concept in the general paradigm of
leadership was personality exemplified in Carlyle's *Heroes and Hero Worship.* By
the middle of this century research had pretty well established that personality
traits were not all that useful in explaining leadership phenomena. Stogdill's
1948 article on "Personal Factors Associated with Leadership" is probably the
major transition point in the shift from dominant particularistic emphasis to a
more universalistic one (it perhaps would be equally appropriate to call it a shift
in the idiographic-nomothetic mix from an idiographic dominance to a nomothetic dominance).[12]

Another question arises at this point. Is the later paradigm of leadership more valid than the earlier one? Or is it that in a society which is undergoing modernization, the earlier paradigm was more valid for that relatively less modern society and the later paradigm is more appropriate for the current relatively more modern society? If so, what becomes of the criteria of validity? Are we forced to join Pontius Pilate and ask "What is truth?" Again, we may be faced with the need to move from a more particularistic orientation toward validity (for instance, content validity) to one that is relatively more universalistic (construct validity, for example).

If we view the hypotheses or generalizations about leadership as mid-level generalizations between the theoretical postulates and theorems of paradigms and the concrete operational definitions of observation of social objects and events, the test of validity may move from an emphasis on isomorphism between generalization and observation (content validity) toward one that emphasizes coherence of observation and generalization with the intellectual underpinning of the paradigm (construct validity). I shall return to this point later to raise the question whether many of our inherited paradigms of administration and organization may not be so out of touch with social reality as to be of relatively low utility for understanding and prediction and may, indeed, be more generative of error than of knowledge.

The issue of the isomorphism of common sense observation and the paradigmatic assumptions is not a new one. There comes to mind the common sense observation of a motionless earth. In this connection it may be instructive to quote Tolstoy's concluding thoughts from *War and Peace*:

> Just as in astronomy the difficulty of admitting the motion of the earth lay in the immediate sensation of the earth's stationaryness and of the planets' motion, so in history the difficulty of recognizing the subjection of the personality to the laws of space and time and causation lies in the difficulty of surmounting the direct sensation of the independence of one's personality.
>
> ... the new view says, "It is true we do not feel our dependence, but admitting our free will, we are led to absurdity; admitting our dependence upon the external world, time and cause, we are led to laws.[13]

So far we have been considering modern science as a confluence of two major currents from ancient and mediaeval times—reason and observation—and have advanced the hypothesis that modernization tends to shift the mix of the two in the direction of increased dependence on universalistic reason. This shift has, on occasion, to fly in the face of common sense observation. Thus, we are led to be suspicious not only of our generalizations but also of our direct experience. If this is indeed the case, then our traditional Anglo-American confidence in the efficacy of experience may be a case of misplaced confidence.

Following this line of reasoning, it may be that we should be more suspicious than we normally are of what we think we are observing and what we think we know. This rather agnostic posture may be called "critical consciousness." I shall later seek to demonstrate that the paradigm shift in educational administration during the present century has been a movement from a paradigm that emphasized naive particularistic observation to one that gave greater importance to the theoretical base of the paradigm, and that there now is movement toward another paradigm, one that reflects greater critical consciousness.

Twentieth-Century Trends in Research in Educational Administration

On June 6, 1933 a series of lectures were given at Stanford in honor of Professor E.P. Cubberley on the occasion of his retirement. John K. Norton gave a paper entitled, "Twentieth Century Developments in Research in School Administration." He stated:

> We may sum up by saying that in 1900 there was little scientific knowledge to guide educational administration in certificating, selecting, supervising, compensating, and retiring teachers. Personal experience and the off-hand advice of his colleagues constituted the superintendent's stock in trade in dealing with these problems. This is no longer true. The careful pooling of opinion, the close observation of varying practices, the collection of facts, and the statement of principles which have been the product of research offer the professionally prepared superintendent of schools indispensible guides. . . .
>
> Today, most school executives recognize that the systematic collection of opinion and empirical experience is essential to intelligent administration.[14]

During the lectures, credit was given to Cubberley for development of techniques of school surveys. Neither space nor knowledge permits a comprehensive review of the survey and its contribution to knowledge of school administration during the early years of this century. One study at about the turn of the century recommended two administrative heads for the system reporting to the Board.[15] The brief discussion indicated that it was assumed that the two would keep each other on his toes. One is tempted to speculate whether the then current paradigm of evolution as a competitive process through which the fit survived was somewhere behind it. The superintendents on the study panel did not register strong objection to the recommendation.

The *Report of the Educational Commission of the City of Chicago* (1899) assumed the same binary nature of administration in the following recommendation: "That the function of the Board be chiefly legislative, the executive work being delegated to the superintendent and business manager."[16]

The Chicago Board of Education had a large national panel of advisors who commented on various recommendations in the Report. One of the advisors, S.T. Dutton, Superintendent, Brookline, Massachusetts, commented as follows:

> In what you propose respecting the two great phases of school management, that pertaining to the business and that of education, you have not only taken high ground regarding the centralizing of authority in the person of two competent experts, but have placed around these executive heads such safeguards as will prevent possible abuses on the one hand and unnecessary interference on the other.[17]

Dutton's response suggests that his paradigm may have been a Hamiltonian checks and balances.

As we are all aware, another paradigm of management, emphasizing efficiency, took shape early in the present century. The conception was eventually captured in the term "scientific management."

Professor Ernest Carroll Moore, head of the Bureau of Education of Yale University prepared a *Report of the Examination of the School System of East Orange, New Jersey* in 1911. He stated:

> It is a principle of scientific management, that in every properly directed undertaking there shall be a planning department whose duty it shall be to learn about all that is being undertaken and done, and to provide plans in accordance with the laws of science. . . .
>
> The one person who is "on the job" all the time, who can know about all that is being undertaken and whether it is being done in such a way as to serve the one ultimate interest of the undertaking and can make plans for the work of all his assistants, and watch their work from day to day, to see that it is being performed properly, is the Superintendent of Schools.[18]

Here we see a radically different image of administration; rather than a natural set of social checks and balances, we see a single head of the school system with authority to see that things get done as he has planned them. We need not go into detail regarding the ways that paradigm differed from the organismic conception that was formulated just prior to the middle of the present century, the primary proponent of which was Chester Barnard.[19] There the emphasis was on cooperation, worker satisfaction, and legitimacy as a base of compliance. It marked a shift from the personalistic authority of the superintendent to the more universalistic base of social integration and legitimacy. The wide adherence to social-psychological conceptions of interpersonal relationships in school systems during the third quarter of the twentieth century seems to have clustered about that paradigm. The current surge of interest in policy and in quasi-legal processes of bargaining, conciliation, arbitration, and the like appear to be moving toward a more strongly universalistic or nomothetic paradigm with a concomitant reduction of the particularism of personality. (It may be of interest to recall that the Greek *nomothetes* were interpreters of the law.)

Another indicator of such a shift from the particularistic toward the universalistic relates to personality. Reference has already been made to S.T. Dutton. In 1903, when he had become professor of School Administration at Teachers' College, he published *School Management.*[20] In the table of contents, Chapter VII, "The Government of the School," commences with the heading "The Power of Personality." It is difficult to conceive that such a treatment would begin in that way today; it might have something to do with policy process or decision-making. Cubberley's discussion, in *The Principal and His School,* is an interesting treatment of the relationships of the superintendent and the principal. He dealt with personal behavior in great detail. He opened the analysis as follows:

> The principal of the school and the superintendent of a school system hold somewhat complementary positions in the administration of a system of public instruction. . . . It is primarily the function of the superintendent to think, and to plan and to lead; it is primarily the function of the principal to execute plans and to follow and to support.
>
> . . . a principal should be able to sense the superintendent's policy, and to carry it out without bothering him continually for details.[21]

The table of contents included chapters on "The First Day of School," and "Intermissions, Lines and Drills." There was an emphasis throughout on the importance of professional knowledge; it was knowledge about specific matters of practice. Such a discussion today would no doubt be conceptualized in terms of the more universalistic concept of competence.

We could go on to further indicators of the paradigm shift from a descriptive, concrete, particularistic orientation toward a more analytic, conceptual, and universalistic orientation. For example, during the early part of the century the following words were frequently used: *facts, information, practice, ought,* and *experience.* After the middle of the century the following were more common: *mental constructs, information theory, is,* and *behavioral science.* Another descriptive distinction was that between legislation and administration as embodied in the dogma propounded in Woodrow Wilson's article of 1887, and the related dogmatic separation of politics and education.[22] Models from decision theory, information theory, and policy sciences have moved the paradigm to a more complex and universalistic status.

Paradigm Shift and Research Literature
in Educational Administration

Nascent science illustrated in the efforts of individuals, contrasted with collective effort, has a long history. The work of Aristotle, Roger Bacon, Copernicus, and Galileo come to mind. Lavoisier was so absorbed in his experimentation that, during the French Reign of Terror, he asked that he be spared the guillotine for a few days in order to complete his experiment.

Science, as a conscious collective effort, however, did not emerge until the late nineteenth century. In the ninth edition of the *Encyclopedia Britannica* (1889) the index did not include a separate treatment of science and scientific method. There was a reference to Whewell's philosophy of the sciences. The eleventh edition (1911) had two index references to science; one was an article dealing with science generally and the other, under philosophy, dealt with philosophy and the natural sciences. In the fourteenth edition (1929, the 1954 revised edition) there were five general references to science as well as many others to particular sciences and scientific matters. The fifteenth edition (1974) does not have an index and so is not directly comparable. There are long articles on the history and philosophy of science and a great many related references. These references to the *Britannica* support the contention that only within the last century has science become institutionalized as a broad social effort and that the major growth has taken place within the present century.

Norton has already been cited to indicate the lack of scientific research in educational administration at the turn of the century. The growing institutionalization of research was reflected in the organization in 1915 of the National Association of Directors of Educational Research, later to become the American Educational Research Association.[23] In 1930 it officially affiliated with the National Education Association and approved establishment of its own official publication, the *Review of Educational Research.*[24] The first issue appeared in January 1931, and the first issue directly related to educational administration appeared in June 1931 under the title "School Organization." The foreword began as follows:

> School organization is one of the parts of school administration which is gradually being subjected to the criticism and examination of scientific investigation. Administrative procedure has not been evaluated by scientific methods so extensively as has teaching procedure because, apparently, evaluation is more difficult in the one case than the other.[25]

It described the historical development of school units, evaluated the status of those units, and treated pupil classification and grouping. It might be characterized as *descriptive-analytic.*

The concentration on organization continued in the first issue on research methods (February 1934) with a chapter on "Methods of Research in School Organization."[26] Triennial reviews of research on school organization continued and were expanded to "Organization and Administration of Education" in the October 1940 issue. The last *Review* of educational administration appeared in 1967[27] and was succeeded by the *Review of Research in Education,* the first volume of which appeared in 1973.

Earlier in this analysis two major themes in scientific development were identified, namely, observation and abstract generalization. It has been noted that research in educational administration during the early part of this century gave primary attention to observation and description of practices (descriptive-analytic). When did abstract generalization become a more prominent theme? The first issue in which a chapter is devoted to theory ("Theory and Structure in Local School Administration") appeared in the issue of October 1952,[28] signalling the early phase of what has come to be called the "theory movement." The focus was still on structure/organization and the introduction to the issue restates the difficulties and diversity of thought confronting the study of administration. The theory movement continued to receive explicit attention until the last issue in 1967, when it was stated in the foreword: "The erstwhile search for 'administrative theory' . . . seems virtually abandoned today . . ."[29]

There has been considerable debate about the meaning of the decrease in "theorizing about theory." To many of us an alternative hypothesis appears plausible, namely, that the abstract generalization theme had become incorporated with the earlier theme of observation and experience, setting the stage for a more mature advance in scientific analysis in educational administration.

A similar progression appears in the *Yearbooks* of the National Society for the Study of Education.[30] The early yearbooks that relate most clearly to educational administration deal primarily with descriptive analysis of current practice under the following titles: *The Relation of Superintendents and Principals to the Training and Professional Improvement of Teachers* (1908), *The Supervision of City Schools* (1913), and *Plans for Organizing School Surveys, with a Summary of Typical School Surveys* (1914). Part II of the Forty-fifth Yearbook (1946), *Changing Conceptions in Educational Administration*,[31] is indicative of paradigm shift. No longer was leadership seen as a matter of personality; it was seen as "social process." Such concepts as planning and policy were used extensively, but nowhere was theory dealt with explicitly. This analysis of the social text of the field suggests that we may usefully treat the period 1900-1950 as one emphasizing descriptive analysis of experience and the period 1950-1970 as one emphasizing theoretical analysis of experience. Indicative of the latter period was the 1964 Yearbook, *Behavioral Science and Educational Administration*.[32]

Is there any evidence that further maturation is now occurring? Immegart's review[33] suggests that the field is still caught in the grip of the relatively atheoretic, particularistic past, and the Campbell-Newell study[34] indicates that a very small group of persons has a basic commitment to research. When we examine the content of the new series of reviews, which commenced in 1973, the theme persisting since 1931 reappears in volume I under the heading "School Organization, Effectiveness, and Change."[35] No longer, however, was there a discussion of the relative complexity of organization versus administration. Rather, the critical issues lay around research variables and methodology. In volume II (1974), theory returns under the heading "Organizational Theory and

Research in Education."[36] The first article, "Models of Educational Organizations" by Corwin, undertook a critical examination of various organizational theories providing "summaries or in-depth critiques of particular pieces of research." Of the Weberian ideal type model of bureaucracy, which had great currency during the theory movement period, he concludes:

> In short these studies of schools confirm an impression gained from studies of other types of organizations, namely that educational organizations take not one but a variety of forms, depending upon the circumstances . . . Most researchers concerned with school organization have not used the ideal type in this way, but it can be viewed as a set of variables. . . .[37]

Is that critical analysis of alternative theories an indicator of an emerging critical consciousness in the field? In the same year (1974) Greenfield undertook a critical challenge of conventional "naturalistic" theories, challenging the definition of theory itself.[38] The discussion was still vigorous at the American Educational Research Association meeting in 1977. These fragments of evidence support the hypothesis that the theory movement phase has shifted to a more mature stage that may roughly be called *critical consciousness.*

In summary, it now seems somewhat justified to think of paradigm shift in educational administration during the present century as directly associated with particularism toward universalism, an indicator of modernization, and roughly recognizable as having three phases, namely: 1900-1950, the descriptive-analytic period; 1950-1970, the theory movement period; and in 1970 the beginning of a period of critical consciousness. This relationship is shown in figure 2-1.

Concluding Observations

Clearly this hypothesis, as it relates to the present, is one developed in medias res and so may be premature. Further developments will, no doubt, reveal the shift more clearly. The recent article in the *Scientific American,* "The Theory of the Rainbow," traces from Aristotle through 1975 the increasing power of theoretical explanation of rainbow phenomena.[39] It is suggestive of the theoretical quest that may still lie ahead of us. Students of research in both educational administration and education generally have noted the low level of explanatory power of existing theories. Griffiths recently commented as follows:

> The major test of theories is the power of the concepts and hypotheses which they generate. I reviewed Volume XII of the *Educational Administration Quarterly* to note the power of hypotheses and relationships among variables. I judged that 11 articles dealt with administrative behavior. In four of the studies *all* of the hypotheses were rejected and *all* tests were non-significant. In four of the studies no more than a

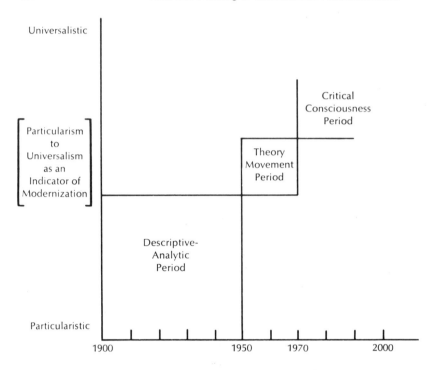

Figure 2-1. The Paradigm Shift in Educational Administration since 1900.

third of the tests resulted in significant relationships. In three, the hypothesized relationships were confirmed.[40]

The above distribution is less successful than would be predicted by chance. One is tempted to speculate that current paradigms of our field are so inadequate that our hypotheses are more inclined toward error than to useful knowledge. How does one know when belief is roughly equivalent to the erroneous belief that the earth was flat and stationary? How is such critical understanding promoted in our consciousness? Are we faced with the need for a paradigm shift similar to that posed by the Ptolemaic theory? If so, then the apparent emergence of a period of a critical consciousness may prove to be a harbinger of further paradigm shifts toward greater explanatory power—another step like that long search for an adequate theory of the rainbow.

Notes

1. Thomas S. Kuhn, *The Structure of Scientific Revolutions,* 2d ed. (Chicago: The University of Chicago Press, 1970).

2. *Method* is used here in the root sense of "a following after" (see Henry George Liddell and Robert Scott, *A Greek-English Lexicon*) from *meta* meaning after and *odos* meaning way. Odos appears in such words as ex*odus, odo*meter and *ody*ssey. Plato used it in the sense of "an inquiry into scientific subjects" and "the mode of prosecuting such inquiry." With his emphasis on the "light" of truth, he saw it as a light from heaven that makes truth known (see *Oxford English Dictionary*). Thus, method here means the procedure used in the pursuit of an inquiry with the intent of casting "light" on the question at hand.

3. P.B. Medawar, "Is the Scientific Paper Fraudulent?," *Saturday Review,* August 1, 1964, pp. 42-43 in which he states: "I mean the scientific paper may be a fraud because it misrepresents the processes of thought that accompanied or gave rise to the work that is described in the paper."

4. R. Oliver Gibson, "Research Trends in the United States," in M. Hughes, ed., *Administering Education: International Challenge* (London: Athlone Press, 1975), pp. 229-235.

5. R. Oliver Gibson and Marilyn Stetar, "Trends in Research Related to Educational Administration," *UCEA Review* 16, no. 5 (July 1975):11-20.

6. Alfred N. Whitehead, *Science and the Modern World* (Harmondsworth, Middlesex, England: Pelican Books, Penguin Books, 1938), p. 13.

7. Ibid., p. 21.

8. Gibson and Stetar, "Trends in Research."

9. Pierre Duhem, *The Aim and Structure of Physical Theory* (orig. pub. 1906), trans. Philip P. Wiener (New York: Atheneum, 1962). See chapter 4, "Abstract Theories and Mechanical Models," passim.

10. Immanuel Kant, *The Philosophy of Kant* (orig. pub. 1793), ed. Carl J. Friedrich (New York: Modern Library, 1949), in part *IX:* "Theory and Practice Concerning the Common Saying: This May Be True in Theory but Does Not Apply to Practice," p. 412-429.

11. Marion J. Levy, Jr., *Modernization and the Structure of Societies,* 2 vols. (Princeton, N.J.: Princeton University Press, 1966), passim, especially pp. 10-71, vol. 1.

12. Ralph M. Stogdill, "Personal Factors Associated with Leadership," *Journal of Psychology* 25 (1948):35-71.

13. Leo Tolstoy, *War and Peace,* trans. Constance Garrett (New York: Modern Library, 1931), pp. 1135-1136.

14. John K. Norton, "Twentieth Century Developments in Research in School Administration," in Jesse B. Sears, ed., *School Administration in the Twentieth Century,* Stanford Pamphlets, no. 4 (Stanford, Calif.: Stanford University Press, 1934), p. 45. Reprinted with permission.

15. The exact citation is not possible.

16. "Report of the Education Commission of the City of Chicago" (Chicago, 1899), p. 13.

17. Ibid., p. 14.

18. *Report of the Examination of the School System of East Orange, New Jersey* (The Board of Education, 1912), pp. 12-13.

19. Probably the most influential source is Chester I. Barnard, *Functions of the Executive* (Cambridge, Mass.: Harvard University Press, 1938).

20. Samuel T. Dutton, *School Management* (New York: Charles Scribner's Sons, 1903).

21. Ellwood P. Cubberley, *The Principal and His School* (Boston: Houghton-Mifflin Company, 1923), p. 19.

22. Woodrow Wilson, "The Study of Administration," *Political Science Quarterly* 2 (June 1887):197-222.

23. See Nancy J. Hultquist, "A Brief History of AERA's Publishing," in *Educational Researcher,* December 1976, pp. 9-13.

24. American Educational Research Association, *Review of Educational Research.* Volume 1 was published in 1931 and continued until volume 40, no. 2, April 1970 as solicited review manuscripts organized around a topic each year.

25. *Review of Educational Research* 1, no. 3 (June 1931):162. Copyright 1931, American Educational Research Association, Washington, D.C. Reprinted with permission.

26. Ibid., 4, no. 1 (February 1934):21-28.

27. Ibid., 37, no. 4 (October 1967).

28. Ibid., 22, no. 4 (October 1952).

29. Ibid., 37, no. 4 (October 1967):276.

30. National Society for the Study of Education, *Yearbook* (Chicago: University of Chicago Press). The first *Yearbook* was published in 1902 and is still in publication.

31. National Society for the Study of Education, *Changing Conceptions in Educational Administration,* 45th Yearbook, part 2 (Chicago: University of Chicago Press, 1946).

32. National Society for the Study of Education, *Behavioral Science and Educational Administration,* 63rd Yearbook, part 2 (Chicago: University of Chicago Press, 1964).

33. Glenn L. Immegart, "The Study of Educational Administration 1954-74" in L. Cunningham, W. Hack, and R. Nystrand, eds., *Educational Administration: The Developing Decades* (Berkeley, Calif.: McCutchan, 1977), pp. 298-328.

34. Roald F. Campbell and L. Jackson Newell, *A Study of Professors of Educational Administration* (Columbus, Ohio: University Council for Educational Administration, 1973), passim.

35. American Educational Research Association, *Review of Research in Education,* vol. 1 (Itasca, Ill.: Peacock, 1973), p. ix.

36. F.N. Kerlinger and J.B. Carroll, eds., *Review of Research in Education,* vol. 2 (Itasca, Ill.: F.E. Peacock, 1974), p. viii.

37. Ronald Corwin, "Models of Educational Organization," in ibid., p. 255. Copyright 1974, American Educational Research Association, Washington, D.C. Reprinted with permission.

38. Thomas B. Greenfield, "Theory about Organization: A New Perspective and Its Implications for Schools," in Hughes, ed., *Administering Education* pp. 71-99.

39. H. Moyses Nussenveig, "The Theory of the Rainbow," *Scientific American,* April 1977, pp. 116-127. I am indebted to Frederick P. Frank of Northern Illinois University for calling this suggestive article to my attention.

40. See chapter 3.

Part II
Assessment of Research from the Practice of Educational Administration

Dr. Pell was wont to say that in the Solution of Questions, the Maine Matter was the *well-stating of them*; wch requires motherwitt, & Logick . . . ; for let the question be but well-stated, it will worke almost of itselfe.

—John Aubrey

3

Another Look at Research on the Behavior of Administrators

Daniel E. Griffiths

When writing this chapter, I had an overwhelming feeling of déjà vu: I have certainly been here before. My previous papers on research in educational administration were attempts to view the field as a whole.[1] In general, I concluded that research in educational administration was not a robust child, and now, twelve years after my last effort, I can report that it is not a robust adolescent—a view shared by Immegart, who did so well in 1975 what I tried to do in 1959 and 1965.[2] The prognosis for a vigorous adulthood is dismal. The major reasons for this progression of sickly stages is that too few professors of educational administration have the interest or the competence to do research. As editor of the *Educational Administration Quarterly,* the only educational administration periodical in the United States that presumes to be scholarly, I am constantly appalled at the papers that we receive. Most of the writing can be typified as "using an atrocious style to spoil what might otherwise have been a mediocre idea."[3]

In contrast to previous papers in which I attempted to be complete and to buttress obvious points with appropriate statistics, I shall give a personal view of the difficulties I see in research in one aspect of educational administration, namely administrator behavior, and raise issues and suggest directions that interested researchers might explore. Further, I shall restrict myself to what I consider to be the three major matters of concern: the level at which research is done, the problem of transferability of research findings from one field of administration to another, and theory development.

Level of Research

C.P. Snow put our problem well when he wrote in his essay "Science and Government": "Most of the concepts that administrative theorists use are at best rationalizations, not guides to further thought; as a rule they are unrealistically remote from the workaday experience."[4] He might have added that the language we use in our research is equally remote.

I have been concerned about doing research and developing theory on the "real" behavior of "real" people for a long time, but only recently did I become aware that my colleagues and I use a rather abstract language to talk about administrator behavior. This was first brought to my attention by Thomas B. Greenfield in Bristol, England, when he called for a phenomenological basis for research in administration. I have since read in phenomenology and have been influenced by David L. Denton, who insists that education, as "first-person experience," must be talked about in terms of the experiences of individual people, not in nomothetic terms. Instead, he notes, virtually all of the words employed in organizational theory refer to "definitions which are established by stipulation, by formal rule, or by ordinary usage."[5] He calls this vocabulary of abstract definitions "steno-language," and he says it cannot be used to talk about everyday experience. He then states a premise:

> Instead of starting with a standardized language, with its cannon of exactness, which precludes all but the most limited use of terms and sentences stating idiographic, novel, open, and multidimensional experience, let us start with that which is given to us in ordinary experience which is sharable, verifiable, mutually observable.[6]

Denton later states:

> Given the objective nature of steno-language, one cannot construct a theory of organization, or a theory of anything, which will be consistent with the presuppositions of steno-language and, at the same time, account for, open the door to, the idiographic, simultaneous, protean characteristics of individual persons in the operation.[7]

He suggests that organization—to be meaningful—must be grounded in the ordinary experience of individuals and talked about in appropriate terms:

> All of this would suggest that to talk of organization with the existential language of our ordinary experience would be to talk of autonomous groups, spontaneous order, workers' and students' and faculties' control, and the principle of federation.[8]

I am not so sure that one would end up with autonomous groups and the like, but I am quite certain that the use of nonabstract language to describe everyday experience would lead us in different directions in research and theory.

This discussion of the abstractness of our organizational language brings to mind a recollection of Heisenberg by one of his students, Felix Bloch. They were out walking and were talking about space. Bloch wrote:

> I had just read Weyl's book, *Space, Time and Matter,* and under its influence was proud to declare that space was simply the field of linear operations. "Nonsense," said Heisenberg, "space is blue and birds fly through it." . . . This may sound naive, but I knew him well enough by

this time to fully understand the rebuke. What he meant was that it was dangerous for a physicist to describe Nature in terms of idealized abstractions too far removed from the evidence of actual observation. In fact, it was just by avoiding this danger in the previous description of atomic phenomena that he was able to arrive at his great creation of quantum mechanics.[9]

One of the achievements of the past twenty years is that we have developed a vocabulary that is now used by professor and practitioner alike to describe administrative situations. Halpin discusses this and laments the fact that the use of the vocabulary demonstrates an understanding that is only "word deep."[10] I am concerned that the use of this sophisticated language is deceptive. For example, I was discussing the creation of the 1972 Fiscal Review Group at New York University with a social scientist now turned management consultant. He accounted for the membership of this Task Force on the grounds that the members (all deans) were the "power elite" of the university selected because their positions in the "power structure" would ensure "compliance." (Note the vocabulary.) The real reasons were these: only the deans understood the budget, and only deans had no routine responsibilities and could be freed for six months to do the work. For a larger example of how sophisticated concepts lead one astray, read Baldridge's study of New York University.[11]

The first concern is the level at which research is done in educational administration; by this I mean two things. First, administrators are studied en masse by means of surveys.[12] Second, administrator behavior is studied through the use of such abstract concepts that the behavior is obscured.

Administrators as Individuals

While there is, no doubt, value in the kind of information that can be gleaned from questionnaires—average age, height, and weight, place in family, religion, birthplace, salary, and so forth—that which is really significant in understanding administrators is omitted. There should be a great deal of research on educational administrators as individuals: how they function in their jobs; how they learn the "territory"; what styles they develop; whether the styles are consistent throughout their careers or change as situations change; what makes them effective; indeed, what is effectiveness in educational administration? It is true that, for instance, some progress was made toward understanding administrator styles in the in-basket studies, but these have not been followed up.[13] Admittedly, the research involved a large number of principals, and we cannot be certain of the style of any one of them. The knowledge we need can be obtained only by the intensive study of individuals through observations, and descriptions should be written in terms of ordinary experiences expressed in ordinary language.

The book *Lyndon Johnson and the American Dream* by Doris Kearns is an example of what I am talking about. Professor Kearns describes in great detail the way LBJ behaved. Following is an abstract of a section discussing his early years:

In 1931 Johnson got a job as congressional secretary to a Texas representative. Moving from Texas to Washington he undertook to "learn" Washington just as he had learned Johnson City where he lived, San Marcos where he went to college, and Cotulla where he taught. He moved into the Dodge Hotel, which was occupied by seventy-five congressional secretaries. His floor had only one bathroom. The first night he took four showers so that he could meet and talk to as many people as possible. The first morning he brushed his teeth and washed his face five times—at ten-minute intervals—again to meet people. He chose five young men who he thought knew the most and made them his teachers. In the cafeteria he would push to the front of the line and gobble down his meal so he could ask questions while others ate. Note that he considered people the chief source of his Washington education, but he also read voraciously. He read *The New York Times, The Wall Street Journal,* the three daily Washington papers, and the Texas papers. Each evening he collected the daily *Congressional Record,* copies of pending bills, pamphlets, booklets, and committee reports and relaxed with them in bed the way others might relax with a good mystery. It was said of him, "This skinny boy was as green as anybody could be, but within a few months he knew how to operate in Washington better than some who had been here twenty years."[14]

The situation in which Johnson was placed determined whether he was successful. He could encompass all the San Marcos Teachers College but not the House of Representatives. The House was too big, with a highly structured, formal authority system. The Senate, on the other hand, fell easily to him. It was small. He got to know everyone. The power structure was sloppy, most of the senators did not care to dominate it, but Johnson did. He could personally confront and coerce every senator. He knew everything about them and used this knowledge to gain his own goals. As President he succeeded in his first two years because he put Kennedy's program through Congress—which he knew so well—but after that things fell apart. He could not learn all the aspects of the Presidency using techniques that were so successful in his early life, and apparently he could not learn new ways. Kearns concluded that the Presidency simply cannot be handled by a man with Johnson's characteristics.

The general approach used by Kearns is of value to us. She described Johnson's behavior using existential language and made attempts to explain the behavior largely by using Freudian concepts. My reaction is that the behavior of LBJ, a most complex human being, must have a better explanation than the fact that his mother disliked his father; however, the theoretical bases for explaining administrator behavior are weak, and it may well be that there is no better way. Nonetheless, the book is an example of one way in which the appropriate data can be collected.

Another source for understanding the people who become administrators is their autobiographies. It is true that there are not many of them, but the ones in existence are revealing. I have in mind Frank E. Spaulding's *School Superintendent in Action in Five Cities.*[15] This candid and completely revealing story tells one more than a dozen of the traditional modern texts tell.

What I am asking for is research on administrators as individuals using either direct observation such as the Kearns study did or systematic analysis of biographies and autobiographies.

Doing Administration

The English have many nice ways with the language. For instance, they say, "Margaret is at Cambridge *doing* mathematics." I believe that administration should be considered as something that people do. In this sense it is similar to other things that people do: medicine, dentistry, mathematics, teaching, and baseball. Since administration is, I believe, something people do, research must be done on the actual practice of administration.

By way of getting started let us review a few days in the life of a university dean.

9:15 a.m. *Chaired meeting of committee convened by the president to prepare a long-range policy for the university's participation in intercollegiate athletics. The committee was comprised of three professors chosen by the Faculty Council, two students chosen by the Student Council, and two deans, one chosen by the president and the other by the chairman. The agenda included: review of plans for new sports center; examination of intramural athletics; and review of statement on the value of intercollegiate athletics.*

10:30 a.m. *Deans Group. A weekly meeting of the five deans of the School of Education, Health, Nursing, and Arts Professions. The meeting lasted through a sandwich lunch. The agenda included: final recommendations on tenure and promotion; discussion of a number of problems relating to the transfer of a research and training center into the school; and report on expanding the school's activity in research in special education.*

2:00 p.m. *Meeting of the Organizational Committee of the Study of the Common Undergraduate Program. The Committee was chaired by the vice-president for academic affairs and was comprised of the deans of the five undergraduate colleges, the five chairpersons of curriculum committees, and two students. The meeting was concerned with final plans for getting the study under way.*

3:30 p.m. *Met with the Director of the Research and Training Center Program of the Rehabilitation Service Administration to discuss problems emanating from a site visit of the school's Deafness Research and Training Center.*

4:30 p.m. *Met with the board of trustees of the school's Para-Educator Center. The discussion was focused on raising money.*

5:30 p.m. *Dinner with the national advisory board of the school's Deafness Research and Training Center. Meeting of the board followed the dinner and lasted until 10:00 p.m.*

Items in the mail included a request from a student to have his grades raised so he could enter graduate school and a copy of a letter from an ophthalmologist to the president of the University demanding that the school be investigated because the dean did not pull a TV tape of a Sunrise Semester session which included an optometrist on a panel of four specialists in learning disabilities. Quite a different day was this:

10:00 a.m. to 12 noon *Chaired faculty meeting. The agenda included: report on the university study of undergraduate education; report of the Faculty Welfare Committee which dealt with faculty loads, retirement benefits, faculty performance ratings, and the IRS action on tuition remission; report from the University Senate dealing with a uniform time module for classes, affirmative action, and some activities of the university board of trustees; and report by the dean on retention and attrition in doctoral programs.*

1:00 p.m. *Met with the assistant dean for administration on a problem dealing with moving a research institute.*

2:00 p.m. *Participated in a doctoral oral as a reader.*

A more typical day was this:

8:30 a.m. *Met with president and central administration of the university to discuss off-campus programs on Long Island.*

9:30 a.m. to 1:30 p.m. *Attended meeting of members of the New York State education commissioner's Task Force on Teacher Education and Certification.*

2:00 p.m. to 4:00 p.m. *Met with school's Department of Music and Music Education to talk about themselves, plans for the future, problems (such as reducing doctoral attrition), and for a review of economic indicators and new programs.*

4:15 p.m. *Met with chairman of Faculty Welfare Committee to discuss problems in two programs.*

5:45 p.m. to 9:00 p.m. *Dinner and welcome of audience to the Peter Agnew Memorial Lecture.*

Several sets of research questions surface after such a recitation, the answers to which would help us to understand administrator behavior and serve as a basis for improved theory.

The first observation is that the dean was constantly involved with other people. Solitary activity was rare and took place before 10:00 a.m. or outside the office. While with a group, the dean was often, but not always, the chairman. The group activity was sometimes policy-making, sometimes problem-solving, sometimes information-receiving, and the dean's work varied with the group. What kind of behavior on the part of the dean would have been most appropriate? Appropriate to what? What skills should he develop? What personality predispositions should be dampened or reinforced? How would the dean know when he was effective?

Every administrator is concerned about how he uses his time. While the days described above do not constitute a scientific sample, they are not atypical. Were these activities the best use of the dean's time? Could he have spent his time more effectively doing other things? What are the criteria for use of time? There are few guides to this set of concerns; there is little knowledge for administrators to use.

There are many questions concerning the authority of the administrator in education. The fact that he is constantly in interaction with people in the organization means that there is the need to talk things out, to negotiate, to bargain, and to do it on a face-to-face basis. What is known and what should be known of the authority position of the administrator in higher education? How does the authority of the university administrator differ from the authority of elementary or secondary school administrators?

I have one last set of questions. Even the brief overview of a few days in the life of a dean that we are considering raises inquiries concerning the physical health and stamina of administrators. How much of the success of an administrator is dependent on his health? Are there people who are less vigorous and are just as effective? Just what part does physical health play in the success of an administrator? Similar questions can be raised about mental health.

In this chapter I have expressed concern about the level of our knowledge about administrators as individuals. I have raised many old questions, most notably that of the criteria of effectiveness. I have stressed the need to study actual behavior by observation and have deplored the abstractness that is now the vogue.

Transferability of Research Findings

I have become increasingly concerned with the uncritical use of theories and research findings from sources other than educational administration. Even the most perfunctory examination of our literature demonstrates that borrowing is the practice rather than the exception. As Immegart has noted, "Educational administration professors simply appear to draw increasingly on the literature of other areas in a 'pure' or applied sense . . ."[16] Many textbook writers have shifted from drawing upon other education sources such as texts, reports, and association publications for content to drawing more broadly on the literature from a variety of professional fields and disciplines.[17] Textbook writers have also moved from the almost exclusive use of research from education and psychology for findings to the use of research findings from other professional fields and disciplines in 1974.[18]

My first attempt to use research findings from another field should have been enough to cause me to question the practice, but it was not. In the process of doing my dissertation (on the leadership of school superintendents) I constructed what I called the Teacher Reaction Form.[19] Twenty of the twenty-two items came from Helen Jennings' study *Leadership and Isolation*.[20] You may remember she studied behavior characteristics of leaders using a population of 450 girls in the New York State Training Schools for Girls. Even her claim that ". . . the institution population does not deviate too radically from the general population"[21] did not deter me. It did not deter John Hemphill either, since he used the same study to develop the LBDQ (Leadership Behavior Description Questionnaire).[22] Well, the story of the Teacher Reaction Form was that, while it was reliable (.90), it had no validity when used with teachers to distinguish successful from unsuccessful superintendents of schools. Not only did the mean total scores not distinguish, but no item had a "*t*" in excess of 1.08. I finished this part of my dissertation by writing, "It may be concluded that such things as sense of humor, ability to make a speech, courteousness, and the like do not distinguish 'successful' from 'unsuccessful' superintendents."[23] I should have added that items that distinguish leaders from nonleaders of delinquent girls do not distinguish successful from unsuccessful school superintendents—for which they should be grateful.

The Teacher Reaction Form and the PBDQ (The LBDQ adapted for use with principals) are highly correlated, as one might expect. When they were used in the in-basket study, there was virtually no agreement between ratings on their form and superiors' ratings of principals.[24] That marked the last time I ever used the Teacher Reaction Form. I wish others could say the same for the LBDQ.

I believe I used the Teacher Reaction Form as long as I did because it was a short, easily administered, highly reliable form and because the belief that administration is administration regardless of the setting. I now question that belief. There are others who are also questioning.

John Millett published *The Academic Community: An Essay on Organization* in 1962 in which he developed this thesis:

> *I believe ideas drawn from business and public administration have only a very limited applicability to colleges and universities.* [Millett's italics.] More than this, the essential ideas about business and public administration, such as they are, may actually promote a widespread and unfortunate misunderstanding of the nature of the college and university in our society.[25]

While Millett's thesis received little support—in fact, the literature of administration developed in the opposite direction—the occasional studies done in higher education as well as critiques tend to verify his point. Hill and French in a study, "Perceptions of the Power of Department Chairmen by Professors," concluded, "The findings reported here tend to confirm the impression of a number of students that colleges are unique kinds of organizations."[26]

In the only comprehensive bibliographical analysis of the administration of higher education that I could find, Olive offers the hypothesis that existing theories of organizational behavior and administration may not be applicable to present-day universities. In support of her hypothesis she says:

> . . . governmental agencies and business corporations have an internal organization which is unlike that of the university. Among the differences mentioned are these: the goals of the university are not specific and clearly defined; the product or service produced is not tangible; the customer (student) exerts limited influence; the employees (faculty) are dedicated to their specialized fields, not to the employing institutions; and the decision-making process is diffused in a way not typical of other forms of organization. Such differences suggest the inadequacy of present theories on problems of university administration and the incontestable and urgent need for new thinking and new approaches to research in this field.[27]

There are few empirical tests of the relevance of theoretical work in one field to another field. One such study, which did attempt to use a theoretical frame developed in industry and government to categorize New York City school personnel, found serious differences.[28] These were summarized as follows:

> A significant distinction between Presthus' and our studies, however, occurs in the fact that some two-thirds of all teachers were found to be either pupil-oriented or intellectuals. Presthus has no categories even remotely resembling these, leading us to question the wholesale and indiscriminate application of studies of business, industry, the military, and the federal government to education.[29]

However, Blau's study, *The Organization of Academic Work,* offers the opposite conclusion. He attempted to determine whether academic institutions and government bureaus and private firms were homologous, that is, exhibited empirical regularities in size, differentiation in structure, and administrative structure. He concluded, "The administrative structure of academic institutions exhibits a remarkable homology with that of other institutions."[30] It may be that if one compares universities and colleges with other organizations on purely structural grounds, without studying how the structures work, they will appear to be similar. Or, it may be the more abstract one's concepts, the more things appear to be the same. Further, as will be elaborated below, the use of a particular model, in this case bureaucracy, may well bias the results the researcher gets.

The only theory developed exclusively from studies of educational institutions known to me is the Cohen, March, and Olsen theory,[31] and it bears no resemblance to any of the theories now in use in educational administration. I would feel more comfortable with the Cohen, March, and Olsen formulation if I could see some clear relationship between their research and the resulting theory; nonetheless, the theory appears to explain certain aspects of university governance. Their theoretical framework can be summarized as follows: Whereas most organizations can be called "organized anarchies" some of the time, public, educational, and illegitimate ones consistently display these characteristics. They operate on the basis of inconsistent and ill-defined preferences—fuzzy goals, if you will; unclear technology, that is, their own processes are not understood by their members; and fluid participation, that is, the members change frequently and devote varying amounts of time and energy to decision-making and, further, the audiences and decision-makers change capriciously. Decision-making in such organizations is described by the authors as the "Garbage Can Model," for obvious reasons.

It would certainly seem that there is no clear evidence to support the contention that administrative theories can automatically be considered to be general or universal. Further, it would appear that the theorists and researchers in educational administration must give very serious thought to the idea that schools, colleges, and universities are institutions that vary in significant ways from IBM, G.E., and G.M.

Educational administration is not the only field in which people are concerned with transfer of knowledge. Lichtman and Hunt reviewed a large number of theories of organization and concluded that "the extreme variability found within and among organizations renders one-sided normative theories less useful in understanding organizational behavior than models that recognize situational contingencies."[32] Whether one can safely borrow research or theory done in a particular type of organization is dependent on whether there is a reasonable degree of isomorphism with the situation in which the theory or research is to be applied. This might be ascertained by applying a set of criteria developed by Katzell[33] and described briefly as follows:

1. Size. The number of interdependent organizational members is a crucial variable when attempting to transfer research findings from one kind of organization to another. A number of researchers have related employee absence and turnover, communication difficulties, job satisfaction, and morale to large size. Although there is a need for more research on problems caused by size, it is clear that what holds for large organizations very well may not hold for small organizations.

2. Interaction and interdependence. This parameter deals essentially with structuring the work environment. Katz and Kahn, for instance, argue that where task interdependence is high, where creative requirements are minimal, and where identification with organizational goals is not required, a hierarchical

authority structure calling for close supervision is indicated. Where the opposite circumstances obtain, a more democratic alternative should be used for maximum efficiency.[34]

3. Personalities of organizational members. The motivations, expectations, abilities, and other personal qualities seem to be of paramount interest in determining policies and practices.

4. Degree of congruence or disparity between organizational goals and the needs and goals of members. Organizations vary according to goal internalization of their members. The extremes are illustrated by workers on assembly lines and scientists in research companies or universities.

5. Who has ability and motivation. As Katzell says:

> ... It would seem necessary to mold the organizational system so that it maximizes freedom of action and initiative for those who can and will take effective action, while eliciting compliance, support, or noninterference from others. Depending on the organizational loci of expertise and dedication, the appropriate work system may vary widely from situation to situation.[35]

I find Katzell's guidelines useful in helping to determine whether a piece of research done in industry, for instance, is applicable to an educational organization. Possibly, a set of rules might be devised to test the transferability of research findings. Another research task that needs doing is the actual testing of research findings together with the publication of that which is applicable to educational institutions. Even this would have to be interpreted with care, since there is such a wide variation among educational organizations.

Contemporary Theory Development and Educational Administration

In this section I shall argue that the paradigm presently used in educational administration is neither useful nor appropriate because it is no longer fruitful in generating powerful concepts and hypotheses; it does not allow us to describe either modern organizations or the people in them; and, as a result, it is not helpful to administrators.[36] I shall further contend that the fault is not so much in the methodology employed as in the substance. In other words, the tools and methods of research (commonly called the scientific method) are adequate, but what the tools and methods are used on is not.

The paradigm consists largely of the Getzels-Guba social systems model, role theory, decision theory, bureaucracy, and varieties of systems theory.[37] These theories hold many assumptions in common. They assume that organizations have goals that the members strive to attain; that there are roles, sets of expectations for the members which are agreed upon (the nomothetic dimension); that behavior is more or less governed by a set of rules (bureaucratic structure); that decision-making is a systematic process; that only legitimate power is employed; and that merit is superior to politics. Administration, organizations, and organizational behavior are viewed as essentially orderly and rational. Organizations function regardless of the individuals within them. These theories of administration are "great man" theories which assume that if the administrator were capable enough he would be able to comprehend and resolve all situations in a satisfactory manner. This is a view of organizations and administration familiar only to a committed researcher of the old school.

The argument is, then, that it is necessary to view organizations with different spectacles, that the theories we have been using have limited our view of what an organization is and how it operates.

There is, however, a basic question that must be discussed first. The question is "What is theory?" and, more particularly, "What is a theory of administration?" As I read various uses of the word *theory* today, I am more and more inclined toward, but have not yet accepted, Conant's position:

> The reader may be reminded that the words *theory* and *hypothesis* are frequently employed to describe both conceptual schemes and models, or pictures, explaining such schemes. A discussion of the definition of theory and hypothesis is often given in elementary texts, but I think such considerations of doubtful value. Because of the ambiguity it is well, perhaps, to avoid as far as possible both words in discussing the evolution of science.[38]

It is disturbing in reading Kuhn, considered by so many in educational administration to be the author of the definitive work in the history of science, to note the loose way in which he uses the words *theory* and *paradigm.* One diligent critic counted at least twenty-two different uses of *paradigm.*[39] Instead of being pleased at this recognition of his creativity, Kuhn discounted the different uses as "stylistic inconsistencies" and claimed to have used the term in only two ways.[40] For us, at this point, the following from Kuhn is of importance:

> Scientists themselves would say they share a theory or set of theories, and I shall be glad if the term can ultimately be recaptured for this use. As currently used in philosophy of science, however, theory connotes a structure far more limited in nature and scope than is required here. Until the term can be freed from its current implications, it will avoid confusion to adopt another. For present purposes I suggest "disciplinary matrix": "disciplinary" because it refers to the common possession of the practitioner of a particular discipline; "matrix" because it is composed of ordered elements of various sorts, each requiring further specification.[41]

I disagree. *Disciplinary matrix* is no improvement at all, and those who pervert the *term* theory will have a field day with *disciplinary matrix*. My view is very similar to that of Blalock:

> Ideally we might hope to achieve a completely deductive theoretical system in which there would be a minimal set of propositions taken as axioms, from which all other propositions could be deduced by purely mathematical or logical reasoning. (Note the similarity to Feigel.) More realistically we might take the model of the completely closed deductive system as an ideal which in practice can only be approximated.[42]

I believe we should attempt to approximate the use of the word *theory* to mean a set of assumptions from which propositions can be deduced by methematical or logical reasoning. I hope that we in educational administration reach consensus on this use and put a stop to the wide usage which has, for all practical purposes, rendered the term useless.

At this point I would remind everyone that there is much in administration that very probably lies outside the scope of theory. The practice of administration is largely an art and reflects the personal style of an administrator and the environment in which the person functions. Much of this lies beyond the reaches of theory as we know it.

Critique of the Current Paradigm

The paradigm currently used in educational administration has conceptual weaknesses, and it is not always useful for describing administrative situations.

Concepts: There is considerable evidence that the current paradigm is inadequate. Gross's work, for instance, calls into question the concept of role as it is used in educational administration.[43] The Aston studies indicate that Weber's concept of a single bureaucratic type is not a universal concept, since bureaucracy takes different forms in different settings. Riemann generally confirmed the findings of the Aston study,[44] but Mansfield contends that abandonment of the bureaucratic type is premature.[45] The evidence is strong enough, however, to call previous thinking about bureaucracy into question.

Systems theories and derivatives thereof also have shortcomings. Wildavsky, in a devastating article in *New York Affairs,* demonstrates convincingly that PERT (Program Evaluation and Review Technique), CPM (Critical Path Method), MBO (Management by Objectives), and PPBS (Program Planning and Budgeting System) rarely work. (In fact, he argues PPBS does not work anywhere in the world.)[46]

The major test of theories is the power of the concepts and hypotheses that they generate. I reviewed volume 12 of the *Educational Administration Quarter-ly* to note the power of hypotheses and relationships among variables. I judged that eleven articles dealt with administrative behavior. In four of the studies all of the hypotheses were rejected or all tests were nonsignificant. In four of the studies no more than a third of the tests resulted in significant relationships. In three, the hypothesized relationships were confirmed. I concluded that the concepts and theories employed in these studies could hardly be called powerful. I suspect that what is published in the *Educational Administration Quarterly* is typical of our field. I recently sat in on a doctoral oral where the thesis that was defended was the sixth on conceptual systems theory. Only one of the six came up with significant findings.

I am not saying that one should not publish nonsignificant findings, but I presume that no one intentionally does studies that come out this way. The presumption is that the theories are powerful and, as such, suggest the possibility of producing significant findings.

Describing Administrative Situations: I shall present only two additional exam-ples of the problems involved in using the current paradigm in describing administrative situations.

Of all the elements of society that have changed, that which has changed most significantly is the individual. Perhaps the case may be made by contrasting two statements, one by Simon in 1950 and the second by Lord Morris in 1974. In discussing the concept of authority Simon, writing in his classic *Administrative Behavior,* said, "The superior frames and transmits decisions with the expectation that they will be accepted by the subordinate. The subordinate expects such decisions, and his conduct is determined by them."[47] Lord Morris, in speaking of the same relationship said, "The peoples do not want to be governed, and clearly they do not believe there is any real and final necessity to be governed."[48] Both statements are a bit extreme; however, each is used to describe a central tendency. Clearly, the way in which people view themselves and the relationships to others in organizations has changed to the point that the theories of administrative and organizational behavior we have been using are no longer applicable. They do not describe organizational behavior, nor do they predict such behavior. They ignore the basic change in authority relationships, which has been under way since World War II and which accelerated in the early 1960s. This is probably the single most important change in organizations.

An interesting test by Bleecher of Barnard's criteria for judging the authoritativeness of organizational communications is also relevant to my point. He found that although teachers understood a set of accountability and assessment criteria issued by the Michigan State Education Department they felt them to be: (1) inconsistent with the purposes of the school organization as they understand them; (2) not compatible with their personal interest; and (3) not able to be complied with, mentally and physically.[49] This was in spite of a lengthy and apparently logical attempt by the Department to set goals of the schools of the state. The theoretical framework of Barnard could not be used to describe what appeared to be a relevant organizational situation.

New Directions

I should like to sketch some of the new bases upon which emerging administrative theories must be constructed if they are to be used to describe administrative situations and to predict administrative behavior.

Garbage Can Theory. Clark and Guba in their study of schools, colleges, and departments of education find that decision-making fits the March, Cohen, and Olsen description.[50]

Environment-Situation. Taking von Bertalanffy's formulation, Emery and Trist developed a concept, "the causal texture of the environment," to account for those processes in the environment that are among the determining conditions of the exchanges between the organization and its environment.[54] Emery and Trist identify four types of causal textures following studies of change problems in hospitals, prisons, and educational and political organizations: placid, randomized environment; and turbulent fields. They also state that most of our troubles arise from the environment itself rather than from within the organization (a conclusion I am not entirely ready to accept). By a process that is not entirely clear, the authors feel that an analysis of the environment resulting in turbulent fields implies that McGregor's Theory Y is the proper course of action. This means that a new set of values must be developed—which they feel will take a generation.

Loose Coupling. Weick puts forth the concept of "loose coupling" as a way of describing organizations. He proposes that elements of an organization are often tied together loosely and that this incorporates a surprising number of disparate observations about organization, suggests novel functions, creates stubborn problems for methodologists, and generates intriguing questions for scholars.[52] I think the concept should be simply "coupling," since there are obvious examples of both tight and loose coupling. While Weick stresses loose couplings, I suggest that one reason why schools innovate so slowly is because they are so tightly coupled to their communities.

Informal Organization. Modern theories have attempted to deal with the attitudes and feelings of people in organizations through the concept of informal organization. The idea was that if the goals of people could not be met through the formal organizations, then the members would join together to seek their goals outside the formal structure. Denton states, "Informal arrangements will develop for the simple reason that the life forces, the spontaneity, the elan, the ordinary experiences of persons overflow the bounds of any organizational chart."[53] Are informal structures central to organizations rather than peripheral as we have assumed? Remember that Chester Barnard developed the concept of informal organization, and he was the president of New Jersey Bell. How would he have viewed the informal organization if he had been a lineman?

Unions. Theories of administration and organization are written as though there were no unions or other formal employee groups existing within organizations. Theories of organization in education must be devised to incorporate the individual as a member of at least two formal groups. I suppose, after talking with my union friends, that there must also be an informal power structure within the union as well as within the educational institution. This means that each individual assumes at least four postures, formal and informal in each organization.

The formal decision-making structure of each school district or university must also be reconceptualized, because the union replaces building faculties in the public schools and senates in the universities as the decision-making body. Although there is no faculty union at New York University, for example, there is a plethora of formal groups all involved in varying ways in the formal decision process. Some of these are: Faculty Council, Deans Council, Student Senators Council, Central Administration Officers Group, President's Office, and the Management Council. There are two focal points at which they meet to develop policy: the Senate Budget Advisory Committee and the Senate. In addition, there are several unions of nonprofessional people whose policy issues are settled through collective bargaining. I have never seen a theoretical formulation that has attempted to incorporate these various elements in a university's decision-making process.

Idée Fixe. Philip Johnson was recently quoted as saying, "Let us celebrate the death of the *idée fixe*. There are no rules, only facts. There is no order only preferences."[54] For us, as administrators and professors of educational administration, it is particularly applicable because our theories have been based on the idée fixe.

The Individual. Although the phenomenologists make a strong case for treating people in theories as individuals without the use of steno-language or categorization, they offer no examples of what this means in practice.

It is true that present efforts at theorizing in educational administration employ concepts stated in sociological, psychological, economic, or anthropological language, and these are abstractions. For instance, we talk of a person occupying a role. Role is a sociological abstraction. The phenomenologist would prefer to speak of the person as a basic fact. As Vandenberg puts it for education, "The task of educational theory is the restoration of the wholeness of educational phenomena as they appear within the educating perspective."[55] The ultimate task for educational administration is, I presume, very much the same.

If the person is considered the basic fact, then his values, his feelings, his attitude, what Denton calls his "soul," would be reproduced in some way. But would we then have a theory? Remember that theories are important only to the extent they give rise to the activities that Kuhn calls "normal science," that is, the testing of hypotheses derived from the theories. If the individual is the basic fact, how is he incorporated into theoretical statements unless steno-language and categorizations are used?

Rather than attempting to build theories in which individuals are central, we must try to construct theories that reflect the actual balance as it exists among people, organizations, and environment so as to be of value in specific situations. As noted, the theories presently employed in educational administration are essentially "great man" theories, which assume that if the administrator is capable enough he will be able to comprehend and resolve all situations in a satisfactory manner. It seems to me that a number of recent studies would lead to precisely the opposite conclusion, namely, there are situations which no administrator, however capable, can comprehend and resolve unless changes are brought about to alter the environment or the organization. I have in mind the Nicholas et al. study of the climates of four elementary schools and the differences in administrative behavior found in each.[56] In addition, there are now several studies that attempt to build classification systems of climates and environments.

An experimental study by Frederiksen et al. employed simulation to test the effect of climate on the people working in it.[57] The major finding was that the mean productivity score, that is, the amount of work completed, is significantly affected by the consistency of climate conditions. More important are the four climates that were contrived and the fact that it was clearly and significantly demonstrated that the climates made a difference in administrative performance.

Clark and Guba conclude in their study of schools, colleges, and departments of education that, "The culture of institutions of higher education is predominately idiographic (that is, emphasizing the self-actualization of the professor) rather than nomothetic (that is, emphasizing the goals of the institution)."[58] Administration in such an organization must surely demand a theory different from that which is appropriate for IBM or the Army, which are far more nomothetic than the university.

If theory is built on observations of organizations—one by one—it seems apparent that individuals (except for the President or certain mavericks) form groups to attain their personal goals and, often, the organizational goals. Thus, public school teachers have developed strong unions and associations designed to achieve the goals of individuals. Even universities in which individuals have traditionally worked on their own are moving toward unionization. The individual as a member of a group of his own choosing is a fact of organizational life.

Development of the New Paradigm

What, then, are some of the dominant ideas which might well be influential in the development of the new paradigm?

1. The end of the idée fixe in modern life. Just as in modern art the artist pictures life in nonrepresentational ways, so too will the social theorist recognize that his work should produce theories that encompass the essence of modern life.

2. Theories will have to develop new approaches to the concept of authority and acknowledge the fact that people do not want to be governed.

3. Because of the change in authority relationships, the key administrative process in organization is very likely to be bargaining and not necessarily collective bargaining. It could very well be that the Barnard-Simon theory, which is essentially a bargaining theory, will be prominent in the new paradigm.

4. New theories are likely to be highly specific and focused on particular types of organization. The search for a general theory of administration will be long delayed.

5. There will be numerous efforts to build theories using ideology and values for axioms, with propositions predicting behavior dependent on the axioms. It is doubtful that these efforts will succeed.

6. Emerging theories will likely use situations and situational variables as axioms.

7. Methodologically, emerging theories will be far more complex than present theories.

8. New concepts entirely different from ones with which we are familiar will be used (for example, coupling).

Summary

I have attempted to point to three directions in which research is needed. These include researching what it is that administrators do; using nonabstract language; and establishing criteria of effectiveness for administrators. I also raised the question of the transferability of research findings, and suggested some guidelines. Finally, I asked for new approaches to developing theories of educational administration.

Notes

1. Daniel E. Griffiths, *Research in Education Administration: An Appraisal and a Plan* (New York: Teacher's College, Bureau of Publications, 1959); and Daniel E. Griffiths, "Research and Theory in Educational Administration," in W.W. Charters et al., eds., *Perspectives on Educational Administration and the Behavioral Sciences* (Eugene, Oreg.: Center for the Advanced Study of Educational Administration, 1965), pp. 25-48.

2. Glenn L. Immegart, "The Study of Educational Administration 1954-74: Myths, Paradoxes, Facts, and Prospects," Paper presentation to conference, *Educational Administration Twenty Years Later: 1954-74* (Columbus, Ohio: The Ohio State University, 1975).

3. Kingman Brewster, *The Report of the President* (Yale University, 1975-1976), p. 11.

4. Charles Percy Snow, "Science and Government," in C.P. Snow, *Public Affairs* (New York: Scribners, 1977), p. 100.

5. David E. Denton, *The Language of Ordinary Experience* (New York: Philosophical Library, 1970), p. 37. Reprinted with permission.

6. Ibid., p. 43. Reprinted with permission.

7. Ibid., p. 139. Reprinted with permission.

8. Ibid., p. 142. Reprinted with permission.

9. Felix Bloch, "Reminiscences of Heisenberg and the Early Days of Quantum Mechanics," *Physics Today* 29, no. 12 (December 1976):27. Reprinted with permission.

10. Andrew Halpin, "The Development of Theory in Educational Administration," in A. Halpin, ed., *Administrative Theory in Education* (University of Chicago: Midwest Administration Center, 1958), p. 288.

11. J. Victor Baldridge, *Power and Conflict in the University* (New York: John Wiley, 1971).

12. David B. Tyack, "Pilgrim's Progress: Toward a Social History of the School Superintendency, 1860-1960," *History of Education Quarterly*, Fall 1976, pp. 257-300.

13. John K. Hemphill, Daniel E. Griffiths, and Norman Frederiksen, *Administrative Performance and Personality* (New York: Teacher's College, Bureau of Publications, 1962).

14. Doris Kearns, *Lyndon Johnson and the American Dream* (New York: Harper and Row, 1976), p. 73.

15. Frank E. Spaulding, *School Superintendent in Action in Five Cities* (Rindge, N.H.: Richard R. Smith Publisher, 1955).

16. Immegart, "Study of Educational Administration," p. 35.

17. Glenn L. Immegart, "The Study of Educational Administration 1954-74," in L. Cunningham, W. Hack, and R. Nystrand, eds., *Educational*

Administration: The Developing Decades (Berkeley, Calif.: McCutchan, 1977), p. 313.

18. Ibid., p. 313.

19. Daniel E. Griffiths, "An Evaluation of the Leadership of the School Superintendent" (Ph.D. diss., Yale University, 1952).

20. Helen Jennings, *Leadership and Isolation* (New York: Longmans-Green, 1950).

21. Ibid., p. 27.

22. Hemphill, Griffiths, and Frederiksen, *Administrative Performance.*

23. Griffiths, "Evaluation of Leadership," p. 125.

24. Hemphill, Griffiths, and Frederiksen, *Administrative Performance,* p. 234.

25. John D. Millett, *The Academic Community: An Essay on Organization* (New York: McGraw-Hill, 1962), p. 4.

26. Winston W. Hill and Wendell L. French, "Perceptions of the Power of Department Chairmen by Professors," *Administrative Science Quarterly* 11, no. 4 (March 1967):572.

27. Betsy Ann Olive, "The Administration of Higher Education: A Bibliographic Survey," *Administrative Science Quarterly* 11, no. 4 (March 1967):677. Reprinted with permission.

28. Daniel E. Griffiths, Samuel Goldman, and Wayne J. McFarland, "Teacher Mobility in New York City," *Educational Administration Quarterly* 1, no. 1 (Winter 1965):15-31.

29. Ibid., p. 30. Reprinted with permission.

30. Peter M. Blau, *The Organization of Academic Work* (New York: John Wiley, 1973), p. 13.

31. Michael D. Cohen, James G. March, and Johan P. Olsen, "A Garbage Can Model of Organizational Choice," *Administrative Science Quarterly* 17, no. 1 (March 1972):1-25.

32. Cary M. Lichtman and Raymond G. Hunt, "Personality and Organization Theory: A Review of Some Conceptual Literature," *Psychological Bulletin* 76, no. 4 (October 1971):283-285.

33. Raymond Katzell, "Contrasting Systems of Work Organization," *American Psychologist,* no. 17 (1962), pp. 102-108 as summarized in Lichtman and Hunt, "Personality and Organization Theory."

34. Daniel Katz and Robert Kahn, *The Social Psychology of Organization* (New York: Wiley, 1966) as reported in Lichtman and Hunt, "Personality and Organization Theory," p. 283.

35. Katzell, "Contrasting Systems of Work Organization," as summarized in Lichtman and Hunt, "Personality and Organization Theory," p. 285. Copyright 1962 by the American Psychological Association. Reprinted by permission.

36. A more detailed discussion of this argument appears in Daniel E. Griffiths, "The Individual in Organization," (The 1976 NCPEA Walter D. Cocking Lecture) *Educational Administration Quarterly* 13, no. 2 (Spring 1977).

37. Daniel E. Griffiths, ed., *Developing Taxonomies of Organizational Behavior in Educational Administration* (Chicago: Rand McNally, 1969); and Daniel E. Griffiths, "Administrative Theory," in R.L. Ebel, ed., *Encyclopedia of Educational Research,* 4th ed. (New York: Macmillan Company, 1969), pp. 17-24.

38. James B. Conant, *On Understanding Science* (New York: Mentor, 1951), pp. 57-58.

39. Margaret Masterman, "The Nature of a Paradigm," in Manfred Kochen, comp., *Growth of Knowledge* (Cambridge, Mass.: Wiley, 1970) as noted in Thomas Kuhn, *The Structure of Scientific Revolutions,* 2d ed. (Chicago: University of Chicago Press, 1970), p. 181.

40. Kuhn, *Structure of Scientific Revolutions,* p. 182.

41. Ibid.

42. Hubert M. Blalock, Jr., *Theory Construction* (Englewood Cliffs, N.J.: Prentice-Hall, 1969).

43. Neal Gross, Ward S. Mason, and Alexander W. McEachern, *Explorations in Role Analysis* (New York: Wiley, 1958).

44. Bernard C. Riemann, "On the Dimensions of Bureaucratic Structure: An Empirical Reappraisal," *Administrative Science Quarterly* 18, no. 4 (December 1973):462-476.

45. Roger Mansfield, "Bureaucracy and Centralization: An Examination of Organizational Structure," *Administrative Science Quarterly* 18, no. 4 (December 1973):477-488.

46. Aaron Wildavsky, "Policy Analysis Is What Information Systems Are Not," *New York Affairs* 4, no. 2 (Spring 1977):10-23.

47. Herbert A. Simon, *Administrative Behavior* (New York: Macmillan, 1950), p. 125.

48. Lord Morris, "Acceptability: The New Emphasis in Educational Administration," in M. Hughes, ed., *Administering Education: International Challenge* (London: Athlone Press, 1975), pp. 13-19.

49. Harvey Bleecher, "Educational Accountability in Michigan: Root and Branch," *Educational Administration Quarterly* 12, no. 2 (Spring 1976):47.

50. David L. Clark and Egon G. Guba, "An Inventory of Contextual Factors and Conditions Affecting Individual and Institutional Behavior in Schools, Colleges, and Departments of Education," RITE Occasional Paper Series, Indiana University (July 1976).

51. P.E. Emery and E.L. Trist, "The Causal Texture of Organizational Environments," in Joseph Litter, ed., *Organizations: Systems, Control and Adaptation,* vol. 2, 2d ed. (New York: John Wiley, 1963).

52. Karl E. Weick, "Educational Organizations as Loosely Coupled Systems," *Administrative Science Quarterly* 21, no. 1 (March 1976):1.

53. Denton, *Language or Ordinary Experience,* p. 140. Reprinted with permission.

54. John Russell, "Anything Goes at the Galleries," *New York Times,* 21

May 1976, p. C1. © 1976 by the New York Times Company. Reprinted by permission.

55. Donald Vandenberg, "Phenomenology and Educational Research," in David E. Denton, ed., *Existentialism and Phenomenology in Education* (New York: Teacher's College Press, 1974), p. 189.

56. Lynn N. Nicholas, Helen E. Virjo, and William W. Wattenburg, *Effect of Socio-Economic Setting and Organizational Climate on Problems Brought to Elementary School Offices,* U.S. Department of Health, Education and Welfare, Cooperative Research project no. 2394 (Detroit: Wayne State University, 1965), p. 169.

57. Norman Frederiksen, O. Jensen, and A.E. Beaton, *Organizational Climates and Administrative Performance* (Princeton, N.J.: Educational Testing Service, 1968), p. 376.

58. Clark and Guba, "Inventory of Contextual Factors." Reprinted with permission.

4

Some Issues in Research on School Organizations

Donald J. Willower

There has been much discussion and some debate in educational administration over such matters as the merits of various research methods, the relation of theory and research, and the relationship of theory and research on the one hand and practice on the other. The purpose of this chapter is to put some issues in these areas into clearer perspective.

Hence, this is not a review of research of the kind available in such standard sources as the *Encyclopedia of Educational Research,* the *Handbook of Organizations,* and the *Review of Research in Education.*[1] It is a more general treatment, a reflective statement on research and its context.

There are many other works of this sort, some of them quite recent. For example, a classification scheme for research in educational administration has been presented,[2] and relevant papers were given at the seminar held in 1975 in honor of Roald Campbell.[3] One was a careful analysis by Immegart of research in educational administration over a twenty-year period along with some exploration of the circumstances that influenced research during that time. Another was an essay by Halpin and Hayes on theory and research over the same span. That paper contained many cogent insights, but in some ways it was a grand pontification—grand in the sense that the Irish use that word and a pontification in the sense that some key judgments were rendered *ex cathedra.*

But we have had a lot of pontification in educational administration with regard to theory and research. The field began to be oriented in those directions just over twenty years ago, and considerable effort and energy are still being expended in debates about theory and research rather than in discussions of specific theories and studies.

Although I am reluctant to do so, I will add to those debates, because I believe it is time for a less introspective, more pragmatic perspective. To that end, selected issues are examined in the three areas mentioned: research methods, the relation of theory and research, and the relationship of theory and research to practice. The main focus is on research on school organizations. However, research is taken broadly, as part of inquiry—the process that seeks grounded explanation—and although the emphasis is on school organizations, some of the points made may have wider application in educational administration and similar fields.

Methods: Advocacy and Results

No one that I am aware of has been audacious enough to argue explicitly that there is one best way to do research on school organizations. However, there has been a remarkable amount of choosing up sides.

Educational research has its main heritage in psychology, stemming primarily from the descriptive, experimental, and measurement aspects of that discipline. In colleges of education, departments of educational psychology typically have been responsible for instruction in research methods, and the faculty members of those departments often have been viewed as experts in research, circumstances that have helped to maintain the dominance of their methods.

Field Methods

Griffiths and Iannaccone both have contended that greater emphasis should be given in educational administration to observational type field studies.[4] I have taken a similar position.[5] However, no one wants to eliminate traditional educational research methods. Rather, a better balance has been sought.

Iannaccone argued that field methods are likely to furnish data with special meaning for theory in educational administration, and he also stated that the content of field studies should have special relevance for practitioners of school administration, since that content arises from descriptions of life within school organizations.[6]

I have stressed an additional value of field studies. They provide unusual opportunities to confront descriptive data and attempt to give them meaning. I give high priority to the cultivation of the scientific temper on the part of both researchers and practitioners in educational administration,[7] and observational type studies offer an arena within which such qualities can be sharpened. To puzzle over, wonder about, and strive to make theoretical sense out of previously disparate data is both a crucial aspect of inquiry and good practice for those who seek to understand how and why something works the way it does.

Halpin and Hayes reacted to Iannaccone's call for field studies in educational administration by warning that should the path he proposed be followed, years would be wasted.[8] Granting that field studies can generate hypotheses, they emphasized the problem of generalization.

Positions on field studies may be influenced to some degree by the units of analysis with which one is most comfortable. Those who take sociocultural systems or organizations as units of analysis seem more likely to take a positive view of field research than those who take individuals as units of analysis. Another division can be made in terms of whether one assigns greater value to getting ideas or to testing them. Field studies have a particular attraction for those in the former category.

Application of several common classification schemes highlights the complexities involved. The empirical-rational or empirical-theoretical distinction is one such scheme. Obviously, field research is highly empirical. Yet, field researchers often carry extensive theoretical baggage, especially if hypothesis formulation is a major objective of their inquiries. Hence, significant elements of the rational or theoretical might also be present.

A popular distinction is that made by William James between the tough- and tender-minded. It is generally accepted that James referred to the tough-minded philosophical naturalist or realist and to the tender-minded idealist, although he contrasted the two without using those terms. Some may employ the tough- and tender-minded dichotomy in a casual way, but correctly used it does not have a clear application in thinking about field studies. I suppose one could argue that a field researcher would be more likely to be a tough-minded metaphysical naturalist than an idealist, but that seems farfetched.

A related distinction has to do with orientations toward truth, to use a word that makes researchers but not philosophers uneasy. The correspondence theory of truth holds those propositions to be true that correspond with observed fact. The coherence theory of truth holds those propositions to be true that harmonize with or fit a system of knowledge. Where does field research fit in these terms? If one chooses to emphasize observation, it fits the correspondence orientation, and if one chooses to emphasize interpretation, it fits the coherence orientation.

Obviously, the orientations and the issues have been simplified to make a point. We want both correspondence and coherence, although Einstein's preference was coherence in a conflict between elaborated theory and the "facts."[9] In any case, it is a mistake to categorize glibly field methods. Rather, the method should be appraised on the basis of its utility in inquiry, and specific studies should be assessed in terms of such criteria as the precision and range of the observations made, the plausibility of the interpretations set forth, and whether the propositions presented were theoretically cogent and fruitful.

Several comments are worth making on the evidence and generalization issues. If the unit with which a field study deals is a sociocultural system of some sort, then a single case is examined. Even if the units treated are more numerous ones, like groups or events, they usually are found in a single setting. Hence there is the argument that too few cases exist to allow for generalization, although the issue in induction is not so much the number of cases observed as it is their representativeness.

Even so, the statement that field studies can generate hypotheses but not test them is correct for most field research. But it is a shade too simple. Obviously, if a hypothesis is formulated as a result of a given field study, it cannot be tested in that study. It is an after-the-fact interpretation. However, what can be said about a case in which a prior hypothesis is examined in the course of a field study? What about a prior hypothesis examined in many field studies? Assuming that the procedural aspects of the research are sound, one can say that the field data either are consistent with the hypothesis or reject it.

The problem of generalization remains, but it is a problem that is not peculiar to field research. It is present in any research, including the more traditional types of educational research. In such investigations, the adequacy of samples, operational definitions, designs, and so on, are important technical questions. They furnish indications of the confidence one can have in the evidence gathered in the research process.

In research that employs statistical analysis, probability applies to comparisons and relationships between operationally defined units. Regardless of the kind of analysis employed, evidence bears directly on such units and their association. It has an indirect bearing on the abstract concepts for which the operational definitions stand, and on the general propositions or assertions, sometimes stated in hypothetical form, that interrelate the concepts. These propositions are direct and unequivocal. They are stated as generalizations, as if the inductive leap has occurred, and it is meaningless to attempt to assign particular probability to such general propositions or to a theory. Here our concern is with the weight of the indirect evidence and with a number of other criteria.[10] Yet, no evidence can be conclusive, even in areas of science that are genuinely advanced. General propositions are never proved. Rather, they are not yet disproved. Moreover, the possibility of new and more tenable propositions, a mark of the self-correcting character of all science, is always present.

In making these comments on evidence and generalization, I want to evoke the tenuousness of all science, especially social science; and I want to emphasize the complexity of the issues involved in generating what Dewey called "warranted assertions."[11] These issues cut across the various branches of science. They are just harder to deal with in the social sciences. To recall them on occasion should bring a touch of humility to everyone concerned with inquiry.

Two of the points made so far might give pause to those who offhandedly derogate the use of field studies. One is that field studies cannot readily be categorized in terms of certain of the dichotomies used, sometimes stereotypically, to classify research methods. The other, which stressed the limitations of evidence and generalization and the provisional character of inquiry itself, provides a perspective that makes choosing up sides with regard to research methods less a matter of scientists versus romantics and more a matter of examining the advantages and disadvantages of various methods.

It has already been suggested that the advantages of field studies include their direct focus on the peculiar subject matter of educational administration and the opportunities presented for the interplay between data and ideas or observations and theorizing. Another is that field research strives to be open to all the features of a total system, not just a narrow aspect of it. This can mean the discovery of previously undefined problems or of important elements or relationships that might otherwise have been missed. Still another plus is the emphasis in field studies on taking nothing for granted and questioning the obvious. This can lead to new slants on old things—something that helps to maintain the vitality of research in a given area. These idea-generating features of the method are apt, since inquiry on school organizations is still at an early stage of development.

The limitations of field research include those usually associated with work on qualitative data. Which events to observe can be a problem. Classification also can be a problem, since it is sometimes hard to place observations in the kinds of general categories necessary to interpretation.

I believe theoretical frameworks can be of great help in deciding both what to observe and in classification. However, some anthropologists contend that field studies should be unhampered by theory and concerned solely with description. In that view, the scope, detail, and accuracy of description become overriding and virtually exclusive considerations. My position is that a substantial conceptual dimension can enhance explanation and thus the value of the investigation. Also, one's conceptual framework should be made explicit. This avoids "pure" descriptions erected on the basis of submerged conceptual schemes. Discussions of field research in educational administration have overemphasized the method's anthropological roots and underemphasized its sociological ones. The distinction is not a sharp one, but the sociological approach tends to be more theory-oriented and more likely to deal with systems, such as organizations, that are appropriate to educational administration.

Another limitation of field methods stems from the difficulty of replication. Replication provides a sense of whether the case observed was a representative one, whether relationships seen in one context pertain in others. It is especially important in the social sciences, where sampling is so problematic.

Replication is difficult in field research, because the setting must remain natural and uncontrolled. Whereas efforts can be made to choose field situations that permit reexamination and refutation of a previously observed relationship, the flow of events in the field dictates what will be possible to observe. Furthermore, inability to control for confounding variables that could be present or absent in different field settings might prevent an objective test of the relationship in question. It is the replication issue and its implications for representativeness that signal caution concerning hypothesis-testing using field methods. At the same time, traditional educational research has had its share of trouble in this connection.

There are two additional problems in doing field studies that should be at least noted. One is ethical and the other is practical. Since field studies are based on extensive descriptions of social settings, they present special problems with regard to the protection of the privacy and dignity of those who are part of the events described. On the practical side, once access is gained, sometimes a major problem in itself, field studies make inordinate demands on time and resources.[1][2]

So we find that field studies have their particular advantages and limitations. But that is true of other research methods. None are panaceas.

Finally, in considering any methodology, a pragmatic criterion should be invoked. More than a few field studies have been conducted on school organizations. Were they worthwhile from the standpoint of gaining understanding about such organizations? I believe that they were, but I invite the reader to examine these works and make his own judgment.[13] In any case, the proposition that field methods should be one among various methods employed in research on school organizations is easy to defend. The method is not new or untried. Its track record is good, and its potentials are well known. Recall Scott's comment that "most of what we know today about organizations and the behavior of their members is known on the basis of field studies."[14] It would seem that precious opportunities might be lost if field methods were not utilized sufficiently in inquiries on school organizations.

Next, some brief comments are made on two additional general approaches. One emphasizes highly quantitative analysis in the study of school organizations, the other is based on phenomenology.

Quantitative Approaches

Advanced quantitative approaches to the study of organizations range from the use of relatively common statistical devices, like multivariate analysis, to the various applications of mathematical models. In the present discussion, it is necessary to distinguish between quantitative approaches that are used primarily as aids to practical decision-making or planning and those that are used as tools in inquiry. An area like operations research falls essentially in the former category.[15] The statistical and mathematical methods used in operations research to model alternative choices for decision-making ordinarily can be employed in descriptive modes in research. However, it appears that such methods have been applied in education primarily in connection with practical decision-making and planning. Moreover, most of the applications lack an intraorganizational focus, dealing instead with such areas as work-force requirements and resource allocation at the regional or state levels.[16]

The use of specialized mathematical approaches to describe decision-making or some other feature of school organizations clearly is a promising arena for development.[17] Computer technology makes even quite complex analyses and simulations feasible. The current problem is the enormous gap that separates statements that acclaim the potentials of these approaches and the use of the approaches in the production of research that helps to account for significant aspects of behavior in school organizations.

If research of this kind gets off the ground, it must attend to the problem of the integration of mathematical expression and the ordinary language of explanation. General systems theory offers one type of terminology that appears to fit well in this regard, but it is only one possibility, since propositions derived from a wide range of theories presumably could be examined using mathematical models and related approaches.

Invoking a pragmatic criterion in this case is of little help. The extent to which mathematical models have been employed in research that adds to our understanding of school organizations cannot be judged because of the paucity of the work. There is a cheering section, and there has been a fair amount of activity on the planning and practical side. But, as far as research on school organizations is concerned, the picture is one of abundant promise but scant production.

In contrast, advanced quantitative approaches like multivariate methods have been much more commonly used in research in educational administration. In fact, calls for the increased use of multivariate techniques and the elimination or at least the reduction of simple two variable designs have become almost routine.

An obvious asset in multivariate analysis is the ability to control for the effects of intervening variables, and the emphasis placed on variance is a reminder of the limitations of probability. On the other hand, because multivariate techniques make it relatively easy to examine a fairly large number of variables, there is some danger that theoretically trivial but easily measured variables will predominate.

There are similarities in certain of the problems that can arise in multivariate analysis and in field studies. Both methods are capable of dealing with numbers of variables, and both require some sort of conceptual scheme to give meaning to the data examined. Studies using either method often have a fishing-expedition quality. In the one, observations are made within a given social setting, and explanations are developed for them. In the other, data are gathered on the interrelations of a number of variables, and an attempt is made to account for the relationships.

Both pay homage to the complexity of the apprehended world. To put it in a clumsy way, the world is multivariate. Theories delimit the world, but their mode of expression is not that of particular observations nor variance any more than probability. Even so, the results of studies using multivariate techniques ordinarily can be interpreted without great difficulty. However, the statement of multivariate relationships in the form of prior hypotheses is awkward. Hence, the null format is usually employed. This can reduce pressures for prior theoretical clarification because it gives the impression that hypotheses actually have been formulated. Moreover, the use of multivariate methods in itself confers a certain legitimation on the research, a legitimation that could mask conceptual impotence. In addition, the treatment of a large number of variables suggests that the area being studied has been adequately covered whether it has or not.

These are potential dangers connected with multivariate methods that should be kept in mind. The last one is shared by field methods. However, multivariate methods lack the flexibility of field methods. Although multivariate analysis often is used to scan a number of variables in a search for relationships, it is limited to those variables the researcher decides to include and which can be suitably measured. In this, it is necessary to guard against the "garbage-in, garbage-out" phenomenon.

Multivariate analysis, like other methods, has its peculiar assets and shortcomings. Like other methods, it should be employed when it is an appropriate strategy for dealing with the research question at issue.

Phenomenology

Recently, phenomenology has been commended as a perspective that should be employed by researchers in educational administration; it has been criticized as amorphously defined, but having some value as a method if not as a theory.[18] Phenomenology as a modern school of philosophy was founded by the German philosopher Edmund Husserl. The basic work by an American is that of Marvin Farber.[19] The journal, *Philosophy and Phenomenological Research,* edited by Farber, is the official organ of the International Phenomenological Society. Among other things, the journal provides a forum for the discussion of issues in phenomenology.

There are several versions of phenomenology, but the method of phenomenological analysis is a common focus. The method is subjectivistic and is based on phenomenological reduction. A key feature of reduction is the suspension of judgment, often referred to as the epoché. All past judgments are held in abeyance, and their referents are "bracketed." That is, the presumption that the referents exist is abandoned, and nothing is taken for granted. What is left is the stream of pure experiences of a given individual.[20] In Farber's words, "The phenomenological datum for analysis is my-experiencing-the-object, whether the latter be real or fictive in character."[21] Perhaps this conveys at least the general tenor of phenomenological analysis.

Recent discussions of phenomenology and research in educational administration have not dealt with phenomenological methods as such. Greenfield, who proposed the use of the phenomenological perspective in research on school organizations in one paper, did not mention the word phenomenology in responding to a criticism of that paper. He did make a strong critical statement concerning the reification of the idea of organization. That suggests a philosophical nominalism, but it is unrelated to phenomenology, since the objects experienced via phenomenological reduction need be neither particular nor existential.

The reification argument is an old and familiar one, a popular target being the notion of society in sociology. However, I believe it would be hard to find anyone today who would contend that an organization is a thing. Like social system, or gravity, or force, it is a concept. The real issue hinges on awareness of the advantages and disadvantages of using the organization as a theoretical unit of analysis as against the relative advantages of using other units of analysis. In any case, it is not a matter of good and evil, but of the preferences of the researcher, which ultimately must be justified by the contribution made by the research to knowledge.

Returning to phenomenology, it appears that phenomenological methods have not been applied in inquiries on school organizations. Hence, it is not possible to invoke a pragmatic criterion. The method appears to have some unusual potentials, but it is not just a new procedural twist that researchers can pick up with a little coaching and practice. At minimum, some depth is required both in the point of view and in the use of phenomenological method.

Although the appropriate stance is one of skeptical open-mindedness, a genuinely informed judgment cannot be made until it is possible to apply a pragmatic criterion or to look at results. Then, at least some evidence would be furnished on whether the method played a key part in research that added to knowledge.

In the search for useful ways of doing research on school organizations, no serious approach should be dismissed because it is unfamiliar or different. Many approaches are needed, not one orthodoxy. To quote Farber, ". . . using one method of procedure would only be possible if all problems were of one type. A . . . plurality of methods is the response to the great diversity of problems."[22] At the same time, doctrinaire approaches and exhortations are out of place. As Homans put it, "People who write about methodology often forget it is a matter of strategy, not of morals."[23] Debates on methods should be cast in terms of their assets and limits and how they can abet the knowledge-getting process. But keep in mind that the most compelling argument for a given method is the publication of theoretically interesting results gained using that method. A pragmatic criterion is fundamental. Advocacy without results eventually is a hollow exercise. In the end, research must speak for itself.

Theory and Research

Conceptual support is indispensible if research is to add to understanding. Hence, the relation of theory and research is a key consideration in assessing the state of inquiry on school organizations.

Essays on the general state of theory and research in this field are often impressionistic and sometimes reflect heavily the bents and biases of their authors. Halpin, who has written on the topic about as much as anyone, made some dire predictions some years ago about the use of theory in educational administration, and since then has periodically announced their confirmation.[24]

His discourses are often penetrating and astute. They are also littered with highly moralistic accounts of the shortcomings and machinations of an unusual assortment of fools, incompetents, and charlatans. These are the faddists mouthing pompous pieties, the self-prostituting grantsmen, and an array of professors and students suffering a shortage of ideas, ignorant of research methods, bereft of wit and wisdom, and dedicated to the subversion of academic standards at Halpin's target institution, Catatonic State University. These accounts can be taken simply as reports on one person's experiences. So taken, one regrets for Halpin's sake that he has run across so many of the wrong kind of people. The recitation of instances of this kind cannot, of course, furnish grounds for conclusions, unless it is demonstrated that the cases described are, in fact, representative of a particular population, in this instance, presumably professors and students of educational administration. The extent to which they are representative is unknown. Halpin does not claim that they are. Actually, they appear to be part real, part fictional embellishments strewn along the final approach to his verdict on theory in educational administration, a verdict couched in the rhetoric of the fumbled torch and the broken ikon.

In any case, the imputation of tainted motives and the recounting of selected horror stories is hardly an appropriate way of exploring theory and research in this or any area of study. Oratorical excesses may titillate but they do not inform. Whatever the state of theory and research in our field, discussions on the topic are better served by less rabid analyses.

Immegart has made what is perhaps the most painstaking appraisal to date of research in educational administration.[25] His investigation, which used several classification schemes in its evaluations, covered work published during the two decades between 1954 and 1974. He concluded that over this time span there was an increase in the quantity of research and some improvement in its quality. His overall assessment was that the state of affairs is neither rosy nor deplorable, but somewhere in between depending on how the evidence is added up. If a general statement is required, slow but tangible progress seems to be a reasonable interpretation. That is also how I described the situation with regard to theory.[26] However, both Immegart's comments on research and mine on theory stressed the uneven and varied character of the work and emphasized how much remained to be done before significant gains could be realized.

There are a host of special problems that arise when one attempts a general assessment of theory.[27] For example, there is definition. It is possible to employ a conventional but rigorous definition of theory that excludes virtually everything reported so far on school organizations. So a more inclusive definition is assumed or used, or phrases like "theoretically oriented frameworks" or "works having theoretical utility" are brought into play. Moreover, some frameworks are well developed, whereas others are mere conceptual fragments. Some are presented so that assumptions, concepts, and general propositions are explicitly set forth, although others lack such clarity. They also vary greatly in the extent to which they are logically coherent and in the extent to which empirical tests of derived hypotheses have been carried out. Immegart's review indicated a lack of agreement on concepts and theories within the field, a fact that he lamented. I am not alarmed by the absence of consensus, given the range of theoretical perspectives available to guide research. It may even be healthy at this stage of inquiry, as long as complete fragmentation is avoided and there is cumulative work around various theoretical orientations.

In any case, general assessments of theory and of research are difficult to make because of the range and diversity of the published works and because there is no universally accepted standards of quality. Nevertheless, I feel at ease with the slow but tangible progress appraisal for both theory and research. The fact that we have not reached some sort of promised land, even though it has been over twenty years since the first papers appeared on theory in educational administration, should not be cause for concern. In this realm, extravagant expectations only sow the seeds of disillusion. The plain truth is that there is no promised land in the domain of inquiry.

This judgment reflects the forever unfinished nature of inquiry itself, but in the present case it is greatly reinforced by the scientifically fragile character of the social sciences that serve as sources of concepts and procedures. Those disciplines have witnessed the ascent and decline of a multitude of theories and methodologies. Crucial experiments have been rare because theories normally have not been in competition. Instead, they have simply represented diverse perspectives just as methods have represented different ways of addressing phenomena or data. Yet, each in its time has typically contributed something to knowledge, and over time cumulative gains have been made.

I suspect that inquiry on school organizations will exhibit a pattern like that of most work in the social sciences. Particular theoretical frameworks will be favored for a period and perhaps will guide numerous empirical efforts. Then the popularity of some frameworks will wane and others eventually will replace them. The same will be true of methods. Through this kind of flow and ebb a variety of ways of seeing and thinking about school organizations will emerge. Each new vista should confer a singular kind of understanding about certain aspects of life in such organizations. The range of approaches employed will result in some debates among respective adherents, but some disputes will be based on personal, ideological, or political considerations rather than on substantive questions of theory or research. Those who crave certainty, or the grand theory, or the one true method, or are threatened by probing examinations of beliefs or of institutions will contribute little of value.[28] The work will be carried forward by those who are lured by the unexplained and those who are skilled in the arts of inquiry.

So much for general assessments of the past and conjectures on the future. To be more specific, there has been a substantial amount of writing and research on school organizations based on, among others, social system theories, role theory, bureaucratic theory, several kinds of leadership theory, and various theories used in attempts to account for organizational change.

As a result of such work, especially that grounded in one or another of the versions of social system theory, I believe we are beginning to develop a much better understanding of what school organizations are like. Work using a social system perspective begins with Waller's portrait of the school as a miniature society.[29] Waller saw teachers and students as members of groups that were in essential conflict, and he depicted various kinds of confrontations and the adaptations they spawned. Included were internal confrontations between the teacher and student groups and external ones between teachers and administrators on the one side and the community on the other. Later, Becker described mechanisms that protect the adult members of the school organization in their relationships with students and parents.[30] Iannaccone documented the part played by educator informal groups in schools, and Jackson's account of life in classrooms detailed important social system features operative at that level.[31] Carlson stressed the mutually mandated relationship between the school and its student clients and catalogued the adaptations of each side, and Miles listed a number of properties that were characteristic of schools as social systems.[32] My colleagues and I reported on the teacher subculture and suggested a number of structures in schools that serve largely latent adaptive functions.[33] Cusick's research furnished a carefully rendered picture of a student subculture, and Lortie provided an extensive analysis of the work life of the teacher.[34] The University of Oregon group also focused on the work or task structures of teaching and has underway a longitudinal investigation of change in schools.[35] The process of change has been examined from a social system perspective in studies by Smith and Keith and by Gross and his associates.[36]

Although the works listed differ considerably in emphasis and detail, they view the school organization within generically similar frameworks. In the most general terms, the school is seen as vulnerable to external environmental pressures and to internal strains generated by the number and variety of clients to be served and the reluctance of some of them concerning the service. In consequence, a wide range of adaptive structures protect the organization and its adult members, whereas others bolster student adjustment. These include social structures like norms and traditions as well as more formal routines and rules. Such structures channel and constrain variety and threat. In Thompson's terms, uncertainty is reduced.[37] Hence, a key focus is the problem of predictability. Predictability is ordinarily fostered by stability, but it is sometimes gained through change.

This perspective on the nature of school organizations and their mechanisms of adaptation helps to explain much about teaching, about the relationships among teachers, students, administrators and other school personnel, and about the problems of change. In my judgment, the perspective is strong on explanation. For example, it is easy to understand that teachers would resist changes that add to their role overload or decrease their status relative to that of students, and it is readily apparent why there are norms in the teacher group that proscribe the criticism of colleagues in front of students. It is equally clear why Sputnik spawned efforts to revise the instructional programs of many schools.

Yet, the connections of specific explanations to more general theory are usually implicit rather than explicit. This is common in the social sciences, where formal theoretical presentations are rare. Even Homans' treatment of Durkheim on suicide, a well-known example of theoretical explication, was confined to a few syllogisms.[38]

It might be a useful exercise if some students of educational organizations were to attempt the logical elaboration of social system theory in propositional form. This could clarify theoretical structure and result in reformulation and perhaps some synthesis. Explication is prerequisite to either and, in this case, has other values as well.

For example, social system approaches often take the school as the unit of analysis. This can result in a tendency to blur distinctions among schools. Hence, the statement of propositions in the form, if p then q, or if p increases, then q will increase, not only adds to logical clarity but also facilitates interschool comparisons of variations in p and q and their relationship.

Different variables with equivalent functions are another kind of complication. Just as in psychological theory, frustration can lead to the different responses of aggression or withdrawal, there are a variety of possible organizational responses to similar circumstances. Thus, the school's adaptive response to student deviance could be extensive routinization and sanctions, norms in the teacher subculture that support forceful pupil control, cooptive efforts, or a mixture of these or other responses. It is difficult to map out conceptually this kind of thing, and to erect the whole implicit theoretical framework is even more difficult. For many, it would also be tedious. It is more fun and less pretentious simply to work with concepts at lower levels of abstraction than can be readily operationalized and studied. Nevertheless, more extensive theoretical explication is called for.

In spite of these problems, the general line of inquiry described has been an especially fruitful one. The publications cited as illustrations were in some cases empirical investigations and in other cases analytical pieces.[39] Many of the empirical studies employed field methods; the analytical pieces were attempts to enhance conceptual integration.[40] A balance of empirical and theoretical effort has been a strength of work with a social system perspective.

Of course, other approaches also have made contributions. Role theory has been represented in a number of studies, notably in an investigation by Gross and others and in the work of Getzels and his colleagues.[41] These two stand out because of their emphasis on the statement of prior hypotheses—a feature missing in much research on school organizations. However, according to several sources, investigations of school organizations guided by role theory are declining.[42]

Bureaucratic theory has not been ignored,[43] but its application has been hampered because the characteristics of ideal type bureaucracy are disjoined in schools.[44] Also, we lack theory-based narrative studies of bureaucratization of the type found in the sociology literature.[45]

Various approaches to leadership represent a major research effort in educational administration. A large number of studies have been prompted by measures that tap leader behavior or perceptions of it. Among the best known are the Leader Behavior Description Questionnaire of the Ohio State University group, the Executive Professional Leadership device of Gross and his associates, Fiedler's Least Preferred Coworker instrument, and Halpin and Croft's Organizational Climate Description Questionnaire.[46] The emphasis on leadership may be overdone in view of conclusions like Packard's that school principals simply do not supervise instruction very much.[47] More than most research, these studies seem to reflect the society and culture, which esteem both decisive leadership and democratic participation. The same appears to be true of work on change in schools, which is often informed by an underlying meliorism.

Another area of theory and research that is relevant is found in the politics of education. Certain work in this area deals with the organization-environment interface and adds another dimension to inquiry on school organizations.[48]

In addition to research guided by various theoretical perspectives, some studies have made a contribution by operationalizing a concept from theory. An example is the application by Kunz and Hoy to school organizations of Barnard's concept of zone of indifference.[49]

The overall picture concerning theory and research on school organizations is hardly that of a wasteland. It is apparent that there is quite a lot of theory-based research and quite a few theories. The theories are those of the social sciences, especially sociology and social psychology. Most are middle range and are presented in narrative form without formal elaboration.

Theories direct empirical attention to given propositions and concepts, and as Merton points out, research sometimes exerts pressures for theoretical reformulation.[50] Research on school organizations seems to have produced little of the latter. The treatment of the postulate of role consensus by Gross and his colleagues,[51] and questions raised concerning the unidimensionality of bureaucracy are examples of exceptions, but mostly our research has involved the assignment of empirical referents for theoretical concepts and the examination of relationships among several such referents. The theories are abstract and hypothetical, whereas the more specific empirical referents are time and place bound, but may furnish special insights about schools as such. For example, testing in teacher groups the proposition, "the greater the social visibility, the greater the conformity to norms" would furnish information on what the norms for teacher behavior were, how widely and intensely they were held, and related items of interest in understanding teachers and schools.

From my standpoint, although theory and research on school organizations are not very mature, they are fresh and full of possibilities. Ironically, one quite virginal area is administration. There have not been enough studies of the processes and work of administration. Relevant investigations of decision-making and work on taxonomies of administration have not yet led to vital lines of inquiry.[52] Descriptions and analyses of managers' work of the type reported by Mintzberg furnish models that could be applied not only at the level of the school principalship but also at the neglected level of the school superintendency.[53] Exploration of administrator socialization, norms, and status systems is another promising possibility.

Asking what school administrators do, and why, are examples of fundamental questions about a basic phenomenon. Such questions direct the search for explanation. Representative samples, adequate methods of observation, precise measures of key concepts, clear-cut classification procedures, longitudinal designs, and sophisticated statistical analyses all can contribute to rigor, but technique is sterile unless applied in the service of cogent ideas that respond to fundamental questions. Hence, we should demand of research on school organizations not only that it be methodologically sound but also that it advance explanation. At the same time, we should be wary of snap judgments. In Parson's words ". . . we can never know whether a research idea or a theoretical scheme is of the first importance until it has been fully worked out and tested in innumerable ways. . . . this requires heuristic acceptance of it for purposes of exploration, development and testing. . . ."[54] Such openness will facilitate theoretical development and exploratory research. But our eventual aim is explanations about the functioning of school organizations that are both logically coherent and empirically grounded. Again, in the end, research must speak for itself.

Inquiry and Practice

Finally, the relationship of inquiry and practice should be briefly considered. Clearly, there is no necessary connection. If reason is a coin of the realm in the affairs of men, for many it is one of lesser value. Even when the spirit, like Dickens' Barkis, is willing, the flesh may be weak. Human behavior often is driven by needs for ego enhancement, by desires for power, money, fame, and assorted will-o'-the-wisps. Perceptions are selective and frequently distorted. The age-old gaps persist between belief and behavior, between values and realities, between knowledge and action.[55] In short, the human condition is full of frailty, and injunctions to put knowledge to use ordinarily preach to the wind.

Even for those committed to the uses of knowledge, applications to practice can be intricate and difficult.[56] The world is far too complex to be captured by the language of inquiry. Furthermore, the fit often is poor in the sense that the existential representation of concepts and generalizations is problematic. Hence, the order that inquiry is said to impose on reality can be hard to operationalize in real situations.

The social and organizational setting within which educational administration takes place further abets the separation of inquiry and practice. The high-external-vulnerability and high-internal-variety configuration of school organizations virtually guarantees that their personnel will be sensitized to potential criticisms, conflicts, and crises. Priority is given to adaptive responses to problems of immediate urgency. The large array of routines that supposedly reduce chaos to order demand considerable attention in themselves.[57] This combination of organizational firefighting and housekeeping can consume administrative time and energy and can diminish the likelihood of efforts to apply theory and research in practice.[58]

The picture, then, is one that features psychological, operational, and social and organizational impediments to the alliance of inquiry and practice. That such an alliance is not a distinctive aspect of the behavior of educational administrators is a reasonable surmise. This is consistent with Hills' report that he rarely found theory or research useful during his one-year stint as a school principal.[59] On the other hand, the dean of a college of education recently remarked to me that his background in organization theory was extremely helpful in his work as an administrator. My experience is somewhat closer to his than to Hills'. But these are self reports that can be quite idiosyncratic.

I stick with the view that theory and research are not extensively used in the practice of educational administration. However, I believe that they can be fruitfully employed in practice and that they should be.

But it will not just happen. Dewey has emphasized the place of deliberation in rational choice,[60] and it would seem that the use of concepts and generalizations about schools requires a conscious effort on the part of the administrator. Hills stated that he had no special plans regarding his approach as a principal and expressed in one instance a preference for doing "what comes naturally" as contrasted with the use of a deliberate strategy. He later considered the argument advanced by a colleague that had he been able to catch himself consciously employing theory it would have meant that he had not sufficiently internalized what he learned, and, like a ballet dancer performing mechanically, he would have failed.[61] The alternatives are that Hills simply did not use theory very much or that he used it so naturally that he was not aware of using it. The latter alternative seems remote. Internalization is one thing, a total lack of awareness on the part of the internalizing individual is another. Unconscious would be an appropriate word, and what is done unconsciously is done uncritically.

At the same time, the easy, natural use of ideas is a desirable aim. In Dewey's terms, deliberation is made habitual. However, activity that is easy and natural need not be unthinking and robot-like. The administrator's world is complex, and it does not come marked with theoretical labels. Whether concepts and theories are used as clues, cognitive maps, or predictors, it would seem that cognition is essential.[62]

However, there are a great many concepts and theories, and there are numerous studies that examine them. Furthermore, over time some will be modified, some disgarded, and fresh ones embraced. Current theories and research furnish content that has the potential to be applied in practice, but that content varies and changes. Some of the content is well grounded, while some is not. This is another reason why the use of knowledge by administrators should be neither unconscious nor mechanical. Deliberation that explores the utility of content for the problem at hand is required. Judgments have to be made. This means no less than the use of scientific methods, the methods of inquiry or reflective methods in Dewey's terms, to assess the implications of science for practice in a specific set of circumstances.[63]

That is why I have stressed over the years the value of the scientific temper and reflective methods for both theorists and practitioners in educational administration. Their joint occupation should be to get handles on how and why school organizations work as they do. A variety of explanations should be sought, and those judged relevant should be treated as hypotheses by practitioners for their particular settings. Anyone who hopes to improve an organization needs first to understand it, and understanding is the chief legacy of inquiry whether its object be the stars, the functioning of the brain, or school organizations.

The crux of the matter is that the alliance of inquiry and practice is as difficult to achieve as it is desirable. Yet, significant lines of work on the relationship of inquiry and practice in the administration of school organizations have not been produced. Here is another area that invites conceptual and empirical clarification. Whatever judgments are made about research on school organizations, it is plain that there is no lack of interesting problems.

Notes

1. See Daniel E. Griffiths, "Administrative Theory," in R.L. Ebel, ed., *Encyclopedia of Educational Research,* 4th ed. (New York: Macmillan, 1969); Charles E. Bidwell, "The School as a Formal Organization," in J.G. March, ed., *Handbook of Organization* (Chicago: Rand McNally, 1965); and Ronald G. Corwin, "Models of Educational Organizations," in F.N. Kerlinger and J.B. Carroll, eds., *Review of Research in Education,* vol. 2 (Itasca, Ill.: F.E. Peacock, 1974).

2. R. Oliver Gibson and Marilyn Stetar, "Trends in Research Related to Educational Administration," *UCEA Review* 16 (July 1975); and R.O. Gibson, "Research Trends in the United States," in M. Hughes, ed., *Administering Education: International Challenge* (London: Athlone Press, 1975).

3. Glenn L. Immegart, "The Study of Educational Administration 1954-74"; and Andrew W. Halpin and Andrew E. Hayes, "The Broken Ikon: Or, What Ever Happened to Theory?" both in L.L. Cunningham, W.E. Hack, and R.O. Nystrand, eds., *Educational Administration: The Developing Decades* (Berkeley, Calif.: McCutchan, 1977).

4. Daniel E. Griffiths, *Administrative Theory* (New York: Appleton-Century-Crofts, 1959), p. 35; and Laurence Iannaccone, "Interdisciplinary Theory Guided Research in Educational Administration: A Smoggy View from the Valley," *Teachers College Record* 75 (September 1973).

5. "The Professorship in Educational Administration: A Rationale," in D.J. Willower and J.A. Culbertson, eds., *The Professorship in Educational Administration* (Columbus, Ohio and University Park, Pa.: The University Council for Educational Administration and The Pennsylvania State University, 1964), pp. 98-99.

6. Iannaccone, "Interdisciplinary Theory."

7. "Reason, Robustness and Educational Administration," Seventh Annual Holloway Lecture (Buffalo, N.Y.: Society of Educational Administrators of Western New York and the State University of New York at Buffalo, 1975).

8. Halpin and Hayes, "The Broken Ikon."

9. Werner Heisenberg, *Physics and Beyond* (New York: Harper and Row, 1971), p. 63.

10. See Donald J. Willower, "Some Illustrated Comments on Hypothesis Construction and Research," *Journal of Educational Research* 56 (December 1962) for an application of such criteria to a particular theory.

11. John Dewey, *Logic: The Theory of Inquiry* (New York: Henry Holt, 1938).

12. This is why I suggested the use of experience audits and logs as proxies for the preferred full-fledged field study. See Donald J. Willower, "Theory in Educational Administration," *Journal of Educational Administration* 13 (May 1975) or *UCEA Review* 16 (July 1975).

13. A good start would be the studies by Laurence Iannaccone reported as part 4 of Daniel E. Griffiths et al., *Organizing Schools for Effective Education* (Danville, Ill.: Interstate, 1962); Louis M. Smith and Pat M. Keith, *Anatomy of Educational Innovation* (New York: Wiley, 1971); and Philip A. Cusick, *Inside High School* (New York: Holt, Rinehart and Winston, 1973).

14. W. Richard Scott, "Field Methods in the Study of Organizations," in J.G. March, ed., *Handbook of Organizations*, p. 261. Scott's definition of field studies is a broad one, but his statement nevertheless suggests how widely field approaches have been used to study industrial and other noneducational organizations.

15. For a work that presents operations research applications to education, see Ralph A. Van Dusseldorp, Duane E. Richardson, and Walter J. Foley, *Educational Decision Making through Operations Research* (Boston: Allyn and

Bacon, 1971). A broad-gauged collection on quantitative models is Hector Correa, ed., *Analytical Models in Educational Planning and Administration* (New York: McKay, 1975).

16. Examples of applications at various levels can be found in James F. McNamara, "Mathematical Programming Models in Educational Planning." *Review of Educational Research* 41 (December 1971).

17. For a study that used such methods to test theory, see Mary E. Lippitt and Kenneth D. Mackenzie, "Authority-Task Problems," *Administrative Science Quarterly* 21 (December 1976).

18. See three papers by T.B. Greenfield, "Organizations as Social Inventions: Rethinking Assumptions about Change," *Journal of Applied Behavioral Science* 9 (September-October 1973); "Theory about Organization: A New Perspective and Its Implications for Schools," in M. Hughes, ed., *Administering Education: International Challenge*; "Theory about What," *UCEA Review* 17 (February 1976); and Daniel E. Griffiths, "Some Thoughts about Theory in Educational Administration—1975," *UCEA Review* 17 (October 1975).

19. Marvin Farber, *The Foundation of Phenomonology* (Cambridge, Mass.: Harvard University Press, 1943).

20. Marvin Farber, "Phenomonology," in D.D. Runes, ed., *Twentieth Century Philosophy* (New York: Philosophical Library, 1947).

21. Marvin Farber, "Experience and Subjectivism," in R.W. Sellars, V.J. McGill and M. Farber, eds., *Philosophy for the Future* (New York: Macmillan, 1949), p. 611.

22. Marvin Farber, "Modes of Reflection," *Philosophy and Phenomenological Research* 8 (June 1948):600.

23. George C. Homans, "The Strategy of Industrial Sociology," *American Journal of Sociology* 54 (January 1949):330.

24. See, among other works, Andrew W. Halpin, "The Development of Theory in Educational Administration," in Andrew Halpin, ed., *Administrative Theory in Education* (Chicago: Midwest Administration Center, University of Chicago, 1958); Andrew Halpin, "Administrative Theory: The Fumbled Torch," in A.M. Kroll, ed., *Issues in American Education* (New York: Oxford University Press, 1970); and Halpin and Hayes, "The Broken Ikon."

25. Immegart, "Study of Educational Administration."

26. Willower, "Theory in Educational Administration." My treatment of theory was neither as systematic nor as comprehensive as Immegart's examination of research. Gibson, in "Research Trends in the U.S.," concluded that theory has neither been aborted nor incorporated into the fabric of research in educational administration, but that the state of affairs is somewhere in between. William G. Walker took an even more positive view. See William G. Walker, "Theory and Practice in Educational Administration: 1973," paper presented at a CCEA regional conference, Suva, Fiji (August 1973). One of the most lucid statements on the issue is by W.W. Charters, Jr., "The Future (and a

bit of the past) of Research and Theory," in Cunningham, Hack, and Nystrand, eds., *Educational Administration: The Developing Decades.*

27. The following points are developed at greater length in Willower, "Theory in Educational Administration."

28. Although many have been critical of the search for *the* theory of educational organizations, I have not found anyone who has advocated such a theory. The idea of a single, grand theory apparently has been a straw man.

29. Willard Waller, *The Sociology of Teaching* (New York: Wiley, 1932).

30. See, among other sources on this research, Howard S. Becker, "Social Class Variations in the Teacher-Pupil Relationship," *Journal of Educational Sociology* 25 (April 1952); and Becker, "The Teacher in the Authority System of the Public School," *Journal of Educational Sociology* 27 (November 1953).

31. Iannaccone's study can be found in Griffiths et al., *Organizing Schools,* and in sources cited therein. The work by Philip M. Jackson is: *Life in Classrooms* (New York: Holt, Rinehart, and Winston, 1968).

32. Richard O. Carlson, "Environmental Constraints and Organizational Consequences: The Public School and its Clients," in D.E. Griffiths, ed., *Behavioral Science and Educational Administration,* NSSE Yearbook (Chicago: University of Chicago Press, 1964); and Matthew Miles, "Some Properties of Schools as Social Systems," in G. Watson, ed., *Change in School Systems* (Washington, D.C.: National Training Laboratory, 1967).

33. See Donald Willower, "The Teacher Subculture," in L.W. Drabick, ed., *Interpreting Education: A Sociological Approach* (New York: Appleton-Century-Crofts, 1971); and Willower, "Social Control in Schools," in L.C. Deighton, ed., *Encyclopedia of Education* (New York: Macmillan and Free Press, 1971).

34. Cusick, *Inside High School*; Dan C. Lortie, *School Teacher* (Chicago: University of Chicago Press, 1975); and Lortie, "The Balance of Control and Autonomy in Elementary School Teaching," in A. Etzioni, ed., *Semi-Professions and Their Organizations* (New York: Free Press, 1967).

35. W.W. Charters, Jr. et al., *The Process of Planned Change in the School's Instructional Organization* (Eugene, Oreg.: Center for the Advanced Study of Educational Administration, University of Oregon, 1973).

36. Smith and Keith, *Anatomy of Educational Innovation;* Neal Gross, Joseph Giacquinta, and Marilyn Bernstein, *Implementing Organizational Innovations* (New York: Basic Books, 1971). On the general topic see Alan K. Gaynor, "The Study of Change in Educational Organizations: A Review of the Literature," in Cunningham, Hack and Nystrand, *Educational Administration: The Developing Decades.*

37. James D. Thompson, *Organizations in Action* (New York: McGraw-Hill, 1967).

38. George C. Homans, "Contemporary Theory in Sociology," in R.E.L. Faris, ed., *Handbook of Modern Sociology* (Chicago: Rand McNally, 1964), pp. 951-953.

39. There is no overlap between these works and those listed as landmarks by Halpin in both the fumbled torch and broken ikon papers. His approach and the fact that he saw so little of worth done since the mid-sixties seemed almost solipsistic. Obviously, my illustrations reflect my own biases.

40. Some field studies have led to lines of traditional work. Ours resulted in a line of research on pupil control and its place in school organizations. The field studies done by investigators at the University of Oregon provided the basis for much of their later research including instruments designed specifically to tap school characteristics deemed important as a result of the earlier work. See Donald Willower "Some Comments on Inquiries on Schools and Pupil Control," *Teacher College Record* 77 (December 1975); and J.S. Packard et al., "Governance and Task Interdependence in Schools: First Report of a Longitudinal Study" (Eugene, Oreg.: Center for Educational Policy and Management, University of Oregon, 1976).

41. Neal Gross, Ward S. Mason, and Alexander W. McEachern, *Explorations in Role Analysis* (New York: Wiley, 1958). This study has been criticized by Kaspar D. Naegele, "Superintendency Versus Superintendents," *Harvard Educational Review* 30 (Fall 1960); and in a book review by Andrew W. Halpin, *School Review* 66 (Summer 1958). For an example of a study using the framework developed by Getzels, see Egon G. Guba and Charles E. Bidwell, *Administrative Relationships* (Chicago: Midwest Administration Center, University of Chicago, 1957). Other work is cited in Jacob W. Getzels, James M. Lipham, and Roald F. Campbell, *Educational Administration as a Social Process* (New York: Harper, 1968).

42. See Willower, "Theory in Educational Administration."

43. For example, see James G. Anderson, *Bureaucracy in Education* (Baltimore: John Hopkins Press, 1968).

44. Keith F. Punch, "Bureaucratic Structure in Schools," *Education Administration Quarterly* 5, no. 2 (Spring 1969).

45. A minor classic of this type is Alvin W. Gouldner, *Patterns of Industrial Bureaucracy* (Glencoe, Ill.: Free Press, 1954).

46. See Andrew E. Halpin, *The Leadership Behavior of School Superintendents* (Chicago: Midwest Administration Center, University of Chicago, 1956); Neal Gross and Robert E. Herriott, *Staff Leadership in the Public Schools* (New York: Wiley, 1965); Fred E. Fiedler, *A Theory of Leadership Effectiveness* (New York: McGraw-Hill, 1967); and Andrew W. Halpin and Donald B. Croft, *The Organizational Climate of Schools* (Chicago: Midwest Administration Center, University of Chicago, 1963). John H.M. Andrews contends that this instrument essentially measures leader-follower relations, which is why it is considered in that category. See John H.M. Andrews, "What School Climate Conditions Are Desirable," *The CSA Bulletin* 4 (July 1965); and Andrews "School Organizational Climate: Some Validity Studies," *Canadian Education and Research Digest* 5 (December 1965).

47. J.S. Packard, "Schools as Work Organizations," paper presented at a

symposium on the organizational characteristics of schools, University of California at Santa Barbara (February 1977).

48. For a review, and a recent book in this area, see Laurence Iannaccone and Peter J. Cistone, *The Politics of Education* (Eugene, Oreg.: ERIC Clearinghouse on Educational Management, University of Oregon, 1974); and Peter J. Cistone, ed., *Understanding School Boards* (Lexington, Mass.: Lexington Books, D.C. Heath & Co., 1976).

49. Daniel W. Kunz and Wayne K. Hoy, "Leadership Style of Principals and Professional Zone of Acceptance of Teachers," *Educational Administration Quarterly* 12, no. 3 (Fall 1976). H.A. Simon's version of Barnard's zone of indifference, zone of acceptance, was used in this study.

50. Robert K. Merton, *Social Theory and Social Structure* (New York: Free Press, 1968), chap. 5.

51. Gross, Mason, and McEachern, *Explorations in Role Analysis.*

52. Two works in these areas are John K. Hemphill, Daniel E. Griffiths, and Norman Frederiksen, *Administrative Performance and Personality* (New York: Teachers College, Columbia University, 1962); and D.E. Griffiths, ed., *Developing Taxonomies of Organization Behavior in Education Administration* (Chicago: Rand McNally, 1969). For an intensive study of the life of an elementary school principal, see Harry F. Wolcott, *The Man in the Principal's Office* (New York: Holt, Rinehart and Winston, 1973).

53. Henry Mintzberg, *The Nature of Managerial Work* (New York: Harper, 1973).

54. Talcott Parsons, "Comment on 'Preface to a Metatheoretical Framework for Sociology' by Gross," *American Journal of Sociology,* no. 68 (September 1961).

55. On this problem see Donald J. Willower "Schools, Values and Educational Inquiry," *Educational Administration Quarterly* 9, no. 2 (Spring 1973).

56. For elaboration, see Donald J. Willower, "Educational Administration and the Uses of Knowledge," in W.G. Monahan, ed., *Theoretical Dimensions of Educational Administration* (New York: Macmillan, 1975).

57. This is a familiar example of goal displacement. See Merton, *Social Theory and Social Structure.*

58. The same, of course, applies to teachers.

59. Jean Hills, "Preparation for the Principalship: Some Recommendations from the Field," *Administrator's Notebook* 23 (May 1975); and Hills, "The Preparation of Administrators: Some Observations from the Firing Line," *Educational Administration Quarterly* 11, no. 3 (Fall 1975).

60. Dewey, *Logic*; and John Dewey, *Human Nature and Conduct* (New York: Henry Holt, 1922).

61. Hills, "The Preparation of Administrators." If I read him right, Hills would be wary of such an argument. See his excellent "The Social-Behavioral Sciences and Educational Administration," in W.G. Monahan, ed., *Theoretical*

Dimensions in Educational Administration. The analogy of the ballet dancer is unfortunate. Hills in the piece just cited used a boater to illustrate his point. The pilot of an aircraft also would be an apt analogy. The activity required of both boater and pilot is more cognitive and less gymnastic than the ballet dancer's, and it is much closer to that needed by the administrator who would blend inquiry and practice.

62. On some of the uses of concepts and theories in educational administration, see W.W. Charters, Jr., "The Role of the Social Scientist," in R.F. Campbell and J.M. Lipham, eds., *Administrative Theory as a Guide to Action* (Chicago: Midwest Administration Center, University of Chicago, 1960); and Griffiths, "Some Thoughts about Theory in Educational Administration—1975."

63. I have argued that such methods should be incorporated in a wide range of activities in school organizations. Put another way mechanisms that institutionalize them should be sought. See Willower, "Reason, Robustness and Educational Administration."

5 Educational Policy Research and the Pursuit of Equality, Efficiency, and Liberty

James W. Guthrie

This chapter assesses the last quarter-century of research on selected dimensions of school administration and educational policy. In this undertaking, we attempt to determine the utility of past research and to appraise the prospects for analytic efforts in the future.

Before embarking on this appraisal it is necessary to (1) define the research realm with which we are immediately concerned, and (2) specify the values by which we intend to judge success or failure. Then, we turn to a summary explanation and critical review of educational administration and policy-related research conducted between 1950 and 1975.

Policy Research Boundaries

The meaning of *policy* has long been subject to debate both among scholars and practitioners.[1] Understandably, policy research is equally subject to ambiguity. However, our concern here is not so much with promoting precise definition as it is with establishing practical boundaries to encompass the research concerns of this chapter. For our purposes, policy research consists of systematic inquiries intended to evaluate the consequences of alternative government decisions. More specifically, we take into consideration the results of research intended to influence regulatory and distributional decisions of school policy-making bodies such as Congress, state legislatures, courts, and local school boards.

Historically, educational policy research has been conducted in school districts or by professors of educational administration and their graduate students. One of the most notable changes in this field over the last quarter-century is the expansion in terms of both numbers and disciplines of the individuals involved. School practitioners and administration professors continue to perform policy-related research; however, their ranks have been joined by economists, sociologists, political scientists, and lawyers. There has even evolved a breed of academic that labels itself "policy analyst," or, with unabashed self-assurance, "policy scientist."

The addition of these disciplines to the domain conventionally dominated by educational administration has resulted in an expansion of the kinds of research conducted, a heightened attention to scholarly rigor, and a proliferation of the journals through which such studies are reported. It is not possible within the scope of this chapter to assess the entire spectrum of the research now done regarding educational policy. Consequently, this appraisal is limited to the last twenty-five years of school administration and policy research conducted on three dimensions: finance, economics, and law.

The "Good" or "Bad" Of It All

How can we know if studies in economics, finance, and law have hindered or helped school administration? Such judgments require a backdrop of purpose or values against which to make an assessment. There exists at least three dimensions upon which such a judgment could be made: empiricism and logic, professional standards, and public values.

Logical Criteria

One could assert that the utility of research undertakings in a practical field such as school administration is to be found in the degree to which it makes schools better. Unless it is taken several steps further, this appraisal standard is useless. The term *better* must be defined. For example, it could be argued that schools are better if students learn more, teachers are happier, or parents are more satisfied. There exist empirical measures that would enable us to judge progress on dimensions such as these.

We have rejected this approach for deriving a baseline against which to judge the utility of contemporary school administration research. There are at least three difficulties involved. First, there is little agreement on the hierarchy of objectives for schooling. Hence, it is hard to know what represents improvement. Second, even when agreement exists, as may be the case with reading and mathematics achievement, test results presently are mixed, and a substantial portion of the evidence suggests that modern day students are not performing as well in school as their peers in the past.[2] Similarly, there are few reasons to believe that teachers or parents are more supportive of their jobs and schools now than in the past.[3] Third, and probably more important, even if we could reach agreement on school objectives and had accurate measures for them, it is difficult to attribute changes to the results of educational research. Alternative explanations of educational outcomes—student background characteristics and school personnel incentive systems, for example—are substantially more powerful.

Professional Criteria

Research specialists in school administration, particularly those who view themselves as policy analysts, frequently conceive of their function as clarifying alternatives. They contend that research is useful if it assists officials in better understanding the consequences of their decisions. This approach assumes that more and more accurate information is a good in itself and that public officials, if better informed, will make better decisions.

We also reject this approach for assessing the utility of school administration research. Our reasons are twofold. First, as is well argued in other publications,[4] there exists no value-free research or analysis. Regardless of the intensity of a researcher's professional ethics, values permeate the analytic process determining selection of research questions, methods to be employed, data to be collected, and interpretation of results. The professional assessment strategy ultimately resolves itself into a larger inquiry of good or bad.

Second, we have no accurate means for determining if decision-makers have become better informed or more conscious regarding the consequences of alternative choices. We could survey a scientifically selected sample, but we would nevertheless be relying on subjective responses of individuals who have a personal stake in the outcome. It is difficult to conceive of a large cross-section of public officials, either elected or appointed, that would readily reveal that they are less or only as well informed today than they were in the past.

Ethical Judgments

Because of the definitional difficulties involved with the foregoing strategies, we have adopted an arbitrary value base against which to assess the merit of contemporary research in school administration. Our approach has been to select three important value dimensions of public policy and examine the extent to which research studies have assisted in extending or reinforcing the ability of this nation's schools to realize these values.

Public Values and Public School Policy[5]

American culture contains three strongly held values which significantly influence public policy: equality, efficiency, and liberty. Government actions regarding national defense, housing, taxation, antitrust regulation, racial desegregation, and literally hundreds of other policy dimensions, including education, are motivated and molded by one or more of these three values. Equality, liberty, and efficiency are viewed by the overwhelming majority of the public as conditions that government should attempt to maximize. They are positions about what is considered good, just, and right. They are beliefs the historical roots of which are deeply embedded in the cultural streams that comprise our common heritage. They permeate the ideologies promulgated by political parties, religions, schools, and other social institutions.

Despite widespread public devotion to equality, efficiency, and liberty as abstract goals, it is almost impossible to pursue these values to their ultimate fulfillment. At their roots, the three desired conditions are inconsistent and antithetical. Pursuit of equality exclusively restricts or eliminates liberty and efficiency. Similarly, complete attention to either one of the other values reduces the remaining two. Consequently, efforts to rearrange society so as to maximize fulfillment of a particular one of the three values are constrained by forces desiring to preserve the status quo of both the others. The three values are always suspended in dynamic equilibrium. The practical relationship between them constantly shifts; the balance at any particular point is fixed as a consequence of a complicated series of compromises made within the political and economic systems.

It can be argued that liberty or freedom is the highest of the three values. Efficiency for its own sake is absent much meaning. The justification for desiring that an endeavor be undertaken efficiently is to conserve resources, which then can be used for other endeavors, thus achieving greater equality or expanding choice. Similarly, equality qua equality appears hollow. Few if any persons desire absolute parity with their peers. Rather, equality of wealth and circumstance can be viewed as desirable means to the end of greater choice.

Education is one of the prime instruments through which American society attempts to promote fulfillment of all three values. Researchers and analysts involved in education are well advised to be informed about and alert to the interaction and tradeoffs among these value dimensions.

Education as a Policy Variable in the Pursuit of Equality, Efficiency, and Liberty

The sixteenth-century Protestant Reformation encouraged education as a means to facilitate individual interpretation of religious scriptures. Similarly, among eighteenth-century leaders of the new republic, the United States, education was viewed as a means to enable one to participate as an equal in the affairs of government.[6] Under these circumstances, education was important to ensure liberty.[7] It was not until the ninteenth century that formal education began to assume significance for economic purposes. The increasing technical complexity of industrialization necessitated a more highly educated work force. This condition provoked widespread provision of public schooling. Schooling was taken as an important contributor to economic efficiency. By the twentieth century, intensified technological development and economic interdependence rendered schooling crucial for an individual's economic and social success. Consequently, schooling assumed new importance from the standpoint of fulfilling the value of equality.

Beginning with the 1954 U.S. Supreme Court decision in *Brown* v. *Board of Education of Topeka*,[8] and continuing with the vast increase in federal government education programs of the sixties and the school finance reform efforts of the seventies, a major portion of mid-twentieth-century education policy has been directed at achieving greater equality. Consequently, we begin our discussion of public values and school administration research by concentrating on equality.

Equality

School administration research efforts related to equality focused on three major reform dimensions in the period from 1950 to 1975: racial desegregation, school finance, and special education. The three are bound together by several common threads, most notably that progress toward greater equality on these dimensions is primarily the result of court cases and other legal actions brought under the Equal Protection Clause of the U.S. Constitution's Fourteenth Amendment. We discuss each of these policy dimensions in order.

Racial Desegregation: It is possible that the topic of racial desegregation has provoked greater public controversy than any other in the last twenty-five years. National guard mobilization, massive public demonstrations, civil disobedience, heated political campaigns, and acrimonious school board recall movements are but partial illustrations of the intensity of the conflict. Although usually not on a physical level, researchers too have been involved in the issue from the outset. The initial U.S. Supreme Court decision in *Brown* v. *Board of Education of Topeka* incorporated social science evidence in support of the view that legally enforced segregation of schools violated the Fourteenth Amendment and was damaging to minority students.[9] In subsequent years, researchers, primarily sociologists, conducted numerous analytic efforts to assess the effects of desegregated schooling. For the most part, results have been ambiguous.[10] No clear path of evidence presently exists as to whether minority students benefit from desegregated school settings. Even the original research cited by the Supreme Court has now been disputed.[11] There are those who contend that the entire school desegregation movement, on balance, has failed. They cite as evidence for their position the fact that more black children attend racially isolated classes today than was the case twenty-five years ago.[12]

Despite the ambiguity of social science desegregation results and the mixed success of northern school desegregation efforts, one facet of the issue emerges with relative clarity. The de jure segregated school systems of southern states, with few exceptions, have been successfully dismantled. This is the case not because of the dramatic findings of policy analysts and researchers, but because of the construction of successful legal strategies. This signals a condition to which we will return in detail. The significant addition that has imputed a measure of success to school administration research during the last twenty-five years is the intervention of lawyers and legal strategies.[13] Previously, a linkage between education research findings and practical reforms was difficult to forge.

Aside from the successful effort by lawyers to construct new legal theories under the Fourteenth Amendment, little effective research has been done on desegregation in the realm of educational administration. Researchers oriented toward political science have attempted to understand community conditions related to desegregation, conflict, and conflict resolution.[14] These endeavors are reviewed elsewhere in this book and are, therefore, not covered here. An important linkage was constructed between racial segregation and financing of schools, but we will describe this dimension in the next section on school finance and equality. Moreover, this research leaned on a lawsuit, *Hobson* v. *Hansen,* for its practical effect.[15] Lastly, a substantial amount of folklore and anecdotal evidence have been amassed by school administrators in districts that have experienced desegregation. However, little of this has been subjected to systematic examination or rigorous validation. This has not prevented a number of self-styled experts from spreading their desegregation homilies and administrative advice around the nation, frequently under the aegis of the American Association of School Administrators.

School Finance: The legal dimension of school desegregation began to peak in the late sixties. It was at this time that the mantle of equal protection was being stretched by lawyers in an effort to include school finance. For more than half a century, academics had described and decried the revenue and taxing disparities resulting from school finance arrangements throughout the United States. Generations of school administration students and school finance experts in training learned of the unequal charters of taxing power granted under existing "Foundation Programs."[16] However, despite literally hundreds of empirical studies, journal articles, and scholarly volumes, little progress was made by states in equalizing the spending power of local school districts.

In 1967, Arthur Wise questioned the constitutionality of state school financing arrangements.[17] Wise, then a doctoral student in school administration at the University of Chicago, contributed to the effort to eliminate inequality, not a new set of fiscal analyses, but, rather, the suggestion of a new legal theory.[18]

Other legal scholars were quick to follow Wise. Subsequently, John E. Coons, with William H. Clune, III and Stephen D. Sugarman, published *Private Wealth and Public Education,* which, in magnificent fashion, dissected the operation of state school finance statutes and fabricated a strategy whereby they could be attacked legally.[19] Coons and his colleagues formulated the principle of fiscal neutrality. "The quality of a child's schooling should not be a function of wealth, other than the wealth of the state as a whole." By providing a negatively phrased decision rule, permitting courts to strike down existing schemes while allowing legislatures to construct a statutory redress of the inequity, Coons rescued the fledgling "equal protection" school finance movement from judicial oblivion. Prior to that time, courts were deciding against plaintiffs on grounds that no judicially manageable solutions were apparent.[20]

The major effort of the contemporary school finance reform movement and the research energy connected with it has been directed at alleviating *intrastate* fiscal inequities. However, there exists another dimension of this reform, which, although not receiving equal publicity, may ultimately have equal or greater effects. We refer here to the suit brought initially in Washington, D.C. by Julius Hobson. This case, actually two separate judgments decided by Judge Skelly Wright,[21] has had a dramatic effect on the *intradistrict* distribution of school resources. In essence, Hobson uncovered evidence that the Washington, D.C. school district was discriminating against black children in its delivery of services. Neither explicit intent nor malice were culprits as much as were the insidious effects of the district's seniority-based personnel policies. In exercising their transfer privileges, senior teachers flowed to white-dominated schools. In so doing, they took with them their higher salaries resulting from added years of service as teachers. Judge Wright's decisions were intended specifically to redistribute school resources within Washington, D.C. However, the case had wider influence. Other school districts were guilty of similar practices, and many moved of their own accord, following *Hobson,* to rectify the situation.[22] In addition, Congress subsequently took note of the decision and made equal distribution of state and local resources a precondition in all states and school districts for receipt of federal compensatory education funds.[23] Consequently, the *Hobson* decisions, and the fiscal analyses on which they rested, have had an influence on school administration practices across the nation.

From its inception in the mid-sixties, the school finance reform movement, based primarily on equal protection arguments, has contributed to the revision of revenue-raising and distribution arrangements in approximately thirty states.[24] This is the case despite the fact that the U.S. Supreme Court issued an opposing opinion, on federal constitutional grounds, in 1973.[25] A number of school finance experts, frequently connected with university departments of educational administration, constructed the evidence for many equal protection suits and testified personally in trials throughout the United States. Charles Benson, Joel Berke, Walter Garms, Robert Goettel, James Guthrie, Michael Kirst, Henry Levin, and Lawrence Pierce were all prominent in this regard. However, as rigorous and complete as were their analyses, the crucial new ingredient in the pursuit of reform was the invention and pursuit of a successful legal strategy.

Special Education: Special education is the latest school policy category to be the focus for substantial reform. The reform has proceeded on two dimensions, the provision of appropriate school services to physically and mentally handicapped students, and the provision of bilingual instruction to non-English-speaking students. The inability of school districts to serve adequately the needs of such handicapped students has long been recognized by school officials. However, as was the case historically with school finance inequities, there appeared no means by which the situation could be altered. Specialized services are extraordinarily expensive; school budgets simply were not stretched to provide them. When state categorical funds were provided for special education, local school districts all too frequently diverted all or a portion of them to subsidize the regular school program. The mid-sixties innovation aimed at rectifying these conditions was the construction of a successful legal theory to mandate change.

The landmark cases are *Mills* v. *Board of Education*[26] and *Pennsylvania Association of Retarded Children* v. *Commonwealth of Pennsylvania*[27] for handicapped students and *Lau* v. *Nichols*[28] for the non-English speaking. These cases have both altered the special education practices of states and local school districts and influenced Congress in enacting the "Education for All Handicapped Children Act."[29] The likely consequence of these movements is to increase dollar spending for special education by billions. Hopefully, these vast increases will result in better school services for such children and, eventually, greater ability for them to lead a fulfilling life.

Efficiency

It is difficult to contend that America's public schools have gained in efficiency over the last quarter-century. During this period average per pupil expenditures nationwide have escalated in an awesome manner. Even when inflation is discounted, the increase is 500 percent between 1950 and 1975.[30] The additional funds have purchased items suggested by conventional education wisdom as facilitating production. For example, class sizes have been reduced, and many categories of instructional and administrative specialists have been added.[31] Despite such added resources, there appear to be no dramatic increases in output. Indeed, to the extent to which standardized test scores are valid indicators of school production, output has diminished.[32]

Efficiency has always been a major concern for educational policy-makers and school administrators. However, there have existed points in history at which particular attention has been accorded the topic. Approximately fifty years ago was a time of such intense interest. This period coincided with the expansion of school administration as a specialized field. In an effort to enhance their professionalism, education officials attempted to adopt for schools many of the efficiency techniques then popular in industry. This movement is brilliantly described by Raymond Callahan in *Education and the Cult of Efficiency*.[33] The last ten years have been a similar period. The desire to discover a means by which greater productivity could be achieved has been motivated, if for no other reason, by startling cost increases.

School administration research devoted to educational efficiency has been inhibited by the absence of comprehensive and appropriate theories and paradigms. For example, the so-called cost-quality studies conducted in the fifties by Paul R. Mort and his colleagues were based on what we have come to see was an incomplete model of school effectiveness.[34] These studies linked school expenditures with student achievement. They also connected expenditures with innovative instructional practices, assuming that such innovations were more productive.[35] The findings bolstered the case for so-called "lighthouse" school districts, wealthy districts pioneering in new educational techniques. Their continuation as high spending districts was justified on grounds that they provided sites for educational research and development. All of education, it was argued, benefited from the spillovers from their fortunate financial circumstances. A flaw in these studies was the failure to control for the background of students. It frequently was the case in the districts sampled that high property wealth was significantly associated with high socioeconomic status of students. The cost-quality model and the research findings were badly confounded.

In the sixties, school effectiveness research was dominated by sociologists. The premier study of this period was the Coleman Report,[36] named after its principal author. This study, in addition to measuring the distribution of school resources and academic achievement by race and ethnic group, attempted to understand the linkage between school resources and student achievement. The study was a massive research undertaking, and it is highly improbable that any other individual or group could have improved on the effort at that time. The Coleman team did construct a more sophisticated model of school effectiveness than existed previously, and this model took student environment and background characteristics into account. Nevertheless, the study was flawed from other perspectives.[37] It has been questioned for a number of highly technical reasons. The most widely noted was its alleged failure to correct for statistical multicollinearity, the coincidence of independent variables. Critics contended that generally, high socioeconomic status (SES) students had available to them high quality school services whereas the reverse was true for low SES students.[38] (This was before the enactment of the Elementary and Secondary Education Act and in advance of the widespread contemporary movement toward compensatory school services.) This correlation, it was argued, accounted for Coleman's third major conclusion, that is, that there were no school effects independent of students' social background.

Following the Coleman report, numerous research efforts were made by economists to conduct school effectiveness studies that improved on the Colemen team's techniques. Initially these studies added little to the body of knowledge regarding school efficiency. A school administrator would have gained little from them to enable him or her to operate an improved school. This point was stressed strongly in a 1972 Rand Corporation report to the President's Commission on School Finance and by Henry Levin, an economist.[39] Several subsequent studies by economists were conceptually more sophisticated and contained more reliable findings.[40] However, the majority of the school effectiveness studies, although more sophisticated and rigorous than their antecedents, have done little to improve school productivity.

Research aimed at understanding school productivity coincided with a popular reform known as the "accountability movement." This was an effort to control wildly increasing school costs and sagging student achievement by employing techniques from the industrial sector. System analysis, management by objectives, program performance budgeting, program evaluation and review techniques, were but a few of the procedures accountability advocates suggested would improve school productivity.

By 1977, this fad had reached its crest, having had little impact on the day-to-day operation of schools.[41] However, the long-range effects may be to handicap more sophisticated efforts to make schooling more efficient.

For the most part, both analysts and accountability advocates have accepted the conventional technical-industrial model of school operation. This model, adopted from the private sector, depends heavily on the following assumptions:

1. The desired outcome of the production process is agreed on and measurable by objective means.
2. There exists a body of applied science or techniques specifying the steps in production.
3. The availability of raw material of a relatively uniform quality and the ability to control or minimize outside influences on production.
4. There exists an incentive structure that motivates both management and labor to improve the quality of the product and produce it at lower costs.

The validity of each of these assumptions for the schooling process is arguable. Seldom is there widespread public agreement on the purposes and priorities of schooling. When there is, the means for measuring school progress are extraordinarily primitive. Schooling continues to be at least as much an art as a science, and many would argue that the science side of that dichotomy presently provides little worthy of the label. Public schools have access to, at most, 20 percent of a student's time. For many children this may be less than their exposure to television programs. The opportunity for outside conditions to confound the schooling process is obvious. Lastly, public schools enjoy a virtual monopoly; the demand for their services is highly inelastic. This induces little motivation for educators to improve the quality of their service. Indeed, schools are notorious for their upside down incentive system, which grants higher rewards the more distant one becomes from instruction.

For these reasons it may be that the technical-industrial model of efficiency and schooling is inappropriate. In its place, one might well substitute either a political or a market model. Each of these alternatives permits judgments to be made in the absence of agreed on and measurable objectives. In one instance, consumer preference is expressed through the ballot and other political mechanisms. In the other instance, preference is expressed by the summary effect of numerous individual choices among products. One model portends of greater politicization of schools, the other suggests a free market remedy and greater private provision of school services. Both models are deserving of greater exploration by policy-makers and researchers than has been the case to date.

Liberty[42]

A third deeply held value that frequently influences the direction of American education policy is liberty. This value provided a major ideological justification for the revolution that gave birth to the United States as a nation. After the war with England, James Madison wrote: "In Europe, charters of liberty have been granted by power. America has set the example, and France has followed it, of charters of power granted by liberty."[43]

For Americans, liberty has meant the freedom to choose, to be able to select from among different courses of action. The desire for choice fueled the historical American affection for a market economy. Competition among producers, along with other benefits, is held to expand the range of items from which consumers can choose. In the public sector, responsive governmental institutions are taken to be a crucial element for the expressions and preservation of choice and liberty.

In the view of those who initially designed the structures of American government, authority was vested in the citizenry, who then delegated the power to govern to selected representatives. A measure of representatives' effectiveness was the degree to which they were responsive to the will of those they governed. Lack of responsiveness eroded power of the citizenry and thus constituted grounds for removal from office.

A second means for preserving liberty was to dispense governmental authority widely. This accounts for the separation of powers between three branches and over various levels of government. Efforts to inhibit accumulation of power also account for the deliberate fragmentation of decision-making authority, specific powers accorded the federal government, some to states, and some powers reserved to the people themselves. Historically, the power to make educational decisions was structured in the same fashion. Centralized authority was viewed as perilous because of the prospect of exerting widespread control and uniformity. Formation of literally thousands of small local school districts, portending both inefficiency and inequality, was intended as an antidote to the accumulation of power. Proximity to constituents, coupled with the electoral process, was taken as a means to enhance governmental responsiveness and preserve liberty.

Governmental Cycles and the Dilution of Responsiveness: American government has evolved through a series of constant adjustments made in response to pressure from three forces: (1) advocates of responsiveness, (2) those favoring greater centralization of authority, a stronger executive, and (3) those espousing the merits of expert, professional management.[44] School governance is no exception to this cyclical emphasis. Representativeness peaked during the Progressive era, and centralized authority and professional management subsequently ascended to prominence. In that this shift in the pattern of governance strongly colors school conditions in the third quarter of the twentieth century, it appears appropriate to review briefly the historical events that comprise this pendulum swing.

School District Consolidation. By 1930, the number of local school districts in the United States had reached its high point—in excess of 125,000 separate units. By 1976 this number had been reduced to approximately 16,000.[45] This drastic reduction in the number of units of a specialized local government took place in a manner so subtle as virtually to escape the notice of political analysts. Nevertheless, it constitutes one of the most dramatic of all changes in America's patterns of government.

There were several motives for the consolidation of thousands of small rural school districts, many of them with only one school, frequently a one-room school at that. It was argued that small school districts were inefficient. Specifically, it was asserted that they were incapable of providing a sufficiently wide array of services, impeded the ability of teachers to specialize, and generally inhibited the attainment of economies of scale in matters such as purchasing and maintenance. Under both the carrot and stick of legislative inducements and penalties, many local schools and school districts were combined into larger units.[46]

Consolidation of local districts took place at a time when the U.S. population was undergoing substantial growth. The size of the average school district increased many times. Consequently, whereas each local school board member once represented approximately 140 constituents, by 1976 this figure had risen to one board member per 2,500 constituents. Representativeness had been diluted to an awesome degree.[47]

Professional Management. Reduction in number of school districts and the increase in population resulted in the creation of many school district organizations that were too large to be managed by school boards themselves. Historically it was the case that board members were directly responsible for matters such as hiring teachers, purchasing supplies, setting school curricula, establishing school regulations, and listening personally to citizens' complaints. In short, for school matters, they performed the three functions of government—rule-making, rule implementation, and rule adjudication.[48] The formation of large districts vastly reduced such practices. It became clear that most school districts would require full-time management. Consequently, beginning in New York in the

1870s and subsequently spreading across the nation, elected school boards employed professional school superintendents and turned over to them the day-to-day operation.[49] Professional dominance was abetted by the turn-of-the-century proliferation of "scientific management" in the private sector, a phenomenon referred to in the previous section on efficiency. Professionalism was bolstered yet further by the discoveries of the muckrakers in the 1920s. The scandalous disease of government was diagnosed as an excess of politics, and the cure was more experts and fewer elected officials. In the process, representativeness was further diluted.

Collective Bargaining. Beginning in the fifties, teachers began to expand their unions to engage more effectively in collective bargaining with school boards. This development was initiated in large cities and subsequently spread to almost every school district in the United States. Increases in organizational size, bureaucratization, and the expansion of administrative levels in large measure probably accounted for teachers' feelings of inefficacy and alienation and prompted them to unionize. Although it frequently is the case that teacher representatives come to the bargaining table with concerns for the welfare of students and respect for the interests of the broader public, their primary allegiance is to teachers' welfare. They cannot legitimately claim to represent the larger public. Nevertheless, duly elected public representatives, school board members, must share decision-making authority with them. The outcome is further to centralize school policy-making and to erode the ability of the general public to participate in the process.

Escalating State Power. Although state government has always held the ultimate legal responsibility for school decision-making, it was the case historically that state government delegated substantial policy discretion to local units of government. However, in the period since World War II, factors such as increasing school costs, politicization of school decisions, and intensified efforts to achieve greater equality of educational opportunity and more efficient use of school resources have heightened state-level participation.[50] A consequence has been to remove a large measure of decision-making discretion from local education authorities.[51] For example, state specifications on dimensions such as the school curriculum, teacher salaries and working conditions, graduation requirements, and school architecture have increased markedly. More decisions regarding schools are now determined by fewer persons. Choice is restricted, the ability of local officials to respond to constituent preferences is constrained, and, at least in a legal sense, local autonomy, liberty, and probably efficiency have been diminished.

Reaction. By the latter half of the sixties, a reaction to the diminished status of representativeness had begun. Requests for change stemmed initially from ethnic enclavess in large cities, which perceived themselves as relatively impotent in affecting the operation of their children's schools. They demanded what was then labeled "community control."[52] For example, several community control experiments were attempted in the New York City schools. The state legislature ultimately recognized the growing political tide by fractionating New York City into thirty-two elementary school districts. In that each of the thirty-two averaged 30,000 students, approximately the size of the entire school system of the city of Syracuse, it could not realistically be characterized as "community control." Nevertheless, each of New York City's local districts was authorized to elect a nine-member local board of education. Thus, New York City's elected school policy-makers grew from 9 to 297.[53]

Reaction to the dilution of representativeness also reached Congress. Federal education acts were amended in the early seventies to mandate parent participation in the making of decisions about the use of federal program funds. Also, by the mid-seventies several state legislatures were requiring formation of parent advisory councils at school sites.[54] Numerous local school districts were voluntarily implementing plans for wider involvement of citizens in school decision-making.

The Role of Research: Administration and policy research has been a mixed blessing with regard to the value of liberty or representativeness. As we have commented previously about education in general, school administration research cycles seem to be influenced strongly by fashionable ideas in the larger society. In the initial half of the twentieth century, when efficiency was a prime private sector concern, researchers were quick to focus on the advantages of larger units. Subsequently, as society has been forced by shortages of various kinds to think "small," researchers are speculating about the possible virtues of small schools and school districts.

The school district consolidation movement between 1920 and 1950 was fueled heavily by the weighty pronouncements of educational statesmen, particularly professors of school administration. Little empirical inquiry was undertaken to assess the validity of the assertion that with regard both to school districts and schools, "bigger was better." The few scale economy studies undertaken assumed that material items were the only important dimensions. Few efforts were made to assess the possible tradeoffs between physical economies and the effects of diminished personal contact and increased alienation on student achievement and discipline. This was clearly the case up to the mid-sixties when James Bryant Conant trumpeted the virtues of larger high schools in his polemic *The American High School Today*.[55] During this period, administration research continued to accept the previously discussed technical-industrial efficiency model. The result was added, even if narrow, evidence for greater consolidation of small schools and districts. By so doing, the unit costs of items such as transportation, durable goods, and specialized classes were reduced.

In the mid-sixties, the pendulum began to swing in the opposite direction. The rate of school consolidation dramatically slowed, and scholars began to question the advantages of large schooling units. The signal for this transition was a remarkable school-size study conducted in the midwest by Barker and Gump.[56] They performed analyses that demonstrated the existence of many interpersonal and academic benefits to students of small, rural schools. Simultaneously, an increasing number of researchers became dubious of the utility of large urban districts. This latter doubt was triggered by the community control demands of various ethnic minorities tired of professional dominance. The decade from 1965 forward produced a cascade of administration research literature focused on decentralization.

Decentralization was featured as the solution to the problems of bureaucracy and large government. Subsequently, however, a more radical reform was put forward—voucher plans. This latter strategy would have decentralized school decision-making all the way down to the individual household.[57] Such an idea, whatever its merits, was extraordinarily threatening to professional educators, so threatening that it was never permitted a widespread test, even on an experimental basis.[58] A more neutral set of ideas began to rise as a compromise between vouchers and decentralization, for example, alternative schools, parent advisory councils, and schools within schools. These concepts were consistent with the "small is beautiful" philosophy popularized by the English economist, Schumacher.[59] However, as was the case with the school consolidation movement a half-century earlier, there was little empirical research conducted to assess the validity of the small-scale solutions.

The advent of unions and collective bargaining for teachers is perhaps the most dramatic change in the public sector, and certainly in all of education, since 1950! It is a topic about which much is written in school administration research circles, but most of what is published on the topic is hortatory and proscriptive. In the decade after 1965, education officials began to accept collective bargaining as a fait accompli, and slowly a body of empirical research findings is beginning to emerge. However, to date, there exists no select groups of definitive works; the field appears to be too embryonic for such a development.

Topics such as the consequence of bargaining methods, effectiveness of conflict resolution mechanisms, effects of strikes on employee morale, and influence of bargaining on teacher salaries in a region increasingly are the subject of systematic analyses.[60] However, with but a few significant exceptions, education researchers are repeating a mistake of an earlier era. They are assuming that the private sector model of collective bargaining is also appropriate for a public sector undertaking such as schooling. Consequently, their analyses typically overlook a number of important possible consequences, primarily the effect of collective bargaining on the ability of the lay public to continue to control public schools.

Patricia Craig and Lawrence Pierce[61] are among the few who have recognized the important differences between private and public sector bargaining. For example, in the private sector, both labor and management are heavily constrained in their actions by the potential effect of their settlement on future sales. If a wage settlement is too high, the product may no longer be price competitive, and sales will decline forcing a loss of employment. This possibility acts to moderate the demands of labor. However, in a monopolistic public sector setting, such as schooling, the market is relatively assured, and the consumer has little opportunity to express dissatisfaction with the settlement. The only avenue available is through the ballot box, and frequently the timing for bargaining may not permit a direct electoral expression of consumer views. Also, the increased financial participation of professional educators, through their unions, in local and state school politics, may dilute further direct expression of lay voters regarding collective bargaining and school policies.

In short, collective bargaining offers the substantial prospect of further altering traditional mechanisms of government control for public schooling, and few administration researchers or policy analysts have pursued the possibility.

Summary and Conclusion

This chapter appraised the last quarter-century of school administration research in the areas of finance, economics, and law. Effectiveness was assessed in terms of research contributions to progress on three public policy value dimensions: equality, efficiency, and liberty.

In the last twenty-five years the United States has made substantial progress toward greater equality of educational opportunity. This is evident on policy dimensions such as racial desegregation, school finance reform, and expanded services for handicapped students. Research efforts appear to have aided these reform movements. However, the significant addition over the preceding periods of history was the formulation of new legal reform strategies involving the Equal Protection Clause of the U.S. Constitution's Fourteenth Amendment. The strategic use of litigation was a sine qua non of the reform effort.

Education appears to have made little progress on the dimension of efficiency, and, on balance, school administration research has not assisted positively. By promoting a dubious paradigm for measuring efficiency—the technical-industrial model of schooling—academic researchers and policy analysts may have hindered progress. Pursuit of additional efficiency concepts, for example, a political or market model, might have enabled efficiency to have been further enhanced.

Liberty, or responsiveness, is the policy dimension on which the least progress has been made. It is likely that schools are less representative of the will of the general public today than at any time in the last seventy years. School administration researchers and policy analysts have done little to rectify this condition. In fact, by accepting uncritically the cost-saving arguments of school and school district consolidation proponents and by not questioning the validity of the private sector model for collective bargaining, they may have abetted the erosion of public control.

Thus, there exist both positive and negative dimensions of the school administration and policy analysis research efforts of the last quarter-century. On the negative side, researchers have been too quick to accept the conceptual schemes and theoretical models prevailing in the private sector. This has contributed to inappropriate analyses and the shortchanging of vital research undertakings. In an even more dismal view, acceptance of inappropriate conceptual models has fostered dubious and debilitating school policies, for instance, school consolidation.

On the most positive side, the twenty-five year period after 1950 was characterized by substantial progress toward greater equality of educational opportunity. This appears to have occurred in large measure because of the formulation of legal theories for invalidating previously existing discriminatory conditions. The availability of a judicial avenue for redressing past evils represented a more effective change strategy, the likes of which social reformers seldom have available to them. However, there exists growing evidence that the equal protection legal strategy may be exhausting its utility. Judicial reforms are themselves not all-powerful. It may be that we have come close to exhausting the school reform potential inherent in the equal protection strategy.[62] This was made evident in New Jersey when the state Supreme Court found itself relatively helpless when the legislature would not adhere to a court mandate to revise the state's school finance distribution arrangements.[63]

If the foregoing observations are judged accurate, then the task facing school administration researchers in the next quarter-century is both to seek more appropriate theories and models and to search for implementation strategies, legal or otherwise, which will prove as powerful for the cause of efficiency and liberty as was previously the case for equality.

Notes

1. See Harold D. Lasswell and Daniel Lerner, *The Policy Sciences: Recent Developments in Scope and Method* (Stanford, Calif.: Stanford University Press, 1951); Yehezkel Dror, *Public Policy Re-examined* (Scranton, Pa.: Chandler, 1968); Dror, "Prolegomena to Policy Services," *Policy Sciences* 1 (1970); and Dror, *Ventures in Policy Sciences* (New York: American Elsevier, 1971).

2. See for evidence, John C. Flanagan, "Changes in School Levels of Achievement: Project *TALENT* Ten and Fifteen Year Retest," *Education Researcher* 5, no. 8 (September 1976):9-11.

3. This point is supported by the survey findings of the Field poll of

public confidence in major social institutions released on May 11, 1977. See the *San Francisco Chronicle,* 12 May 1977, p. 12.

4. See, for example, Harold A. Larrabee, *Reliable Knowledge* (Boston: Houghton Mifflin Co., 1948).

5. The following discussion draws heavily from chapter 2, "Public Values and Public School Policy," in Walter I. Garms, James W. Guthrie, and Lawrence G. Pierce, *School Finance: The Economics and Politics of Public Education* (Englewood Cliffs, N.J.: Prentice-Hall, 1978). © 1978, Reprinted by permission.

6. See Frederick Rudolf, ed., *Essays on Education in the New Republic* (Cambridge, Mass.: Harvard University Press, 1969).

7. For added discussion of this topic see chapter 1 in John W. Gardner, *Excellence: Can We Be Equal and Excellent Too?* (New York: Harper and Row, 1961).

8. *Brown v. Board of Education of Topeka,* 347 U.S. 483 (1954).

9. The U.S. Supreme Court offered the following as evidence in support of its position: Kenneth B. Clark, *Effect of Prejudice and Discrimination on Personality Development* (Mid-century White House Conference on Children and Youth, 1950); Helen L. Witmer and Ruth Kotinsky, *Personality in the Making* (New York: Harper, 1952); Max Deutscher and Isidor Chein, "The Psychological Effects of Enforced Segregation: A Survey of Social Science Opinion," *Journal of Psychology* 26, no. 259 (1948); Chein, "What Are the Psychological Effects of Segregation under the Conditions of Equal Facilities?" *International Journal of Opinion and Attitude Research* 3, no. 229 (1949); T. Brameld, "Educational Costs," in R.M. MacIver, ed., *Discrimination and National Welfare, A Series of Addresses and Discussions* (New York: Institute for Religious and Special Studies, 1949), pp. 44-48; Edward F. Frazier, *The Negro in the United States* (New York: Macmillan, 1949), pp. 674-681; and Gunnar Myrdal, *An American Dilemma* (New York: Harper, 1944).

10. The effectiveness of racial integration as a strategy for improving minority student school achievement has been the subject for substantial argument among social science researchers. Early interpretations of Coleman Report findings suggested that integrated schooling had a beneficial effect on the school performance of black students. See James S. Coleman et al., *Equality of Educational Opportunity* (Washington, D.C.: U.S. Government Printing Office, 1966). This general conclusion was subsequently thrown into question by the research of David Armor, which asserted that integration was associated with no positive outcomes for minority children. See David J. Armor, "The Evidence on Busing," *The Public Interest* 28 (Summer 1972):90-126. Armor's position has itself been subject to dispute. See Thomas F. Pettigrew et al., "Busing: A Review of the Evidence," *The Public Interest* 30 (Winter 1973):88-114.

11. See Mark Yudof, "Equal Educational Opportunity and the Courts," *Texas Law Review* 51, no. 3 (March 1973):437.

12. See for evidence, U.S. Commission on Civil Rights, *Racial Isolation in the Public Schools* (Washington, D.C.: U.S. Government Printing Office, 1967).

13. See Betsy Levin, "Recent Developments in the Law of Equal Educational Opportunity," *Journal of Law and Education* 4, no. 3 (July 1975):411-447; National Institute of Education, *Education, Social Science, and the Judicial Process* (Washington, D.C.: U.S. Department of Health, Education, and Welfare, June 1976); and Donald C. Horowitz, *The Courts and Social Policy* (Washington, D.C.: The Brookings Institution, 1976).

14. See Frederick M. Wirt, *Politics of Southern Equality: Law and Social Change in a Mississippi County* (Chicago: Aldine, 1970).

15. *Hobson* v. *Hanson,* 269 F. Supp. 401, 515 (D.D.C. 1967); and *Hobson* v. *Hanson,* 327 F. Supp. 844, 859 (D.D.C. 1971). Known as *Hobson I* and *II.*

16. This is a school finance arrangement devised by Strayer and Haig and promoted subsequently by Paul R. Mort; it only partially equalizes local taxing and spending ability. Above a per pupil spending minimum this plan permits conditions of local property wealth to influence strongly local school spending.

17. Arthur E. Wise, "The Constitution and Equality, Wealth Geography, and Educational Opportunity," (Ph.D. diss., University of Chicago, 1967). Wise initially presented his thesis in a 1965 issue of *The Administrator's Notebook* published by the Midwest Administration Center at the University of Chicago.

18. Wise later authored *Rich Schools, Poor Schools: The Promise of Equal Educational Opportunity* (Chicago: University of Chicago Press, 1968).

19. John E. Coons, William H. Clune, III, and Stephen D. Sugarman, *Private Wealth and Public Education* (Cambridge, Mass.: Harvard University Press, 1970).

20. For an example of the nonjudiciable problem see *McInnis* v. *Shapiro,* 293 F. Supp. 327.

21. *Hobson* v. *Hanson,* 269 F. Supp. 401, 515 (D.D.C. 1967); and *Hobson* v. *Hanson,* 327 F. Supp. 844, 859 (D.D.C. 1971). Known as *Hobson I* and *II.*

22. See R. Martin and P. McClure, *ESTA Title I, Is It Helping Poor Children?* (Washington, D.C.: NAACP Legal Defense Fund and the Washington Research Project, 1969).

23. The result was the so-called "Comparability Guidelines," which were issued by USOE in 1971.

24. Education Commission of the State's records.

25. *Rodriguez* v. *San Antonio Independent School District,* 337 F. Supp. 380.

26. *Mills* v. *Board of Education,* 348 F. Supp. 866 (D.D.C. 1972).

27. *Pennsylvania Association of Retarded Children* v. *Commonwealth of Pennsylvania,* 334 F. Supp. 1257 (E.D. Pa. 1971); and 343 F. Supp. 279 (E.D. Pa. 1972).

28. *Lau* v. *Nichols,* 414 U.S. 564.

29. P.L. 93-142.

30. Figures derived from the USOE publication: National Center for Educational Statistics, *A Century of Public School Statistics* (Washington, D.C.: Department of Health, Education, and Welfare, 1973).

31. National Center for Educational Statistics, *The Condition of Education,* 1976 ed. (Washington, D.C.: U.S. Government Printing Office, 1976).

32. See Flanagan, "Changes in School Levels of Achievement."

33. Raymond E. Callahan, *The Cult of Efficiency* (Chicago: University of Chicago Press, 1960).

34. A review of the cost-quality inquiry and some of its successors is provided by William E. Barron's chapter, "Measurement of Educational Productivity," in W.E. Gauerke and J.R. Childress, eds., *The Theory and Practice of School Finance* (Chicago: Rand McNally, 1967), pp. 279-308. An earlier review of such efforts is provided in Paul R. Mort, "Cost Quality Relationships in Education," in R.L. Johns and E.L. Morphet, eds., *Problems and Issues in Public School Finance* (New York: National Conference of Professors of Educational Administration, 1952).

35. For example, L.H. Woollatt, *The Cost-Quality Relationship in the Growing Edge* (New York: Columbia Teachers College Press, 1949).

36. Coleman et al., *Equality of Educational Opportunity.*

37. For a summary of Coleman Report criticisms see James W. Guthrie et al., *Schools and Inequality* (Cambridge, Mass.: M.I.T. Press, 1971).

38. Ibid.

39. Harvey Averch et al., *How Effective Is Schooling: A Critical Review and Synthesis of Research Findings* (Santa Monica, Calif.: Rand Corporation, 1972); and Henry M. Levin, "Measuring Efficiency in Educational Production," *Public Finance Quarterly* 2 (January 1974):3-24.

40. For example, Richard J. Murnane, "The Impact of School Resources on the Learning of Inner City Children" (Ph.D. diss., Yale University, 1974); and Anita A. Summers and Barbara L. Wolfe, "Which School Resources Help Learning Efficiency and Equity in Philadelphia Public Schools?" *Federal Reserve Bank of Philadelphia Business Review* (February 1976).

41. James W. Guthrie, "The Political Economy of School Productivity" in J. McDermott, ed., *Indeterminacy in Education* (Berkeley, Calif.: McCutchan, 1976).

42. See the discussion in F.A. Hayek, *The Constitution of Liberty* (Chicago: University of Chicago Press, 1960).

43. Bernard Bailyn, *The Ideological Origins of the American Revolution* (Cambridge, Mass.: Harvard University Press, 1967), p. 55.

44. The cyclical nature of governmental reforms is described by Herbert Kaufman in *Politics and Policies in State and Local Government* (Englewood Cliffs, N.J.: Prentice-Hall, 1963), chap. 2.

45. *A Century of U.S. School Statistics* (Washington, D.C.: U.S. Department of Health, Education, and Welfare, 1974); and Jonathan Sher, *Economy, Efficiency, and Equality. The Myths of Rural School and District Consolidation* (Washington, D.C.: National Institute of Education, 1976).

46. For an assessment of the research findings related to school and school district size, see James W. Guthrie, "The Scale of Government and the Success of

Schools," paper prepared for the Berkeley-Stanford NIE-sponsored seminar on education research.

47. The evolution of school governance is described in James W. Guthrie, Patricia A. Craig, and Diana M. Thomas, "The Erosion of Lay Control," in National Committee for Support of Public Schools, *Public Testimony on Public Schools* (Berkeley, Calif.: McCutchan, 1975).

48. Gabriel A. Almond, "A Functional Approach to Comparative Politics," in G.A. Almond and J.S. Coleman, eds., *The Politics of Developing Areas* (Princeton, N.J.: Princeton University Press, 1960), pp. 3-64.

49. Theodore L. Reller, *The Development of the City Superintendency of Schools in the United States* (Philadelphia: Published by the author, 1935); David B. Tyack, *The One Best System* (Cambridge, Mass.: Harvard University Press, 1975); and Joseph M. Cronin, *The Control of Urban Schools* (New York: The Free Press, 1973).

50. See James W. Guthrie and Paula H. Skene, "The Escalation of Pedagogical Politics," *Phi Delta Kappan* 54 (February 1973), pp. 386-389; and Les Pacheco, "The Politicization of Education at the State Level: A Case Study of California, 1947-72" (Ed.D. diss., University of California, Berkeley, 1974).

51. For added evidence on this point see Tyll van Geel, *Authority to Control the School Program* (Lexington, Mass.: Lexington Books, D.C. Heath & Co., 1977).

52. See Henry M. Levin, *Community Control of Schools* (Washington, D.C.: Brookings Institution, 1970).

53. See Melvin Zimet, *Decentralization of School Effectiveness* (New York: Teachers College Press, 1973).

54. For example, by 1975, California, South Carolina, and Florida had enacted statutes requiring school site advisory councils.

55. James Bryant Conant, *The American High School Today* (New York: McGraw Hill, 1959).

56. Roger G. Barker and Paul V. Gump, *Big School, Small School* (Palo Alto, Calif.: Stanford University Press, 1964).

57. See John E. Coons and Stephen D. Sugarman, *A Model Statute for Family Choice in Education* (Berkeley, Calif.: Institute for Governmental Studies, 1973).

58. David H. Cohen and Eleanor Farrar, "Power to the Parents? The Story of Education Vouchers," *The Public Interest*, no. 48 (Summer 1977), pp. 72-97.

59. E.F. Schumacher, *Small Is Beautiful* (New York: Harper and Row, 1975).

60. For example, see Jay G. Chambers, "The Impact of Collective Bargaining for Teachers on Resource Allocations in Public School Districts: The California Experience," *Journal of Urban Economics* 4 (July 1977):324-339; and Donald R. Winkler, "Absenteeism and Sick Leave Policy in the Public Sector," paper written with the support of NIE Grant No. NIE-G-74-0044.

61. Lawrence G. Pierce, "Teachers' Organizations and Bargaining Power

Imbalance in the Public Sphere," in National Committee For Support of Public Schools, *Public Testimony on Public Schools* (Berkeley, Calif.: McCutchan, 1975).

62. This is a point brilliantly assessed by David Kirp in "School Desegregation and the Limits of Legalism," *The Public Interest,* no. 47 (Spring 1977), pp. 101-128.

63. The court case was *Robinson* v. *Cahill,* 62 N.J. 473, 303 A. 2d. 273 (1973).

Part III
Assessment of Research on Educational Administration from the Disciplines

"Scanty attention is paid to problem diagnosis and the tendency is to concentrate on problems which conform to readily available solution paradigms."

<blockquote>
—Michael Eraut, "Promoting Innovation in Teaching and Learning: Problems, Processes and Institutional Mechanisms," Higher Education 4, no. 1 (1975).
</blockquote>

6

The School as a Formal Organization: Some New Thoughts

Charles E. Bidwell

Rereading one's own work inevitably is painful. Nevertheless, to prepare this chapter I was forced to reread "The School as a Formal Organization" (Bidwell 1965). As a consequence of this rereading, I shall review some of the more evident limitations of my 1965 approach to school organization, viewed from my 1977 perspective. This review will point to a set of problems that, as a sociologist, I believe are central to further research on educational organizations.

School Organization: A Review

It is striking to me now how silent or at least how hesitant I was in 1965 about three related questions: school productivity, change in schools, and the connectedness of schools and their environments.[1]

I suppose that my silence on productivity and change and my hesitance about environments—my view of schools as stable, strongly bounded organizations—should not be surprising. The environments of schools were relatively placid when I wrote: teacher's strikes were largely confined to the biggest cities, distributive justice in schooling and the rights of children in school were not yet issues, and effects of declining birth rates were not yet apparent. This naturally reinforced my easy assumption of strong boundaries and organizational stability in schools. But more important, early in the sixties, organizational theory was still within the era of closed-system formulation. Indeed, this strand of organizational theory remains vigorous (for example: Blau 1970; Blau and Schoenherr 1971), although no longer unchallenged. Closed-system theories have approached organizations as if they were machines. The organization-as-machine is a system that remains undisturbed by events outside its boundary, unless a prime mover of some kind—most often in these theories either an entrepreneur or top-level administrator—intervenes to change parts of the system or change the ways existing parts act on one another. Moreover, the action of such a prime mover is used to account for the machine's existence in the first place.

This Newtonian version of organizational theory sets aside problems of dynamics and environments. The prime mover's intervention accounts for both, but as an unanalyzed given. The mechanistic approach also turned our attention away from productivity. From the assumed strength of the organizational boundary derives the notion of a single feedback channel from product markets to the organization—the prime mover himself, who may found a new kind of organization to capitalize on unsatisfied demand and available resources (viz., Stinchcombe 1965) or adapt an existing organization to changed market conditions. More elaborated notions of feedback from environment to organization cannot be analyzed adequately within the purview of the closed-system theorist.

Nevertheless, I do find in my chapter the beginnings of a dynamic approach to school organization. I took pride at the time that I wrote it (and I still do) that it gave strong emphasis to process—not processes of organizational change, to be sure, but processes of schooling. I viewed these processes as more or less uniform throughout the population of schools; nevertheless, I did formulate them as a dynamic equilibrium between contradictory forces. I would like to spend a little time on this aspect of my chapter, since it points toward an understanding of dynamic relationships between the structure of schools and processes of schooling.

Because of my emphasis in 1965 on schooling processes, I gave organizational structure a less dominant position than is characteristic of closed-system theories. I did so because I viewed the structure of schools as reciprocally related to schooling—as a response to the nature of the work to be done and as a fostering and constraining context within which it takes place.

In short, I was required to examine organizational technology—in the present case the practical principles and codified means of instruction—and to trace the influences of this technology and school structure on one another. Like my Chicago colleagues, Robert Dreeben and Dan Lortie, I found the codified means largely absent. I would now put the point more precisely and say that while specific tools and procedures of instruction are available, the decision rules for their combination and application to cases are a strong function of the preferences of individual teachers. I suggested that the major effect of practical principles was to be found in the way changing conceptions of learning (for example, the movement from faculty to dynamic psychology as the basis of learning theory) affected teachers' conceptions of the tasks of teaching—that is, what kinds of learning teachers were to foster and what aspects of the student and of the class, collectively, were pertinent. I then attempted to account for coordination and control in schools as an adaptation to regularities of teachers' work—regularities that were generated by these conceptions in the absence of rationalized instructional procedures.

Although I did not use the term, mine was a *sociotechnical* theory of school organization. I assumed that schools had strong boundaries, but I did not assume that these boundaries were impermeable. The principal external influence on school organization, however, came not from local or variable sources, but from a teaching technology that I treated as if it were uniform and generalized throughout the population of schools. If school organization were stable, as I implicitly assumed it to be, the stability came from the stability of technology (that is, principles of practice). Thus I treated the stability of organizational form as specific to historical periods defined by the rise and fall of theories of learning (cf., my brief discussion of the replacement of faculty by dynamic psychology and of monitorial by age-graded school organization).

Interestingly, the major sociotechnical theories of organization, early challengers of closed-system theory, appeared at about the same time as the *Handbook of Organizations* (March 1965). Woodward's first monograph, *Industrial Organization,* was published in 1965, and Thompson's *Organizations in Action* two years later (Woodward 1965; Thompson, 1967). Indeed, a third interesting sociotechnical discussion, from the same "absence of codified means" perspective as my own, was Perrow's *Handbook* chapter on hospitals (Perrow 1965).

Woodward and Thompson—the latter only to the extent of his sociotechnical propositions—are highly deterministic. They view organizational structure as an adaptation to technical exigencies. Moreover, although Thompson's theory, especially, is widely regarded as an open-system theory of organization, it is in fact a control system theory in which managerial action forms the one link between environments and otherwise-buffered organizations. In contrast to closed-system structuralism, however, these theories do focus our attention on productivity, since the indicator of structural adaptation is value-added in production—for Woodward, who studied economic organizations, the profitability of the firm.

An obvious tautology derives from this measure of adaptation, but I find the technological determinism more troubling. As in my *Handbook* chapter, I still would prefer to leave open the possibility of reciprocal causation throughout the organizational system. In principle, there is no reason not to expect organizational structure or demography to stimulate technological adaptation.

Public schools, for example, for other than technological reasons, often must enroll large numbers of students relative to the money they have to spend on instruction. Age-graded instruction (and perhaps concomitant age-specific theories of learning), programmed instruction, audio-visual instruction and team-teaching, among others, may be seen as technological adaptations to the demographic exigency of size of the student population.

There is another tautology in sociotechnical determinism. Although I tried to keep technology and structure conceptually distinct (as did Perrow), Woodward and Thompson define technology in structural terms—not as practical principles, tools, procedures of work, or decision rules about work, but as elements of production organization itself (for instance, the specialization or interdependence of work roles). Hence, neither Woodward nor Thompson inform us about the causal location of more precisely specified technological variables in the organizational system.

I still prefer (as I did implicitly in my chapter and as Perrow did in his) to regard production organization as a distinctive component of organizational structure that is directly but reciprocally related to technology (and also affected by organizational demography and the full range of environmental input to an organization). In this view, production organization mediates between other structural elements (such as the morphology of control) and technological, demographic, and environmental variables.

In saying this, I do not mean to deny the importance of technology in the study of school organizations. Instead, I would suggest that theories of organization have not been precise or analytical enough in their treatment of technology; therefore, to address problems of school productivity or of change in school organization, we first must be precise and analytical about the technology of teaching. The elements of this technology comprise a large component of the resources that must be combined in the process of schooling, and they presumably constrain the combinatorial process. Moreover, I have argued that technology and organizational structure are in a mutually adaptive relationship, which, therefore, as it changes is a part of change in organizations. Technology also sets limits to organizational adaptation to other (demographic and environmental) elements of the organizational system—no less in schools than in organizations of other kinds.

I have mentioned organizational demography several times as a component of organizational analysis, and in my *Handbook* chapter I did attend to the composition and reproduction of school populations—especially to the ways in which students, teachers, administrators, and board members are recruited (Bidwell 1965). But I did not carry this aspect of my discussion far enough. I only toyed with even the apparently simple (but fundamental) notion of size, whether of the total school population or of its several components—a set of variables that has proved so tantalizing but vexing in Blau's theory and in the commentary of his critics (see Meyer 1972). Moreover, I limited myself to consequences of population composition for the normative integration of schools, ignoring its possible connections with elements of structure, technology, or input from the environments.

This unfortunate limitation came, ironically, from my concern with teachers' work. Given my assumption that instruction is constrained mainly by practical principles rather than by procedural codes, it seemed to follow that the major source of organizational control over work process would be found in the specific constellation of conceptions of instruction held by teachers and students and, secondarily, in those held by administrators. Hence I saw the composition of school membership, through its effect on this constellation of conceptions, as the chief organizational constraint on instruction—with recruitment indirectly affecting the constellation because of its influence on composition.

Thus, I saw the main sources of control over instruction not in administrative structure but in the mechanisms of organizational recruitment—an indirect form of organizational control that left instructional work open to the vicissitudes of the daily life of school buildings and classrooms and to any forces inside or outside the school that might impinge on it (for instance, a Wallerian "separate culture of the school," or the family origins of students). From this view derived an important contradiction in my chapter. The very procedural diffuseness of technology opened the school to its environment to a much greater extent than my implicit closed-system theory should have suggested.

I did discuss certain countervailing forces, among them another set of conceptions—school administrators' belief in the virtues of rationalization—and the long-run sequential interdependence of instructional activity (essentially the same notion as Thompson's "long-linked" technology). But in view of the low level of procedural systemization of teaching and the low short-run interdependence of instructional activities, these countervailing forces looked very weak. Hence, I emphasized what I called the "structural looseness" of school organization and Waller's (1932) classic treatment of the contradictions and dilemmas of teachers' work. Note that these contradictions and dilemmas were not inherent in the structure of schools but derived from the conceptions held by students, parents, teachers, administrators, and community leaders about the place of school in the daily round of life and about the proper content and form of schooling. I saw the conduct of instruction as shaped less by the location of the school's members and constituents in the structure of the school, and more by their location in the structure of society—in only an apparent paradox a technological link between environment and school, and the only such link that I was prepared to see.

The Study of Organizational Change

Now I would like to turn from reflections on past work to tasks for the present and future. I opened by suggesting a research agenda centered on the related problems of the productivity and dynamics of schools, and thus necessarily on school-environment exchange. In fact, I look toward a dynamic theory of educational production. But I think our first step toward such a theory must be description—the careful, baseline description of the organizational structure of schools. I do not mean aimless description, for I believe this initial reconnaissance should center on school structure as a cybernetic structure of control. It should be conducted across school systems carefully selected to represent the full range of observed values on a series of parameters that, theoretically, we would expect to affect the control structure of schools.

Our theoretical base may well be eclectic, since no one theory of organizational control presently is clearly ahead on the points of evidence. But I myself would begin from the idea of formal organization as a variety of social organization and turn to propositions from modern human ecology about the emergence of cybernetic structures in human populations (for example, dominance relations among niches).

Modern human ecology, I believe, provides the single most promising avenue for the development of dynamic open-systems theory of *any* variety of social organization. The specification of propositions drawn from human ecology to formal organizations is most promising (see Hannan and Freeman 1977; Warriner 1978; Aldrich 1979). These propositions center directly on (1) the emergence of organizational structure as a continuing adaptation to the exigencies of more or less rapidly and evenly changing environment, technology, and organizational membership and (2) the functions of structural adaptation in mediating between these exigencies and organizational productivity.

Moreover, although there is strong emphasis on controlling mechanisms in the adaptive process, these mechanisms are viewed as pervasive throughout the organization's division of labor. There is no need to assume that they are comprised only of managerial action. Finally, despite the strictures of the more polemical advocates of human ecology (for example: Duncan and Schnore 1959; Schnore 1961), there is no reason to exclude from the analysis the behavior of individual actors within organizations. Quite the reverse, as certain of my later comments will suggest.

Modern human ecology suggests five key parameters or sets of parameters for analysis: population size (for schools best measured by pupil enrollment), population heterogeneity (especially the age, sex, and racial/ethnic heterogeneity of the study body), the stability and availability in relation to population size of resources from the environment to sustain the population (especially revenues per pupil, but perhaps the content, distribution, and efficiency of aggregation of local community preferences for educational services), and, finally, at least a rough measure of the complexity of the technology employed by the school.

I earlier argued and still would contend that instructional technology is relatively undeveloped as a set of procedural decision rules. This fact suggests that the technological variables may not differ markedly across schools. Nevertheless, the main purpose of my proposed descriptive reconnaissance is to discover possible variability of control structures in schools and, if such variability exists, to find the covariation of these structures with sociologically fundamental parameters of population, environment, and technology that constrain social organization. Therefore, we should try to determine the empirical range of technological variability that schools do display and possible structural correlates of variation within this range. My earlier comment on instructional technology pointed to teachers' (and others') conceptions of instruction as central constraints on structure, but in a large sample survey of the kind I am suggesting, such conceptions are difficult to measure reliably and expensive to measure at all.

We should not forget, however, that school systems (rather more than local schools) conduct other kinds of production besides instruction, and as one approach to technological complexity, at least at the school system level of analysis, we might measure the sheer number of "product lines" (for instance, in addition to instruction, health care, food service, or pupil transportation). Within instruction itself, we might measure the number of subject areas offered, the number of high school tracks, and the number of age-groups served (for example, K-6, K-9, K-12 school districts). I realize that the number of district sets of production activities is a very rough indicator of technological diversity, but especially with reference to control systems, these crude measures may be revealing.

John Kasarda and I have conducted a descriptive reconnaissance of all the school districts in Michigan, designed very much like the one that I have just outlined. This study relies on quite extensive data about these districts that enable us to measure salient characteristics of their staff and student membership, attributes of the technologies employed by the districts (both instructional and noninstructional), detailed aspects of their division of labor and other structural properties, student achievement gain (at several grade levels) in verbal and quantitative skills, and high school student attrition and college-going rates. These data are available for a five-year time series (1969-1970 through 1973-1974), allowing limited longitudinal, as well as cross-sectional, analysis.[2]

So far as their control systems are concerned, these districts appear in certain key ways to be loosely coupled systems—not in the relaxed meaning that Karl Weick (1976) recently has given to this term, but in the more precise denotation of Herbert Simon (1962). Vertical control relationships form near-decomposable hierarchies,[3] whereas horizontal relationships display exceedingly low levels of interdependence.

There are several items of evidence for the conclusion that the Michigan school districts are loosely coupled. In contrast to repeated findings for economic organizations and for certain other kinds of organizations in the public sector [for example, Blau's state employment agencies (Blau and Schoenherr 1971) and Meyer's (1977) municipal finance bureaus], variation in the division of production labor (such variables as specialization of instruction, ratios of supporting professionals to teachers, and segmentation of instruction) has no appreciable effect on either the relative size or specialization of administration. This finding holds true both cross-sectionally among districts and longitudinally (over our five-year span) within them. The same finding, furthermore, obtains for the clerical staffs of the districts.

Investigators like Blau have found that increases in organizational size (measured as the proportion of front-line operating staff) foster a more complex division of labor and, through this intervening variable, foster proportionate increases in the number of administrators (although these effects generally occur at a rate lower than the rate of increase in size). Our finding is different. Division of labor in instruction does not intervene between size (whether the proportionate number of pupils or of teachers) and either the size or specialization of district administration.[4]

However, the size and specialization of district administration are correlated with size of operating front-line staff and division of labor in the nonprofessional, noninstructional sector of district production (the number, and internal specialization, of such noninstructional activities as maintenance, food service, or pupil transportation, for example). This is exactly what the earlier findings on other kinds of organizations would lead us to expect.

At the same time, the size of staff and the division of labor in instruction and other professional production components are strongly correlated with the size and heterogeneity of pertinent pupil cohorts, because these attributes of the student membership of the districts affect the specialization of staff roles. The measures of student heterogeneity include the diversity of academic ability or prior school performance, socioeconomic standing of the family, and racial-ethnic composition.

Nonprofessional production also is correlated with total size of the student body, but less strongly. Cohort-specific correlations are essentially zero. Moreover, there are internal dependencies in this sector that are not found in the instructional-professional component. For example, the number of teachers and of psychological specialists are uncorrelated once pupil input variables are controlled, but if a district hires any skilled craftsmen at all, they tend to be hired as sets of complementary skills. This finding suggests that there is weaker lateral interdependence between front-line staff roles in the instructional than noninstructional sector of the Michigan districts.

Moreover, although the proportionate size of the administrative cadre, the intensity of the administrative division of labor, and the number of administrative levels are to a degree dependent on the size and complexity of nonprofessional production, these aspects of administration are mainly functions of phenomena outside the organizational boundary—for example, the proportion of per-pupil revenues received from federal sources, the stability of revenues, the per-pupil valuation of real property in the district, and several rough indicators of the stability and homogeneity of community preferences for educational services.

In short, the larger, the more variegated, or the less stable are fiscal and political inputs to a district, the larger the relative size of the administrative component, and the more specialized it tends to be. These relationships obtain at the central office level. At intermediate levels of administration, the main rule is simply one school, one principal, so that the number of principals is a direct function in the short-run of the number of schools and in the long-run (like the number of teachers) probably of the size of student cohorts. Moreover, although the number of supervisors of instruction and the number of teachers are correlated, both also are correlated with pupil enrollment. The relationship between teachers and supervisors disappears when we control for pupil enrollment. But the correlation of either with enrollment does not disappear when we control for the other.

Our findings for the clerical component are most interesting. Below the central office, the number of clerks, like the number of principals, obeys the rule of one-per-school. At the central office level, the proportionate size of the clerical staff is correlated with the intensity of the nonprofessional division of production labor, but it is associated still more strongly with phenomena outside the organizational boundary. These are similar to the external sources of administrative variability, but the most powerful among them are inputs to the district that require record-keeping (for example, the proportion of revenue from grants-in-aid). The one strong internal correlate of the relative size of the central office clerical staff is the presence of a specialized attendance office, which in turn is related to the socioeconomic and ability/performance hetero-geneity of the student body (especially above the sixth grade).

Kasarda and I have interpreted these findings as indicating weak lateral integration of the key production activity—instruction. Instructional units and roles evidently are not strongly interdependent, for they make little demand on the district's coordinative or communicative capacity. Nonprofessional functions and roles, however, are more strongly integrated laterally, and they make such demand. Vertical relationships in the instructional and professional sectors are extremely attenuated, precisely for this reason. Low interdependence requires little in the way either of information flow between roles and positions or of administrative control. This finding suggests that low lateral interdependence may be a necessary (although probably not a sufficient) condition for the emergence of near-decomposable hierarchies in organizations.

By contrast, administrative and instructional/professional activities and roles appear to be quite responsive to events in their own specific environments—the school or classroom responding to the immediate attending student population (and no doubt to a local parental and public constituency), and the central office responding to the fiscal and political resources available in the district's local community and in the state capital and Washington.

To put the point perhaps a little too strongly, neither instruction (or its professional support) nor administration is loosely coupled with its own task-specific environment, but these components are indeed lossely coupled with one another, both laterally (low interdependence) and vertically (near-decom-posability).

Kasarda and I have no evidence of the generalizability of our findings beyond Michigan, although they are consistent with our earlier less detailed findings on the school districts of Colorado (Bidwell and Kasarda 1976). They also are consistent with the theoretical frame within which I have been arguing. For my present purposes, I should like simply to take these Michigan findings as an example of what one might turn up in a descriptive reconnaissance of schools and of how such a survey could inform a conceptualization of the organizational structure of schools.

If one in fact were able to achieve such a baseline conceptualization, how would it inform our approach to the issues of organizational change and productivity in education? Let me begin with the question of change and continue to draw for illustration from the Michigan study.

Dutiful sociologists that we are, Kasarda and I scrutinized our deviant cases—those districts in which administrative structure and the division of labor in instructional and other professional activities did covary. Sensitized by current concern with declining enrollments and revenues, we had expected districts faced by such decline to be disproportionately represented among our deviant cases. We had expected declining enrollment to reduce both revenues and demand for instruction and that these reductions, in turn, would reduce the specialization of both administrative and front-line professional staff. The covariation between the structure of administration and front-line professional activities, then, would have been largely, if not entirely, spurious—reflecting the structuring effects of variation in enrollment and revenues.

The facts, however, were different. The declining districts were not overrepresented among the deviant cases, so for the moment we turned away from them to compare districts with growing, stable, and declining enrollments. Although our data incorporate a series of only five years, so that our conclusions about change must be very tentative, over this short period we found that districts faced with growing, declining, and stable enrollments all followed the same hiring rule—to expand or reduce the teaching/professional work force proportionately in response to experienced growth or decline of enrollment (subject to distortions induced by variation in pertinent labor markets, teachers' contracts, and the like). Since the administrative structure was affected by other, independently acting forces, the administration-teaching force correlation was consistently low in each of these three groups.

We also found that as revenues expanded and contracted, at a given enrollment level, our school districts increased and decreased per-pupil allocations of instructional-professional staff; they buffered against input fluctuation in the light of inelasticities elsewhere in the budget by rationing pupils' shares of teachers' time. Rationing, remember, is the buffering device that Thompson (1967) expected when an organization is unable to smooth out such fluctuations, either by acting on its environment (for instance, by incorporating suppliers) or by stockpiling inputs. These ideas of Thompson's remind us of a very important set of variables to include in a dynamic theory of organizations— the structure of the "industry" or "industries" within which a population of organizations is located.

The analytical components of industry will depend on the problem one studies; for present purposes, the especially pertinent components are the legal framework within which the industry's member organizations operate [see Hirsch's (1975) comparison of the drug and recording industries] and technology, which I assume is, relatively speaking, uniform within industries.

Like many (but not all) public organizations, schools enjoy a legally based near-monopoly within a service area (the district boundary). Legal constraints also make it difficult for them to acquire suppliers of fiscal or material resources or to stockpile these resources (for example, by carrying over annual budget surpluses, operating their own text-publishing units, or borrowing in the short-run to purchase surplus amounts of, say, fuel or maintenance supplies at favorable prices). Moreover, conventional understandings about teaching prevent stockpiling student inputs (for example, staggering admissions to spread them out evenly over school terms or years), while the very monopolistic position of school districts constrains against interdistrict arrangements for equalizing student inputs across districts. I should guess that the substitutability of teachers would make stockpiling teachers unattractive, even if it were possible.

In sum, legal and technological conditions in the industry of education, the latter including low interdependence between instructional roles and units, suggest that loose coupling is a successful environmental adaptation by schools. Linear addition and subtraction of roles and units in instruction accommodate changes in the volume of instruction, while there are few interdependencies among them to constrain this accommodation. The principal functions of administration thus center on: monitoring the environment to provide information about demand and sustenance for the system's services; minimizing barriers to linear adaptation (for example, negotiation with teachers' unions); maintaining an adequate flow of funds (for example, obtaining grants-in-aid, meeting requirements for fiscal accountability, lobbying with state legislators and departments of education, and campaigning for bond issues); and managing political support (for example, keeping political fences mended in the local community).

This discussion should not be taken to exclude structural variability within industries or to suggest that there is only one successful structural adaptation to a given industry environment. On the first point, there are three especially likely sources of structural variation—variation within industries in market structures, legal provisions specific to sets of organizations within an industry, and variation around the central tendency of the key production technology.

For the case of education, note on the first of these possibilities the segmentation of markets by locality (that is, the attendance district) and on the second the differing provisions of law and state administrative regulation governing public and private schools. On the third possibility, technological variability, let me return to the deviant cases that Kasarda and I found in Michigan. There are certain variables that discriminate systematically between the relatively few districts in which there is strong correlation, and the larger number with a weak correlation between the division of instructional/professional labor and the proportionate size and complexity of administration.

The districts in which there is a strong correlation are peculiarly characterized by a level of teaching specialization sufficiently refined so that the subject matter areas of the curriculum are finely divided, and each teaching position is uniquely assigned to a division. Examples from mathematics are teachers of calculus or of analytic geometry; from social studies, teachers of European or American history; or from music, teachers specialized by instrument. When the division of instructional labor in a school district reaches this level, its net direct effect is to increase the proportionate number of instructional supervisors (although not their specialization) and, indirectly through this supervisory increase, to heighten the proportionate size of the central office clerical staff.

Evidently a highly refined division of instructional labor does increase communicative and coordinative problems within the subject matter components of the teaching force. At the same time, the accompanying growth of lower-level instructional supervision itself generates an added flow of communication—probably vertically between supervisors and local schools and between supervisors and central office administrators. This flow requires extra clerks. Supervisors, however, probably because they are almost always responsible for entire subject-matter segments, are not themselves interdependent; thus, we would guess, arises the failure of relative increase of the supervisory component to affect the relative number of central office administrators.[5]

We searched for historical and environmental correlates of a highly specialized teaching force and found three, none of them surprising—the size of the secondary enrollment, the occupational and educational levels of the adult population, and the age of the district. The first two of these relationships are nonlinear. There is a threshold of enrollment below which it evidently is too expensive to intensively subdivide teaching positions. Moreover, this intense division of instructional labor is located almost entirely within those districts that serve communities that have high proportions of the college-educated and professional and upper-managerial occupations within their adult populations.

With district age the relationship is linear. The older the district, the more specialized its teaching force is likely to be. The relationship with age, I think, reflects the salience of what I have called practical principles (or better, the lack of procedural specification of these principles) in instructional technology. These principles give fairly wide latitude to traditional practice. The effects of enrollment size and occupational and educational characteristics of the adult population show interesting consequences of market variables—here the volume of demand and, we surmise, the structure of preferential demand for schooling. Our guess is that these preferences are mainly for advanced college preparation; hence, the high level of instructional specialization that we have observed.

These findings are cross-sectional. Our five-year time series is too brief to reveal much in the way of lagged relationships among these variables. Nevertheless, we do find that two to three years after the proportion of secondary school enrollment from highly educated and professional-managerial homes reaches about 60 percent, teacher specialization begins to increase. The contrary trend is not visible, probably reflecting the relative short-run inelasticity of a teaching force to compositional change in enrollment.

What do our findings imply for the study of organizational change in schools? For my speculative purposes the similarity between our cross-sectional and time-series findings encourages me to take the cross-sectional findings as rough indicators of dynamic relationships.

Aldrich and Pfeffer (1976) have discussed two major approaches to the study of organizational change—which perforce (as my entire argument here suggests) must be the dynamic analysis of organization-environment correlations. One approach, developed especially by Hannan and Freeman (1977), is an application of population ecology to populations of organizations. This approach concerns itself with long-run changes in the prevalence of organizational forms. It takes as given initial morphological variation (for example, the invention of new organizations to make new products or existing products in new ways). Then it asks how these variations are selected (according to a principle of relative success in obtaining sustenance for organizational activities). Then it asks how the selected variations are retained (largely according to the principle of slack in exchanges between existing organizations and their environments).

A second approach Aldrich and Pfeffer call the resource dependence approach. Deriving largely from the work of Thompson (1967), Zald (1970), Child (1972), and Pfeffer (1976), this approach is concerned with dynamics within organizations (rather than within populations of organizations), and it pictures organizations as intentionally constructed systems for providing services to, and taking resources from, an environment. Here the organization is viewed as both proactive and reactive, in part capable of creating its own environment. The principal source of either reactive or proactive response to environmental change is managerial decision (a concept that embraces the possibility of an internal organizational polity, precisely because of the multiple possibilities for response that an environment presents).

The Michigan findings that I have presented are of a *measurement* order apparently more consistent with the ecological than with the resource dependence approach, because the measures do not index behaviors. Yet my interpretations have turned often to implied managerial decisions, though as only one among numerous sources of structural change in the Michigan districts, as the notion of the near-decomposable hierarchy implies. In fact, I think that a satisfactory, comprehensive treatment of the dynamics of organizations generally, and of schools in particular, must incorporate both approaches. Indeed the dynamic properties of populations of organizations can be understood largely as a process of natural selection.

To do so, we must assume initial states on the salient parameters of what I have called industries—existing laws, technological means, resource availability, and demand for products. We would then correlate the rates of structural invention, organizational establishment, and organizational demise with these parameter values. This is precisely what Stinchcombe (1965) attempted in his article in the March *Handbook* (1965). To the extent that industries foster high levels of interorganizational competition, are segmented into locally differentiated markets, and contain variable legal provisions and alternative technologies, we would expect these rates to be high. Organizational form within the industry then would tend toward uniformity within regions of uniform environment and technology.

To the extent that the parameter values are low, we would expect these rates to be low, and, over time, we would expect organizational form within the industry to become highly uniform, as a result not of competitive survival but of a mimetic process. (Here one must assume also that these same parameter values foster free and inexpensive information flow throughout the industry.) Variability at a given time around the dominant structural tendency then would be understood according to deviation from the central tendency of the parameter values. Only massive changes in these parameter values would affect change in the retention of the dominant organizational form.

This analysis is precisely what we find in recent historical treatments of the spread of public education in the United States (see Tyack 1974) and lies behind my conclusion that loose coupling is a successful adaptation by schools to technology and environment.

Note that the population ecology of organizations need not exclude intentional action by organizational elites on the environment. Such action can effect large-scale changes in industry parameters which alter the dynamics of natural selection. But the ecological analyst need not attend to these processes unless he wishes to explain change in the industry itself. Note also that such ecological studies require long time series and cross-industry comparison to the extent that industries foster uniform adaptive patterns and high rates of organizational retention.

When we speak of organizational change, however, we refer typically not to population dynamics or long-run adaptation, but to shorter-run structural alterations within organizations. To the extent that these changes respond to cyclic fluctuations in environments, such studies have limited implications for the population ecology of organizations. But to the extent that the changes respond to secular, technological, or environmental trends, they can be seen as components of structural invention that underlie the variability of organizational form that is basic to the natural selection of organizations.

Our Michigan findings pertain to within-organization adaptation. To conduct a within-organization study of this kind, we begin with a baseline model of the form of the organization. We assume as a central process, the intentionality of actors in the organization, although we are not limited to intentional decisions to alter structure.

As in ecological analyses of organizational populations, parameter values of the organization's industry are central variables, but now as constraints on, or stimuli to, organizational action (for instance, the mutability of technology or laws governing the responsibilities of organizations or defining their domains of autonomous activity). But we are equally concerned with deviations from these parameter values as they pertain to specific environmental conditions for the organization we are studying.

From this point forward, given the present rudimentary state of behavioral theory of organizations, I believe that we must reason from presumed effect to presumed cause rather than the reverse. We initially must gather two kinds of data: measures of temporal variation in inputs to the organization of technology, and measures of demand for products and of resources to sustain the organization. We also must obtain measures of deviation over time from the baseline organizational pattern. In this measurement, we must be careful to gather data at sufficiently frequent and numerous time points to reveal precise lagged relationships—no easy task! We must then correlate in lagged fashion the measures of inputs and structural deviations.

We also may examine the persistence of these deviations and search for the input stabilities that are likely to foster such persistence. We must be careful to consider inputs as configurations containing multiplicative as well as additive relationships. For example, our Michigan findings suggest that increased enrollment may foster a more intensive division of instructional labor only (or do so more powerfully) when demand for specialized instruction also is present. If we are ambitious enough, we may measure specific environmental properties likely to generate the inputs we observe.

If systematic correlations do occur, we can infer behavior of actors in the organization—seen as attempts to solve the problems generated by the inputs that we have measured. Such interpretation will attend to the baseline structure and to limits set by the value of industry parameters, or local variations thereof. We here must consider structural inventions, and also imitative process, as industry conditions affect the flow and cost of information. Similarly we must attend not only to structuring but also to environment-changing or technology-changing innovation.

Such studies will require fairly large samples of organizations within industries and reliable measurement of the pertinent variables. Hence, at this stage of the study of intraorganizational dynamics, aggregative and unit measurement is essential.

But all this is only a first stage. If we are to understand the dynamic processes that underlie any observed input-structure correlations, we must study directly the behavior of organizational actors that intervenes between input and structural change. It is not enough to infer such behavior, as at the first stage of work. This analysis may center on single managers or decision-makers or on organizational polities. It must comprehend ways that behavior in organizations is affected by the composition of the organization's membership and the social relations among them that are induced by the baseline organizational form.

The earlier work of Simon (1969), Cyert and March (1963), and the resource dependency theorists has opened this subject matter, but I do not find in them the precise propositions that link information-processing, problem identification, or problem-solving with structural change. Peter Abell (1975) and his colleagues have made an excellent beginning toward the formal treatment of the effect of existing organizational structure on decision process, but I know of no adequate systematic treatment of the effect of decision-making on structural change.

Hence my belief that we must use findings from first stage survey studies to pinpoint organizational settings, that is, varying constellations of input and structural conditions within industries, in which we can conduct detailed case studies necessary to construct behavioral theories of organizational dynamics.

The field for such work in education is wide open. Schools are in newly dynamic environments. Moreover, if our Michigan findings do generalize, schools display a baseline morphology that is of unusual interest. Indeed we may wish to study in schools essentially two different behavioral or decisional fields—one represented by local schools and classrooms in relation to their specific instructional technologies and within-community environments, the other represented by central offices, their multiple functions and technologies, and their several local, regional, and national environments.

The Study of School Productivity

Let me now turn to the study of school productivity, which I have asserted is related to the study of organizational change. If we are to understand organizational change, we clearly must understand processes of exchange with the environment and, thus, the ability of an organization to create value-added in production in ways that generate favorable terms of trade with sources of capital, labor, materials, and political support. If we want to understand the conditions that influence the creation of value-added (for example, the academic effectiveness of schools), we must understand how resource inputs are combined in the production process, how this combinatorial process is affected in varying structural contexts, and what surely must be a reciprocal relationship between change in production activities and change in structure.

Nowhere in organizational sociology have we proceeded very far in these directions. So far as schools are concerned, I think, in company with my Chicago colleagues, that the main problem is our failure to conceptualize instructional technology. I know of no good theoretical base for this conceptualization, no more now than in 1965. Therefore, we must work toward more adequate conceptualization of technology by the naturalistic observation of schools and classrooms at work. Behavioral studies in microlevel school settings, then, are an essential step toward the analysis of school effectiveness.

There is, of course, a considerable literature by economists on educational production functions (see Thomas 1971) and a smaller one by sociologists on the effectiveness of schools. These studies all come to the same point—that considering between-school or district variance in achievement test scores, various measures of resource allocation do affect academic outcomes. These effects are larger when the measurement is aggregated to that level of school organization where, presumably, resources are received by students and have their effects—that is, measurement at the track or classroom level (see Summers and Wolfe 1975; Rosenbaum 1976; Alexander and McDill 1976), rather than at the school or district level (see Bidwell and Kasarda 1976). Most of the findings are straightforward, indicating that the higher the quality of resources (for instance, teacher experience) and the more of them per student (for example, teacher-pupil ratios) the higher students' average levels of attainment.

Occasional findings are of greater interest and theoretical suggestiveness, especially Summers and Wolfe's findings at the classroom level of statistical interactions between such student traits as prior performance and such teacher traits as years of experience (in relation to individual attainment by students), and Brown and Saks' (1975) finding at the district level that revenue allocation rules used by school boards can affect the distribution of student achievement.

There are many technical quibbles that can be raised about these studies, but I wish to pass them by to point to a more serious problem—the absence in even the most interesting of these works of a systematic conceptualization of the production process in schools. As a result, the production-function work of the economists and the organizational effectiveness research of the sociologists amount to the same thing—a not-very-rigorously-argued sociological analysis in which school resources or inputs are treated without careful attention to the distinction between the disbursement and receipt of resources. The form of the process through which multiple resources are combined into instruction, how the combinatorial process may be conditioned by values of the organizational context of schooling, and the conceptualization of the student as a factor in educational production are scarcely touched.

Even though instructional decision rules may be primitive, what kinds of procedures accompany varying conceptions of education (my "practical principles")? Are there other systematic covariations of procedure with organizational structure, aspects of student input, or other components of the organizational ecosystem?

Since I take instructional procedures to intervene between structure and value-added outcome and to react back on structure itself, information about procedural variation (its dimensions, range of dimensional variation, and interrelations among dimensions) and about its organizational and value-added correlates is essential. Without this information, production-functions cannot be specified (ultimately in terms of costs), and until they are specified we can only examine, at whatever level of aggregation, correlations between patterns or amounts of resource allocation and outcome. This is the present state of research on school productivity.

Note especially that, although these studies have measured resource availability, they have not measured resource use, while the interlevel connections in school systems between allocation and use are neither measured nor thought through. The consequences of district level decisions about teachers' salaries for the training or experience and consequent instructional procedures of particular teachers in particular classrooms are an example. Note, too, in these studies, inattention to events below the school level. For example, the social-organizational characteristics of classrooms, the forms and content of teaching activities, and teaching-learning relationships all remain beyond their purview. But without attention to the microlevel of active schooling (educational production), there is no way for us to tie together events at the school or district and at the track or classroom levels.

With better conceptualization of instructional technology, we will be able to ask how schools as organizational structures adapt to and constrain the procedures of teaching. If the notion of school systems as loosely-coupled is indeed correct, we may find that these interconnections center less on the administrative management of instruction (which may scarcely exist or exist only in rare places) than on the consequences of environment-organization exchanges at each level of the district for such exchanges at every other level. We should find that actors at one level compete with those at other levels, at least in the short-run, for resources available to sustain their work.

For example, I have suggested that the form of central offices is mainly adaptive to characteristics of the fiscal and political environments of the district. As these characteristics become more complex and unstable, the relative size of administration seems to grow. Given the postulated near-decomposability of school districts, unless administrative growth is accompanied by proportionate increases in revenues, there will be less money to spend on production staff or materials. Kasarda and I have interpreted in just such terms our finding, first in Colorado and now in Michigan, of negative returns from administrative growth to school effectiveness. Similarly, increases or decreases in the size of student cohorts will limit or expand funds available for administration (given conventional class-size assumptions), perhaps resulting in change in the amount of revenue input or change in political support.

In short, if school district structure is indeed nearly decomposable, the most interesting formulation of organizational constraint on schooling activity (even at the behavioral level) may be the classic ecological model of the interniche competition within an ecosystem for sustenance. One consequence of such competition is the formation of coalitions and alliances (commensal groupings), which takes us back to the study of the organization as a polity, but by a different route.

Unless we can specify the parameters of teaching technology and their functional relationships, however, we cannot know either the terms of competition (whether among niches or commensal groups) or the mechanisms through which the allocative results of such competition are translated into outcomes of schooling. Hence my main conclusion—that the first steps in the study of organizational change in schools and the organizational effectiveness of schools must be complementary survey analysis of the organizational morphology of schools and the naturalistic case study of teachers and students at work.

Notes

1. Throughout this chapter I shall use the word *school* to denote both schools and school systems. If statements apply only to the one but not to the other I shall so indicate.

2. Parallel data are available for each of the schools in the Michigan data, but our work at the school level is only now beginning.

3. A near-decomposable hierarchy is a vertically differentiated set of units, in which the strata are strongly bounded. That is, events in one stratum only weakly affect events in the strata below.

4. There is one obvious exception. As enrollment increases, the segmentation of instruction (the number of classrooms and schools) increases, with subsequent growth in the number of principals and school clerks.

5. The division of instructional labor that I have described is centered, of course, at the secondary school level. There may be other aspects of this division of labor elsewhere in the districts that have similar form and effects, but that we could not measure because of limited formal specialization of teaching below the secondary level.

References

Abell, Peter, ed. *Organizations as Bargaining and Influence Systems.* London: Heineman, 1975.

Aldrich, Howard E. *Organizations and Environments.* Englewood Cliffs, N.J.: Prentice-Hall, 1979.

Aldrich, Howard E. and Pfeffer, Jeffrey. "Environments of Organizations." *Annual Review of Sociology,* 1976, pp. 79-105.

Alexander, Karl L. and McDill, Edward L. "Selection and Allocation within Schools: Some Causes and Consequences of Curriculum Placement." *American Sociological Review* 41 (1976):963-980.

Bidwell, Charles E. "The School as a Formal Organization." In *Handbook of Organizations,* edited by James G. March, pp. 972-1022. Chicago: Rand-McNally, 1965.

Blau, Peter M. "A Formal Theory of Differentiation in Organizations." *American Sociological Review* 35 (1970):201-218.

Blau, Peter M. and Schoenherr, Richard A. *The Structure of Organizations.* New York: Basic Books, 1971.

Brown, Byron W. and Saks, Daniel H. "The Production and Distribution of Cognitive Skills within Schools." *Journal of Political Economy* 83 (1975):571-593.

Child, J. "Organization Structure, Environment and Performance—the Role of Strategic Choice." *Sociology* 6 (1972):1-22.

Cyert, Richard M. and March, James G. *A Behavioral Theory of the Firm.* Englewood Cliffs, N.J.: Prentice-Hall, 1963.

Duncan, Otis D. and Schnore, Leo F. "Cultural, Behavioral, and Ecological Perspectives in the Study of Social Organization." *American Journal of Sociology* 65 (1959):132-146.

Hannan, Michael and Freeman, John H. "The Population Ecology of Organizations." *American Journal of Sociology* 83 (1977):929-964.

Hirsch, Paul M. "Organizational Effectiveness and the Institutional Environment." *Administrative Science Quarterly* 20 (1975):327-344.

March, James G., ed. *Handbook of Organizations.* Chicago: Rand-McNally, 1965.

Meyer, Marshall. "Size and the Structure of Organizations: A Causal Analysis." *American Sociological Review* 37 (1972):434-441.

Meyer, Marshall and Brown, M. Craig. "The Process of Bureaucratization." *American Journal of Sociology* 83 (1977):364-385.

Perrow, Charles. "Hospitals: Technology, Structure and Goals." In *Handbook of Organizations,* edited by James G. March, pp. 910-971. Chicago: Rand-McNally, 1965.

Pfeffer, Jeffrey, "Beyond Management and the Worker: The Institutional Function of Management." *Academy of Management Review* 1 (1976).

Rosenbaum, James E. *Making Inequality.* New York: Wiley, 1976.

Schnore, Leo F. "The Myth of Human Ecology." *Sociological Inquiry* 31 (1961):128-139.

Simon, Herbert A. "The Architecture of Complexity." *Proceedings of the American Philosophical Society* 106 (1969):467-482.

Stinchcombe, Arthur L. "Social Structure and Organizations." In *Handbook of Organizations,* edited by James G. March, pp. 142-193. Chicago: Rand-McNally, 1965.

Summers, Anita A. and Wolfe, Barbara L. "Disaggregation in Analyzing Educational Equity Issues—Methods and Results." Unpublished paper from ETS-NBER Workshop on Economics of Education. Princeton, N.J., 1975.

Thomas, J. Alan. *The Productive School.* New York: Wiley, 1971.

Thompson, James D. *Organizations in Action.* New York: McGraw-Hill, 1967.

Tyack, David. *The One Best System.* Cambridge, Mass.: Harvard University Press, 1974.

Waller, Willard M. *The Sociology of Teaching.* New York: Wiley, 1932.

Warriner, Charles K. "Teleology, Ecology and Organizations." Unpublished paper presented to the Midwest Sociological Society, Milwaukee, Wisc., April 27, 1978.

Weick, Karl. "Educational Organizations as Loosely Coupled Systems." *Administrative Science Quarterly* 21 (1976):1-19.

Woodward, Joan. *Industrial Organization: Theory and Practice.* London: Oxford, 1965.

Zald, Mayer N. *Organizational Change: The Political Economy of the YMCA.* Chicago: University of Chicago Press, 1970.

7 The Uses of Political Science in the Study of Educational Administration

Frederick M. Wirt

This chapter reviews from a political science perspective the conceptual and theoretical problems of research in educational administration. This is not done by reviewing all the growing flood of literature, which outpaces even the most current literature reviews.[1] Rather, I will summarize this research in order to answer the following set of questions: How have political science concepts and theories been used to generate questions and problems for the study of educational administration? How productive have these studies been? And, what future studies seem likely, employing such ideas from the political science perspective?

There is much presumption in all this, of course, because to summarize, criticize, and prophesy all in one effort makes it seem more certain than I truly feel. Given the problems of research, to be noted later, and the diversity of scholars at work, I prefer to put these thoughts less with the serene certainty of a Christian with four aces, as Mark Twain said, than with the attitude of Montaigne that "To know much is often the cause of doubting more."

Theory, Concept, and Current Research

The central query that initiates this analysis has been put: "What concepts and theories from political science have been used to generate questions and problems for the study of educational administration?" That question is typical of the recent interest by some members of the two disciplines of political science and educational administration in coming together for mutual interests. As Harman has noted, this morganatic marriage stems both from changes within the disciplines as well as within the public environment in which schools are embedded. The marriage also has been blessed by the presence of research money and eminent scholars.[2] In this union, as in all marriages, some do different things. For there has emerged one group committed to a primary framework of analysis, and another group that eschews it in order to employ traditional concepts of political science. The result has been a Maoist "Let a thousand flowers bloom"—great for gardens but painful for an intellectual marriage.

The prevalent analytical framework, which some term "theory," is that of

133

David Easton's systems analysis, by now so familiar that it is rarely footnoted. From his first essay on education as a political system,[3] many students have used the familiar elements of the construct to frame their work. "Support" of the system framed a decade or more of political socialization studies, in which the school's role appears minimal.[4] The national political system's "conversion" of "demand inputs" structured studies of the creation of the Elementary and Secondary Education Act (ESEA) of 1965.[5] Kirst and I summarized the extant literature in the early seventies within that framework, with special studies of "feedback"; a more recent collection is organized by all stages of the Eastonian model.[6]

But alongside this systems analysis research there has always existed the use of traditional political science concepts to study "the politics of education," as it came to be called. In the sixties, Masters and his colleagues compared three states' school policy processes from an interest group perspective, while others searched for community power systems and the school role therein.[7] In the seventies, a freshet of studies appeared, lacking broader theoretical focus but turning over new ground in familiar concepts of political science and throwing new light on aspects of educational administration.

We can see this by merely listing the subjects of recent major books. The meaning of *representation* was applied to administrators,[8] and *voter linkages* to school referenda decision-making;[9] the consequences of *equality* were tapped for desegregation politics;[10] the intergovernmental fisc of *federalism* was examined in a set of states;[11] the role of *pressure groups* in local school politics was explored in a national sample of districts and in the national politics of universities;[12] and policy-making for schools was explored at the local level in community conflict over governmental structures;[13] at the national level in the interactions of *Congress and the Presidency;*[14] and at the state level among *legislatures, governors,* and other political actors.[15] The highly traditional *legal analysis* continued, but was applied to school authority.[16] What such authority meant in *implementation* (the new term for the old *administration*) was suddenly given new empirical meaning in studies of the effects of national school policies on state and local authorities.[17] And a flood of school finance analyses surrounded the new challenge to the basis of that financing.[18]

This is a rich collection suddenly to emerge on the scene, but note that little if any of it is rooted in systems analysis. This profusion of familiar political science concepts as the basis of research,[19] rather than overarching theory, emphasizes that Easton does not dominate the field. Rather, the field is one of multiple new starts that is a recognizable stage in the history of ideas. Like the confusion of plant classification before Linnaeus in the eighteenth century introduced the ultimately successful organizing scheme, there are many vineyards in the house of intellect in the politics of education at this time. In short, because no master theory directs the questions and problems to be formulated for research, how is that direction accomplished?

The Nonstrategy for Selection of Research Problems

In this section, I wish to show how a discipline selects key research questions in the politics of education. My argument is threefold: that this selection is influenced by the absence of causational theory at the middle or grand level, by the nature of political science as a discipline, and by a resulting strategy, or nonstrategy, which I term the "free-enterprise model."

Heruistic versus Causational Theory:
"What's It All About, Alfie?"

In the physical sciences, on which much of social science qua science is based, theory directs attention to crucial concepts and generates hypotheses, which are then operationalized and tested. At its core, such theory is causational, that is, it seeks to test empirically certain statements about cause and effect drawn from the theory. For example, in political science a recent middle-range theory about the prime motivating force working on legislators is the so-called "electoral connection," that is, their need for reelection causes them to apply crude cost-benefit evaluations to their own voting decisions. Testable hypotheses can be derived from this theory to determine whether that theory better explains their behavior than do constituency representation pressures, party affiliation, and values, and so forth.[20]

But that form of thinking is not what systems analysis was designed for, as Easton has repeatedly pointed out; thus, he never termed his ideas a "theory." Rather, he constructed what he termed a "framework of analysis," which in essence is a heuristic concept. That is, the construct consists of a set of sequential categories of behavior but without any causational theoretical components about what moves the sequence—except for "crisis" that sets off the whole thing, rather like the old Rube Goldberg devices.

For example, this framework posits that "demands" from the social environment trigger the processes of the political system, which "convert" some of the demands into "outputs." But because there are different kinds and intensities of demands, different kinds of conversion processes, and different kinds of outputs, the systems framework does not enable us to hypothesize which patterns of these three factors are associated causally. Salisbury and Heinz have expanded on this aspect, theorizing that it is the pattern of the demand— fragmented versus unitary—that shapes the kind of policy output, with the policy-making system mediating between the two.[21] But that theoretical development occurred without reference to systems analysis; it was a stage in current thinking by political scientists about the relationships between pressure groups and patterns of policy.[22] Similar theoretical development has also transpired without reference to Easton in the recent interest in what occurs after a bill becomes a law, so to speak, or the court writes "it is so ordered."[23] Here the theoretical focus is on those factors that develop in implementation so as to narrow or widen the gap between what was intended by legislature and court and what was achieved in practice.

Some of this is the traditional mode of the case study of a singular event in a single place; Pressman and Wildavsky's *Implementation* study of one city and one federal program shares much with the several decades of case studies in the Inter-University Case Study Program.[24] More richly theoretical and generalizable are studies of a single policy's implementation across a number of school districts, as with school prayer, desegregation, and ESEA policies,[25] or of the implementation of a number of policies within the same jurisdiction.[26] Here, familiar concepts of the systems analysis framework are expanded, and directed hypotheses are explored, but the framework itself is not used directly.

What we have in systems analysis, then, is no more than an enlarged metaphor, relating an unorganized world of experience to a familiar metaphor. It may be, as Landau has convincingly argued, that this is possibly the best "theory" of which the social sciences are capable at this time, and that, indeed, the metaphor is possessed of several utilities.[27] Thus, such a metaphor (1) sorts our experiences into roughly similar categories; (2) detects the presence of deviant cases from these categories and thereby stimulates thinking about expanding the categories or stimulates insight into an underlying theory (rather than having theory develop cumulatively);[28] and (3) provides a testing ground for what a theory should look like. But systems analysis for long has been recognized as *not* the kind of theory that generates hypothesis-testing, now considered the basis for social sciences.[29]

There are obvious consequences for problem selection from this first characteristic of political science research on educational administration. With no single star to guide them, scholars select problems as the winds of swirling preferences move them. Familiar lenses of political science are turned on new fields of school politics, with little attention to whether what we learn about school policy origins, policy-making, and implementation is comparable to other policies, or whether important distinctions arise from the very nature of our school authority.[30] The appearance is yeasty, even exciting, with every person a specialist in his or her focus, rather like the early days of community power study, when an individual wrote of a single place and championed a parochial view of reality as the general one. It is exciting maybe, but hardly designed to direct us to the significant questions on which we might better focus our energies. It certainly does not provide us with a comprehensive picture of "What's it all about."

Disciplinary Influences on Problem Selection:
The Grooves of Academe

Another influence on problem selection comes from the very nature of a scholarly discipline, which both focuses the attention of its members on some question but not others, and which strives not to be infected by the pragmatic, programmatic concerns of those in the public arena whom the scholar studies. The latter is the familiar chasm between pure and applied intellect, which runs through science, both hard and soft.

Nor is the interest of political science so solidaristic, because as a discipline it has been characterized by disagreement, not accord, on its primary purposes and methods.[31] It studies a great range of activity deemed "political," while there is also great division over how to study these objects. This particular split has come between an earlier and a more recent persuasion. The former included those who believe the major emphasis should be on description and analysis of institutions and values of *homo politicus*; this was traditional emphasis until the post-World War II period. Then the "behavioral persuasion"[32] emerged, seeking to apply methods of natural science to political behavior and testing empirical propositions in order to build up a systematic and predictable world picture. Borrowing from sociology and economics (occasionally from psychology), the new type used research techniques and quantitative methods considered better for achieving these purposes. I need not further detail this internecine warfare in political science, if for no other reason than that the issues in conflict cannot be agreed on, because the sides cannot agree on the methods for arriving at agreement. Not unlike the Capulets and Montagues in their passions over the matter (although a Romeo and Juliet have been known to canoodle together from time to time), the two sides of academe have set themselves into opposing grooves, with cries of "unclean! unclean!" issuing back and forth.

The consequences for this section's main question must be extracted from this account of an almost religious war. That is, how does all this affect the formulation of questions and problems in the study of educational administration? It means just that the literature reflects this split between traditional and behavioral emphases. That fact underlies the difference between the kinds of studies referred to in the previous section, as any current collection of writings on the politics of education will show. Even a journal as heavily behavioralist as the *Social Science Quarterly* will still carry a few pieces in the traditionalist mode in a special issue on educational problems and policies.[33] In short, problem selection is a function of one's disciplinary preference in subject matter and in analytical mode as well, depending on one's groove of academe.

Further, within each of the two divisions of political science there are influential elite figures who direct attention to questions that they deem significant for research. And few leading political scientists have emphasized the politics of education. There are several measures of this avoidance behavior. For example, only three presidents in the entire history of the American Political Science Association (APSA) have written on the subject of this chapter. David Easton's name is preeminent, and almost exclusive; Charles Merriam wrote almost a half-century ago on citizenship training; and Eulau wrote one article on it decades later.[34]

Moreover, there is a paucity of articles on the politics of education in the journals of the discipline. True, political socialization studies were prominent in the sixties, but interest now has faded, to judge from the handful to turn out for such a panel at the 1976 APSA annual convention. This journal reaction may well have been justified when few were writing on this topic. But to judge from the growing number of panel papers at the American Educational Research Association (AERA) and even APSA conventions, from the dissertation subjects, and from the appearance of occasional journal articles now, there is much good work out there seeking an outlet. The time may now be ripe for the founding of a journal in educational politics and policy, which fits between the political science journals and the *Education Administration Quarterly*. Such a publishing format would help legitimate young scholars, both in political science and education administration departments, in their efforts.

But none of this obviates the fact that the influential figures of political science have not sought to direct their efforts to studying the largest number of political units in the nation—school districts—which involve the largest amount of domestic expenditures, which attract citizens to the most numerous elections, and which precipitate the most frequent exercise of popular sovereignty in referenda. So it is that one of the consequences of this discipline is that problem selection has been influenced by indifference to this research potential. Inaction is as much a policy decision as action, whether in the public arena or in university life. What, then are the larger implications of these sections' discussions for the selection of questions and problems?

The Operative Model of Problem Selection:
The Free Enterprise of Academia

All this suggests to me a particular model of the formulation of research questions about educational administration. This model shares much with the classical notions of free enterprise in the economic marketplace.

First, there are diverse, but not too numerous, producers of these scholarly goods as signified by the recent spate of books and articles. Second, there is a market for such goods signified by: interest groups who use research to substantiate their demands; the growing number of people in two disciplines interested in reading and discussing the subject; the growth of the Special Interest Group on the Politics of Education of the AERA; the growth in university courses in this field, usually in graduate schools of education; and the growth of graduate programs to train education policy analysts, such as at Berkeley or Stanford. All these are signs of what we can call "consumers" of these scholarly products.

But, third, there are scarce goods to be allocated in this scholarly system. The absence of influential, elite political scientists means the status of such study is in short supply. Too, there are only a limited number of research funding sources, and their investment interests are often limited to the traditional school subjects of instruction and finance. Too, few government bodies encourage this emphasis, so official authority to back the endeavor is limited, and those bodies that do back it often have their own purposes in view, to which scholarship must be bent.[35] Fourth, some producers have more resources than others for such research, so the competition is not equal.

Fifth, not all producers have the same information; this condition of imperfect information is less so than before because of the growth of the special AERA group noted, the recent yearbooks of the National Society for the Study of Education,[36] and the continuing interest of the University Council for Educational Administration (UCEA) in training administrators in social science orientations and methods.[37] Still, many political scientists with potential interests to contribute to such scholarship do not know of it because they read primarily their own journals, which have few such articles.

Sixth, as noted, there is no authoritative body of scholars to direct the selection of questions and problems; indeed, the very concept is antithetical to our notions of academic freedom. This means that the academic market place is subject to faddish surges of interest whenever persons and money come together accidentally. This fad quality—not unlike the erratic behavior of the stock market—can be traced in changing intellectual efforts, for example, interest in the early sixties in community power and educational administration, in systems analysis and the school system, in political socialization, and now in the politics of the innovation in school policy.

What we can see in this model, as inferred (admittedly roughly) from the published and informal behavior of the field, is that there are no criteria of significant research, other than those provided by the status of those suggesting that scholarly tides move their way. That condition prevails because of the absence of any theory that could direct us to the significant questions and problems for research. Thus, we see the faddish quality of research in this field over the last fifteen years or so.

Nor is this lack of theory the only basic condition in problem selection. For it is the case that this lack interacts with the entrepreneurial nature of the discipline, with the independent spirit of academic freedom in which the discipline is rooted, and with the absence of sufficient resources (including information) to accumulate knowledge. For it is the lack of cumulative knowledge that is the final hallmark of this model. Those books published recently and cited earlier do not add up to a body of knowledge, unless one has Frankenstein in mind as a body. Certainly it is not what is meant by that term in other disciplines or what is inherent in the phrase *corpus juris*—a set of systematic, interrelated, agreed-on propositions about reality, which are rooted in tested experience. Yet I will in the next section return to a few, generally supported findings that we can offer with some confidence.

Missing from this model is another mechanism, that mysterious presence of the economic model, the "invisible hand" that regulates the generation and dissemination of tested findings. There may be an "invisible college" at work, scholars specializing in the politics of education, but I have not seen it direct anyone anywhere. A substitute regulator might be "conventional wisdom," but, as noted throughout this chapter, there is not in this research that degree of acceptance needed for the term "conventional," although many would question that any "wisdom" inhered in this research. In short, in the absence of any regulative mechanism—whether an idea or body of authorities—scholars here pick what interests them (either as social activists or as social theorists), what they can find the money to underwrite, and what they think might be new enough to find a publishing outlet. Clearly, then, any effort to predict from this state of affairs what problems should be selected involves great uncertainty. Indeed, one thinks of Heisenberg's principle when confronting the next set of questions: namely, how productive have these studies been?

Assessment of the Research Literature

If there is not a cumulative, theoretically based body of knowledge, is there still something to be learned about the political aspects of educational administration in the existing research? That is, I have been asked to assess how productive these studies have been, namely, what do we know, what studies have been most useful, and which are the least useful—all for the purpose of assessing how this research may have informed the practice of educational administration. What follows can only sketch the answers, given space constraints.

What Do We Know?

I find four statements to be rather widely supported by the prevalent research, whatever the mode of analysis.

1. *Educational administration is "political" in two senses.* There is agreement that this concept of "political" means authority over the allocation of resources and values—a heritage of systems analysis thinking. This judgment exists in at least two forms. First, educational administration is the *object* of activity from political influences outside the school walls. These external forces may be community groups, state and federal governments, or private forces, such as professionals or foundations. Second, educational administration is the *subject* of political activity, that is, its practitioners can—by their mobilization of resources, skill of leadership, and knowledge of the social territory—shape policy and behaviors within the school system. Educational administration as the subject of political activity, although expressed under other names, is the essential message of the usual textbook used in graduate courses in schools of education. But this conceptual understanding also appears in the current writing

discussed earlier.[38] There is however, an even longer tradition of viewing educational administration as a massive, invulnerable bureaucracy that is the enemy of local control, the ruler of all its surveys.[39] But the notion of school administrators as the object of political activity which constrains them leads to a second finding.

2. *Educational administration is increasingly subject to a politically turbulent environment.* I have developed this thesis in considerable detail quite recently,[40] so it needs but a sketch here. This process of politicization of the environment consists of significant school constituents—parents, teachers, taxpayers, minorities, students—sharply disagreeing with the traditional allocation of resources in school policies—respectively, accountability, collective negotiations, finance reform, desegregation, civil rights. Further, these groups, stimulated by new ideas and illuminating events outside the district, have turned to outside authorities and resources to influence local authorities to reallocate resources. In one form or another, many of the books cited earlier deal with facets of this political turbulence arising over these groups and their issue demands.[41]

3. *School politics shows variety, based on community differences, in size and status.* That is, the political context for educational administration varies by different demands placed on it, flowing from different mixes of population; that is a familiar finding in the study of urban politics also.[42] So its emergence in the study of local school politics in recent studies is no great surprise.[43] Even the local school site can show such variation in demands and administrator political styles.[44] This finding reminds us that there is no single American political system but rather a mosaic of different mixes of life styles and policy preferences, all interacting within dynamic networks of communication and a "family of governments."[45]

4. *This new school politics may be reshaping the behavior of school administrators.* In this increasingly intense and complex politicized environment, there is some evidence that the political role of the administrator—once only implicit—has become much more overt. Too, this changing context may be sensitizing administrators to this new politicization and reshaping their professional role. This sensitization is inferable from the growth of panels on the politics of administration at conventions of the AERA, American Association of School Administrators (AASA), and National School Boards Association (NSBA); from the recent popularization of this viewpoint in the administrators' major journal;[46] from the development of new training programs for educational administration in such subjects as teacher negotiation skills, desegregation techniques, students' rights, and so on; and in empirical studies showing the adjustment of administrators to the community's participatory role.[47] The thesis of role reexamination is found among big city superintendents in the last decade and among superintendents adapting to community and board expectations in different kinds of communities.[48] It is implicit in the rise in a few

graduate schools of new programs for educational administration, oriented to training practitioners for their political environment and political role or to defining new careers in policy evaluation.

In short, there is substantial evidence that educational administrators operate in an environment increasingly hostile to their once prevalent notions of separation of school and politics, hostile to their traditional presumption of the inherent correctness of judgments arrived at "professionally,"[49] and hostile to the immunity of school policy and administration from democratic control. Too, the reactions of the administrators may be more adaptive than once thought, for new styles may be emerging to meet new demands on the profession.

What Studies, or Lines of Inquiry,
Have Been Most Useful?

Again, good answers are not possible for this query, because the absence of theory provides us with no criteria of utility. But with the blind temerity that has characterized the rest of this paper, I suggest the answer be directed to the utility for three groups—administrators, policy-makers, and scholars of school policy.

For Practicing Educational Administrators: One test of this transfer effect might be to review which studies are cited or discussed in administration association journals, or which are referred to in the leading textbooks of administration. Certainly the growth of the AERA special interest group suggests that this research is getting into the graduate training of future administrators. So maybe it is time for the UCEA to restudy the advent of social science training, particularly that discussed here, in schools of education.

I note several trends that suggest some use for our scholarly efforts. Schools of education are now hiring political scientists; there are new curriculum modules in the politics of education in traditional educational administration training programs, or in new ones like Nova University's; and there has been at least one major research program for Ph.D. candidates in this field in the Campbell-Mazzoni comparative state study. But the studies may be of greatest utility when based on the local politics of education, particularly if they have the practical implications spelled out for practitioners.[50] As I will note later, these professionals seek the "bottom line" of scholarship, namely, detailed advice on such activities as program innovation and strategies for dealing with community challenges or for staff and curricular changes to meet desegregation needs. Of course, they would also find great use in anything that enables them to manage their administrative environment, that being the continuing interest of the profession from its inception. Our articles in scholarly journals do almost none of this, of course, nor do most of the works cited earlier, although these instrumental consequences should be more often attempted by scholars.

For School Policy-Makers: For this scholarship to have use for policy-makers, it would require them to have training to understand or translate it. Because so much of it is cast in the social science methodology, which asks different questions and seeks different information than does the policy-maker,[51] there seems to be a current disenchantment between the two types. However there is also an impressive array of social scientists (although very few political scientists) acting as consultants on controversial policy problems—such as desegregation, finance reform, and teacher negotiations. Here an important translation function is being performed, for hopefully there is some wisdom in such scholarship, and certainly it is prudent to have policy informed by sound knowledge. No one has performed a study of this fusion of academe and the policy arena for education,[52] but I suspect there is not much consulting done by those with degrees or training in political science.[53] But we do not know much of whether policy-makers use such advice—or under what conditions they do, a much more interesting question. We may see more of this transfer function, however, in the next generation, as those trained in education policy analysis move into the public arena.

For Scholars of the Politics of Education: I suggest that for political scientists there has been more utility in work that explores:

1. Mass-elite linkages (the old "community relations" and the new "demand input" studies). Why would this be useful? These incorporate the educational policy system within the larger democratic system, with all its policy-making linkages. In the process, there occurs the demythologizing of the notion of school policy as somehow different from that arrived at for other services.[54]

2. Vertical linkages of school policy-making, that is, the institutional and political factors that impinge on the local education authority (LEA) from external sources. Why would this be useful? This work incorporates into our traditional, well-researched understanding of American federalism the LEA, which was for too long viewed as autonomous. Again, one result is the demythologizing of the notion of local control.[55] Moreover, it broadens the utility of case studies, so often used to study the politics of education.

3. Problems of program change in a democratic, federal system, that is, when there is demand for change in the volume, quality, or distribution of a public service, we know from other policy fields that contextual factors impede that delivery (widening the gap between output and outcome, in Eastonian terms). Why would this be useful? Because so many policy ventures have been experienced in the last decade or more, seeking to alter the distribution of educational resources and hence outcomes, that it has opened up as never before our thinking about all policies' implementation. Thus it appears that school may

be only a special case of the general process of innovation. The gloomy predictions of the last five years about the limits on innovation's acceptance by target groups are now confronted by more optimistic evidence that federal school programs did accomplish many of their goals.[56] This interest is part of the larger interest of the discipline in the "so what?" studies of post-decision-making events.

Another way of estimating productivity is to ask which research has been least helpful.

What Studies Have Been Least Useful?

Again, the lack of theory deprives us of criteria of inutility, but plunging ahead I can use the same three groups to frame an answer.

For Practicing Educational Administrators: I fear that the studies in the national politics of education are least useful, despite local administrators' experience with expanding federal requirements. The problem is that such studies are difficult to relate to the everyday concerns of the local scene. Too, I fear the same is true of political socialization studies, even though here the local implications are immense. For this research has shown that schools play little role in this process, that when they attempt it in the form of civics courses their effects are very few, and—from local experience—that getting too close to examining the real basis of local politics generates extramural opposition from aroused groups with something to protect. But the abominable level of civics knowledge reported regularly on national tests of students' knowledge—and confirmed by every political scientist facing college freshmen in the introductory course—should send someone a message that something is not being done well in the schools. Finally, I fear that some recent emphasis on analytical methods of studying educational policy does not go across well locally. These techniques train persons to evaluate policy alternatives in order to choose better those that are most applicable. Such techniques do have an application to local administrators, as Mann has shown, but many of these administrators have few options from which to choose, according to other analyses.[57]

For School Policy-Makers: I suspect that less useful for this group are those volumes cited earlier, which are detached from policy implications. Policy-makers, I have noted, read little social science research anyhow, even when they commission it,[58] until pressure groups pick on the studies to meet their special interests. Note the slow reaction to the Coleman Report after it first emerged, until desegregationists used it to back their goals and later others to justify scaling down programs and budgets in this field. Such pressure groups are policy-relevant consumers of scholarship who translate it into so-called action research. That process is clearly evident in school finance reform, with the symbiosis among Chicago and Berkeley scholars, the Ford Foundation, and minority and civil rights pressure groups—a full story yet to be told. In any case, this translation function for policy-makers is poorly documented, hence little understood, in the study of the politics of education, just as little is known of the diffusion of knowledge in general. So it is the political potential of scholarship that makes it useful, but because there are fewer pressure groups than there is scholarship, much of the latter will seem irrelevant to policy-makers who are sensitive only to loud voices.

For Scholars of the Politics of Education: Because, as noted, there are no accepted criteria here of what to study, those subjects are least useful in which scholars express little interest. We seem currently to have little interest in: community power studies (although someone should be studying this within a state context); economic models of democracy applied to education policy-making, although it does appear in evaluating referenda decisions;[59] linkages among political parties, partisan identification, and school policy-making as a facet of mass-elite studies.[60]

This section, in discussing most and least useful studies, has suggested tentatively a schedule of research items. So I need not expand on them in response to the question, "To what extent has the research informed the practice of educational administration?" The tersest answer is: probably some, but not much. This is no council of despair, however, if one considers how recent the research in this area by political science is, and the time it takes for new concepts and findings to work their ways into the training and practice of professionals.

Too, the "problems that have been encountered in research using concepts and theory from political science" have been treated in passing earlier in this chapter.[61] Harman has well summarized these in three major forms. Researchers here lack community, boundary definition, and research priorities.[62] Indeed, he finds this the case in Australia as well as the United States.

A Research Agenda with Implications for Educational Administration Practice and Policy-Making

This brings me to the final question, "What trends and directions for inquiry are suggested by using concepts and theory from political science?" My response here takes the form of a research agenda with specific implications for the making and implementation of school policy. The objective is to combine items of scholarly and practitioner interest, if possible.

The Comparative Politics of Education

We are at a stage in the study of the U.S. politics of education that it would be illuminated and strengthened if we were to apply some of our findings to an international comparison. A larger pool of experience always helps us test tentative findings, and comparative study is ideal for that. There is little scholarship here that compares the same policy, institution, or political process in a number of nations, as I have noted elsewhere.[63] Such study would be linked back twenty-five centuries to one of the original bases of political science, Aristotle's *Politics* and his comparative study of city-state constitutions. However, for the policy-maker or administrator, all this might seem quite remote. But these other sites do provide testing grounds for new policy ventures, a belief that underlies the current joint effort of Ford and NIE to study comparatively the financing of education. Too, the information that something works elsewhere is particularly important evidence for Americans, who are so grounded in pragmatism.

State Power Structure and State Policy Cultures in Education

We need much information about how state school authority eventuates in LEA action, if any. We might conceive of a "state power structure" in school policy-making and implementation, including a distinctive way of looking at the many dimensions of school policy that constitute what I have elsewhere termed a "state policy culture." Preliminary evidence of a fifty-state study suggests the latter has some empirical reality, particularly among regions.[64] Too, the Cambell-Mazzoni study of a set of states' policy-making agencies and actors points to interstate differences. But we have little research on the vertical interactions between what the state capital does (or does not do) and how the LEA responds. It seems likely that there are variations among the states in the degree to which centralization exists. And, the explanation of these observed differences, as Kerlinger reminds us, is the basic question of social science. But it is also of utility for policy-makers and practitioners to understand how policy ventures might fare when channeled down through the labyrinths of federalism, whether from the perspective of Washington or of the state capital, or from the view of legislature, executive, or state education agency.

The Relative Autonomy of School Policy among Policy Areas

Next, do we have any local autonomy left? That ideology runs through the history of public education, we all know. But a curious dichotomy arises today in the popular belief in it and the scholars' doubt about its existence. The latter find for education that higher authorities or professional norms currently shape much of the resources and programs of the LEA. There seems to exist what I have elsewhere termed, not local control, but a politics of residual decision-making for the LEA.

Too, we may be seeking autonomy, or the lack of it, in school policy as some special feature of that policy domain, when in other policy domains the same condition could also prevail. Peterson put it well:

> If such comparative research shows school boards to be typical, rather than atypical, in their autonomous decision-making patterns, one must seek explanations for such autonomy by looking at the general character of modern, urban societies, which conduct their affairs through complex bureaucracies directed by specially trained professionals. On the other hand, if school politics are particularly autonomous, one must continue to look for explanations . . . to certain features of this particular arena of public policy.[65]

Here we are dealing with a basic concern of political science, namely, in democratic systems what accounts for the shifting balance between the demands of popular participation and those of professional bureaucracy? What about the balance between citizens' desires for local control and national leaders' concern to normalize public services? Such questions go to such study areas as mass-elite linkages, the nature of bureaucracy, the responsibility for the use of power, representation, and others.[66] And, because these are all questions with which policy-maker and administrator must struggle every one of their workaday lives at every level of government, so knowledge from this domestic, comparative analysis could inform their need to act wisely.

Political versus Environmental Influences
upon State-Local Policy Outputs

Political scientists for fifteen years have been pursuing any trace of the alleged independent effects of political forms on state-local policies, as against the effects of the socioeconomic environment (resources). The evidence has been largely on the side of the socioeconomic being the major influence, a needling finding for those who center their scholarship on political experience. But we need to know more, because this research is faulty.[67] We need to know how such influences, political or socioeconomic, affect local autonomy, school quality, and decisional structures (including administrators' behaviors). Sometime we will have to determine if such independent variables of politics and economics are linked to effects on students and their education, for example, on academic achievement, civic orientation (including political efficacy),[68] personal growth, life adjustment, and so forth.

That last reminds us of the debate over whether schools affect the polity or the polity the schools,[69] and that we assume that there exists some association among school quality, the education that children receive, and the political system. In this web, the study of educational administration is necessarily caught by its professional responsibilities. The scholars of the politics of educational administration must ask questions that are both theoretically significant (for the body of social theory) and also pragmatically useful. It has been the issue of "softness" (read: no theoretical significance) that has in the past separated social science disciplines and the study of education in general. The push of the practitioner for utility repels those whose interest is in the development of theory. Yet the former, needing to know how to do the job well and prudently, has limited, if any, interest in the latter's concerns.

Educational Policy Analysis

The items sketched as a research agenda suggest to me an even larger area where both the needs of theory and of utility can come together, and that is in educational policy analysis. I urge consideration of this area as the major thrust for educational administration research and training in the next decade. By policy analysis we mean four things usually, although not often distinguishing them: (1) *description* (reporting behavior and values of actors and resources); (2) *explanation* (evaluating the influence of implementation conditions on policy impacts); (3) *criticism* (beyond explanation to the questioning of policy in terms of alternative choices that could or should have been made); and (4) *forecasting* (predicting to the future from observation of past and current patterns of events).[70]

As education becomes, in March's term, a "declining industry," where the steady-state level of resources must be competed for against policy-makers and citizens no longer assured of education's purity of heart, there will be an even greater need for more skilled training in policy analysis of these kinds. Currently, there is an important market consideration, namely, that there are job openings for people better trained in the concepts and skills of analysis of policy, including the education. But there is also a great scholarly consideration in this refocus, that is, the conceptual richness and complexity, as well as the numerous disciplines interested, in policy analysis. From this potential marriage of the utilitarian needs of practitioners of education and the intellectual interests of scholars of educational administration, an exciting process is at hand.

We will still be "waiting for Godot" of theory, both in political science and educational administration. But meanwhile, before that coming, we can do some work that is intellectually significant and practically useful in education policy analysis. What that entails, however, would require another chapter to set forth.

Notes

1. These reviews are: Frederick M. Wirt, "American Schools as a Political System: A Bibliographic Essay," in Michael Kirst, ed., *State, School, and Politics* (Lexington, Mass.: Lexington Books, D.C. Heath & Co., 1972); Paul Peterson,

"The Politics of American Education," in Fred Kerlinger and John Carroll, eds., *Review of Research in Education II* (Itasca, Ill.: Peacock, 1974), pp. 348-389; and Grant Harman, *The Politics of Education: A Bibliographic Guide* (Brisbane: University of Queensland Press, 1975). The most current are the separate essays by Jay Scribner and Richard Englert, and by Frank Lutz in J. Scribner, ed., *The Politics of Education,* 67th Yearbook, N.S.S.E., part II (Chicago: University of Chicago Press, 1977), chaps. 1-2.

2. Grant Harman, "Continuities and Research Gaps in the Politics of Education," *Social Science Quarterly* 55 (1974):267-269.

3. David Easton, "The Function of Formal Education in a Political System," *School Review* 65 (1957):304-306.

4. The most recent, which also reviews that literature, is Harmon Zeigler and M. Kent Jennings, *Governing American Schools* (N. Scituate, Mass.: Duxbury, 1974).

5. Eugene Eidenberg and Roy Morey, *An Act of Congress* (New York: Norton, 1969); Stephen Bailey and Edith Mosher, *ESEA: The Office of Education Administers a Law* (Syracuse, N.Y.: Syracuse University Press, 1968); and Philip Meranto, *The Politics of Federal Aid to Education in 1965* (Syracuse, N.Y.: Syracuse University Press, 1967).

6. Frederick M. Wirt and Michael Kirst, *The Political and Social Foundation of Education* (Berkeley, Calif.: McCutchan, 1975), first published as *The Political Web of American Schools;* and Frederick M. Wirt, ed., *The Polity of the School: New Research in Educational Politics* (Lexington, Mass.: Lexington Books, D.C. Heath & Co., 1975).

7. Nicholas Masters, Robert Salisbury, and Thomas Eliot, *State Politics and the Public Schools* (New York: Knopf, 1964); Ralph Kimbrough, *Political Power and Educational Decision-Making* (Chicago: Rand McNally, 1964); and Arthur J. Vidich and Joseph Bensman, *Small Town in Mass Society* (Princeton, N.J.: Princeton University Press, 1958).

8. Dale Mann, *The Politics of Administrative Representation* (Lexington, Mass.: Lexington Books, D.C. Heath & Co., 1976); and Harry Summerfield, *The Neighborhood-Based Politics of Education* (Columbus, Ohio: Merrill, 1971).

9. Howard Hamilton and Sylvan Cohen, *Policy Making by Plebiscite: School Referenda* (Lexington, Mass.: Lexington Books, D.C. Heath & Co., 1974).

10. David Kirby et al., *Political Strategies in Northern School Desegregation* (Lexington, Mass.: Lexington Books, D.C. Heath & Co., 1973).

11. Joel Berke and Michael Kirst, eds., *Federal Aid to Education* (Lexington, Mass.: Lexington Books, D.C. Heath & Co., 1973).

12. Zeigler and Jennings, *Governing American Schools;* and Lauriston King, *The Washington Lobbyists for Higher Education* (Lexington, Mass.: Lexington Books, D.C. Heath & Co., 1974).

13. Zeigler and Jennings, *Governing American Schools;* Joseph Cronin, *The Control of Urban Schools* (New York: Free Press, 1973); Paul Peterson, *School Politics Chicago Style* (Chicago: University of Chicago Press, 1976); and Diane

Ravtich, *The Great School Wars: New York City* (New York: Basic Books, 1974).

14. Larry Gladieux and Thomas Wolanin, *Congress and the Colleges* (Lexington, Mass.: Lexington Books, D.C. Heath & Co., 1976); Chester Finn, *Education and the Presidency* (Lexington, Mass.: Lexington Books, D.C. Heath & Co., 1977); and Norman Thomas, *Education and National Politics* (New York: McKay, 1975).

15. Roald Campbell and Tim Mazzoni, Jr., *State Policy Making for the Public Schools* (Berkeley, Calif.: McCutchan, 1976); Frederick Wirt, "Educational Politics and Policy," in H. Jacob and K. Vines, eds., *Politics in the American States*, 3d ed. (Boston: Little, Brown, 1976), chap. 8; and Gladys Kammerer, "The State University as a Political System," *Journal of Politics* 31 (1969):289-310.

16. John Hogan, *The Schools, the Courts, and the Public Interest* (Lexington, Mass.: Lexington Books, D.C. Heath & Co., 1974); and Tyll van Geel, *Authority to Control the School Program* (Lexington, Mass.: Lexington Books, D.C. Heath & Co., 1976).

17. Jerome Murphy, *State Education Agencies and Discretionary Funds* (Lexington, Mass.: Lexington Books, D.C. Heath & Co., 1974); a broader review is found in Jay Scribner, "Impacts of Federal Programs on State Departments of Education," in E. Fuller and J. Pearson, eds., *Education in the States: Nationwide Development since 1900* (Washington, D.C.: National Education Association, 1969), chap. 11; Mike Milstein, *Impact and Response: Federal Aid and State Education Agencies* (New York: Teachers College Press, 1976); Paul Berman and Milbrey McLaughlin, *Federal Programs Supporting Educational Change*, vol. 4, *The Findings in Review* (Santa Monica, Calif.: Rand Corp., 1975); and Harrell Rodgers and Charles Bullock, *Coercion to Compliance* (Lexington, Mass.: Lexington Books, D.C. Heath & Co., 1976).

18. This is most currently set out in a volume by Walter I. Garms, James W. Guthrie, and Lawrence G. Pierce, *School Finance: The Economics and Politics of Public Education* (Englewood Cliffs, N.J.: Prentice Hall, 1978).

19. For a recent collection of this kind, see Samuel Gove and Frederick M. Wirt, *Political Science and School Politics* (Lexington, Mass., Lexington Books, D.C. Heath & Co., 1977).

20. David A. Mayhew, *Congress: The Electoral Connection* (New Haven, Conn.: Yale University Press, 1975).

21. Robert Salisbury and John Heinz, "A Theory of Policy Analysis and Some Preliminary Applications," in Ira Sharkansky, ed., *Policy Analysis in Political Science* (Chicago: Markham, 1970), pp. 39-60.

22. Theodore Lowi, "American Business, Public Policy, Case Studies, and Political Theory," *World Politics* 6 (1964):677-715; see also Robert Salisbury, "An Exchange Theory of Interest Groups," *Midwest Journal of Political Science* 13 (1969):1-32.

23. See the review by Willis Hawley of this discipline's shift in Scribner,

Politics of Education, chap. 11.

24. Jeffrey Pressman and Aaron Wildavsky, *Implementation* (Berkeley, Calif.: University of California Press, 1973).

25. William Muir, *Prayer in the Public Schools* (Chicago: University of Chicago Press, 1967); Frank Way, Jr., "Survey Research on Judicial Decisions: The Prayer and Bible Reading Cases," *Western Political Quarterly* 21 (1968):189-205; Rogers and Bullock, *Coercion to Compliance;* Murphy, *State Education Agencies;* and Michael Giles et al., "The Impact of Busing on White Flight," *Social Science Quarterly* 55 (1974):493-501.

26. Frederick M. Wirt, *Politics of Southern Equality* (Chicago: Aldine, 1970); and Peterson, *School Politics Chicago Style.*

27. Martin Landau, *Political Theory and Political Science* (New York: Macmillan, 1972), chap. 3.

28. Thomas Kuhn, *The Structure of Scientific Revolutions* (Chicago: University of Chicago Press, 1964); for a critique, see Landau, *Political Theory,* chap. 2.

29. Gerald Sroufe, "Political Systems Analysis and Research in Educational Administration: Can the Emperor Be Clothed?" (Paper presented at the AERA national convention, 1969); Jerome Stephens, "The Logic of Functional and Systems Analysis in Political Science," *Midwest Journal of Political Science* 13 (1969):367-394; Michael Kirst and Edith Mosher, "Politics of Education," *Review of Educational Research* 39 (1969):623-640; and Laurence Iannaccone and Peter Cristone, *The Politics of Education* (Eugene, Oreg.: University of Oregon Press, 1974), chap. 2.

30. This is an important criticism raised by Peterson, "The Politics of American Education."

31. On the discipline's theory, see Albert Somit and Joseph Tanenhaus, *The Development of American Political Science* (Boston: Allyn and Bacon, 1967).

32. Heinz Eulau, *The Behavioral Persuasion in Politics* (New York: Random House, 1963).

33. "Education: Problems and Policies," *Social Science Quarterly* 55 (1974). I have sought to combine these two modes in recent collections of advanced research on this subject; see Wirt, *Polity of the School;* and, see Gove and Wirt, *Political Science and School Politics.*

34. Charles Merriam, *The Making of Citizens: A Comparative Study of Methods of Civic Training* (Chicago: University of Chicago Press, 1931 and Teachers College Press, 1966 reissue); and Heinz Eulau, "Political Science and Education: The Long View and the Short," in Kirst, *State, School, and Politics,* pp. 1-9.

35. Richard Dershimer, *The Federal Government and Educational R&D* (Lexington, Mass., Lexington Books, D.C. Heath & Co., 1976).

36. Including that just issued, Scribner, *Politics of Education.*

37. Jack Culbertson et al., *Preparing Educational Leaders for the Seventies* (Columbus, Ohio: University Council for Educational Administration, 1969).

38. For example, Mann, *Politics of Administrative Representation;* and Summerfield, *Neighborhood-Based Politics of Education.*

39. For example, David Rogers, *110 Livingston Street* (New York: Random House, 1968). For a challenge to the thesis, see Peterson, "Politics of American Education."

40. For an overview, see Frederick M. Wirt, "Political Turbulence and Administrative Authority," in L. Masotti and R. Lineberry, eds., *The New Urban Politics* (Cambridge, Mass.: Ballinger, 1976), pp. 61-89. For the local level, see Wirt, "Social Diversity and School Board Responsiveness," in P. Cristone, ed., *Understanding School Boards* (Lexington, Mass.: Lexington Books, D.C. Heath & Co., 1975), chapter 10; for the state level, see Wirt, "Educational Politics and Policies," and Wirt, "State School Policy Cultures: Power Linkages Between State and Local Policy Making," in Scribner, *The Politics of Education.*

41. For example, Mann, *Politics of Administrative Representation;* Kirby et al., *Political Strategies;* Hogan, *The Schools, the Courts, and the Public Interest;* and Rogers and Bullock, *Coercion to Compliance.* Demonstrating the extent of the constraints on local authority is the major thrust of van Geel, *Authority to Control.*

42. This forms a standard section of any urban politics text; for example, Robert Lineberry and Ira Sharkansky, *Urban Politics and Public Policy*, 2d ed. (New York: Harper and Row, 1974). For a review of this research, see Brett Hawkins, *Politics and Urban Policies* (Indianapolis, Ind.: Bobbs-Merrill, 1971).

43. Zeigler and Jennings, *Governing American Schools;* a review of this literature is Wirt, "Social Diversity." For its consequences on desegregation struggles in the North, see Kirby et al., *Political Strategies;* and Eldon Wegner and Jane Mercer, "Dynamics of the Desegregation Process: Politics, Policies, and Community Characteristics as Factors in Change," in Wirt, *Polity of the School,* chap. 8.

44. Summerfield, *Neighborhood-Based Politics.*

45. Edith Mosher, "The School Board in the Family of Governments," in Cristone, *Understanding School Boards,* chap. 2.

46. See *Phi Delta Kappan* 57 (October 1976).

47. Mann, *The Politics of Administrative Representation.*

48. Larry Cuban, "Urban Superintendents: Vulnerable Experts," *Phi Delta Kappan,* December 1974, pp. 279-282 (based on his Ph.D. diss., School of Education, Stanford, 1974). See also Zeigler and Jennings, *Governing American Schools.*

49. That there is more politics than suspected, even in curriculum decisions, is argued in Wirt and Kirst, *Political and Social Foundation in Education,* chap. 10; and William Boyd, "The Changing Politics of Curriculum Policy Making for American Schools," *Review of Educational Research,* Fall 1978:577-628.

50. For example, see the concluding section of Mann, *Politics of Administrative Representation;* and all of Al Smith, Anthony Downes, and M. Leanne

Lachman, *Achieving Effective Desegregation* (Lexington, Mass.: Lexington Books, D.C. Heath & Co., 1972).

51. See the exchange between the two sets in Gove and Wirt, *Political Science and School Politics,* especially chap. 4.

52. It has been done elsewhere, though; see Arnold Meltsner, *Policy Analysis in the Bureaucracy* (Berkeley, Calif.: University of California Press, 1976).

53. Gary Orfield and myself in school desegregation, for example, and Michael Kirst and Norman Thomas in school finance reform.

54. Robert Salisbury, "Schools and Politics in the Big City," *Harvard Educational Review* 37 (1967):408-424; and Peterson, "Politics of American Education," is useful for evaluating this research concern.

55. An early statement of this perspective is Roald Campbell and Robert Bunnell, *Nationalizing Influences on Secondary Education* (Chicago: Midwest Administration Center, University of Chicago, 1963); a mid-sixties Carnegie survey that demonstrated this constraint is Robert Bendiner, *The Politics of Schools* (New York: Harper and Row, 1969); but see Zeigler and Jennings, *Governing American Schools,* for another view.

56. For a review of a variety of Great Society programs, which the authors contend demonstrate much more success than the current mind-set holds, see Sar Levitan and Robert Taggart, *The Promise of Greatness* (Cambridge, Mass.: Harvard University Press, 1976). For a review of the reasons underlying the surprising success of Southern desegregation, see Rodgers and Bullock, *Coercion to Compliance;* and Giles et al., "Impact of Busing."

57. Dale Mann, *Policy Decision-Making in Education* (New York: Teachers College Press, 1975); for the implications of contemporary shifts in state and national policy-making for local administrators' control, see van Geel, *Authority to Control.*

58. One reason is the jargon, obscurantism, and data presentation problems. A recent Rand study of desegregation contained about a hundred tables and graphs in 150 pages; even my interest dulled at the prospect of plowing across these waves of data.

59. For example, Robert Goettel, School of Education, SUNY-Albany, has closely analyzed the ties between community characteristics and support of tax referenda, finding little association in the usual SES measures. For an intensive analysis of voter motivations based on attitude surveys, see Hamilton and Cohen, *Policy Making;* this literature is reviewed systematically for its propositions and their empirical support in Philip Piele and John Hall, *Budgets, Bonds, and Ballots* (Lexington, Mass.: Lexington Books, D.C. Heath & Co., 1974). For its applications to parochial schools, see Daniel Sullivan, *Public Aid to Nonpublic Schools* (Lexington, Mass.: Lexington Books, D.C. Heath & Co., 1974).

60. Some of these components, especially political party and school policy, have limited study; an exception is Paul Peterson, "The Politics of Education

Reform in England and the United States," *Comparative Education Review* 17 (1973):160-179. Salisbury, "Schools and Politics in the Big City," earlier suggested the utility of a partisan politics of education, but most writers ignore the possibility of such linkages coming into being.

61. And more thoroughly in Frederick M. Wirt, "Reassessment Needs in the Study of the Politics of Education," *Teachers College Record* 78 (May 1977):401-412; and Peterson, "Politics of American Education."

62. Harman, "Continuities and Gaps," pp. 269-271.

63. A fuller statement of aspects of such a shift is found in Frederick M. Wirt, "Concepts and Strategies for Research in the Comparative Politics of Education." (Paper presented at the AERA national convention, April 1977.) For such work in two modes, see Peterson, "Politics of Education in England and the United States"; and David Cameron and Richard Hofferbert, "The Impact of Federalism on Education Finance: A Comparative Analysis," *European Journal of Political Research* 2 (1974):225-258; both are reprinted in Wirt, *Polity of the School.*

64. See Wirt, "State Policy Culture," and the literature cited therein.

65. Peterson, "Politics of American Education," p. 57 (typescript). Reprinted with permission.

66. That is why I find Mann, *Policy Decision-Making in Education,* so important for tracing these interrelated questions.

67. For this critique in detail, see Peterson, "Politics of American Education."

68. I suggest rethinking the usual finding of limited school effects on civic orientation, because of the new politicization of local schools in recent years, which may well have provided students with new blunt, direct influences on their political views; this possibility is outlined in Frederick M. Wirt, "Current School Policy Making and Political Learning," *Society* 14 (May-June 1977):46-48.

69. See the differences in perspective that flow from this dichotomy in Eulau, "Political Science and Education."

70. Ronald Johnson, "Research Objectives for Policy Analysis," in K. Dolbeare, ed., *Public Policy Evaluation* (Beverly Hills, Calif.: Sage, 1975), chap. 3; and Eugene Meehan, *The Foundation of Political Analysis* (Homewood, Ill.: Dorsey, 1971).

Part IV
Methodological Considerations and Variables Affecting Research

... [F]or me at least, theory (as activity) begins with a question, a contradiction, a paradox, a puzzle—not with an answer ... Inquiry really gets off the ground when one moves from topic to question. The step tends to cut away ... all kinds of research embroidering the obvious.

—James David Barber, "Strategies for Understanding Politicians," *American Journal of Political Science* 18, no. 2 (May 1974):448-449.

8

Management of Educational Organizations and Implications for Research

William H. Meckling

Does educational management have distinctive features? Is it significantly different from the management of other kinds of organizations? This chapter addresses these questions and the implications of the answers for the behavior of educational managers and for research on educational management.

What Knowledge Is Useful to Managers

In recent years many business schools, like those at Stanford University and the University of Chicago, have introduced either general or specialized programs in not-for-profit management. In part, at least, those programs are rationalized on the grounds that managing not-for-profit organizations has much in common with the management of for-profit organizations. Management, defined in very general terms, does have much in common across organizations. Whether they function in for-profit or not-for-profit organizations, managers have two major responsibilities—first, making decisions, and second, overseeing their implementation. Four classes of knowledge are useful to managers in carrying out those two responsibilities:

1. cause-and-effect relationships or principles
2. techniques and methodology
3. institutional knowledge or description
4. communication skills

Cause and Effect Relationships

Statements of cause and effect are principles, or theories, or laws in the scientific sense. They are generalizations in the sense that they are considered applicable, relevant, or useful in a variety of situations. They are also, thereby, abstract; they ignore, as unimportant, many aspects of specific situations.

Principles or generalizations are the sine qua non of prediction in the "if A, then B" sense. All purposeful behavior, including management, implies a theory relating action to result. This is true from the most trivial act to the most far-reaching policy. When a manager asks his secretary to type a letter, he has a theory about how she will react. When he advertises, he has a theory about how advertising affects sales. When he establishes salary policy, he has a theory about how compensation will affect hiring and retention. The theory may be tentative and vague, the action may even be exploratory, but unless there is some notion of a cause-and-effect relationship, behavior cannot be regarded as purposeful, that is, managerial.

Knowledge of cause-and-effect relationships (theory) is central to all management, whether it is decision-making or the implementation of decisions. A primary objective of management research should be to systematically develop a body of theory useful to managers. By a systematic body of theory, I mean a set of related propositions that are logically consistent. Geometry provides an example. The propositions are related in the sense that they are logically derivable from a common set of axioms. In the social sciences, the axioms come down to a model of man, that is, a set of propositions that capture the essence of man's nature and from which behavioral propositions are deduced.

Economics, among the social sciences, has perhaps gone the furthest in carefully specifying a model of man to serve as a basic building block in constructing a systematic body of theory. I have elsewhere characterized this model of man as REMM—resourceful, evaluative, maximizing man.

1. Each individual cares; he is an evaluator:

   (a) He cares about almost everything: Knowledge, wealth, the plight of other individuals, prestige, rules of conduct, the weather, etc., etc.;

   (b) If we designate those things which he values positively as "goods," then he prefers more goods to less. Goods can be anything from objects of art to ethical norms;

   (c) Valuation is relative. The value attached to a particular unit of a good depends on the bundle of goods the individual enjoys with that unit. The value of a unit of any particular good decreases (at an increasing rate) as the individual enjoys more of it relative to other goods.

   (d) Individual preferences are transitive, i.e., if A is preferred to B, and B is preferred to C, then A is preferred to C. The phrase "rational man" is often used to describe the whole set of character-istics with which economists endow the individual. Semantically, it seems better to restrict the use of the term rationality to the transitivity characteristic of preferences.

2. Each individual is a maximizer. He acts so as to enjoy the highest level of value he can. To be of any relevance, this proposition must

presuppose some limit (the limit, of course, is not satiation) on the aggregate level of value attainable, and some freedom of action to the individual . . .

The Role of Resourcefulness. The model of man which makes him a maximizer and gives him a value system is formally incomplete in one important respect. It says nothing about the individual's ingenuity—his ability to conceive of changes in his behavior or in his environment and to foresee the consequences thereof . . . Human beings are not only capable of learning about new opportunities, but they can, and actively do, seek out and even create new opportunities. In applying this model, i.e., in predicting the consequences of changes, say in relative prices, economists must (and implicitly do) endow the individual with knowledge, ingenuity, and intelligence, though they do not always agree on what levels are appropriate.[1]

If the social sciences are ever to develop a systematic theory of the behavior of organizations, I believe it will have to be founded on a model of man very much like REMM. Whereas using something like REMM is a necessary condition for developing a systematic body of theory about educational management, it is far from a sufficient condition. Most of the research effort required to develop a body of useful theory will consist of careful scientific testing of alternative hypotheses in order to weed out those that are falsified.

Techniques and Methodology

Managers have, no doubt, always used induction and deduction in problem-solving. In recent years, however, there has been a dramatic growth in the use of formal techniques (or tools) in both decision-making and operations. In part the tools and techniques are new (for example, linear programming) and in part they already existed, but were seldom used by managers (for example, classical statistics). Progress in management hardware—including but not limited to computers—has provided much of the impetus for these developments.

A deliberate distinction is drawn here between techniques and methodology. Techniques are formal tools for solving problems. Most of what is taught in quantitative courses in business schools falls under the heading of techniques, for example, regression analysis, linear programming, differentiation, integration, and matrix algebra.

Methodology encompasses all of deduction and induction, including propositions that cannot be quantified and hence need not involve mathematical or statistical techniques. More importantly, methodology also includes knowledge about how to structure problems—for example, how to decide what costs are relevant to a particular decision, or how to view a problem as a sequential decision process involving the acquisition of new information at each stage. In the context of structuring problems, methodology merges with principles and generalizations. The structuring of a problem always requires more or less abstraction, that is, a decision on what the important variables are and what can be neglected. Thus, the way one structures a problem depends very critically on what one believes about cause-and-effect relationships. Indeed, what one even identifies as a problem is conditioned by knowledge of cause-and-effect relationships.

Institutional Knowledge or Description

In making decisions and carrying them into effect, managers must also make extensive use of purely descriptive or institutional knowledge that is highly specialized to the particular organization and its context.

Communication Skills

One class of resources that managers manage is human resources, and managing humans requires skill in communicating or, more broadly, in interpersonal relations. Even if there are no specific courses designed to teach these skills in formal programs of management preparation, students should improve their communication and interpersonal relations skills as part of their education. At a minimum, this means writing and engaging in group activities as part of the formal curriculum.

Distinctive Features of Our Educational System

Much management research is general in applicability, that is, it is relevant to management in a variety of organizational settings, including educational organizations. This is particularly true of research on managerial techniques. Quantitative techniques such as operations research models and statistical methods, for example, are not specialized to particular organizational forms. Thus, it makes sense to talk about research in *educational* management to the extent that the educational system displays unique institutional or organizational features. The U.S. educational system does have certain basic features that distinguish it from the normal for-profit organization:

1. Education in the United States is predominately financed through taxation. Although private universities and colleges, and even private elementary and secondary schools, exist, tax revenues dominate as the source of revenue at every level of education. Even private universities and colleges depend on government funds for research, scholarships and fellowships, and institutional

students loans. Because much of the educational funding is provided by government, educational managers are not subjected to the discipline of consumer (students and parents) satisfaction to the same extent as managers of profit-making enterprises.

2. Education is not only predominately financed through government but also is largely socialized; that is, most educational organizations are literally government organizations. At the elementary and secondary level private schools, mostly denominational, educate only a small fraction of the annual student flow. At the level of universities and colleges, the proportion of students in private educational settings is higher, but even there the vast majority of students attend governmentally operated institutions.

The socialization of education means that the control system that conditions managerial behavior in the educational sector is political in nature. Parties interested in controlling educational policy can do so only through control over political behavior. The politicization of educational policy has fostered the organization of powerful special interest groups (lobbies), whose objective is to control such policy. Teacher organizations, such as the National Education Association, are a prime example, but there are many others, such as the American Association of Universities. Further, in the case of educational employee organizations, political activism is combined with unionism.

3. At the elementary and secondary level in the United States there is very little competition among educational institutions. This is itself an outgrowth of the socialization of education. Students (and parents) generally have little or no choice about which particular school they (or their children) will attend. They are assigned to schools on the basis of place of residence. This geographic assignment of pupils to schools also serves to weaken the consumer's influence on the educational managers.[2] Local control of schools, however, combined with the opportunity for parents to move from one independent school district to another, to some extent moderates the monopoly power of elementary and secondary schools.

Constraints on the Educational Manager

From the point of view of the educational manager, these distinctive features of the educational system help determine the constraints and the reward system the manager faces. In most cases resources to produce education are made available to the manager as part of a "budget" process. The manager has responsibility for using those resources, subject to a set of constraints, also imposed from above. For state-operated schools, and to some extent even for private schools, these constraints are imposed directly or indirectly by elected officials.

Nominally, the objective of the educational administrator is to maximize the educational output with given resources. He is presumed to have knowledge of the production function of education, that is, what educational output can be produced with alternative combinations of inputs he could purchase with his budget.

In practice, the constraints that the educational manager faces are likely to significantly restrict the alternative combinations of inputs he can choose. The manager's budget is not likely to come to him as a lump sum, which he can use as he sees fit. Rather, it is likely to come to him already allocated by purpose, and accompanied by constraints on his authority to reallocate from one purpose to another, for example, from salaries to visual aids or from maintenance to books. Since educational managers are often intimately involved in preparing budgets for submission to public bodies for approval, budget constraints may not be as binding as they at first blush would appear. Other constraints, however, cannot be so easily avoided. This is particularly true of constraints designed to benefit various special interest groups, especially teachers. As a practical matter, educational managers are not free to reward teachers on the basis of merit; and that statement applies not only to public school teachers at the elementary and secondary levels but also to faculty in state university systems, to faculty of city universities, to community college faculties, and the like. Educational managers in state-operated institutions are also not completely free to choose class sizes or curriculum content.

Performance Evaluation and Rewards for Educational Managers

Managerial constraints aside, there remains in our model of the educational manager's behavior—as a resourceful, evaluating, maximizer—a question of how diligently he will pursue the objective function we have prescribed for him, namely, maximizing educational output for a given budget. The strength of the manager's efforts to maximize educational output will depend on how closely the system of rewards he faces is tied to that objective. There are many reasons for suspecting that those ties will not be very strong. For one thing, those who are responsible for hiring, firing, and promoting educational managers are not likely to accept maximizing educational output as *the* objective for the educational system. To the extent that the ultimate employers of educational managers are elected officials, and given the political influence of minority special interest groups (for example, teachers), it seems very unlikely that educational managers will be rewarded on the basis of educational output. It seems much more likely that their performance will be evaluated in terms of how they serve the influential special interest groups.

Even if employers of educational managers wanted to evaluate and reward educational managers on the basis of educational output, they would be hard pressed to do so. Evaluating and rewarding managers in accordance with productivity is a problem even in for-profit organizations. There, at least, there is a reasonably well defined objective function—maximizing the value of the firm. Moreover, there is an external market in which the firm is continuously being evaluated. In the case of corporations, there are highly organized markets in which claims (shares of stock) on the firms are bought and sold. The existence of such external markets provides an objective measure of the performance of management. The institution of private property plays an important role in this connection in for-profit organizations. Because of private rights in resources, the costs of misusing resources and the benefits from effectively using resources are imposed on the owners. Thus, corporate managers tend to be evaluated on the basis of how efficiently they use resources.

Nothing comparable exists in the case of educational organizations. There are no owners to capture the gains from providing education more efficiently. Moreover, since education is itself sold only in the case of private schools, colleges, and universities, educational managers are required to meet only a very weak market test for their product.

Implications for Research in Education Management

The unique organizational features that characterize the production of education in the United States pose both challenges and opportunities for research in education management. The educational system provides a laboratory for researchers interested in finding out how alternative organizational and institutional arrangements affect individual behavior and the performance of organizations. Developing a body of theory about how such organizations function is a prerequisite to making policy recommendations about how education might be improved. Building such a body of theory, however, is not an easy task. What theory we have about political processes is rudimentary at best, and education for the most part is supplied by government.

Moreover, research in this area is confronted by serious measurement problems. We can measure achievement in such skill areas as reading and computation reasonably accurately, and we can measure knowledge of various subject areas such as physics or biology with reasonable accuracy. It is much more difficult, however, given the institutional arrangements in education, to measure the value of various skills and knowledge, and it is the value added that is the ultimate test of the performance of educational organizations.[3] One fact, although generally not recognized, is that curriculum decisions, whether to teach more mathematics and less social studies, or what kind of mathematics to teach, cannot be made intelligently except in terms of the relative value of those alternatives.

At the level of the educational manager, himself, perhaps the most serious knowledge deficiency we face is with respect to the nature of the educational production function, that is, about what educational output can be generated with alternative combinations of input. Earlier, I characterized the special expertise of the educational manager as that of effectively converting educational inputs into outputs. "Inputs" in this context includes buildings, teachers, visual aids, books, and so forth; but it also includes kinds of teachers—for example, the extent to which their training focuses on educational methods rather than in terms of academic disciplines—class sizes, grading policies, instructional methods, and so forth. The truth is we have only very crude notions about how various combinations of these inputs will affect educational output.

Research Methodology

At the most general level, any question exploring methodological approaches for research on administration or management has only one answer. We know only one method for research. It is the scientific method. It consists of systematic construction of hypotheses, testing those hypotheses, rejecting those that are falsified, and then going on to new hypotheses that will better explain phenomena we observe or that will explain a wider range of phenomena.

From the viewpoint of one outsider, two issues could be raised about research in educational management, which are in a sense methodological. One is how scrupulously researchers in this field have adhered to the precepts of science. It is my impression that educational researchers are much more likely to let their personal value judgments influence the interpretation of research findings and the choice of subjects for research than is true in other fields. The other is that the standards for evaluation of research in education have generally not been as strict as those applied in other areas. The statistical techniques employed, for example, are generally less powerful than those used in economics. Moreover, there is much less insistence on rigor in stating hypotheses and deducing conclusions therefrom. There is, of course, always the danger that by demanding more rigor in research a subject area will be reduced to formal logic or elegant mathematics. Research in educational management can move substantially in the direction of more rigor and more sophisticated techniques before that becomes a real danger.

Notes

1. William H. Meckling, "Values and the Choice of the Model of the Individual in the Social Sciences," *Schweizerische Zeitschrift fur Volkswirtschaft und Statistik,* Bern, Switzerland, December 1976; and forthcoming in Karl Brunner, ed., *Man and Society* (Boston: Martinus Nijhoff Publishing Co., 1979). Reprinted with permission.

2. A much wider range of choice is available to students choosing among colleges and universities. Higher education in the United States is unique in this respect. State monopoly of higher education is characteristic of virtually all the rest of the world. The fact of competition in higher education in the United States no doubt explains why American institutions of higher learning have come to dominate the international scene, whereas no such claim can be made for our elementary and secondary educational system. That hypothesis, at any rate, would itself be an interesting subject for educational research.

3. We can infer something about the value to individuals of alternative educational programs and of alternative educational institutional arrangements from comparative studies of earnings of students with varied educational backgrounds.

9 Ideas versus Data: How Can the Data Speak for Themselves?

Thomas B. Greenfield

Grau, teurer Freund, ist alle Theorie,
Und grün des Lebens goldner Baum.

My worthy friend, gray are all theories—
The verdant tree of life alone is green.

—Goethe, *Faust*

There is no point in talking about data and methodology unless we are also prepared to talk about our ideas and beliefs—theories if you like—which give meaning to data and power to methodology. Too frequently we forget the perspectives and assumptions that determine how we approach data and what we see in them. And we regularly ignore the fact that in the realm of social reality the data themselves may have their own perspective, which may differ sharply from that which the researcher seeks to impose on them. Social scientists take as their study human life, but in research on organization and administration they are apt to ignore experience as part of life and to forget that it is imbedded in the lives of individuals. One person's experience is inaccessible by any direct means to the experience of others. How then are we to understand our own experience and that of others? This major existential question faces everyone; even more so must the social scientist find it an unavoidable and perplexing puzzle.

Yet anyone who takes seriously the usual texts on research and theory in administrative studies is likely to come away with the impression that the workings of social systems and the place of individuals in them are fairly well understood. After all, researchers wielding powerful tools have amassed this knowledge through a process that is arcane but indisputably successful. Their methods and terminology imitate those of physical science, while invoking at the same time the mystique of the medical profession. The standard methodology speaks of controlling variables or holding them constant. It talks of treatments, subjects, and effects as though understanding administrative process and life in organizations were in no way qualitatively different from Galileo dropping objects of different weight from the leaning tower of Pisa or Fleming observing penicillin mold devour bacteria in the agar of his petri dishes.

So confident have some social scientists become in their experimental methodologies and assumptions about them that a distinction between "hard" and "soft" data finds ready acceptance as the touchstone for separating valid research from that which is barely removed from the obvious unreliabilities and subjective impressions of sheer journalism. In the usual parlance of social researchers, hard data are those derived in real numbers from reliable instruments. Soft data, in this way of talking, are said pejoratively to rest only on somebody's perception, expressed usually in words. And this form of expression further invalidates soft data, for they are now ill-fitted if not totally unacceptable for quantitative analysis.

By turning the tables on these categories of thought, we may see another contrast—that between "cheap" data and "hard" data.[1] In this way of thinking, cheap data are those that researchers obtain in large quantities at minimal cost. Such data can be herded into a computer with little difficulty; there they can be analyzed in the twinkling of a solid state system and disgorged in forms ready-made for presentation to annual conferences or scholarly publications. It is not necessary for cheap data to reflect the experience of individuals or to illumine the quality of relationships among them. Cheap data do not have to explain why they exist or what sense they make in their own right. It is sufficient that they find their meaning from the logic of the mathematics to which they are susceptible. Human interpretation of them is not required. If cheap data fail to confirm hypotheses or theories to which they are fitted, that shortcoming is no reason to abandon them; rather it is evidence that the researcher needs more data and more sophisticated methods for gathering and analyzing them. Hard data, in contrast, do not spring from a facile act of creation; they are difficult to identify, handle, and interpret. They speak meaningfully and powerfully for individuals in specific situations, yet they find a larger significance as well. They show how individuals' sense of themselves and their world has consequences in that world, and they suggest how these meanings and consequences can be expressed in typifications, symbols, or theories that provide fresh insights into social reality.

Methodology as an End in Itself

If these observations seem extreme, I invite the sceptics to review, as I have done recently, the current empirical research in the field of educational administration. At the 1977 Conference of the American Educational Research Association, Division A presented a session on recent research devoted to such well-accepted areas of study as leadership, organizational climate, bureaucracy, supervision, and the future of organizational changes in large school districts.[2] Could any array of five topics better represent major concerns of the field over the past decade or more?

As critic for the session in which these studies were presented, I was struck first by the heavy reliance in the studies on quantitative data and what has come to be standard methodology. Their authors used hard data—but cheap data. The sophistication of their techniques and the skill with which they used them are not in question here. Indeed, the researchers used a formidable array of weapons from the statistician's armamentarium to bring order into large arrays of data. From my perspective, the meaning and validity of such studies are in question. In reviewing them I was struck secondly by the fact that their findings never served to shake or reshape the initial theory, whether the research hypotheses were confirmed or not. The outside observer dropping in on such a session would leave convinced that the theoretical study of administration was making immense strides through such research, and that it could only be some kind of unusual perversity that delays the application of such knowledge for the amelioration of the many problems that beset the educational enterprise. But then it is entirely typical of such studies that the data do not serve, as one might expect, to test the theory; instead it is the data that are to be judged by accepting the theory a priori as the standard of validity. I will return to this point again, but let me say now why I raise these questions.

The combination of readily accessible computer technology with prevailing notions about the unique explanatory power of experimental design has placed advanced statistical techniques at the command of all would-be social researchers and schooled them to believe that these are not just *some* methods of inquiry into social reality, but *the* methods of such inquiry. Thus to unlock the secrets of the social system, researchers need only take time to follow the instructions in a manual with a name like "Data Analysis Package for the Social Sciences" and listen, perhaps, to the advice of a helpful expert on computer software. Eigenvalues, factor scores, Wilks' lambda, discriminant functions, obliquimax rotations, multiple linear regressions, and a host of other bizarre but puissant servants are placed immediately at the command of the researcher: Pandora's box and the sorcerer's apprentice. Do we know what these servants are doing for us? If we do not, then it is certain that the techniques themselves will not bring meaning where none before existed. The sophistication of data analysis cannot make up for the emptiness or irrelevance of the concepts to which they apply.

As researchers we must remind outselves of some elemental lessons from our introductory textbooks on methodology. Reliability is not validity. Correlation does not imply causality, even if the correlation is large and reliable. The question we must continually ask ourselves as researchers is whether the view of the world we get from our current highly quantified technology squares with the view of persons whose actions we we are trying to explain.

Explaining variance in an array of data is not the same as explaining behavior as an actor in a social situation sees it. Do real individuals see leadership as a set of bipolar factors set orthogonally in twelve-dimensional space? Do they think bureaucracies come in two dimensions representing hierarchy and expertise?[3] They may, but it is an obligation of the researcher to show that they do. Otherwise the realities of the researcher's world are confined to their minds and to the workings of their computers. The logic of the researchers' analysis can have no force in the everyday world unless it conforms to the logic that people use in everyday situations. Unless there is a close match between the world as researchers construct it and the world as people perceive it and act in it, the researchers' efforts to establish social truths will be a self-contained and ultimately self-deluding pastime.

Validating Theory[4]

In the standard view of research, its purpose is to test the adequacy and the truthfulness of theoretical constructs. A long- and well-accepted logic in research requires researchers first to have a theoretical view of the world and then to test it stringently against reality by collecting empirical data through operationally defined procedures. In contrast, Kuhn and Feyerabend argue that theory is never disconfirmed by empirical research. If findings are inconsistent with the theory, we are likely to disbelieve them or to search for other data that fit better with the theory.[5] Or more commonly and subtly, the researchers' theories and methodologies themselves ensure that the data will be consistent with the researchers' initial assumptions.

By conventional standards, the studies in the AERA symposium are useful, because they begin with a clear notion of what they expect to find. Our research logic teaches us that observation without theory is blind. But I would caution that observation within theory and prescriptive methodology predisposes us to see what theory knows to be true. In this regard I have some strong reservations about the use of factor analysis and multiple regression as methodological devices for testing theory. My reservations stem from the high degree of latitude that these methods give researchers for interpreting their results. For example, few methods of factor analysis yield unique results. What a factor is depends on what the researcher is satisfied with. Typically, researchers keep rotating their factors until something interpretable emerges. And the criterion for interpretation comes inevitably from the theory with which the researcher began. Korfhage explains how this process works: "The number of factors retained for rotation was determined by balancing three criteria: Kaiser's criterion, Cattell's scree, and interpretability."[6] And Terenzini and Pascarella tell us: "Each factor has been given a tentative name which was felt to represent the underlying construct tapped. The reader is cautioned, however, against attributing surplus meaning to the factors beyond the scales which characterize them."[7] Whereas these authors always point out the limitations of their findings, as they do in the passages above, it may be doubted whether those who quote their findings will remember not to attribute surplus meaning to the mathematical constructs their findings are based on.

And I have a minor quibble about the manner in which variance is reported as "explained" in those studies using factor analysis. It has apparently become standard practice in reporting results to deal only with common variance. As a result, the researchers are able to claim that their factors are "explaining" a large part of variance. The proportion of variance explained would certainly drop if the factors were compared to total rather than to common variance. My suspicion is that the factors would look much less substantial against total variance, and for this reason, the researchers prefer to deal only with common variance. Again the assumption here is that the world really looks the way the researchers' theoretical and methodological assumptions say it looks, and if it doesn't, it should. Noncommon variance, after all, contains error. In excluding noncommon variance, the researchers appear to be saying that the error is attributable to the world, not to the researchers' assumptions about it.

The tendency of researchers to ignore error variance has been noted in scholarly circles, but with little obvious effect on the practices recommended in research textbooks. In an article published over a decade ago, Schutz drew attention to the consequences of failing to consider error variance in assessing the meaning and practicality of experimental research. He pointed out that researchers typically subordinate error variance to an incidental role, while at the same time they elevate the final test of the hypothesis as the ultimate criterion for judging the value of research. According to Schutz, this practice has had "an unfortunate effect on the behavior of educational researchers," in that it leads them to mistake statistical significance for substantive and practical meaning. He also deplored the situation in which "even our most highly respected research journals fail to report the magnitude of the error term or any data that would permit its computation."[8] This cavalier dismissal of information that does not fit the hypothesis perhaps helps to create the widening gulf between common-sense understandings of social reality and the increasingly obscure rituals of researcher-statisticians. In this situation, researcher-statisticians perhaps sense a crisis of confidence and call on the laity in priest-like fashion to trust their statisticians. For example, Benjamin, in reflecting on attempts to train British civil servants in the statistical methods of social science, advises the nonstatistician as follows:

> The good administrator must be prepared to trust his statistical advisers provided that he can be sure that they are technically competent and professional in their approach, just as a good administrator entrusts his subordinates with authority.[9]

The major point to be made here is that far from being tested in these studies, theory is used as the standard for interpreting data. Data become meaningful when they fulfill the predictions of the theory. And even when the data let the theory down, as they do in Korfhage's study, she responds as many other researchers do in the situation by saying that what we need is more research, more variables, more data. After all, the paradigm can't be wrong, can it? She concludes:

The inconsistent appearance of predicted paradigm-related differences suggest that paradigm [sic] is not sufficiently powerful to account for departmental variations. This is not to suggest that the use of paradigm [sic] has been exhausted or that it should be disregarded in investigations of academic units. What this suggests is that additional variables should be considered in order to more thoroughly describe the departmental context.[10]

In case anyone believes that the kind of thinking I have been criticizing is limited to papers presented at scholarly gatherings, it is useful to look at a recent policy-oriented research carried out with the explicit purpose of bringing rigorous economics to bear on an issue that educators had apparently been too soft-minded to look at under the hard light of scientific analysis. The question Summers and Wolfe set out to solve is an old and important one in education: What is the effect of school resources on educational achievement? After proclaiming that, "Educational achievement, like shoes, canned tuna, and clean streets can be regarded as the output of a production process," these economists set out to resolve the class-size question by correlating every quantifiable variable in sight and submitting the whole thing to multiple regression analysis.[11] The results are illuminating, but not in the way the authors conceived them to be:

Library books: As one more book per pupil is added to the library, pupil achievement growth declines by .5 months.

Class size: Being in a class of 34 or more reduces achievement growth by 2.1 months. Being in a class of 28 to 33 rather than a class of less than 28 has no effect on students who scored at grade level in third grade, a negative effect on low achievers, and a positive effect on high achievers.

Sixth grade Teacher's [sic] Experience: Teacher's [sic] experience has a positive effect on average and above average students. A student who is at grade level in the third grade (=3.8) will increase achievement growth by .6 months for each three additional years of teacher's experience (to 11 years). A student scoring 5.0 will increase by 1.3 months per three additional years experience. Below grade level, down to 2.0, additional experience has no effect. Below that, it reduces growth.[12]

Surely, even the most convinced supporter of scientific analysis would not advocate removing library books to increase pupil achievement. If the effects claimed for class size and teaching experience are to be understood at all against the complexities of the reported interactions, they suggest the possible conclusion that some students learn better than others whatever the size of the class and the experience of the teacher. Such an outcome is hardly a new finding in the scientific world or a revelation among the realities policy-makers recognize as compelling. Although their findings can be of little use for policy-making, it seems unlikely that the researchers will alter their belief in educational achievement as the product of an ordered and well-understood production process.[13] Thus theory helps us to see and not to see. Let us look at how this happens.

What we see depends in large measure on what we believe we are going to see. It may be argued indeed that we see, hear, and feel nothing without first having ideas that give meaning to our experience. Knowledge and learning, therefore, have to do with acquiring new ideas—new categories for perceiving reality. In trying to understand reality, we require concepts or categories that enable us to make sense of that which William James called "the blooming welter" of phenomena around us. As aids for understanding, we use larger frameworks and models—theories, if you like—which provide us with reservoirs of ideas for understanding the world around us. These frameworks or models are images of reality, which we carry in our minds and which we use as templates to stamp meaning into the world around us.

This argument rests on propositions that were established in the earliest era of Western thought. The philosophers of ancient Greece and Asia Minor argued long over image and reality and often made their points through analysis of everyday experience. For example: Some travellers approach a tower which they see first from a distance. From this perspective, the tower appears round. At close quarters, however, they see that the tower is "really" square. With this truth in mind, the traveleers continue on their journey. On looking back at the tower from a distance once more, they find that it again looks round, though they now "know" that it is square.

That we require ideas to understand our experience and to perceive reality is generally accepted as a principle of epistemology. What is in dispute is where the ideas come from and whether they represent—although possibly in flawed form—the ultimate reality of the world. In many cases, the ideas we use to understand the world run quite contrary to direct observation and common experience. Zeno's paradoxes prove that motion from point A to point B will never be accomplished in a world based on the notion of a continuum consisting of isolated elements. Feyerabend points out how this line of reasoning supports Parmenides' theory of "the unchanging and homogeneous one which is contradicted by almost everything we know and experience." Feyerabend goes on to show how this odd notion plays a role even today in the theory of general relativity and in Heisenberg's insight that "the basic elements of the universe cannot obey the same laws as the visible elements."[14] For Plato also, and philosophers of the naturalistic school, the images or forms we need to understand the world lie behind that which we immediately perceive as reality. In his allegory of the cave, Plato saw people as being chained in darkness so that they could see only shadows cast on the wall in front of them. In this allegory, reality lies outside of the cave—outside of man's immediate experience. Ordinary mortals therefore require help, if they are to see things as they really are. For Plato, it was the philosopher who could provide such help. In our time, we are likely to believe that it is scientists who give us access to knowledge. In these views, knowledge is not easily come by; that which we have should therefore be cherished and accepted. Certainly we know that scientists have theories that are very hard to understand and that are built only by painstaking research in which the theories are subjected to stringent tests. Once tested, scientific theories are powerful, because they tell us what things are and how they really work.

In the view that I have elsewhere argued in some detail,[15] the images we use to understand the world around us are man-made and socially maintained. This view rejects the naturalistic assumptions, which suffuse much of research on organization theory. Under naturalistic and Platonic assumptions, theory is something that scientists build, largely from the armchair, by thinking up ultimate explanations for the phenomena observed. Contrary to accepted opinion, Kuhn has argued that such theory is never open to disproof and serves instead as a consensual agreement among scientists about what procedures shall constitute scientific activity and hence which explanations will count as scientific explanations.[16] Does the sun go around the earth, or the earth around the sun? The Ptolemaic astronomers had no difficulty in fitting all kinds of facts into a system that saw the sun revolving about the earth. Copernicus did not batter down the old theory with new scientific observations. Instead, he showed that the old facts could be fitted into a different theory, if we believed that the earth were revolving around the sun. In both cases, the image of what we believe to be determines what we see. The process of scientific inquiry confirms that we really do see what theory says should be there. It fails to test whether the original concept or belief is true.

Feyerabend demonstrates how both reason and empirical observation supported the Aristotelian and Ptolemaic view of the structure of the heavens and the mechanics by which they moved.[17] A stone dropped from a tall tower fell at the base of the tower, not some distance from it, as it would surely do if the earth were hurtling through space at the rate of many miles per second. Ergo, the earth stands still. And ergo the whole social system that supports such reasoning it also right. Feyerabend also shows why the telescope that Galileo constructed to demonstrate the truth of a heliocentric cosmos failed to convince the scholars of the day.[18] Galileo could see that it proved Copernicus right, but they couldn't. It failed to convince the sceptics partly because of physical limitations in the telescope, but mostly because the viewers of that time had not yet learned to see what Galileo was convinced was there to be seen. Both the theory and the experience to understand and interpret the evidence from telescopic observations were lacking. Only faith in a new order of things, in a new method of inquiry, and in a new cosmology could bring one to see the rightness of the heliocentric view.

For Copernicus now stands for progress in other areas as well, he is a symbol for the ideals of a new class that looks back to the classical times of Plato and Cicero and forward to a free and pluralistic society . . .

. . . The ideas survived and they can *now* be said to be in agreement with reason. They survived because prejudice, passion, conceit, errors, sheer pig-headedness, in short because all the elements that characterize the context of discovery, *opposed* the dictates of reason *and because these irrational elements were permitted to have their way.* To express it differently: *Copernicanism and other "rational" views exist today only because reason was overruled at some time in their past.* (The opposite is also true: witchcraft and other "irrational" views have *ceased* to be influential only because reason was overruled at some time in *their* past.)[19]

Can There Be One Best Theory of Experience?

The power of the image to shape what we see is even more potent in social affairs than in the natural world. Strangely, this truth has largely been ignored in organization theory, where research has become more and more technically sophisticated, while attention to the validity of its concepts dwindles. Kuhn points, for example, to research by Bruner and Postman in which subjects were asked to identify cards in a deck that included both "normal" cards and "anomalous" cards, for instance, a red six of spades and a black four of hearts.[20] When subjects were shown the cards briefly and asked to say what they were, they would first transform the anomalous cards into normal ones and then, with longer exposure, begin to say things like, "that's the six of spades, but there's something wrong with it—the black has a red border." Some subjects never could see the anomalous cards for what they were. One of them exclaimed, "I can't make the suit out, whatever it is. It didn't even look like a card that time. I don't know what color it is or whether it's a spade or a heart. I'm not even sure now what a spade looks like. My God."

In naturalistic science, there is usually only one theory accepted at a given time as the best explanation of phenomena in the field to which it applies. Whereas the consequences of this one-theory-at-a-time approach are certainly important in the physical sciences, the limitations of their theoretical assumption are of immense importance in the social sciences. As Weber noted some time ago, atoms do not care whether physicists' theories are accurate. People, on the other hand, have a stake in social theory. The theory is about them, and someone is going to take action on the basis of the theory as though it were true. If, as Weber argues, there are various perspectives for seeking and understanding social phenomena, social scientists are making moral judgments at the same time they are selecting a model, framework, or theory from which to view social organization.[21] And if, as Kuhn and Feyerabend argue, theories are overthrown through intellectual revolutions, not through "the findings of research," social scientists may readily deceive themselves and fail to note the imperial role which their theories play in imposing meaning on reality.

There is a strong tendency in modern science to deal with new theories and hypotheses according to what Feyerabend calls the "consistency principle."[22] The consistency principle arises from the belief that things are what they are and cannot be otherwise. So that is why we must accept the version of them that best conforms to our reasoning and to observation within such reasoning. The consistency principle eliminates new theories, hypotheses, and methodologies, not because they are inconsistent with the facts, but because they are inconsistent with previously established theories. To combat the consistency principle, Feyerabend recommends testing hypotheses that run at variance to or directly against well-established theories, because such as approach provides "evidence which cannot be obtained in any other way. Proliferation of theories is beneficial for science, while uniformity impairs its critical powers."[23] And he goes further:

> Unanimity of opinion may be fitting for a Church, for the frightened or greedy victims of some (ancient or modern) myth, or for the weak and willing followers of some tyrant. Variety of opinion is necessary for objective knowledge. And a method that encourages variety is also the only method that is compatible with a humanitarian outlook.[24]

The basic problem in the physical sciences is how to understand a world beyond our direct experience. This problem is solved by imposing meanings on observed behavior and reasoning whether the behavior is consistent with the explanation. In social reality, it is experience that is the unknown. And the problem is how we come to understand our experience and to communicate it to others. R.D. Laing echoes Max Weber when he says:

> Natural science knows nothing of the relation between behaviour and experience. The nature of this relation is mysterious . . . That is to say, it is not an objective problem. There is no traditional logic to express it. There is no developed method of understanding its nature. But this relation is the copula of our science—if science means *a form of knowledge adequate to its subject.* The relation between experience and behaviour is the stone that the builders will reject at their peril. Without it the whole structure of our theory and practice must collapse.[25]

If we regard learning and experience purely as behavior about which we must theorize, we are likely to misconstrue its meaning and to distort seriously our understanding of it. The atom cannot speak for itself, even if we think there is reason to give credence to the theory that says atoms exist. Neither can the amoeba speak for itself, although we can see it moving, if we take the time and care to learn how to see with a microscope. But people can talk, and they can say what they experience and how they came to understand that experience. No one can experience another's experience, but we may come to understand it. People can speak. They can speak with words, with silence, with the look on a face, the movement of an arm, the posture of the body. The events we see in social reality can speak. Social data can speak. They can speak for themselves, although it is not altogether clear how they do so or how we are to understand them. R.D. Laing hammers home this point, and it is one that has been made often and often ignored in administrative and organizational studies:

> Natural scientific investigations are conducted on objects, or things, or the patterns of relations between things . . . Persons are distinguished from things in that persons experience the world, whereas things behave in the world. Thing-events do not experience. Personal events are experiential. Natural scientism is the error of turning persons into things by a process of reification that is not itself part of true natural scientific method. Results derived in this way have to be reassimilated into the realm of human discourse.[26]

The physical world does not care what hypotheses we hold about it. Or, if it does, it never says so. But people care, and they go through elaborate exercises to prove that their beliefs are right. If observation and the facts fail to support our beliefs, we are likely to fall back on what we call reason. Neither the physical scientist nor the social scientist can afford to ignore this reasoning process, because it is the process by which we come to understand the world around us. Some examples may clarify this point. Feyerabend gives several examples of how scientists behave when they are confronted with facts that conflict with or apparently refute their theories. Newton shored up such discrepancies in his own theories by ad hoc hypotheses and explanations. In a more usual response, scientists simply retain the theory and forget its shortcomings.[27] When confronted with discrepancies between data and theory, Barrow, who was Newton's teacher and predecessor at Cambridge, chose to believe the theory and then reflected on his decision: "All which does see, repugnant to our principles. But for me neither this nor any other difficulty shall have so great an influence on me, as to make me renounce that which I know to be manifestly agreeable to reason."[28]

Young draws attention to the subjectivity of even the hard subjects in the school curriculum and quotes from a study on the sociology of mathematics to contrast the views of the mathematician, Hardy, with those of the philosopher, Wittgenstein.[29] Hardy holds that: ". . . 317 is a prime number, not because we think so, or because our minds are shaped one way rather than another, but *because it is so* because mathematical reality is built that way." For Wittgenstein, however, it is *we* who are inexorable, not mathematics:

With endless practice, with merciless exactitude; that is why it is inexorably insisted that we shall all say "two" after "one," "three" after "two" and so . . . Our children are not only given practice in calculation but are also trained to adopt a particular attitude towards a mistake in calculating.

Our ideas and our experiences are subject to human intervention. One generation trains another and it is these patterns and processes of institutional reality-making that we must come to understand, as Laing makes clear:

From the moment of birth, when the Stone Age baby confronts the twentieth-century mother, the baby is subjected to these forces of violence, called love, as its mother and father, and their parents and their parents before them, have been. These forces are mainly concerned with destroying most of its potentialities, and on the whole this enterprise is successful. By the time the new human being is fifteen or so, we are left with a being like ourselves, a half-crazed creature more or less adjusted to a mad world. This is normality in our present age.[30]

Other Voices, Other Rooms: Other Images, Other Theories

If the logic of this critique is accepted, what are its implications for the conduct of inquiry in administration? First, it seems to me that we need to take our theories more seriously in one sense and less seriously in another. We need to be more serious about our theories, because they represent not just possible views of reality, but views that people believe in and which they think of as true. We need to take them less seriously when it comes to proving or testing them. I doubt that theories are ever tested by what researchers do to them. They are given meaningful and stringent tests when people attempt to act in accordance with them. When people engage in meaningful acts of leadership or when they act in terms of a specific set of values, researchers and theoreticians may glimpse the world as other people see it rather than as their own assumptions and methods of observation allow them to see it.

For example, leadership is acknowledged to be a dynamic and complex phenomenon. Yet LBDQ-based research has been content now for many years to explain it in procedures that are unusually restrictive and static.[31] At best, the LBDQ gives us a single Brownie camera snapshot of a complex and obscure process. We know that much went on before we took the photograph; we know that much will go on after it; and we know that our fuzzy LBDQ snapshot represents only a tiny part of what was going on at the time it was taken. None of these limitations appear to shake our faith in a concept of leadership whose chief virtues may be that it offers immediate results and quantitative data, which we know how to handle. We know too that the future is incredibly hard to predict or control in any meaningful way. Yet we are willing to delude ourselves that Delphi techniques, for example, show the future rather than our own reflected images—through a glass, darkly.

Something of this deception and its futility is caught by Van Veen, Nabokov's mime of time, who muses on the connections between past, present, and future realities:

> What we do at best (at worst we perform trivial tricks) when postulating the future, is to expand enormously the specious present causing it to permeate any amount of time with all manner of information, anticipation, and precognition. At best, the "future" is the idea of a hypothetical present based on our experience of succession, on our faith in logic and habit. Actually, of course, our hopes can no more bring it into existence than our regrets can change the past. The latter has at least the taste, the tinge, the tang, of our individual being.[32]

The essential point is to consider the images that we have of ourselves, of social reality, and of our future. Is leadership better-conceived as twelve kinds of behaviors described in terms like "consideration," "initiating structure," and "tolerance for ambiguity," or is it better seen, as Cohen and March see it, as a man sitting at the wheel of a skidding car: what he does at the moment is of marginal importance compared to other forces, which got him into the situation in the first place and which will largely determine its outcome.[33] These images of leadership are very different, and no amount of research is likely to prove either one. What we should be paying more attention to is the kind of questions we can ask and explore with the different models.

Researchers should be paying more attention to the initial theories and assumptions they have about the world and how knowledge can be developed and used. Researchers need theories and models, but they also need to spend more time looking at the theories as theories. What are the implications of seeing social reality one way as opposed to seeing it another? What are the moral consequences if we believe in one theory rather than other possible ones? How do different people at different places or times regard the same phenomena or social processes?

Answering such questions can make us more aware of the consequences of working within a specific theoretical perspective, and it may make us more tolerant of the existence of other possible perspectives. I would argue for research that attempts to look at social reality from a variety of perspectives and particularly from the perspective of different actors in a given social situation. In this approach, the researchers become interpreters of social reality, whose task is to explain the human condition to their fellow man. How that condition can be changed, or how it ought to be changed, are larger and more difficult questions to answer. But it is to these questions that researchers should turn if their work is truly to extend our knowledge.

In conclusion, let be briefly outline some other images of reality that seem to me possible and fruitful avenues for research. I have not chosen them to make any kind of exhaustive or prescriptive list. Rather, I have chosen some that stand in sharp contrast to ideas that have long dominated our field and that I would go so far as to say have suffocated alternative ideas while producing little of substantive and lasting value of their own.

Organizations in Environment

Administrative theory has long embraced the notion of the organization as a system that responds promptly and purposefully to changes in its environment. The image is that of an organism that must adapt to its environment in order to survive in it. Changes in the environment—be they changes in ideology, technology, or human values—are, therefore, felt within the organization and responded to. This benign relationship between organizations and their environments is one which is particularly congenial to the liberal, freedom-loving thought that prevails among the nations of the West. It means that the institutionss of society can generally be left alone to work out their own salvation, or if intervention is required between organizations and their environments, it is only to ensure better flows of information so that the processes of adaptation and mutual adjustment may move unimpeded to their natural end—achievement of human purposes in their best and most effective forms. Human intention, to say nothing of human passion, scarcely enters this process. Notions of human greed, duplicity, love and commitment, or sheer frailty, aging, and mortality have no place in this vision of the organization.

Stafford Beer, who speaks of cybernetics as "the science of effective organization" and who is described as an international consultant in the application of that science, denies that organizations are simply "entities."[34] They are instead:

> Dynamic viable systems, and their characteristics are in fact outputs of their organizational behavior. The variety that is pumped into them is absorbed by regulating variety, through an arrangement of amplifiers and attenuators. A system that, through this kind of exercise in requisite variety, achieves stability against *all* perturbations, is called a homeostat.[35]

Recognizing that there are a few facts that fly in the face of a theory that defines organization as being by its own nature well-adapted to its environment, Beer goes on to note that there are indeed some organizations that do not adapt to their environments and may more likely resist adaptation. He thereupon immediately adds an ad hoc proposition, which runs directly counter to the main body of this theory. As Feyerabend notes, this is exactly the same kind of solution, that Newton adopted when empirical observations ran counter to his theory of light.[36]

Beer's solution to the nonadapting organization is to identify a part of it which perversely, and against all reason, just will not play the adaptation game. And who is it that lets the theory down in this disappointing fashion? Bureaucrats, of course.

> Yet buried inside the institution is a nucleus which retains its home-ostasis by ignoring not only external change but the primary function of the institution itself. This nucleus is the special kind of homeostat that produces itself. And it is this nucleus that I call the bureaucracy. By this term I am not simply referring to paper-pushing but to an institution within the institution that exists—narcissus-like—in self-regard.[37]

So there we have it again. The data—this time in human form—have betrayed the theory. Therefore, the behavior of bureaucrats has to be identified as a special case quite distinct from the rest of us whose behavior can then still be seen as fulfilling the requirements of the main theory.

Contrary to Beer and the other systems thinkers whose ideas prevail in administrative studies, Weick takes a very different approach to the organization-environment relationship in his largely misunderstood and and long-neglected work, *The Social Psychology of Organizing*.[38] In Pondy's helpful phrase, what Weick does is to "bring mind back in."[39] He conceives organization in social-psychological terms, in terms of how people see it and its environment. There is, therefore, no necessary connection between organization and a benign environment except as ideas, intentions, and motives are held in the human mind and given reality through specific recognizable actions. Weick ignores the standard questions in organizational research: "What is real?" and, "What must organization therefore pay attention to?" He asks instead the same kind of question that William James posed in 1869. With deliberate emphasis in his text, James asked, *"Under what circumstances do we think things are real?"* and answered, "Each world *whilst it is attended to* is real." In drawing attention to James's classic essay, Goffman points out that it gives a "subversive phenomenological twist" to the reality question.[40]

Weick asks a similar subversive question about organization and environment realities and grounds his answer in George Herbert Mead's social psychology.

> ... Man notices those stimuli which permit him to do what he wants to do ...

> The predominant model of man adopted by organization theory is one in which the human is essentially reactive to the environment contingencies that occur. The environment can be inside or outside the organization, but in either case the actor essentially reacts to it as given.

However, instead of adapting to a ready-made environment, it is entirely possible that the actors *themselves* create the environment to which they adapt.[41]

I know of no educational studies beginning with the premise that the organization controls its environment and adapts it to the ends of persons within it. The idea abounds in other kinds of writing however. The behavior of the oil cartel in 1973 is but one obvious example. Someone suddenly decided that oil was in short supply and that there was no reason why those who depended on it should not pay through the nose for it. The result shifted vast wealth from one part of the world to another and had profound effects on world economies, which are still staggering in attempts to adjust to this simple idea.

In his book on the Viet Nam war, *The Best and the Brightest,* Halbertsam gives another poignant example of how organizations control their environment:

The American military and propaganda machine uncritically passed on the lies of a dying regime . . .

As the war effort began to fall apart in late 1962 and early 1963, the Military Assistance Command in Saigon set out to crush its own best officers in the field on behalf of its superiors in Washington. It was a major institutional crisis, but Washington civilians were unaware of it. It was not as if two different and conflicting kinds of military reporting were being sent to Washington, with the White House able to study the two and arbitrate the difference. The Saigon command systematically crushed all dissent from the field; the military channels did not brook dissent or negativism.[42]

Passage and Career

Gail Sheehy's *Passages*[43] reminds us that human life has phases or stages like the scenes of a play in Shakespeare's famous image. "All the world's a stage," says Jaques in *As You Like It,* "And one man in his time plays many parts," from the infant "mewling and puking in the nurse's arms," to the "last scene of all . . . sans teeth, sans eyes, sans taste, sans everything." Each stage has its typical behavior and problems. Many of the middle phases are marked by the failure and reformation of goals for life and career. The transitions from phase to phase are marked by crises, by events that the individual abruptly perceives as symbols of passage from one phase to another, from one reality to another. How people within different phases intersect within a single organization would provide a rewarding field of study. For example, students in high school are in that phase of life where all physical, intellectual, and sexual powers are at their peak. They are likely to be indifferent to these powers, however, and to think of them as permanent and of themselves as immortal. To the thirty-year-old teacher becoming aware of his balding head or her spreading hips, the contrast between their bodies and those of their students may be cause for infinite regret or disillusionment. The enormous investment of themselves into careers that they have pursued for a decade or more is no longer supportable. "Can all this effort be worth it?" they ask themselves, and begin to fear the answer is "No." They then are likely to look for new definitions of themselves and of their work.

Halbertsam sees similar differences between the perspective of officers in the field and the perspective of those who directed the war from Washington or comfortable quarters in Saigon. The men in the field were:

> . . . all combat veterans of other wars, men who had been specially selected for these slots. They were neither hawks nor doves, . . . but they wanted to win the war . . . They were in their late thirties and early forties, and they understood at least some of the political forces the Vietcong represented. Finally, they were living where the war was taking place, and they thought it was a serious business sending young men out to die, and if you were willing to do it, you also had to be willing to fight for their doubts and put your career on the line. To the Saigon command, then and later, Vietnam and the Vietnamese were never really a part of American thinking and plans; Vietnam was at best only an extension of America, of their own careers, their own institutional drives, their own self-image.[44]

Normal/Abnormal: Motivated/Deprived

James Herndon got his first job as a teacher in George Washington Junior High School where he taught English and Social Studies to grades 7, 8, and 9. Almost all the students were black and came from what the other teachers generally agreed were "deprived" backgrounds. Despite the teachers' best efforts, the average achievement in the school was two grades below standard. In a remarkable book, *The Way It Spozed To Be,* Herndon describes his experiences with his students over a period of a year. The students are irreverent, often rebellious, sometimes intellectual, and well representative of a wide range of human hopes and limitations. At the end of his year, Herndon is fired. He has thought too much about the school as an institution, seen through too many of its vanities and deceptions, and been too successful in dealing with the students as human beings. The book is full of unique insights about people and how they treat each other in school.

Herndon questions the assumption that the failure of otherwise tried-and-true educational methods is caused by the deprived backgrounds of certain students. Instead he argues that schools fail students generally, and that this failure is simply hidden from us by the adaptive and compliant behavior that some students learn from their homes. He notes that the unruly, seemingly atypical children whom his school labels "The Tribe" are not qualitatively different from other children in their reactions to school. The "normal," motivated, and well-behaved children we see in middle-class school know things The Tribe does not. But what have the two groups learned in school that is different? Seen in this light, the difference between the two kinds of students is like the difference between the so-called normal and the abnormal personality, if we believe there is no fundamental difference in quality between the two. The abnormal personality is merely revealing processes that the normal masks and controls more successfully. We may think here of Goethe's insight: There is no crime of which I could not believe myself capable. Thus, in social affairs, it is the exceptional cases, the extremes, the deviant, and the delinquent that give us insight into the dynamics at work in our own behavior.

And so Herndon comes to see The Tribe's response to school as the one that motivated children have learned to suppress. The motivated children have adapted to school, and this adaptation makes it appear that school works, that it actually teaches children things that they would not otherwise know or find out for themselves elsewhere. Herndon advances this argument:

> I began . . . to think that The Tribe's reaction to this teaching was not different, only more overt, violent, and easily seen than that of this imaginary normal or "non-deprived" child. In short that where the middle-class kids were learning enough outside of the classroom or accepting the patterns of conformity and behavior more readily and easily so as to make it seem that they were actually learning in school, The Tribe, unable to do this, was exposing the system as ineffective for everyone. It wasn't working for them, it wasn't working for anyone, I felt; only with The Tribe, it was more painful when it didn't work.[45]

Thus Herndon explores the usual assumption of school, which accepts the analogy that normal is to abnormal as motivated is to deprived. If normality and abnormality are founded basically on the same human processes, then motivation and deprivation are similarly bound together. In this perspective, it is not sufficient to say that educational methods fail because children are deprived. The issue becomes what forces shape what we call motivated and deprived children and what the school's role is in these processes.

Education as Domestic Service

Herndon is not the only observer who on the basis of personal experience concludes that schools are failing and that what goes on in them amounts at best to a cruel hoax or at worst approaches a positive evil. The list of despairing voices about school is long.[46] The evidence from hard-nosed research on the effects of schools is not much more reassuring. When researchers try to answer the question, "What does school teach children?", they are apt to say that school may account for a lot, or perhaps for nothing. The answer the researchers get depends on the way they toss their data into the computer and on the causal links that they assume to exist among their variables.[47]

Images that show the school as a spent force, as a failing institution, are now coming to the fore in realms of pure scholarly inquiry. In one of the most interesting of these, March likens contemporary schooling to the institution of domestic service in eighteenth-century England. Like contemporary educational institutions now, domestic service then involved a large part of the population, provided a major avenue for people to rise in the social and economic order, helped to set standards for beliefs, behavior, and morality, and was generally regarded as an important and necessary institution in society.[48] March's point, however, is that domestic service is no longer with us as a mainstay of society and that, like this now defunct institution, contemporary schools will go into a decline as public faith in them recedes and as alternative social forms and activities take their place. The end of this process would see schools as an "archaic curiosity" like the vanished forms of domestic service.

This decline means more for schools than the reduction in enrollments they are now experiencing as a result of falling birthrates and the changing age structure in society. The decline bespeaks rather the ebbing of faith in schools and the beginning of a search for credible forms to replace them. Even as people know now that they can feed, clothe, and dress themselves without the help of servants, so also they are coming to believe they can dispense with schools and still educate their children. We are witnessing the death of the ideas by which we organized pupils, teachers, and principals into schools. This transition recalls the earlier loss of another notion—the notion that once brought us pantries, parlors, butlers, and the upstairs maid. Seeing our schools in extremis, March says we should accept the inevitable and stop trying to keep the failing system alive. With a better grasp of these realities, we might at least plan intelligently for the future and also help the old system to die with dignity and grace.[49]

March's image of the school as an analogue to domestic service is not important as a prediction of things to come. Rather, it finds its significance as an expression of what some people believe school now is. What we believe is what we hope to make true; we are likely to strive to make others accept our beliefs as realities. The questions we should ask about such an image is, "Who holds it?" and "What are they doing about it?" Such images might then be traced in the ideological battles that swirl around school and contrasted as to their history, current impact, and apparent consequences.

The Student as Battered Child

As a final image of what schools are and what is going on in them, let me report a brief incident observed recently in a school.[50] The classroom is that of a male teacher, one who is creative but who sets high standards. The children are in both grades 5 and 6. The instructional design of the room is open, a little chaotic. There is much activity, talk, concentration, and work. The school itself is in a working-class district and many of the children come from immigrant families. The teacher is sitting at his desk working. At such times, the children may line up and wait to talk to the teacher, but sometimes they may simply approach him and begin talking directly to him, even if he is already dealing with another student. Two girls are already with the teacher when Armando approaches and leans over the front of the teacher's desk.

Teacher: [Vehemently to Armando] Will you please not be so *rude?*

Armando: [Softly] What did I do?

Teacher: Can you not see me discussing this with these girls?

Armando: [Reply inaudible]

Teacher: Do you think you're the only one in the classroom that I have to deal with?

Armando: [Reply inaudible]

Teacher: Then take your hand off my desk and get in line like anyone else.

Armando: Sir . . . they're not in line.

Teacher: I don't intend to argue the point with you—you don't understand what I'm telling you, do you? [Armando moves over and stands behind the girls]

Teacher: If you can think of a reason why I should deal with you before anyone else, I'd be pleased to hear it. [Carries on with the girls as before; Armando's face is fallen.]

Using Glaser and Strauss's methods of comparative analysis, we may ask what image this interchange suggests.[51] One which comes to mind is that of the battered child. The adult who batters a child—sometimes an infant, sometimes to death—does so when some action of the child appears unreasonable, provocative, or deliberately calculated by the child to flout the intentions of the adult. The adult assumes that both the child and the adult are operating from essentially the same assumptions about proper behavior, with similar understandings of the situation they both are in, and with equal responsibility for it. When a child behaves in a way that seems to question or ignore these assumptions and understandings of the adult, the adult—usually a man—feels perfectly justified in striking the child. Resistance by the child is interpreted as further evidence of the child's rejection of reasonable and agreed-upon rules.

What happened when Armando approached the teacher's desk? The image here suggests that the teacher strikes the child with powerful emotional blows for failing to recognize instantly the terms that the teacher is using to define the situation. This is a conversation among civilized adults, and in such a situation another adult does not rudely interrupt. That Armando did not recognize this situation under the normally free-flowing, slightly ambiguous rules of an open classroom cost him some heavy emotional penalties.

Conclusion

This chapter has dealt with ideas that determine methodology and give them meaning and validity. It argues that our ideas about the world determine what procedures we will use for creating data and what facts we will see as important and meaningful. The attempt to reach an encompassing and consistent set of theories that explain social reality and order all its so-called facts is a mistaken path. The explanation of physical realities must still contend with theoretical and logical conundrums. Even more puzzling is the interpretation and explanation of social reality. We do not know how to unravel it. From this dilemma we should conclude that we should permit and encourage alternative and even conflicting theories. From these premises, it follows that methodologies must also be open and eclectic.

In organizational and administrative studies, we have generally looked to a narrow range of theoretical ideas to bring order into the phenomena we seek to explain. And we have shifted interest away from the substantive theoretical issues and placed our reliance on the advancement and perfection of quasi-experimental and quantitative methodologies. These methodologies remain obediently within the domains and assumptions recognized by the prevailing theories, so that no challenge to these theories is possible through their approved methodologies. I have suggested some alternative images or conceptions of what organizations are and what processes go on within them. The list offered is, however, merely suggestive and heuristic. Accepting such ideas about the general processes of rational discovery and about the possible nature of organizations raises a considerable difficulty for research in the field. The methodologies appropriate to the assumptions I am making about organizations are not well developed. It seems to me, however, better to set out on these uncharted seas with whatever means insight and reason offer than to continue believing that our present methodologies offer reliable and accurate maps of what these domains contain. I am not sure how we can let the data of organizational reality speak for themselves. But believing that they can do so may be the first step in giving them voice.

Notes

1. This discussion is based on distinctions made by Malcolm Levin in, "Demystifying Program Evaluation." (Unpublished paper, Toronto, Ontario Institute for Studies in Education, 1976.)

2. Session 20.06 of the American Educational Research Association National Convention, "Questionnaires in the Study of Administration" (New York, April 1977).

3. These ways of speaking about the world are used exclusively by social scientists, although the events they describe are part of common experience. Current empirical inquiries into bureaucracy and leadership typically rely on complex statistics and advanced computer technology to find meaning in concepts that otherwise have no obvious connection to what people do. Cf. Mary Korfhage, "Leader Behavior of Academic Department Chairpersons in High and Low Paradigm Disciplines," and James Balderson, "The Bureaucratization of Teacher Behaviour Scale and the Measurement of School Organization Structure." (Papers presented to Session 20.06 of the AERA National Convention, New York, April 1977.)

4. An abridged portion of this section appeared in Thomas B. Greenfield, "Reflections on Organization Theory and the Truths of Irreconcilable Realities," *Educational Administration Quarterly* 14, no. 2 (Spring 1978):5-6. Reprinted with permission.

5. Thomas Kuhn, *The Structure of Scientific Revolutions* (Chicago: University of Chicago Press, 1962); and Paul Feyerabend, *Against Method: An Outline of an Anarchistic Theory of Knowledge* (London: New Left Books, 1975).

6. Korfhage, "Leader Behavior," p. 9. Reprinted with permission.

7. Patrick T. Terenzini and Ernest T. Pascarella, "An Assessment of the Construct Validity of the Clark-Trow Typology of College Student Subcultures," *American Educational Research Journal* 14, no. 3 (Summer 1977):234. This paper was also presented at the session referred to in note 2.

8. Richard E. Schutz, "The Control of 'Error' in Educational Experimentation," *School Review* 74, no. 2 (1966):152-153. See also McNamara's discussion of ω^2 in this book.

9. Bernard Benjamin, "Teaching Statistics and Operational Research to Civil Servants," *The American Statistician* 26, no. 4 (October 1972):23.

10. Korfhage, "Leader Behavior," p. 18. Reprinted with permission.

11. Anita A. Summers and Barbara L. Wolfe, "Which School Resources Help Learning Efficiency and Equity in Philadelphia Public Schools?," *Federal Reserve Bank of Philadelphia Business Review,* February 1976, p. 6. Reprinted with permission.

12. Ibid., pp. 24-27. Reprinted with permission.

13. See Doris Ryan and Thomas B. Greenfield, *The Class Size Question* (Toronto: Ontario Ministry of Education, 1975), pp. 232-285.

14. Paul Feyerabend, *Against Method: Outline of an Anarchistic Theory of Knowledge* (London: New Left Books, 1975), p. 58. Reprinted with permission.

15. Thomas B. Greenfield, "Theory about Organizations: A New Perspective and Its Implications for Schools," in M. Hughes, ed., *Administering*

Education: International Challenge (London: Athlone Press, 1975), pp. 71-99; and Greenfield, "Organization Theory as Ideology," *Curriculum Inquiry* 9, no. 2 (1979 forthcoming).

16. Kuhn, *Structure of Scientific Revolutions.*

17. Feyerabend, *Against Method,* pp. 69-161.

18. Ibid., pp. 124-125.

19. Ibid., pp. 154-155. Reprinted with permission.

20. Kuhn, *Structure of Scientific Revolutions,* pp. 63-64.

21. J.E.T. Eldridge, ed., *Max Weber: The Interpretation of Social Reality* (London: Michael Joseph, 1971), pp. 11-19.

22. Feyerabend, *Against Method,* p. 35.

23. Ibid.

24. Ibid., p. 46. Reprinted with permission.

25. Ronald D. Laing, *The Politics of Experience and the Bird of Paradise* (New York: Pantheon, 1967), p. 17. © R.D. Laing, 1967. Reprinted by permission of Penguin Books Ltd. See Weber's statement that the individual is the "basic unit" of social action in H.H. Gerth and C. Wright Mills, *From Max Weber: Essays in Sociology* (New York: Oxford, 1958), p. 55.

26. R.D. Laing, *Politics of Experience,* p. 53. © R.D. Laing, 1967. Reprinted by permission of Penguin Books Ltd.

27. Feyerabend, *Against Method,* p. 59.

28. Ibid., p. 60. Reprinted with permission.

29. Michael F.D. Young, "Curriculum Change: Limits and Possibilities," *Educational Studies* 1, no. 2 (June 1975):130, quoting Hardy and Wittgenstein in David Bloor, "Wittgenstein and Mannheim on the Sociology of Mathematics," *Studies in the History and Philosophy of Science* 4, no. 2 (August 1973):4. The source of the following two quotes from Hardy and Wittgenstein is given in Bloor.

30. Laing, *Politics of Experience,* p. 50. © R.D. Laing, 1967. Reprinted by permission of Penguin Books Ltd.

31. Thomas B. Greenfield, "Research on the Behaviour of Leaders: Critique of a Tradition," *Alberta Journal of Educational Research* 14, no. 1 (March 1968):55-76.

32. In Aaron Wildavsky, "Does Planning Work?" *The Public Interest* 24 (Summer 1971):104 © by National Affairs, Inc. Reprinted with permission of the publisher and the author.

33. Michael D. Cohen and James G. March, *Leadership and Ambiguity: The American College President* (New York: McGraw-Hill, 1974).

34. Stafford Beer, *Designing Freedom* (Toronto: Canadian Broadcasting Corporation Publications 1974, and London & New York: John Wiley, 1974), p. 13.

35. Ibid., p. 77. Reprinted with permission.

36. Feyerabend, *Against Method,* p. 59.

37. Beer, *Designing Freedom*, p. 78. Reprinted with permission.

38. Karl E. Weick, *The Social Psychology of Organizing* (Reading, Mass.: Addison-Wesley, 1969).

39. Louis R. Pondy and David M. Boje, "Bringing Mind Back in: Paradigm Development as a Frontier Problem in Organization Theory." (Paper, Department of Business Administration, University of Illinois, 1976.)

40. Erving Goffman, *Frame Analysis: An Essay on the Organization of Experience* (New York: Harper and Row, 1974), p. 2ff. Goffman shows the similarity between James' thinking on perception and reality, and that of later phenomenologists and interactionists.

41. Weick, *Social Psychology of Organizing*, pp. 26-27.

42. David Halbertsam, *The Best and the Brightest* (New York: Random House, 1972), p. 248. Reprinted with permission.

43. Gail Sheehy, *Passages: Predictable Crises of Adult Life* (New York: Dutton, 1976), p. 12.

44. Halbertsam, *Best and Brightest*, pp. 249-250. Reprinted with permission.

45. James Herndon, *The Way It Spozed To Be* (New York: Bantam, 1969), p. 79.

46. See Miriam Wasserman, *Demystifying School: Writings and Experience* (New York: Praeger, 1974) for a collection of experience-based reports to support this position.

47. See Frederick Mosteller and Daniel P. Moynihan, eds., *On Equality of Educational Opportunity* (New York: Random House, 1972); William G. Spady, "The Impact of School Resources on Students," in F.N. Kerlinger, ed., *Review of Research in Education*, no. 1 (Itasca, Ill.: Peacock, 1973); and L.F. Schoenfeldt, ed., "Symposium Review of Jencks et al., *Inequality*," *American Educational Research Journal* 11, no. 2 (1974):149-175.

48. James G. March, "Commitment and Competence in Educational Administration," in Lewis B. Mathew et al., eds., *Educational Leadership and Declining Enrollments* (Berkeley, Calif.: McCutchan, 1974), pp. 132, 140.

49. Ibid., p. 133.

50. I am indebted to Elaine Batcher for the record of this incident. In addition to observing it, she suggested the image of the battered child as a comparative frame for understanding it. She is studying emotion in children's experiences of a classroom. Reprinted with permission.

51. Barney G. Glaser and Anselm Strauss, *The Discovery of Grounded Theory: Strategies for Qualitative Research* (Chicago: Aldine, 1967).

10 Practical Significance and Mathematical Models in Administrative Research

James F. McNamara

An editorial inaugurating a new department in the *Educational Researcher*—"R&D in Progress in Schools"—by Richard Schutz was concerned with the difference between academic research on schools and operational research in schools.[1] According to Schutz the difference is in terms of context and communication, and not in terms of methodology or merit. Schutz notes further that context differences are rather apparent but that communication differences in the sense of availability and frequency of reporting mechanisms heavily favors research on schools. Conceding that research on schools and research in schools both can be conducted by either a school or extra-school agency, research in schools is typically an intraschool activity, and research on schools is characterized as an extra-school agency activity. Finally, Schutz points out that there is little value in transforming one kind of research into the other, although both are important to research-and-development progress in education.

Even though this analysis was initially derived for the larger educational research-and-development community, there are no compelling reasons to alter the description for operational and academic research activities in educational administration. Further, there is little question that both kinds of inquiry—academic and operational research—have potential for contributing to knowledge and theory development in educational administration. The value of academic and operational studies is of paramount import in this respect. How can the credibility of research and research findings be established? And, can the credibility of both academic and operational research be ascertained in the same way?

It is important to explore systematically the extent to which critical assessments of design and analysis shed light on the credibility of research in an area and the extent to which such assessment provides leads for knowledge production and synthesis or theory development. In this chapter I wish to demonstrate that an interest in critical appraisal of research designs and data analysis procedures should be viewed as a highly relevant research priority not only from the point of view of conducting research but also in terms of reporting research within the professional arena. It is unfortunately frequently the case that consumers of research in educational administration, and some researchers themselves, often view descriptions of research design and statistical methodology as less interesting than the discussion of final results.

In light of Schutz's distinction between research *on* schools and research *in* schools, and the corresponding need to attend more accurately to the similarities and differences of these two inquiry orientations, this chapter is divided into two major parts. The first part will concentrate on academic research. Here one approach for conducting a critical appraisal of design and method will be illustrated. The appraisal will center on a single research issue, the distinction between statistical and practical significance. In the second part, the concern will be with operational inquiries.[2] Since there is a dearth of reporting of these kinds of studies in the educational administration literature, and since there is no available precise assessment procedure (such as practical significance with academic studies), the design and analysis considerations that should guide operational research will be identified first. Then an actual operational research effort, one also illustrating a mathematical modeling approach, will be discussed and analyzed. The chapter will close with an overview of selected contemporary research issues that appear to have been given relatively low priority in some professional sectors.

Statistical and Practical Significance[3]

Two kinds of statistical tests of particular interest to researchers are those that test for the significance of relationships and those that test for the significance of differences.[4] To determine whether there are significant differences among two or more groups, researchers frequently employ a single classification analysis of variance. This set of statistical decision rules allows one to specify directly the statistical significance associated with the test of an experimental hypothesis of interest. Practical significance, on the other hand, depends on an accurate estimate of the strength of a statistical association. The practical significance assessment usually follows the design employed in tests for the significance of relationships, and often begins by asking, "How much of the variance in a criterion measure can be accounted for by a prediction measure?"

Both statistical and practical significance use the information reported for an F test. This can be illustrated using the analysis of variance (ANOVA) results reported in a study by Shetty and Carlisle, which attempted to analyze faculty perceptions regarding the success of a management by objectives (MBO) program implemented in a major land grant university.[5]

Independent Variables in the ANOVA Design

A total of 109 professors was grouped according to three professorial characteristics: professorial rank, tenure status, and length of service in the university.

The number of groups for each of these three independent variables is given in table 10-1. Hence it can be observed that tenure status has two groups. Moreover, 62 of the 109 professors participating in the study were tenured, whereas the remaining 47 participants were not.

Criterion Variable in the ANOVA Design

To formulate a single criterion variable Shetty and Carlisle first solicited faculty perceptions regarding the success of the MBO program on ten dimensions of interest. These ten responses were then averaged to provide a single indicator for each of the 109 faculty members.

To examine the relationships between various faculty characteristics and perceived success of the MBO program, three ANOVA tests were developed using the null hypothesis of no difference among means. For all three tests, statistically significant differences were reported. These results are also shown in table 10-1. Following an obvious trend for most statistical studies reported in the *Educational Administration Quarterly*, the authors' decision to reject the null hypotheses terminated the formal statistical analysis, and they proceeded to describe what they believed to be the relationship between perceived program success and each faculty characteristic.

Table 10-1
Relationship between Faculty Type and Success of MBO Program

Faculty Type	N	Mean Scores	Standard Deviation	F Ratio
Professorial rank				
Professor	24	3.051	.497	7.97
Associate professor	29	3.181	.532	$(df = 3,105)$
Assistant professor	41	3.542	.592	$(p < 0.001)$
Instructor	15	2.864	.386	
Tenure				
Tenured	62	3.160	.500	3.07
Nontenured	47	3.356	.665	$(df = 1,107)$
				$(p < 0.10)$
Length of service				
1-3 years	32	3.416	.607	4.59
4-7 years	34	3.335	.537	$(df = 2,106)$
7 years or more	43	3.045	.552	$(p < 0.02)$

Source: Y.K. Shetty and H.M. Carlisle, "Application of Management by Objectives in a University Setting," *Educational Administration Quarterly* 10, no. 2 (Spring 1974). Their corrected table appears in vol. 10, no. 3 (Autumn 1974). Reprinted with permission.

ANOVA Designs: Rejection of the hypotheses of no differences between population means is tantamount to the assertion that the independent variables do have some statistical association with the criterion scores. However, the occurrences of statistically significant differences say nothing at all about the strength of the association between independent variables and the criterion of interest, and in no sense can one infer from only these results that important degrees of association necessarily exist.

If the formal statistical analysis in the Shetty and Carlisle study had not been terminated immediately following the rejection of the hypotheses of no differences, they might have used the ANOVA results of table 10-1 to formulate several questions that influence the relationship between practical and statistical significance. Consider just the following:

1. How does one relate the F ratio of 7.97 obtained for the analysis of professorial rank with the F ratio of 3.07 for the tenure data?

2. Does the larger F test value of 7.97 necessarily imply that a more important degree of association exists between the independent variable of professorial rank and the criterion variable indicating the perceived success of the MBO program?

3. How significant is the level of significance at which the null hypotheses were rejected for these variables? (How much more significant is the test value for professorial rank, $p < 0.001$, as compared to the test value of $p < 0.02$ for length of service?)

There are several statistical techniques that can be used to evaluate practical significance concerns such as those suggested in these three questions.[6] Assuming that Shetty and Carlisle were investigating a defensible criterion variable, their analysis might begin by suggesting that each of the three independent variables is practically significant to the degree that it accounts for the variance of the dependent variable. If one of their independent variables accounts for all the variance in criterion scores, it affords a perfect basis for the prediction of the criterion variable. If one of their independent variables accounts for none of the variance of the dependent variable, it has no utility in predicting the dependent variable.

Index Values for Practical Significance

One of the most frequently applied statistical techniques for estimating the proportion of the variance of the dependent variable (Y) accounted for by a given independent variable (X) is a statistical index called ω^2 (Greek omega, squared). Viewed either as a proportion of variance in Y accounted for by X or as a relative reduction of uncertainty, this index, ω^2, can assume values ranging from zero to unity, and is similar to two other indices, the intraclass correlation and the correlation ratio. When ω^2 is 1.0, the independent variable correlates exactly with the dependent variable. On the other hand, when ω^2 is zero, the knowledge of the independent variable does not reduce in any way uncertainty about the dependent variable. In general, the higher the value of ω^2, the greater the practical significance for the association of X and Y.

For a univariate analysis of variance with one independent variable,

$$\text{est. } \omega^2 = \frac{SS(B) - (k-1) \cdot MS(W)}{SS(T) + MS(W)} \tag{10.1}$$

where $SS(B)$ = sum of squares between groups

   $SS(T)$ = sum of squares total

   $MS(W)$ = mean square within groups

   k = number of levels of the independent variable

This formula allows direct estimation of ω^2 from the summary table of ANOVA results. In the case where a complete summary table of ANOVA results is not presented, it is usually possible to construct the needed information from available data.

Constructing ANOVA Tables: It is not uncommon for tables of results to show only sample size, means, standard deviations, and F ratios. A review of table 10-1 information on the Shetty and Carlisle study provides an excellent example of this form of reporting. When at least this amount of information is provided, the ω^2 estimate can be derived using the following method. Let $i = 1, 2, \ldots, k$ represent each group. By definition:

$$\bar{X} = \Sigma[N(i) \cdot \bar{X}(i)]/N \tag{10.2}$$

$$SS(B) = \Sigma[N(i) \cdot [\bar{X}(i) - \bar{X}]^2] \tag{10.3}$$

$$SS(W) = \Sigma[\Sigma x^2(i)] \tag{10.4}$$

where

$$\Sigma x^2(i) = [N(i) - 1] \cdot S^2(i)$$

$$MS(B) = SS(B)/(k-1) \tag{10.5}$$

$$MS(W) = SS(W)/(N\text{-}k) \tag{10.6}$$

$$SS(T) = SS(B) + SS(W) \tag{10.7}$$

$$F = MS(B)/MS(W) \tag{10.8}$$

and where $\bar{X}(i)$ = mean of observations in group i (group mean)

$\overline{X}$ = mean of all N observations (grand mean)

N = number of observations in ANOVA design

$N(i)$ = number of observations in group i

$\Sigma x^2(i)$ = the sum of squared deviations for all observations in group i

$S(i)$ = the standard deviation for all observations in group i

$MS(B)$ = mean square between groups

and other terms are defined as given in equation 10.1.

For example, if one wished to estimate ω^2 for the F test associated with length of service, substitution of information from table 10-1 produces

$$\overline{X} = \frac{32(3.42) + 34(3.34) + 43(3.05)}{32 + 34 + 43} = 3.25 \qquad (10.2a)$$

Continuing,

$$SS(B) = 32(0.17)^2 + 34(0.08)^2 + 43(0.20)^2 = 2.86 \qquad (10.3a)$$

$$SS(W) = 31(0.61)^2 + 33(0.54)^2 + 42(0.55)^2 = 33.86 \qquad (10.4a)$$

$$MS(B) = 2.86/2 = 1.43 \qquad (10.5a)$$

$$MS(W) = 33.86/106 = 0.32 \qquad (10.6a)$$

$$SS(T) = 33.86 + 2.86 = 36.72 \qquad (10.7a)$$

$$F = 1.43/0.32 = 4.50 \qquad (10.8a)$$

The obtained F value of 4.50 compares closely with the F value of 4.59 shown in table 10-1. Applying equation 10.1 with this ANOVA information yields:

$$\text{est. } \omega^2 = \frac{2.86 - (2)(0.32)}{36.72 + 0.32} = .0599 \qquad (10.1a)$$

In something less than lay parlance, this figure says that the independent variable, length of service, accounts for about 6 percent of the criterion variance. If these calculations were repeated for the independent variable of professorial rank, the estimated ω^2 value would be 0.1611, which suggests that approximately 16 percent of the variation in the criterion scores can be accounted for by the independent variable, professorial rank.

An Alternate Formula: The amount and type of information represented in table 10-1 are not, however, always reported. Summary tables in any form are often replaced in organization inquiries with only a report of F values and the appropriate degrees of freedom for the test [for example, $F(2,106, 4.59, p < 0.02)$], making the previous derivation of values seem only an entertaining intellectual exercise. Even for these cases, however, ω^2 can still be estimated directly using an alternative form of the basic formula.

In a single classification ANOVA we have

$$F = MS(B)/MS(W), \qquad (10.9)$$

which can also be written

$$F = \frac{SS(B)/df(1)}{SS(W)/df(2)} \qquad (10.10)$$

where $df(1)$ equals $(k-1)$, $df(2)$ equals $(N-k)$, and N is the total number of observations in the test. Solving 10.10 yields

$$SS(B) = F \cdot (k-1) \cdot MS(W) \qquad (10.11)$$

By definition

$$SS(W) = (N-k) \cdot MS(W) \qquad (10.12)$$

$$SS(T) = SS(B) + SS(W) \qquad (10.13)$$

Using equations 10.11 and 10.12, equation 10.13 can be rewritten as:

$$SS(T) = F \cdot (k-1) \cdot MS(W) + (N-k) \cdot MS(W) \qquad (10.14)$$

Substituting for $SS(B)$, $SS(T)$, and $MS(W)$ in 10.1 produces

$$\text{est. } \omega^2 = \frac{F \cdot (k-1) \cdot MS(W) - (k-1) \cdot MS(W)}{F \cdot (k-1) \cdot MS(W) + (N-k) \cdot MS(W) + MS(W)} \qquad (10.15)$$

Factoring out $MS(W)$ from 10.15 yields

$$\text{est. } \omega^2 = \frac{F \cdot (k-1) - (k-1)}{F \cdot (k-1) + (N-k) + 1} \qquad (10.16)$$

Where F is the numerical value for the ANOVA test, N is the total number of individuals in the sample, and k is defined as in equation 10.1.

For the case $F(2,106, 4.59, p < 0.02)$—which happens to be the information for the length of service variable in table 10-1—this formula produces

$$\text{est. } \omega^2 = \frac{(3-1)(4.59) - (3-1)}{(3-1)(4.59) + (109-3) + 1} = 0.0618 \qquad (10.16a)$$

Allowing for round-off error, it can be seen that this value for ω^2 is the same estimate that was derived by using equation 10.1. For the professorial rank data with $F(3,105, 7.97, p < 0.001)$, the formula yields

$$\text{est. } \omega^2 = \frac{(4-1)(7.97) - (4-1)}{(4.1)(7.97) + (109-4) + 1} = 0.1611, \qquad (10.16b)$$

which again corresponds to the estimates found when equation 10.1 was applied.

t-test: In the special case where $K = 2$, single classification ANOVA results are often expressed in terms of a pooled variance t-test value rather than an F ratio. In this case $t^2 = F$, and either 10.16 or the more familiar formula found in most elementary research and evaluation texts can be used. It is:

$$\text{est. } \omega^2 = \frac{t^2 - 1}{t^2 + N(1) + N(2) - 1} \qquad (10.17)$$

Since $N(1) + N(2) = N$ and $t^2 = F$, the equivalence of 10.16 and 10.17 for a single classification ANOVA can be seen in the substitution given below. Substituting $k = 2$ in 10.16, we get

$$\text{est. } \omega^2 = \frac{(2-1)F - (2-1)}{(2-1)F + (N-2) + 1} = \frac{t^2 - 1}{t^2 + N - 1} \qquad (10.18)$$

Using the tenure variable case with $F(1,107, 3.07, p < 0.10)$, the equivalence of 10.16 and 10.17 can be illustrated as follows:

$$\text{est. } \omega^2 = \frac{(2-1)(3.07) - (2-1)}{(2-1)(3.07) + (109-2) + 1} = \frac{3.07 - 1}{3.07 + 62 + 47 - 1} = 0.0186$$

The Advantage of the Alternate Formula: The advantage of 10.16 is that it is applicable in all cases and does not require the reconstruction of a complete ANOVA table. The reduced time and effort also means fewer opportunities for miscalculations.

A Reassessment of the Data

How does the addition of information regarding practical significance affect the interpretation of results? The answer to this question can be illustrated using any of the variables from table 10-1. For instance, the relationship between tenure status and the dependent variable is viewed as significant statistically ($p < 0.10$). However, the estimated ω^2 value of 0.0186 suggests that approximately 2 percent of the variation in the criterion of interest is associated with variation in the independent variable.

An alternative, but consistent, way to interpret these results is to view ω^2 as a measure of the relationship between being a member of a particular group (tenured or nontenured) and having a particular level of perceived success. For this interpretation, the ω^2 value of 0.0186 indicates that a knowledge of group membership tells us virtually nothing about expected level of perceived success. Thus, despite the findings of statistical significance, the conclusion of no important degree of association or practical significance would appear justified.

An immediate advantage of ω^2 is that it provides a more accurate representation of association between variables in the Shetty and Carlisle study than does the magnitude of the F ratios reported in table 10-1. This increased differentiation of statistical tests results (which formerly could be considered homogeneous only in the sense that they were all "significant") communicates a great deal more information about experimental test results.[7] This advantage can be illustrated by returning to the three questions raised earlier:

1. How does one relate the F ratio of 7.97 obtained for the analysis of professorial rank with the F ratio of 3.07 for the tenure data?

2. Does the larger F test value of 7.97 necessarily imply that a more important degree of association exists between the independent variable of professorial rank and the criterion variable indicating the perceived success of the MBO program?

In answer to both questions, although the F ratio for professorial rank is approximately 2.6 times that associated with the tenure data, this ratio is misleading and inappropriate for direct comparisons. The presence of different numbers of degrees of freedom rules out the comparison of one F ratio with another.

3. How "significant" is the level of significance at which the null hypotheses were rejected for these variables? (How much more significant is the test value for professorial rank, $p < 0.001$, as compared to the test value of $p < 0.02$ for length of service?)

Regarding probability levels associated with the F tests, is the F ratio for professorial rank, $p < 0.001$, twenty times more significant than the F ratio for length of service, $p < 0.02$? That is, is the independent variable of professorial rank twenty times more effective in predicting the same criterion variable?

Again, although a fair-sized body of folklore would suggest that such is the case, this is also an inappropriate comparison on which to base interpretations.

The Educational Administration Quarterly Analysis

Since the statistical analyses of several studies published over the past twelve years in the *Educational Administration Quarterly* (*EAQ*) follow the path taken by Shetty and Carlisle, it should be of interest to describe briefly this sequence of events.

Richard Schutz characterized the path in this manner:

> The logic in making the test of the null hypothesis is as follows. If the obtained F ratio exceeds the tabled ratio, the experimenter rejects the null hypothesis and infers that the independent variable did indeed have an effect. If the obtained F value does not exceed the tabled value; the experimenter fails to reject the null hypothesis; since the effects of the independent variable do not exceed those which could be expected to occur by chance 95 or 99 times out of 100, he infers that the independent variable had no effect. One's decision concerning the rejection of the null hypothesis customarily terminates the formal statistical analysis. That is, one finishes the "results" section and enters the "discussion." If the obtained F or t ratio is "significant," there is something to discuss. If the ratio doesn't "achieve significance," one is very disappointed, and it is doubtful that the report of the research will ever be published.
>
> The subordination of error variance to an incidental role and the concomitant elevation of final test of the hypothesis has had an unfortunate effect on the behavior of educational researchers. Despite the lip service that has been devoted to the distinction between statistical significance and practical significance, our statistical procedures have simply not mediated any systematic method of handling practical significance.[8]

To provide some indication of how ω^2 can be used to illustrate the consequences of basing the interpretation of data entirely on significance testing, each article in the first twelve volumes of the *EAQ* that reported an ANOVA or t test was examined. For each test that resulted in a rejection of the null hypothesis of no difference, the ω^2 was calculated as a means to measure the practical significance associated with these rejection decisions.[9] A tabulation of these calculations appears in table 10-2.

If this analysis reflects a more general trend for academic research either conducted in or endorsed by educational administration, the results are discouraging. This experience was informative, however; it did reveal some general characteristics for studies that have appeared in *EAQ* over the past years. These include:

Table 10-2
Practical Significance Tests for Findings Reported in the
Educational Administration Quarterly

Omega Squared Ranges		Volumes of the EAQ				Percent (1-12)
		(1-6)	*(7-11)*	*(12)*	*(1-12)*	
.0001	.0099	52	8	16	76	26.39
.0100	.0199	15	7	26	48	16.67
.0200	.0299	4	6	14	24	8.33
.0300	.0399	3	9	4	16	5.56
.0400	.0499	2	9	6	17	5.90
.0500	.0599	4	1	1	6	2.08
.0600	.0699	1	5		6	2.08
.0700	.0799	1	6	3	10	3.47
.0800	.0899	4	6	4	14	4.86
.0900	.0999	1	1	3	5	1.74
.1000	.1999	5	15	20	40	13.89
.2000	.2999	1	12	3	16	5.56
.3000	.3999	2	1	1	4	1.38
.4000	.4999	1	2		3	1.04
.5000	.5999	1			1	0.35
.6000	.6999	1			1	0.35
.7000	.7999		1		1	0.35
Number of tests		98	89	101	288	100.00
(Number of studies		7	14	10	31)	

1. Only one of the thirty-one articles using either t or F tests reported ω^2 values. No other statistical method of estimating variance percentages was applied in the thirty-one articles.

2. Three additional articles failed to report t or F information necessary to calculate ω^2. In all three cases this included a failure to specify the degrees of freedom associated with the test. Hence, it is not possible to estimate directly the extent to which the independent variables in these three studies accounted for variance in the corresponding dependent variables.

3. At least 60 percent of the formal statistical analyses followed almost to the letter the sequence of events characterized by Schutz.

4. An interest in replicating previously published *EAQ* studies was not detected.

5. A rationale for decisions regarding the selection of an appropriate sampling procedure and the determination of sample size, as well as a specification of how the investigator dealt with nonsampling errors such as nonresponse bias, were noticeably absent in a majority of the thirty-one articles.

6. Also noticeably absent from the explanations of statistical analyses were any informative comments on the power of specific F tests—that is, an integrated treatment of the consequences associated with both Type I and Type II errors.

7. In some ANOVA studies the same independent variable is used to assess

significant differences for fifteen or more distinct criterion variables, without any reference to the possibility that one or more of the resulting individual F test differences might be due merely to chance since the set of F tests is not statistically independent. For example, if one uses the same independent variable for testing at the .05 alpha level significant differences associated with ten distinct criterion variables, the probability of finding at least one significant difference (among the set of ten independent tests) that is due to chance alone is $1-(1-0.05)^{10}$, or approximately 37 percent. (The situation with respect to dependent tests is even worse in this regard.)

8. In some cases, a series of n single classification, univariate ANOVA tests should have been replaced by a single n-way univariate design that provides explicit opportunities to explore interactions as well as main effects.[10]

9. Opportunities to use multivariate ANOVA designs or other multivariate statistical methods were also bypassed.

The distributions presented in table 10-2 lead to the following general comments:

1. The number of studies using ANOVA designs appears to be increasing over time. Twenty-four of the thirty-one studies applying these designs were published in the second 6 volumes.

2. Approximately one-third of the statistically significant test results, as well as one-third of the studies using ANOVA designs, appeared in volume 12 alone.

3. In volume 12 approximately 56 percent of the statistically significant differences had a ω^2 of less than 0.03. Thus, despite the findings of statistical significance, the conclusion of no important degree of association or practical significance would appear justified in almost all of the fifty-six cases.

4. If it is correct to assume that each study was investigating defensible criterion variables, and we link this assumption with the fact that, over the past twelve years, 63 percent of the statistically significant results reported in the *EAQ* have a ω^2 value of less than 0.05, it is entirely possible that several of the already published discussion sections in these thirty-one articles should be rewritten or at least viewed with caution.[11]

Classifying Practical Significance Results

If a consensus could be reached that the relationship between an independent and dependent variable would have a practical significance only when ω^2 was at least 0.10, then volume 12 would yield twenty-four practically significant results and seventy-seven results that did not meet this criterion.

If the consensus value for deserving a high rather than low practical significance status required ω^2 to be greater than 0.20, then all issues of volume 12 would have four high (and ninety-seven low) practically significant test results. If it were agreed to set the cut-off value at ω^2 greater than 0.299, then only 1 of the 101 results reported in table 10-2 would meet practical significance status.

This hypothetical classification illustration leads to two questions. First, what is an appropriate ω^2 value for the test of an experimental hypothesis to yield a practically significant result? In most educational research studies the use of practical significance indices are rare. In one national-based EAQ study, however, the author imposed an ω^2 requirement of at least 0.10 for practical significance.[12] In that study all statistically significant tests failed to reach the established criterion limit. Accordingly, the researcher's report attributed the statistically significant differences to sample size rather than to any actual strong association between variables. In general, it is safe to say that the required ω^2 value for practical significance probably is best determined by the nature of the study and the variables involved.[13] However, ω^2 values should still be reported, and authors should inform their readers as to their position on ω^2 requirements for practical significance associated with each hypothesis tested in a study.

Second, how often do readers mistakenly assess the significance of studies based on results given in EAQ? This question has no direct answer. There is no way of determining how often the EAQ is consulted or cited as a reference for various decision situations encountered either in field settings or in theory development and the design of research studies. Although some researchers might argue that research findings presented in the EAQ are almost never used to reach critical decisions in actual organizational settings, the fact still remains that we do not have adequate direct means for estimating how often administrators on state, local, and national levels make use of EAQ findings. This is true particularly when a discussion section provides an opportunity to duplicate and circulate research conclusions that support an administrator's viewpoint or preferred alternative.[14]

Theory development and research studies almost always involve the preparation of a review of related research. Here again, there is no readily available direct evidence on the extent to which theorists and researchers use the findings of EAQ studies in their work. Moreover, when they do include EAQ studies, it is difficult to gauge accurately the extent to which they attempt to relate statistical and practical significance as a means to improve their critical assessments of prior research findings. Hence, it is possible not only that EAQ articles might be used extensively in current reviews of research, but also that this use is largely restricted to merely referencing or counting the number of statistically significant differences on criterion variables of interest.

Implications and Future Directions

Most researchers agree that ω^2 communicates a good deal more information than the traditional F value. It provides a measure of the strength of an effect regardless of sample size and, thus, provides a more accurate representation of the degree of prediction. Moreover, since ω^2 is calculated directly from ANOVA results, it creates no difficulty for the investigator.

With this in mind, ω^2 should be reported in professional journal articles, reviews of research, technical reports, and dissertations. Also, ω^2 values should be in the forefront when any researcher finishes the results section of his or her study and enters the section on discussion of significant findings.

Whereas the foregoing treatment of practical significance has centered almost exclusively on the application of ω^2 as a means to determine the importance and magnitude of differences identified in standard statistical tests of significance, the purpose of this analysis is not to imply that this index represents a statistical procedure just recently entered in the educational research literature. In fact, the ω^2 was used by Schutz in 1966 to assess the practical significance of research findings reported in educational research journals. However, the analysis does illustrate that in 1978—twelve years later—this rather straightforward and uncomplicated approach (or its equivalent) still has not found its way into the research literature published in the *EAQ*. Moreover, it is safe to say that the value of ω^2 analysis has been frequently overlooked in recent issues of other educational journals.[15]

Professors who train future researchers might initiate one or more of the following activities to demonstrate that ω^2 values communicate a good deal more information, and thus provide educational researchers with more accurate measures of the relative reduction of uncertainty that can be directly linked with particular studies.

In seminars devoted to research design, an interesting project might be to conduct a practical significance (ω^2) analysis on all recently completed doctoral dissertations. When classification errors (low ω^2 values for highly significant difference tests) are encountered, students could be asked to prepare revised interpretations and discussions of dissertation results. Comparisons of original and revised versions provide excellent means to illustrate the consequences of viewing tests of significance as the ultimate objective.

In seminars devoted to theory development or knowledge synthesis, professors should encourage students to compute and include ω^2 values (or their equivalent) for each research study reviewed. In the past, probability values (for example, $p < 0.01$) have generally been used to support theories. The intent there would be to suggest that ω^2 values rather than probability values should be used to indicate the satisfaction students have with elements of their theoretical framework.

If professors are able to locate current operational studies where the probability values associated with mean difference ANOVA tests were highly significant but the ω^2 values were extremely low, they might use a seminar group to conduct an organizational analysis (case study) to determine how administrators and other policy-making groups in the organization actually used the results of significant-differences tests in subsequent decisions (that is, reporting results to the public, creating new priority issues, preparing press releases, changing teacher assignments, or implementing new instructional designs). Analysis of an actual organizational example and the real consequences that are uncovered in that setting may be far more convincing to graduate students, whose immediate professional interests center primarily on practice rather than theory development and verification.

All three of these suggested alternatives are designed to give students, as well as professors, the confidence to note the following. When highly significant ANOVA test results are accompanied by extremely low ω^2 values, one would do well to follow the advice of McNeil and his colleagues who interpret this situation as "knowing something for sure about very little."[16]

Mathematical Models in Operational Research

Since operational research findings are not reported in the educational administration literature, it is not feasible to conduct an extensive appraisal of the value of existing operational inquiries. Further, statistical approaches are not available for assessing the credibility of findings and analyses in these studies generally, as is the case with academic inquiries. This is indeed unfortunate, since a comparative approach with both kinds of research would contribute valuable insights on the differences and similarities of these two research orientations within the profession. However, it is important to maintain an interest in the validity of operational inquiries in terms of both design and the interpretation of research findings. The position taken here is that criteria for demonstrating the value of research results are ultimately intuitive, cannot be derived from some meta criterion, should include but extend well beyond the variance issue referenced in the earlier discussion of ω^2, are likely to change when the context and reporting requirements are altered, and, more important, cannot be separated from concerns to improve methodology used in either operational or academic research.

Operational research is expected to provide reliable and valid information that is useful to teachers, administrators, board members, and clients of the school. This necessitates a variety of considerations not ordinarily directly relevant in academic research. Moreover, the context in which operational research is conducted requires special attention to the goodness-of-fit between methodological techniques and evaluation problems.

Any attempt to accurately describe the similarities and differences between operational and academic research orientations requires one to explicitly address this goodness-of-fit issue, especially as it applies to the development of relevant mathematical models. Accordingly, I will identify several research considerations that should affect directly the construction of operational research models, and then I will briefly describe an actual operational research effort that illustrates how one might use a mathematical-modeling approach in a public school district resource allocation study will be provided.

Model Construction

Research problems encountered in constructing mathematical models are no different from those encountered in developing other types of operational research projects. Bernstein identifies the following:

> While all procedures need to fit the demands of the research problem, in evaluation research certain aspects become particularly problematic for purposes of design and data analysis. These include (1) specification of the research question(s) to be addressed; (2) selection of the appropriate population to test the hypotheses; (3) selection, assignment, and maintenance of subjects in treatment categories; (4) designation of a system that provides for early estimates of immediate program effects; later, more conclusive estimates of intermediate effects; and estimates of long-range effects; and (5) selection of data sources and/or analytic procedures that can serve as correctives for defective design strategies arising from constraints on the research.[17]

The specification of research questions can be contrasted as follows. In academic research, the researcher frequently begins with one or more criterion variables and hypothesizes about factors that would predict these variables. To deduce hypothesized relationships, one usually examines theoretical statements about the phenomenon of interest. In operational research, the procedure is often reversed. A researcher begins with an independent variable such as a program, a set of actual teaching strategies, or a particular intervention, and to assess how the independent variable affects a set of more or less vaguely identified goals.

This reversal presents a variety of demands. For example, the researcher often needs to learn from persons administering the actual program what the specific goals are. It is also necessary to specify the level of changes in the goal measures that will be relevant apart from whether such changes are statistically significant. It is further necessary to identify the important program of intervention inputs, to assess the degree to which persons administering the program or intervention agree with that definition of inputs, and to assess the degree to which the program of intervention is implemented in the actual environment in accordance with the definitions.

Once a researcher has satisfactorily specified the research questions and identified both criterion and independent variables, the next task is to select the appropriate study population and corresponding sample. In academic research, the sample is normally defined according to its appropriateness for testing hypothesized relationships. In operational research, the sample (population) has already been defined by virtue of its relationship to the program or intervention being evaluated. Hence, the task is not to determine an appropriate sample, but rather to determine how the available sample can be used and dealt with analytically.

Critical in this sense with operational inquiries are problems such as student attrition and attendance in inner city schools. Researchers also often encounter design problems associated with teacher turnover and multiple treatment effects when students are participating in several programs or interventions. The implication here is the following: In the initial stages of planning a research design for an operational inquiry, the need is not only to assess where the available sample violates necessary assumptions (for example, equivalent rates of attrition and student attendance patterns), but also to construct analytic procedures that provide some correction for defects resulting from the use of a less than optimal design. When the design is specified in the form of a mathematical model, corrective measures such as poststratification (from sampling theory) and alternative forms of covariance analysis are frequently applied.

Resource Allocation: An Arena for
Operational Inquiries

Since the release of the Equality of Educational Opportunity Survey in 1966, an increasing number of studies have been conducted on factors affecting the learning of children.[18] This includes the efforts of economists, who have attempted to estimate the changes in different learning outcomes that can be linked with changes in the level of specific school resources and inputs. In this type of resource allocation study, multiple linear regression techniques are the most commonly used functional form to estimate the relationships between outcomes and inputs. The largest number of these studies are based on available samples and do not permit random assignment of students to appropriate treatments to control for other factors that affect achievement.[19]

Efforts to reduce the threats to validity and to improve the methods of public school resource allocation studies have led to the following design considerations identified by Richard Murnane: using the individual child as the unit of observation, using longitudinal information on school inputs (including detailed information on each child's teachers), controlling for prior achievement, estimating different structures or models for different categories of children, including as many outputs of the schooling process as is possible, and separating peer group influences from those of the child's own background.[20]

It is extremely difficult for any single research project to satisfy all these conditions. This is especially true in conducting urban school district resource allocation studies, where outcome measures are seldom available in a convenient form linking individual student progress data over several academic years with relevant classroom variables, peer effects, teacher characteristics, treatment conditions, and background variables.

An Example: A recent study that illustrates the use of mathematical-modeling in operational research is one conducted by Murnane.[21] He examined the impact that school resources have on the cognitive achievement of black inner city children in elementary schools in New Haven, Connecticut.

Based on the application of multiple linear regression, his analysis was directed toward two general resource allocation concerns. The first part of the analysis initially examined the effect of the classroom as a whole on the achievement of children. Then the effects of specific classroom-related variables were considered. The second part of the analysis examined the relationships between characteristics of teachers and their effectiveness in teaching certain subjects or certain types of children.

The identification of variables included in the analysis, and the specification of the relationships among these variables, were summarized in thirty hypotheses.[22] The hypotheses were developed to represent the effects of school resources on learning outcomes and to reflect a more direct emphasis on important administrative decisions such as the hiring and placing of teachers and the determining of which children shall be classmates.

For analytic purposes, three samples were developed from available data on two cohorts of students. Cohort one, a third-grade group, was studied for a single academic year. Cohort two was examined for the period they were in second grade and third grade. The measures of cognitive achievement were standard scores on Metropolitan Achievement tests in reading and mathematics.

Murnane used three regressions. The three models and the logic for each can be summarized as follows. In the first model, year-end achievement was dependent on prior achievement, background characteristics, and school attendance. The assumption of this model was that the effect of a year of schooling was independent of the school and classroom environments. In the second model, year-end achievement was dependent on the child's classroom and the variables in the first model. This model's assumption was that the classroom environment was critical to the effect of a year of schooling. In the third model, year-end achievement was dependent on the school the child attended and the variables in the other two models. (The second model is, therefore, more disaggregated than the third. If there were no differences among classrooms, however, the second model collapses into the third model.) The assumption of the third model was that the school environment was critical to the effect of a year of schooling.[23]

The first of Murnane's hypotheses was the general hypothesis of the study.[24] It explored this question: If one wants to predict a child's achievement at the end of a school year, and one already knows the child's achievement at the beginning of the school year and certain characteristics of the child's background, is it also important to know to which classroom the child is assigned for the school year? The second and third hypotheses were included to investigate the breakdown of differences among classrooms into intraschool and interschool differences. Essentially the second and third hypotheses allowed for the testing of the second and third models.

For all three samples in the Murnane study, the first hypothesis was rejected at the 0.01 significance level for mathematics. The second and third hypotheses were rejected at the 0.05 level for all cases.[25] These findings give strong support to the hypothesis that significant quality differences among classroom environments do exist. Moreover, the results of this study suggest that the differences among classrooms consist of both differences within the schools and differences among schools. The interested reader is encouraged to examine the research report in more detail.

It should be noted that the Murnane investigation exhibited the following desirable characteristics from among those identified earlier: the individual child was the unit of observation, longitudinal information on reading and mathematics was employed, detailed information on individual classrooms was matched with student data, interviews were used to frame hypotheses, and three samples of students were analyzed. Hence, there was an attempt to use available district records to examine the replicability of research results.

Implications: The substantive results of the Murnane study are probably of principal interest to decision-makers or those who allocate resources within the New Haven schools. One reason this might be the case is the fact that school district studies analyze data regarding the *effectiveness of a particular program of intervention in a particular setting.* Given the unique characteristics of a district's approach to instruction, its instructional environment may not match that found in any other district.

However, the report does provide public school administrators with an excellent example of how fact-finding and exploratory analysis in a single district might be structured, using mathematical-modeling and a regression framework to integrate and relate several sources of information likely to rest in different school ledgers, periodic reports, or separate computerized information files. If this general approach to analysis has the possibility of adding a new dimension to current administrative inquiries, then we will most likely need to reexamine ways existing school district record and reporting systems can be modified, since most of the information for these regression studies still require extensive manual data collection efforts. This appears to follow even in school districts currently maintaining elaborate computerized information systems.

On this point Hanushek makes the following observations based on a study of a relatively large urban school system in California:

Major school systems across the country routinely collect and store enormous amounts of data about the educational process, but these data are seldom processed in a way that is helpful to decision making in the school systems. The central lesson to be learned from the single system analysis . . . was how existing data collected by most school systems could be tabulated to provide an evaluation tool to decision makers. The heavy investment by local schools in data processing equipment and management information systems has largely been directed at improving accounting within schools; too little effort has been directed at improving decision making about the educational process itself. Without excessive effort, local school systems could develop supplemental evaluation information to aid in hiring teachers and deciding among programs.[26]

In his analysis of research-and-development in progress in schools, Richard Schutz noted that operational research is typically an intraschool agency initiative, whereas academic research is usually an extraschool agency initiative. The Murnane report represents one exception to that tendency in operational research.

Future Directions

The differences between research *on* schools and research *in* schools represent an essential consideration in assessing what factors affect the quality of research and in evaluating individual studies. The appraisal of selected *EAQ* studies (academic inquiries) employing the consideration of practical significance called into question the adequacy of statistical analyses and, thus, the value of these studies. Criteria for determining the credibility of operational research were viewed as intuitive and inseparable from concerns to improve methodology.

Since the intents of this appraisal of inquiry are to focus on research problems and questions and to explore new directions for improving inquiries in the area of decision-oriented research, it seems appropriate that this chapter should conclude by suggesting some future directions for the use of quantitative methods in educational administration. To address this issue, the 1973 University Council for Educational Administration (UCEA) monograph, *Quantitative Analysis in Educational Administration Preparation Programs*, was reexamined with a view to how its recommendations might be extended to take advantage of insights and directions encountered in more recent literature.[27]

Research on Schools

If one's interest is primarily oriented toward conducting research *on* schools or exploring recent developments in design and analysis, the following deserves investigation.

Theory Construction and Verification: Most writings on theory in educational administration appear to agree on the need for more adequate theories, but there is less consensus on what strategies would be most useful in constructing such theories. In the past several years, the literature in the social and behavioral sciences has contributed to the understanding of the process of moving from the verbal theories that abound in organizational studies to more rigorous formulations in terms of mathematical models.[28] This approach includes: (1) the possibility of causal analysis and inference without experimental manipulation, which is critically important in organizational studies where political, practical, and ethical problems narrow the possibilities for implementing classical experiments; (2) the opportunity to first construct causal diagrams and flowgraph analyses and then to specify the corresponding structural equations; and, finally, (3) the means to estimate and evaluate these theoretical systems from the standpoint of testing their correspondence with reality. In light of such developments, the author holds that it is both possible and desirable to invest in a sustained effort aimed toward a closer integration of theory-building with quantitative empirical research and mathematical-modeling.

Applications of Mathematical Models: A careful examination of current research in the social sciences suggests that a wide variety of statistical methods and mathematical techniques are applied to a number of the research problems typically encountered in organizational inquiries.[29] However, within educational administration efforts are still concentrated on elementary statistical tests, which are seldom very informative, particularly when the variables found to be associated are not thoroughly understood in advance. Moreover high statistical significance levels have often been misunderstood by the statistically naive as measures of association. To be sure, the reduction of research and theory-building to focus exclusively on mathematical studies should be avoided. On the other hand, it is important to explore more actively and persistently how mathematical models accurately applied in the social sciences could also be used to introduce greater precision into all administrative discourse.

One step in this direction might be a careful review of the correspondence between statistical and other mathematical methods (reported in the new twelve-volume monograph series on quantitative applications in the social sciences) and the type of data analysis problems frequently encountered in educational administration research.[30] Particular attention here should be given to methods such as the multivariate analysis of qualitative data to explore interactions among nonmetric or categorical variables, cohort analysis as an appropriate technique for either survey research designs or historical inquiries that rely on archival data, and time series analysis as a means to study change. Organizational theorists should specifically examine the monograph on ecological inference, which treats the research issue of failing to consider the possible effects of making inferences to individuals from aggregate data.[31] Any of these research issues (such as the multivariate analysis of qualitative data or the problem of ecological inferences) would provide more than an adequate framework for conducting a critical appraisal similar to the one offered for the distinction between practical and statistical significance in the *EAQ* studies.

Researchers with predilections toward ethnography and field study methods could profit from a careful examination of a recent three-part symposium on mathematical explorations in anthropology conducted at the annual meetings of the American Association for the Advancement of Science.[32] The findings of this symposium clearly indicate that anthropological methods are by no means completely incompatible with those of sociology, economics, or the administrative sciences, even when they focus on quantitative analytical techniques and similar methodologies.

Knowledge Synthesis: In a recent UCEA publication Culbertson notes that one purpose of investing in synthesis is to produce newly organized bodies of knowledge that reflect a restructuring of concepts and research findings about selected aspects of educational organizations or administrative leadership.[33] Although such efforts typically center on a specific discipline (such as the politics of education and the economics of education) or are interdisciplinary (for issues such as leadership), these need not proceed according to the homogeneity assumption—the case where all research entries are assumed to be of equal quality. The discussion of the distinction between statistical and practical significance illustrated how a critical review of research (one form of synthesis) might benefit from the use of a single quantitative technique, ω^2, to avoid acceptance of all reported findings as they appear in the literature.

Two more general quantitative strategies that can contribute important analytical insights in knowledge synthesis are secondary analysis and meta analysis. Consider the following. Statistical inference follows the so-called hypothetico-deductive paradigm, which consists of three steps: hypothesizing a model for something unobservable; deducing the observable consequences; and undertaking an empirical study to demonstrate that the consequences expected in the observations are actually observed in the data. If the data fit our expectations, we are encouraged to accept the model as an accurate representation of the unobservable reality. Since more than one model may have the same implications for the data one observes, our acceptance is always provisional and subject to modification as other findings or ideas for models become available. Secondary analysis enters at this point. It encourages investigators to test alternate conceptual models and usually proceeds by introducing different mathematical models to represent these alternate conceptual frameworks.[34]

Meta analysis involves a statistical reanalysis and integration of a large collection of prior empirical findings to produce more generalizable estimates of central tendencies and variability.[35] This form of statistical integration should be particularly beneficial in educational administration, since sampling plans employed in different studies often pose severe limitations regarding the external validity of individual studies.

Reporting Research Findings

If one's primary interest centers on reporting research findings or locating new quantitatively oriented research domains, the following deserve consideration.

Graphics and Reporting: Efforts to specify more effective strategies for reporting or disseminating quality empirical research findings—within the profession and to boards of education, public sector policy groups, or task forces and citizens' advisory councils—should consider emerging developments in social graphics—that is, the graphic representation of social indicators and other quantitative social data.

Initial explorations might concentrate on the efforts of the Graphic Social Reporting Project, which the Bureau of Social Science Research began in 1971. Originally, the project explored implications for social indicator reporting presented by recent developments in display and communications technology. Here the emphasis was on "kinostatistics," which include graphics in media other than the printed page, particularly cinematic and electronic media capable of kinetic, audiovisual communication; computer-generated rather than hand-drawn displays; and interactive rather than passive systems. More recently the project has been reoriented to consider as well the principles and practices of social graphics applicable to traditional and technologically simpler modes of representation. All project activities are synthesized and reported in a single bibliographic text with over one thousand entires and abstracts.[36] Less ambitious, but perhaps more immediately relevant for practicing administrators, are guidelines for reporting test scores developed by the National School Public Relations Association and the graphics reporting strategies for community action groups developed by the Institute for Responsive Education.[37]

Statistics as Legal Evidence: In their recently published text, *Statistics and Public Policy* (1977), Fairley and Mosteller have clearly specified the likely foci for contemporary courses in statistical methods taught in public policy programs located in schools of government, public affairs, and administration of law schools.[38] In addition to emphasizing the basic tools of probability and statistical inference, their introductory treatment not only illustrates statistical techniques with examples where policy plays a major role, but also points to themes related to statistics in the analysis of policy. Among these themes receiving increased attention is the issue of statistics as legal evidence.[39] Although their illustrations concentrate primarily on the application of conditional probability and the utility of Bayesian methods in presenting evidence to the courts, their discussions on the admissibility of alternate forms of data into a court of law are both extensive and insightful.

Efforts to elaborate and interpret such developments for educational policy analysis would appear to be a highly relevant research project for exploring new applications of mathematical models in educational administration. Findings from these inquiries should be of particular interest to urban school districts, which are consistently required by the courts to undertake and report the results of large-scale empirical studies that point to either the effectiveness of, or the unanticipated consequences following from, the implementation of mandated student and faculty intervention programs.

Research in Schools

If the primary interest centers on research *in* schools, one might consider the following development in operational research.

An Example: To provide some indication of the general direction of research-and-development in schools, the author examined the 118 large-scale operational research projects completed during the 1975-1976 school year by the Research and Evaluation Division of the Dallas Independent School District's Department of Research, Evaluation and Information Systems.[40] To be sure, this is an exemplary rather than typical department. The department has a current operating budget of approximately $4.7 million, with $2.5 million allocated to the research and evaluation division. This division has twenty-eight senior evaluators and project directors with earned doctorates and fifty additional support staff classified as evaluation specialists and technical support personnel. The department was formed during the 1969-1970 school year, when the district received a grant of $2.4 million dollars from a local foundation to support development activities in the district.

The Dallas Independent School District (DISD) is one of the seven largest Texas urban school districts that presently operate research and evaluation departments.[41] In six of these seven districts (which include Dallas), the general framework identified for allocating departmental resources, designing individual projects, and assessing the practical as well as standard scientific criteria for quality research is the CIPP model of evaluation developed by the Phi Delta Kappa National Study Commission on Evaluation. (CIPP represents an abbreviation for four general types of interrelated evaluation studies: context, input, process, and product evaluations.)[42]

This framework views operational research as the process of delineating, obtaining, and providing useful information for judging decision alternatives. For information to be useful, the model requires eleven criterion elements to be satisfied.

The first four criterion elements—internal validity, external validity, reliability, and objectivity—are designed to represent standard scientific criteria. Specifically, they deal with the characteristics of research design and analysis that allow one to make statements about relationships among the variables in a specific research study and the extent to which these relationships also apply for other settings and samples. Within this framework they are viewed as necessary but not sufficient conditions to judge the value of operational research.

The six practical criterion elements provide a useful way to look at operational research as an activity centrally concerned with the linkage between information and organized action. Although these six criterion elements are essentially intuitive, each explicitly or implicitly involves interaction with a receiver. The first three practical criteria—relevance, importance, and scope—are logically interrelated and are used to specify the boundaries for fact-finding, data collection, and data analysis. The other three practical criteria—credibility, timeliness, and pervasiveness—center on the communication of research findings, a point that Schutz notes is critical for understanding the differences between research *on* schools and research *in* schools.

The eleventh factor—the prudential criterion—deals with cost effectiveness decisions regarding the allocation of personnel, time, and other departmental resources to particular projects.

The eleven criterion elements lead to several comments on the operational research efforts in the DISD. Efforts to satisfy the traditional scientific criteria result in the following observations regarding future directions for quantitative methods in operational inquiries:

1. Most projects are supported by two sets of technical reports. The first set are published prior to implementation and treat the conceptual or theoretical base for projects as well as the validity, reliability, and other design issues one normally associates with standard scientific criteria. The second set of research reports are usually prepared following the completion of the project and include data analysis and the technical interpretation of results.

2. Alternative forms of multivariate analysis are frequently used in several of the 118 projects identified.

3. Experiments are often constructed to provide information for comparing and contrasting different instructional alternatives implemented within the district. In current research-and-development terms, these studies are more likely to be called natural rather than quasi-experimental designs.[43]

4. Formal statistical analyses include tests for the significance of relationships as well as those that test for the significance of differences. These tests often require a need to relate both cost and effect analysis.[44]

5. Since operational research designs frequently require measures on all sample units, several studies use descriptive as well as inferential statistics to more accurately represent school district parameters.

6. To improve the utility of demographic information, index numbers—similar to those used in other large-scale data reporting systems or social indicator projects—are developed.

7. Sampling procedures have also been developed to derive new information from data already contained in the district's computerized information base.

The attention given in the DISD to practical criteria of relevance, importance, and scope can be observed in the following trends:

1. To expand the scope of information presented to the Board of Education, several reviews of research on specific policy issues were undertaken and the findings presented during the 1975-1976 school year.

2. The importance of operational research as a continuing activity in the district can be seen in several studies that reflect an emphasis on longitudinal data, time series designs, and the effective use of archival data in cohort analyses.

3. Long-range planning appears to be an important domain of interest and includes extensive projection reports on enrollments, facilities, staffing, and finance.

4. The district's testing program reflects a priority to measure behavior in both cognitive and affective domains. Particular attention is given to accurate measurement and descriptions of the district's alternate "climates" for learning.[45]

5. The scope of analysis is also extended by developing and communicating to the Board of Education formal reports of exemplary instructional programs in other school districts. In these reports a deliberate effort is made to explain exactly how both quantitative and qualitative indicators were applied to determine the success of these instructional programs.

Efforts to satisfy the other three practical or user-centered criteria—credibility, timeliness, and pervasiveness—result in the following observations:

1. In addition to the two sets of technical reports, a brief (approximately four pages) abstract is prepared for each project completed by the department. In general, the abstract is nontechnical and includes summaries of the project's purpose, origin, design, and results.

2. The abstracts are published annually and widely circulated within the district. They are also available to other DISD patrons on request.

3. To increase the range of interest in evaluative information, the department meets regularly during the academic year with a subcommittee of the Board of Education.

4. To increase the use of the evaluative information, quarterly reports on the status of all operational inquiries in progress are forwarded to the superintendent.

5. To increase the number and type of requests for evaluative information, a special applied research group has been formed within the department to prepare ad hoc information requirements for the district.[46]

6. To increase daily interaction between the evaluation staff and other district personnel, several members of the department reside on project sites rather than in the central office.[47]

A more elaborate case analysis of the DISD and implementation of the CIPP model—not our primary intent—would involve an analysis of several additional organizational factors and administrative predilections that surround the context in which operational research is conducted and reported. To be sure, it would be necessary to examine latent as well as obvious research priorities. Among the less obvious priorities for the application of mathematical models in the DISD would be: the district's administrative commitment to long-term program experimentation and revision based on operational findings;[48] the priority placed on reporting the accuracy of various types of data entered in the district's information system;[49] the goodness-of-fit between the research reporting schedule and actual decision dates in the district's administrative and instructional program calendars as well as the correspondence between reported index numbers and the individual measures they represent;[50] and a comparison of research costs with the costs of the decisions that will be made on the basis of the evaluative information (the prudential criterion).

Administrative Technology: The literature in educational administration has continuously referenced the value of employing so-called administrative technologies, which are usually found in the management science literature and in handbooks on organizational development and planning strategies. More specifically, these include techniques such as program evaluation and review techniques (PERT), management by objectives, program planning and budgeting system (PPBS), delphic inquiries, zero-based budgeting, survey feedback and consultation in organizational development, trend-impact analysis, educational production functions, decision tree analysis, linear programming, policy-capturing models, Monte Carlo simulations, nominal group techniques, functional and cost-centered budgeting, and cost-benefit analysis.

Academic and operational researchers, interested in reporting the practical utility of a particular technique but unwilling to spend time in school districts, may have systematically overlooked the most appropriate set of applications. Until the literature in educational administration, such as that recently inaugurated in the *Educational Researcher*, places a higher priority on publishing articles on research-and-development progress in schools, opportunities to conduct comprehensive critical appraisals, reviews, or syntheses of administrative technologies will remain largely more an ideal than a reality.[51]

Secondly, with respect to graduate training in educational administration, the actual design and successful implementation of administrative technologies in operational settings require a working knowledge of descriptive as well as inferential statistics and a general understanding of quantitative methods used in management operations.[52] University-based programs devoted to the preparation of school administrators (who must assume the responsibility for managing the research-and-development activities in school districts or other organizational settings) might increase their effectiveness by devoting explicitly a part of the formal preparation program to the application of quantitative methods and data reduction strategies that are essential for successful implementation of the administrative technologies.[53]

Utility of Mathematical Models and
Quantitative Methods

If educational administration intends to seriously enter the debate on the utility of mathematical models and quantitative methods in either academic or operational research, the profession would be well advised to critically examine and reference the extensive social and policy science literature that addresses this topic.

In the immediate future we are likely to observe "point-counterpoint" discussions in educational administration on the value of mathematical models and quantitative models to advance the state of the art in decision-making, research, or the development of theory. Although it is usually constructive to note particularly poor studies which in effect endorse an antitheoretical position by merely throwing a large inventory of variables into a regression equation with the intent of selecting out some subset that accounts for the most variance, or to discount the value of factor analytic inquiries by referencing studies where the investigators failed to employ any theoretical insights regarding the reduction of their original correlation matrices, these citations, taken as the last word, fail to address adequately the issues pertaining to either the limits or the advantages of mathematical models for educational administration.

Opportunities to enhance perspectives and to accurately define the relevant issues for debate have been treated extensively in the social and policy science literature, a knowledge base frequently claimed to be most appropriate for research and the instructional content of administrator preparation programs. If this literature is used for more careful fact-finding, researchers might study the following: the 1963 American Academy of Political and Social Science symposium, which treated the utility and inutility of mathematics in the study of economics, political science, and sociology;[54] the National Academy of Sciences reports on new directions in the mathematical sciences;[55] recommendations from the Association for Institutional Research on new directions for quantitative applications in academic administration;[56] and the survey of the social and behavioral sciences conducted under the joint auspices of the Committee on Science and Public Policy of the National Academy of Science and the Policy Committee of the Social Science Research Council. This survey indicates that schools of applied social research will turn to scholars trained in mathematics, logic, and operations research to assist in the development of new methodologies, alternate planning strategies, and programs of study relevant to public administrators.[57] To sharpen explanations for the limitations of mathematical models, the distinctions in the educational planning literature between teaching by the numbers and planning on the basis of numbers should be studied more carefully.[58] The emerging literature on management misinformation systems,[59] the number of "numbness" issue in administrative reporting,[60] the problems associated with the transfer of system analysis from the aerospace industry to public administration and policy studies,[61] and the critical appraisals of computer simulations to capture the dynamics of social systems[62] should be examined as well.

As a final word, the findings of Deutsch and his colleagues, who have identified and analyzed conditions favoring sixty-two major advances in the social sciences since 1900 should not be overlooked.[63] Their analysis indicates that the sixty-two major advances (achievements or breakthroughs) typically combined theory, methods, and results as opposed to one of these elements as a sole focus of interest. In light of these findings, they claim the long-standing quarrel about whether to emphasize theory, methodology, or empirical results seems "ill-conceived," since important advances in any one of these three aspects of social science is likely to lead to advances in the other two. It is of more than passing interest that Deutsch and his colleagues have observed that quantitative problems or findings (or both) characterize two-thirds of all major achievements in the social sciences between 1900 and 1965, and that five-sixths of these advances (those explicitly linked to quantitative problems and findings) were made since 1930.

Notes

1. Richard E. Schutz, "Research in Schools," *Educational Researcher* 5, no. 5 (May 1976). This position is similar to the distinction between decision-oriented and conclusion-oriented inquiry in Lee J. Cronbach and Patrick Suppes, eds., *Research for Tomorrow's Schools: Disciplined Inquiry in Education* (New York: Macmillan, 1969).

2. Operational research is sometimes viewed as "applied decision theory." In this chapter, operational research, or research in schools, refers to the application of scientific methodology to problems related to the functioning or operating of a specific organizational unit such as a public school district. For example, see J.E. Brooks, "Operational Research in Educational Administration," *Education and Urban Society* 3 (1970):7-40.

3. Portions of this section appeared in James F. McNamara, "Practical Significance and Statistical Models," *Educational Administration Quarterly* 14, no. 1 (Winter 1978):48-63. Reprinted with permission.

4. The author acknowledges his debt to the article by Richard E. Schutz, "The Control of 'Error' in Educational Experimentation," *School Review* 74, no. 2 (1966):151-158. Much of the design of this section and the secondary analysis of statistical tests reported for volumes 1 through 12 of the *Educational Administration Quarterly* parallels the treatment of practical significance presented in this source. Assistance in clarifying issues associated with the differences between statistical and practical significance and between tests for the significance of differences and tests for the significance of relationships was

also found in Richard M. Wolf, "Data Analysis and Reporting Considerations in Evaluation," in W. James Popham, ed., *Evaluation in Education* (Berkeley, Calif.: McCutchan, 1974); and W. James Popham, *Educational Evaluation* (Englewood Cliffs, N.J.: Prentice-Hall, 1975).

5. Y.K. Shetty and H.M. Carlisle, "Application of Management by Objectives in a University Setting," *Educational Administration Quarterly* 10, no. 2 (Spring 1974):65-81. Although analysis here focuses only on the ANOVA results, several questions might also be raised regarding the credibility of the sampling plan, the failure to treat the nonresponse bias given a reported questionnaire return rate of 46 percent, the general integrity (validity) associated with the questionnaire, and the means by which questionnaire responses were aggregated and averaged to yield a single criterion measure.

6. For one such technique, ω^2, an excellent treatment appears in W.L. Hays, *Statistics for Psychologists* (New York: Holt, Rinehart and Winston, 1963). Some criticism of using ω^2 as an index of the strength of a statistical association is treated in Gene V. Glass and A. Ralph Hakstian, "Measures of Association in Comparative Experiments: Their Development and Interpretation," *American Educational Research Journal* 6, no. 3 (1969):403-414.

7. When a specific study is to be viewed as nonexperimental rather than experimental, some statistical handbooks (such as Hays in note 6) suggest that a more appropriate index for estimating variance is η^2. Specifically, η^2 is the squared "correlation ratio" that results when ANOVA designs are solved using multiple regression techniques. Hence, it is the ratio $SS(B)/SS(T)$. This index is also described in any text on linear models such as K.A. McNeil, F.J. Kelly, and J.T. McNeil, *Testing Research Hypotheses Using Multiple Linear Regression* (Carbondale, Ill.: Southern Illinois University Press, 1975). The η^2 values for the Shetty and Carlisle ANOVA results are 0.186, 0.077, and 0.028, which are slightly higher but do not represent any real departure in magnitude from the ω^2 estimates. The author will continue to use the ω^2 index in this analysis with the understanding that η^2 could also be readily calculated for any of the ANOVA test results.

8. Schutz, "Control of 'Error',". Reprinted with permission of the University of Chicago Press. (© All rights reserved.) (One obvious exception to this approach is Raymond S. Adams et al., "School Size, Organizational Structure and Teaching Practices," *Educational Administration Quarterly* 6, no. 3 (Fall 1970):15-31. The seventy-two ω^2 estimates for this study appear in the column of table 10-2 labeled volume 1-6. All seventy-two index values were reported in the *EAQ* article along with an interesting discussion of the influence of these ω^2 estimates in interpreting the findings of the study.)

9. For another approach to interpreting standard statistical tests of significance of studies reported in the *EAQ*, see the 1972 appraisal of educational research reported in J.K. Brewer, "On the Power of Statistical Tests," *American Educational Research Journal* 9, no. 3 (1972):391-401. For those who wish to use this model, it is suggested that careful attention be given to the

different cases described in J. Cohen, *Statistical Power Analysis for the Behavioral Sciences*, 2d ed. (New York: Academic Press, 1976).

10. For example, see the author's discussion of an alternate statistical model for the Shetty and Carlisle study in "Practical Significance and Statistical Models," *Educational Administration Quarterly* 14, no. 1 (Winter 1978):48-63.

11. A more exact interpretation is the hypothetico-deductive paradigm for statistical inference, which consists of three steps: hypothesizing a model for something unobservable, deducing the observable consequences of the models, and undertaking an empirical investigation with the intent to test whether the consequences expected in the observations are actually apparent in the data. If the data fit expectations, the investigator is encouraged to accept the model as a correct representation of the unobservable reality. However, acceptance is always provisional. If the data do not conform to expectations—clearly the case for several *EAQ* findings—something is wrong. Since there are several valid reasons for the failure to meet expectations, the author suggests that these study findings be viewed with caution. For example, the models may be invalid, the deductions for model consequences could be incorrect, or the actual data could be inadequate or defective. A more detailed treatment of the consequences of statistical inference in model construction is given in R. Darell Bock, *Multivariate Statistical Methods in the Behavioral Sciences* (New York: McGraw-Hill, 1975).

12. See note 8.

13. Cohen (in *Statistical Power Analysis*) suggests the following operational guidelines for the behavioral sciences in terms of correlation coefficients: for small effects, $r = 0.10$; for medium effects, $r = 0.30$; and for large effects, $r = 0.50$. His position implies that a large effect would be encountered when at least 25 percent of the variance of the dependent variable is attributable to the independent variable.

14. See W. Anderson, "How Not to Let Your Board and Superintendent Be Hoodwinked by 'Research'," *American School Board Journal* 9, no. 3 (1978):391-401.

15. James F. McNamara and David H. Gill, "Practical Significance in Vocational Education Research," *Journal of Vocational Education Research* (forthcoming).

16. McNeil, Kelly, and McNeil, "Testing Research Hypotheses."

17. This excerpt from "An Overview" by Ilene N. Bernstein is reprinted from *Sage Contemporary Social Science Issues* 23 (1976):8 and originally appeared in *Sociological Methods & Research* by permission of the publisher, Sage Publications, Inc. The discussion of problem formulation and sample selection relies extensively on this source.

18. For example, see Harvey A. Averch et al., "How Effective is Schooling? A Critical Review and Synthesis of Research Findings," Rand Corporation, Santa Monica, California (March 1972), R-956-PCSF/RC.

19. For a recent study following this format, and one illustrative of what is

implied by Schutz's reference to an extraschool-agency initiative, see Anita A. Summers and Barbara L. Wolfe, "Which School Resources Help Learning Efficiency and Equity in Philadelphia Public Schools?," *Federal Reserve Bank of Philadelphia Business Review* (February 1976).

20. These design considerations are detailed in Richard J. Murnane, *The Impact of Resources on the Learning of Inner City Children* (Cambridge, Mass.: Ballinger, 1975), p. 25.

21. Murnane, *Impact of Resources*. The description of Murnane's research has been taken directly from this source. The model descriptions presented in this section are represented in a slightly different notation, but the functional forms are consistent with those provided in the Murnane text.

22. These hypotheses are detailed in ibid., chaps. 3, 4.

23. Ibid., p. 33.

24. Most of the hypotheses of the study were tested using one-tailed t tests. Some were tested using two-tailed tests as indicated in ibid.

25. A summary of the information used to test these three hypotheses appears in ibid., table 3-1, p. 35.

26. Reprinted by permission of the publisher, from Eric A. Hanushek, *Education and Race: An Analysis of the Educational Production Process* (Lexington, Mass.: D.C. Heath and Company, 1972), p. 125. Copyright 1972, D.C. Heath and Company.

27. See James E. Bruno and James N. Fox, *Quantitative Analysis in Educational Administrator Preparation Programs*, ERIC/UCEA Series on Administrator Preparation (Columbus, Ohio: University Council for Educational Administration, 1973). More recent interpretations by James E. Bruno are given in *Educational Policy Analysis: A Quantitative Approach* (New York: Crane, Russak and Co., 1976).

28. See Hubert M. Blalock, Jr., *Theory Construction: From Verbal to Mathematical Formulation* (Englewood Cliffs, N.J.: Prentice-Hall, 1969). See also David R. Heise, *Causal Analysis* (New York: Wiley, 1975); Herbert B. Asher, *Causal Modeling*, Series on Quantitative Applications in the Social Sciences no. 3 (Beverly Hills, Calif.: Sage Publications, 1969); and James G. Anderson, "Causal Models in Educational Research: Nonrecursive Models," *American Educational Research Journal* 15, no. 1 (Winter 1978):81-98.

29. For organizational studies see Rocco Carzo and John Yanouzas, *Formal Organization: A Systems Approach* (Homewood, Ill.: Dorsey Press, 1967).

30. Eric M. Uslaner, ed., *Series on Quantitative Applications in the Social Sciences*, nos. 1-12 (Beverly Hills, Calif.: Sage Publications, 1977).

31. This is generally treated in the literature under the title, "ecological fallacies." See Laura I. Langbein and Allan J. Lichtman, *Ecological Inference*, Series on Quantitative Applications in the Social Sciences, no. 10 (Beverly Hills, Calif.: Sage Publications, 1977); and Irving H. Siegel, *Aggregation and Averaging*, Methods for Manpower Analysis no. 1 (Kalamazoo, Mich.: W.E. Upjohn Institute for Employment Research, 1968).

32. Paul Kay, ed., *Explorations in Mathematical Anthropology* (Cambridge, Mass.: MIT Press, 1971). See also the discussions of enumeration and the use of descriptive statistics in Harry F. Walcott, "An Ethnographic Approach to the Study of School Administrators," *Human Organizations* 29 (1970):115-122, and his book *The Man in the Principal's Office: An Ethnography* (New York: Holt, Rinehart and Winston, 1973).

33. Jack Culbertson, "Linking Agents and the Sources and Uses of Knowledge," in N. Nash and J. Culbertson, eds., *Linking Processes in Educational Improvement* (Columbus, Ohio: University Council for Educational Administration, 1977).

34. Leigh Burstein, "Secondary Analysis: An Important Resource for Educational Research and Evaluation," *Educational Researcher* 7, no. 5 (May 1978):9-12.

35. Gene V. Glass, "Primary, Secondary and Meta Analysis of Research," *Educational Researcher* 5, no. 10 (November 1976):1-4.

36. Barry M. Feinberg et al., *Social Graphics*, The Graphics Social Reporting Project (Washington, D.C.: Bureau of Social Science Research, Inc., 1975).

37. See *Releasing Test Scores: Educational Assessment Programs, How to Tell the Public* and *Putting Words and Pictures about Schools in Print* (Arlington, Virg.: National School Public Relations Association); Lloyd Prentice, *Words, Pictures, Media: Communication in Educational Politics* (Boston: Institute for Responsive Education, 1976).

38. William B. Fairley and Frederick Mosteller, *Statistics and Public Policy* (Reading, Mass.: Addison-Wesley, 1977). Additional insights on selecting, conducting, and reporting statistical analysis in public policy studies appear in Arnold J. Meltsner, *Policy Analysis in the Bureaucracy* (Berkeley, Calif.: University of California Press, 1976).

39. Hans Zeisel, "Statistics as Legal Evidence," *International Encyclopedia of the Social Sciences* 15 (1968):246-247; and R. Cullison, "Identification by Probability and Trial by Arithmetic: A Lesson for Beginners in How to Be Wrong with Greater Precision," *Houston Law Review* 6 (1969):471-483.

40. Each of the studies is described in William J. Webster, *Abstracts of Research and Evaluation Reports* (Dallas, Tex.: Dallas Independent School District, Department of Research, Evaluation, and Information Systems, December 1976).

41. See Edward M. Jackowski, "The Functions, Products and Financial Support of Urban School District Research Departments in Texas" (Ph.D. diss., Department of Educational Administration, Texas A & M University, December 1974).

42. Daniel L. Stufflebeam et al., *Educational Evaluation and Decision Making*, Report of the Phi Delta Kappa Commission on Evaluation (Itasca, Ill.: Peacock, 1971).

43. See, for example, the discussion of natural experiments and ecological validity in Urie Bronfenbrenner, "The Experimental Ecology of Education,"

Educational Researcher 5, no. 9 (October 1976):5-15; and the description of heuristic experiments in Abraham Caplan, *The Conduct of Inquiry* (San Francisco: Chandler, 1964).

44. This procedure is described in William J. Webster, "Cost and Effect Analysis: An Example," *Educational Economics* 1, no. 3 (1976):10-16.

45. See William J. Webster, "What's the Score on Testing?" (Paper presented at the Thirty-fourth Annual Convention of the National School Boards Association, Houston, Texas, April 6, 1974).

46. See William J. Webster, "The Organization and Function of Research and Evaluation in a Large Urban School District" (Paper presented at the Annual Meeting of the American Educational Research Association, Washington, D.C., March 31, 1975).

47. This is especially true for the department's Developmental Project Branch, responsible for process and outcome evaluations of new and innovative instructional programs undertaken on an experimental or trial basis.

48. See Nolan Estes, *Marshalling Community Leadership to Support the Public Schools* (Bloomington, Ind.: Phi Delta Kappa Educational Foundation, 1975).

49. On the importance of accuracy in school information systems, see Henry Dyer, *How to Achieve Accountability in the Public Schools* (Bloomington, Ind.: Phi Delta Kappa Educational Foundation, 1973).

50. Ibid., pp. 32-34.

51. The value of these strategies is well illustrated in William Foley, "Analysis and Educational Decision Making: Toward a Theory into Practice" (Doctoral Thesis, Department of Educational Administration, Teachers College, Columbia University, August 1976).

52. Robert J. Thierauf, *Decision Making through Operations Research* (New York: Wiley, 1970); and Russell L. Ackoff and Patrick Rivett, *A Manager's Guide to Operations Research* (New York: Wiley, 1963).

53. Similar recommendations are given in Robin H. Farquhar, "The Social Sciences in Preparing Educational Leaders," in J. Culbertson et al., eds., *Social Science Content in the Preparation of Educational Leaders* (Columbus, Ohio: Merrill, 1973); and Lewis B. Mayhew and the Stanford University University School of Education Committee on Administration and Policy Analysis, *Educational Leadership and Declining Enrollments* (Berkeley, Calif.: McCutchan, 1974), especially pp. 179-180.

54. James C. Charlesworth, ed., *Mathematics and the Social Sciences* (Philadelphia: The American Academy of Political and Social Science, 1963).

55. Harvey Brooks, ed., *The Mathematical Sciences* (Washington, D.C.: National Academy of Sciences, 1968).

56. David P. Hopkins et al., eds., *Applying Analytic Methods to Planning and Management*, New Directions for Institutional Research, no. 13 (San Francisco: Jossey-Bass, 1977).

57. William Kruskal, ed., *Mathematical Sciences and Social Sciences* (Englewood Cliffs, N.J.: Prentice-Hall, 1970).

58. Russel G. Davis, *Planning Human Resource Development: Educational Models and Schemata* (Chicago: Rand McNally, 1966).

59. Russell A. Ackoff, "Management Misinformation Systems," *Management Science* 14 (December 1967):B147-155.

60. W. David Maxwell, "Number Numbness," *Liberal Education* 59, no. 4 (December 1973):405-416; and Frederick W. Hill, "Statistics, Liars, and Figures," *American School and University* 48, no. 3 (November 1975):19-20.

61. Ida R. Hoos, *Systems Analysis in Public Policy: A Critique* (Berkeley, Calif.: University of California Press, 1972).

62. David Berlinski, *On Statistical Analysis: An Essay Concerning the Limitations of Some Mathematical Methods in the Social, Political and Biological Sciences* (Cambridge, Mass.: MIT Press, 1976).

63. Karl W. Deutsch et al., "Conditions Favoring Major Advances in Social Science," *Science* 171, no. 3970 (1971):450-459.

11 Toward a Methodology of Policy Research in Educational Administration

Emil J. Haller and
Kenneth A. Strike

It is a truism in our field that research in educational administration has little effect on administrative practice. Like most truisms, however, we suspect that this one is only partially correct. That is, it appears that research has affected practice, but in ways that are not patently obvious. Its effects are discernible, it seems, but over relatively long periods of time, in what practitioners do not do rather than what they do, and in the justifications offered (or not offered) for actions rather than in the actions themselves.

For example, more than a decade after *Equality of Educational Opportunity* and its numerous progeny, the very rapid growth of resources allocated to compensatory education programs has leveled off, if it is not actually declining. This shift in practice—this change in allocation decisions—is at least partly a consequence of numerous studies whose findings failed to validate the expected gains in pupils' cognitive skills. Apparently Congress has become dubious of such educational interventions, and Headstart, for example, is now funded more for political reasons than for educational ones.[1] Had the results of the Westinghouse (and other) evaluations been uniformly positive—had the black-white achievement gap in the early grades been erased—the monies allocated to Headstart would surely have increased, and that program would be an important and integral part of the operation of every sizable school system, rather than the organizational appendix that it currently is.

Similarly, whereas teachers' organizations continue to press for higher wages, it is becoming increasingly rare to hear these demands justified on the grounds that better salaries mean better teaching, and, consequently, an improvement in pupil learning. School board members no longer buy that rationale.

One final example of the effect of research on practice may be found in a different arena, the courts (although in this case practice has been affected in ways other than what researchers intended). On reading the major desegregation cases from *Brown* v. *Board of Education of Topeka* to the present, one is left with the distinct impression that the courts are becoming less inclined to offer social science research (either as evidence for a finding of violation or as a justification of a proposed remedy) than they were in the immediate post-*Brown* period. It appears that federal justices may be suffering some disillusionment with social science research. Perhaps, along with Cahn, judges would not have citizens' constitutional rights stand on so flimsy a foundation.[2] In any event, the "omnipresent Mr. Pettigrew" (to quote Yudof's felicitous, if somewhat sarcastic, phrase[3]) is less in evidence in the courtrooms of the land than was formerly the case.

Nevertheless, the commonplace notion that administrative research has had little impact on administrative practice contains more than a kernel of truth. In this chapter we would like to examine the nature of the relationship between the two, with particular attention to the question of an appropriate methodology for practice-oriented research. We will approach this task by specifying a conception of research programs in an applied field, a conception having its roots in a model developed for the hard sciences by Imre Lakatos,[4] and later adapted to the research endeavor in education by Strike.[5] Based on this conception, we will then note some of the methodological implications of the model for research in educational administration.

Before we begin, however, let us note that although this whole exercise implies the desirability of a closer connection between the study of administration and its conduct, we are aware that the costs of forging such a connection may be considerably beyond our present awareness—or our eventual willingness to pay. But that is a different subject. For the moment let us state as a premise that educational administration is an applied field of endeavor; it is, to quote the sponsors of the seminar giving rise to this book, "the organization, direction, control and management of all matters pertaining to the operation of education or an educational organization." The study of educational administration involves, therefore, the study of the consequences of deliberate choice regarding the operation, control, and so forth, of schools.

An important domain of choice, we believe, is that of educational policy. Indeed, it is evident that policy and policy studies are a major growth area in the applied social sciences. Thus, we conclude that research on educational policy should be a significant facet of our total investigative effort. To date this does not seem to be the case, although there are important exceptions to this conclusion, notably in the area of school finance. One reason for this relative neglect, we believe, is the lack of a comprehensive conceptualization of the epistemology of the policy research process, coupled with a conception of the methods appropriate to such an epistemology. This chapter is intended as a step in that direction.

A Model of Policy Research in an Applied Field

Let us begin by noting what seems to be a commonly accepted distinction between basic and applied research. To use the terms of Cronbach and Suppes, the distinction is one between "conclusion-oriented" and "decision-oriented" inquiry.[6] On the one hand, the intent of the former is to arrive at generalizable, parsimonious, and descriptive statements of the way the world works—to directly or indirectly contribute to theory. The methods of this research are ultimately derived from some philosophy of scientific rationality. On the other hand, the intent of decision-oriented research is to produce information that will aid in making more rational choices among competing courses of social action. Whereas the methods of this second form of research may also derive from an epistemology of scientific rationality, they are conditioned in important ways by the world of action. For example, differences in audiences (disciplinary colleagues versus political actors), timing (few constraints versus definite ones), and language (disciplinary concepts versus everyday language) are said to impinge in important ways on methodological choices.

There is yet no agreed-on methodology for decision-oriented research (using methodology in its sense as the study of method), although promising starts have been made.[7] Instead, we have a number of ad hoc suggestions, primarily based on the experiences of some of our colleagues who have been involved in it. What is needed is a more comprehensive view of scientific research conducted in the context of public policy-making, from which a methodology may be developed. This portion of this chapter is intended to provide one possible view of such research.

For a considerable period of time a particular view of the nature of the scientific enterprise has dominated our conception of research. This view, perhaps best represented by Karl Popper, was that rationality in science could best be conceived as the interplay of theoretical formulations and empirical research designed to test those formulations.[8] That is, science has presumed to progress through a process of deductively derived falsifiable propositions, which were then subect to rigorous empirical test. Falsification was critical to this process. In fact, the capacity to be empirically falsified was the criterion of a good hypothesis. Further, it was efficient to seek to falsify a proposition, since empirically confirming one, even a large number of times, is not logically sufficient to confirming the theory on which it was based, whereas one instance of falsification was supposed to be sufficient to refute it. This view of the nature of scientific research has dominated the field of educational administration, evidenced best, perhaps, in the writings of Griffiths.[9] Thus, the growth of the scientific study of educational administration was seen to depend on the derivation of critical explanatory hypotheses and a diligent attempt to refute them.

More recently, Kuhn[10] and more importantly for our purposes, Lakatos,[11] have proposed an alternative view of science. In particular, these writers note that Popper's conception is a poor description of the actual progression of a scientific research program. Specifically, Lakatos argues that scientific theories are rarely if ever refuted by empirical findings. Rather, theories are routinely saved from experimental refutation through the introduction of what he terms "auxiliary hypotheses." Theory-saving is possible because theories are composed of concepts that lack direct empirical referents. Thus, each empirical test of a theory necessarily involves a further set of propositions—the auxiliary hypotheses—designed to map the concepts onto the world. For example, the theoretical concept of social class is routinely transformed into socioeconomic status and thence to occupation, education, and income of the head of household. Should an experiment produce negative results, that is, the theoretically predicted outcome does not occur, the researcher is in no way compelled to forfeit his theory. Logically, he knows only that at least one of the premises on which he reasoned to his predicted outcome is false; he does not know which premise. In such situations researchers typically do not give up the theory, but rather they alter or substitute among their auxiliary hypotheses and try again. This is to say that researchers are, in practice, relatively more strongly commited to the basic theory guiding their work than to the auxiliary hypotheses necessary to empirically validate it.

All of us engage in this sort of theory-saving. The conclusions of our research reporting no significant differences (and there is a great deal of this kind) typically contain suggestions for refining measurements, including new variables, and altering hypotheses. Such suggestions, when carried out in future studies, would, we like to think, yield the coveted statistical significance and, hence, tend to validate the underlying theory. Rarely does an investigator conclude that, since the predicted outcomes were not forthcoming, the theory is either incorrect or at least inapplicable to school administration. This is not to say that there is anything wrong with these activities; indeed we shall suggest that this sort of activity is a basic part of rationality. It is merely to illustrate the ubiquity of a practice and its import for Lakatos' contention.

This view implies two things of import for us here. First, Lakatos suggests that there are three components of a scientific research program: the theoretical hard core—the basic theoretical commitment, which is relatively immune to refutation; the auxiliary hypotheses—the additional assumptions necessary to map the theory onto the world; and finally, the data—the facts or empirical regularities that the theory is intended to explain. Second, a research program is best evaluated not on how well its theory explains the data at any given time, but rather on the changing nature of its auxiliary hypotheses. That is, a research program is seen as *progressive* if its auxiliary hypotheses are not ad hoc, are parsimonious, expand the range of data to which the theory applies, generate new predictions, and are anticipative rather than reactive to new phenomena. Conversely, *degenerating* research programs are characterized by auxiliary hypotheses that become increasingly ad hoc, less parsimonious, do not expand the data base, and are reactive to new data. Research programs, thus, are seen to undergo a process of growth and decay in a context of competition among alternative theoretical frameworks. In contrast to Popper's views, the science does not progress through a process of refutation of theories, nor for that matter, through a revolutionary overturning of an established paradigm, as in Kuhn's view, but rather through the slow accretion of auxiliary hypotheses, which mark one research program as degenerating and a competitor as progressive. In short, old theories, like old soldiers, never die.

An analogue of this model of hard science has been proposed by Strike, a model intended to be applicable to areas of applied research.[12] Analogous to the theory in this scheme is a *normative-theoretical hard core*, a systematically interconnected set of empirical theories about how the world operates and normative or ideological beliefs regarding desired end states. In the case of education, for example, the normative-theoretical hard core may consist of an ideological system centered on the value of free-market competition and a belief in equality of opportunity in that competition. Connected with these normative commitments in the hard core are essentially theoretical notions concerning the role of schooling in insuring equality of opportunity. Thus, for example, schooling is viewed as a mechanism by which individuals can be assured of an equal chance in the competition to secure society's benefits. Put another way, education is viewed as a mechanism for breaking any relationship that might exist between a person's home background or ascribed characteristics (such as race or sex) and his eventual occupation, income, or power.

Policies are analogous to auxiliary hypotheses in this formulation. They are regarded as plans of action, which implement the values of the normative-theoretical hard core. Policies also reflect additional empirical and normative assumptions about how these values may be achieved. Like auxiliary hypotheses, therefore, policies are attempts to map a more fundamental conception onto the world. As in the Lakatos model, this mapping operation may fail; that is, the expected outcomes may not follow on a policy's implementation—individuals' incomes may continue to relate to their race. When this occurs, rather than rejecting the hard core (by, for example, directly redistributing income) other policies are implemented that are intended to correct the deficiencies of their predecessors while still attempting to realize the values of the hard core.

Obviously, adopting a policy does not, in itself, produce the envisioned change in the world. Policies must be implemented, and they are implemented not once but many times. That is, they are converted into actions in many different locations, by different actors, and over a period of time. Since these locations, actors, and times differ from each other in numerous and important ways, the nature of these implementations will vary considerably. For example, a preschool compensatory education policy may involve a heavy emphasis on reading readiness in one school district, cultural enrichment in another, and a mix of the two in a third. Such variation arises from several sources: the fact that policies are typically vague and require administrative interpretation at several levels, a variation in political constraints among different sites, variation in available resources, and difference in clients' perceived needs. These variations in implementation are usually so great as to render problematic whether or not an action carried out in the name of a given policy is an instance of that policy. In a real sense, administrators charged with implementing a policy make that policy.[13] Policy implementation, thus, requires additional assumptions generated at the site, which are added to those involved in generating the policy itself.

Policy outcomes correspond to the data in the original hard science model. Figure 11-1 illustrates the basic components of the model.

To complete the analogy to a basic research program, a feedback loop is obviously required. That is, research on the results of implementing a policy leads to modification of the assumptions on which it was based. As in the Lakatos model, it is suggested that negative policy research results do not modify the normative-theoretical hard core. Rather, such results are reflected onto the auxiliary hypotheses—the policies—and new policies result. When research and policy-making interact in this way, a rational policy research program results. Figure 11-2 diagrams the relationship.

It is possible to apply this model of a policy program at various analytical levels—from the organizational to the social. In the former case, concern with a single policy-implementation-result link (for example, P_1, I_a, R_a), the research problem may be seen as an instance of program evaluation. The question is whether or not a policy, as interpreted and implemented at a particular site, is producing the desired effects. In the latter case, we may conceive of the progression of a large number of court decisions over the last eighty years as a series of national policy decisions relating to education and race. Here each

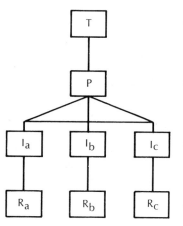

• The normative-theoretical hard core.

• The policy-generating process: The normative-theoretical hard core in conjunction with additional assumptions yields conclusions concerning recommended courses of action.

• Implementation: Policies combined with additional assumptions peculiar to each site of implementation are translated into specific programs and acts.

• Results: Actions produce consequences at each site which are studied and reported by researchers.

Figure 11-1. Components of a Policy Research Model.

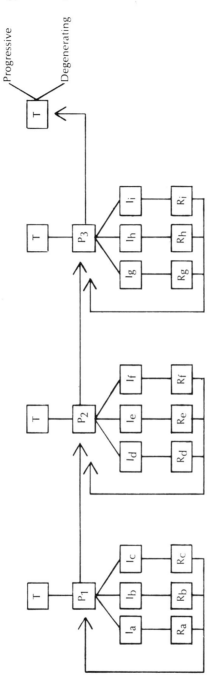

Figure 11-2. Diagrammatic Representation of a Policy Research Program.

decision may be viewed as a successive attempt to implement a normative-theoretical hard core, and the so-called landmark decisions are those marking a change in policy following on the perceived failure of its predecessor. Thus, for example, from a policy intended to realize equality of opportunity by insuring equality in school facilities (*Plessey*), we have moved to one seeking the same end by insuring racial equality in access to those facilities (*Brown*), and finally to a policy of equality in access to privileged classmates, or "racial balance" (*Swann*).

Pursuing the analogy, then, the model suggests that policy programs are to be evaluated in much the same way as scientific research programs. That is, a policy program is to be judged according to the degree to which it is succeeding in implementing the values of the hard core—that is, the degree to which it is progressing or degenerating. Further, the research aspect of the program is to be assessed by the degree to which it produces information relevant to rational policy change.

Implications For Research Methods

In the preceding section we have briefly described a model of policy research in an applied field such as educational administration. Before turning to its implications for research methods, several of its features should be noted. First, insofar as it is a model of rationality, it is a description of scientific, not political rationality. That is, it is concerned with the degree to which policies are warranted by data regarding their effects, rather than the degree to which they are warranted by political considerations—for example, the legitimacy of the process that generates them or their acceptability to policy-makers and constituents. It is certainly the case, however, as Braybrooke and Lindblom have pointed out, that there are severe limits to scientific rationality in the policy-making process.[14] Second, the model is avowedly normative. It is a description of how research in an applied field might be done if the goal were to make it as informative as possible to policy-makers.

It seems to us that there are several implications in the model for research methods in the study of educational administration, some of which we will briefly note. First, and perhaps most obviously, the model implies the importance of determining the direction of a policy research program—whether it is progressing or degenerating. Whereas the bulk of policy research may focus on trying to get a program to work, we also need to be able to decide when the program is unworkable—when it has degenerated to the point that some other approach should be taken. What is needed, therefore, is a methodology for making such a determination, including criteria to distinguish a progressive from a degenerating policy program. In regard to the latter, the following are some possibilities:

1. Evidence of the erosion of the hard core. A program might be thought of as degenerating if, for example, policies begin to be implemented that are founded on assumptions contrary to those in the hard core. This could be construed as a declining commitment to the basic normative belief system. Policies that manipulate the distribution of rewards rather than (as the standard liberal version of equality requires) the manipulation of opportunities come immediately to mind. Much of the controversy over preferential admissions seems to exhibit confusion over such central values.

2. Level of political support. Policies being maintained, in the face of mounting evidence of their inefficacy, through escalating political support, suggest a degenerating program. Headstart may provide an example.

3. Excessive social costs. A situation in which the only policies capable of achieving success are ones that involve too high a social cost suggest a degenerating program. For example, if only state-rearing of children could eliminate inequalities of opportunity arising from family background, the policy research paradigm might be seen to be degenerating.

4. Unanticipated outcomes. Even when a policy is successful in producing the outcomes desired, it is virtually certain that it is also producing unanticipated consequences of both a desirable and undesirable kind. Should the quality of the latter be perceived as persistently outweighing the intended desired outcomes, the policy program may be conceived as degenerating.

5. Predictability. Policies whose outcomes remain unpredictable may contribute to the degeneration of a program. That is, when success is apparent in some implementations but not in other seemingly similar ones—when policymakers or administrators are unable to ascertain the conditions that distinguish the former from the latter and, hence, are unable to predict success in any given implementation—the program may be thought of as degenerating.

6. Ad hoc or excessively complex policies. A program may be thought to be degenerating when policies have no intimate connection with the hard core, when they are added with no rationale other than their necessity for solving some problem, or when they become far-fetched or highly complex.

7. Inconsistency or vacuity of the hard core. Problems or difficulties in a policy program may be solved by altering the meaning or interpretation of the hard core. A hard core may be held to be degenerating when its current meaning or interpretation becomes inconsistent or vacuous.

The reader may wish to propose other criteria for distinguishing a progressive from a degenerating policy program. In any case, regardless of the specific criteria one used, the value of this conception of a policy research program, we believe, is to suggest the importance of deciding when to stop. Research in an applied field should, it seems to us, address the possibility that a series of policies and their available alternatives are unworkable, and that a reconsideration of the normative-theoretical hard core from which they are derived is in order. Such research necessarily would be of a philosophical and historical nature—a mode of inquiry relatively rare in educational administration, dominated as it has been by a commitment to empiricism and hypothesis testing.

However, we have claimed that in most research attention is not focused on the evaluation of the hard core, but on finding policies to implement it. Perhaps the major implication of our model, therefore, is that a substantial proportion of the research in an applied field such as educational administration should be addressed to improving the quality of the information in the feedback loop. The model assumes that policies and their implementations are critical variables determining results in educational institutions. A further assumption is that the purpose of research is to enable us to reflect on the consequences of policy adoption and implementation, to modify our choices accordingly, and thus to achieve more successfully the values embedded in the hard core. Thus, policies take the position of the central independent variables in our research efforts. Other variables should be considered when they can be shown to have a significant effect on policy-making or implementation.

To a remarkable degree this has not been the case, as even a cursory review of journals such as the *Educational Administration Quarterly* will show. The pages of these journals are filled with articles dealing with the effects of organizational climate, leadership styles, organizational structures, and beliefs about pupil control on various and sundry aspects of schools. Many of these studies are informative regarding the theoretical conceptions from which they are derived, and, indeed, the good ones also enlighten us regarding the social operation of educational institutions. However, they have in common a relative disregard for administratively manipulatable variables. It is unclear, for example, why (much less how) an administrator or policy-maker might go about changing an organization's climate.

Our view suggests that such variables are of interest to the administrator when they function to facilitate or retard rational policy-making and implementation. Studying these variables, thus, might be rendered both more useful and more illuminating if their connection to the process of policy-making and implementation were explicit. That is, these variables take on increased practical *and* theoretical significance when they are linked to a framework explicitly concerned with action. An obvious way to forge such a linkage is to treat them as intervening variables conditioning the outcomes of a specific policy or its implementation. For example, an excellent study of the effects of hierarchical differentiation (organization structure) on group decision-making in an educational setting is that of Bridges, Doyle, and Mahan.[15] That study, however, would have been considerably more useful had it been concerned with examining the effects of hierarchical structure on the interpretation and implementation of a consequential policy in schools, rather than on the solution of the "doodlebug problem"—a laboratory exercise with no obvious analogue in administrative action. Generally then, the model implies a priority for our research efforts in educational administration. Of first rank are studies that investigate the effects of deliberate choices among alternative courses of social action—policies—on the desired outcomes implicit in the basic normative beliefs from which the policies are derived. Studies of other variables of more purely theoretical interest—for example, organizational structure—are to be considered of secondary importance, until they can be shown to influence policy implementation or results.[16]

Just as the model suggests that policies should play a central role in our research as independent variables, it also suggests the direction we should look in selecting our dependent variables. Obviously, when policies are explicit and well formulated, and their intended outcomes are clear, those outcomes are the most appropriate candidates for the position of dependent variables. However, those who have engaged in policy or evaluation research will recognize that intended outcomes are rarely explicit, either in the policy itself or in the mind of its formulator or implementor. Instead, a major responsibility of the researcher is to make them explicit.[17]

One source for identifying the objectives of a policy is, of course, the norms embedded in the hard core—the social values the policy is intended to realize. These norms are, themselves, often unarticulated. Thus, the researcher may have the task of constructing the normative-theoretical hard core such that the policy under investigation can be treated as an attempt to realize it.

It should be noted here that our model implies that formulating objectives for a set of policies is not simply a matter of discovering or inventing a set of intentions for the administrator or policy-maker. Rather the researcher is attempting to construct a coherent set of norms and values in terms of which the policy under consideration becomes plausible. The objectives of administrators or policy-makers for a given set of policies may, after all, have more to do with organizational maintenance or personal advantage than for accomplishing something of social utility. Our model suggests that the researcher who attempts to construct or reconstruct objectives for a policy need not be conceived as simply imposing his pet research interests over the real concerns of the decision-maker. He may instead be relating policy to a more comprehensive set of social values. Our model indicates that objectives occur in a theoretical context, that they can be made objects of rational assessment, and that educational researchers have a responsibility to engage in such an assessment. This responsibility is easily ignored, and, indeed, there are often seductive reasons for doing so. That is, we suspect that the relative lack of clarity concerning policy outcomes does tempt us to substitute our own pet research interests for those of the policy-maker or for those approximate to the policies under consideration. When that happens the researcher winds up answering a question for which the policy-maker has no need of an answer, and the view that research is useless is reinforced.

In this regard it is important to note that social science theory has a useful role in identifying outcomes. As noted, even where policy outcomes are explicit, it is virtually certain that other unintended or unanticipated consequences will accompany a policy implementation. The identification and assessment of such consequences is an important aspect of policy research, and social science theory can be very useful in that endeavor. For example, a few years ago one of us had an opportunity to participate in a research project designed to assess the effects of a planning-programming-budgeting (PPB) system on school districts. Conceptualizing the system as a form of bureaucratization, it was possible to identify several potential effects which were unintended by either the developers of the system or its adopters. As it turned out, few of the intended benefits were achieved, whereas several of the unintended (and undesired) outcomes were evidenced, and those outcomes were perceived as fatal by the adopting school district. These effects might have been overlooked had concern been only with the explicit intentions of the system.

Another methodological implication of the model derives from the importance of predictability of outcomes in real systems for real actors. The obligation to make, implement, and modify current policy in light of its results is essentially an obligation to understand the consequences of decisions and actions. Thus, there is a need to be able to predict consequences, not only (or even) to explain them. The social sciences, like all sciences, are ultimately concerned with the development of explanations. That, after all, is what theory is supposed to do. We sometimes forget that, whereas science is concerned with understanding, practitioners and policy-makers are more often concerned with prediction. Indeed, many "savvy" administrators, the ones whom most observers would term successful, often seem entirely unable to explain why things worked out the way they did—why a decision had the effect they desired. In short, they had no explicit theory that guided their decisions.[18] What they did have was an exceptional ability to predict the consequences of their acts. Now it is true that a good explanatory theory may also be a good predictive one, but that is not necessarily the case. (Some philosophers hold that the ability to explain entails the ability to predict. Even so, it does not follow that a good explanation will have manipulable independent variables or that it will predict the consequences of the actions available to the administrator.) And it is certainly true that good predictions are not necessarily based on good explanations. An example of this is the relatively successful predictions of college success that admissions people routinely make, based on a few numerical scores. Yet those scores certainly do not constitute a theory of academic achievement. Sometimes we suspect that the meaning of the criticism leveled at academic research by practitioners—that it is too "ivory tower" and "not in touch with the real world"—is simply another way of making this point. It is a plea for research to be relevant to their real concern, which is not so much to understand their world but to make it predictable. In this regard, one of the virtues of the model presented is that, in philosophical terms, it is a model of practical rather than theoretical reasoning. It suggests how to be rational in the domain of action rather than the domain of understanding.

This focus on prediction rather than explanation suggests that research models of a policy's impact might well allow for a bit more redundancy than is currently viewed as desirable. Put in the language of regression equations, higher R^2s are to be sought, even if the cost of achieving them is the inclusion of atheoretical (but correlated) variables in the equation.

A related methodological point also derives from the importance of prediction. That is, we may wish to reconsider the common strategy of holding constant confounding variables—for instance, the background characteristics of students—when examining the effects of a policy change. Such a strategy may well hide more than it reveals and partially account for the frequency of our no-significant-difference findings. These findings are particularly unfortunate in policy research, where they may result in abandoning a policy that was in fact working for some subset of its target population. For example, Jennings and Niemi, while concurring with the findings of other researchers that social studies curricula have little effect on students' political knowledge, did find such effects when black pupils were examined separately.[19] Had they adopted the common practice of entering race in a regression equation along with their other independent variables, such a finding might not have been made. Background conditions are never constant for policy-makers or practitioners—either across time or across settings—hence the researcher may miss relevant policy outcomes by artificially making them so. Put another way, the variation in implementations noted earlier represents a phenomenon to be capitalized on, not one to be "washed out" in a statistical manipulation.

A further methodological implication of the model derives from the indirect path from policy to outcomes. Obviously the nature of an implementation may have important consequences for the effectiveness of a policy. Thus, research in an applied field must attend to the implementation as well as to the policy itself. This point has been made in different ways by Charters and Jones[20] and by Coleman.[21] The latter calls for what he terms "social audits" in the conduct of policy research. These audits are to be carried out by tracing the flow of resources from the point of disbursement to their point of impact on the intended recipient. It is those resources experienced by the recipient that are to be related to the policy outcomes, not those resources disbursed. However, it is surely of interest to policy-makers to know the relative loss of resources experienced under different implementations. Thus, there are at least two possible causes of a finding of "no effect" in policy research. The resources as experienced may be ineffective, or the resources as disbursed may never reach their intended recipient. Unless policy research traces these resources through the implementation process, there is no way of telling which of these causes of a no-effect finding is the correct one. Note, generally, that a policy can often be defended against failure by deflecting criticism onto auxiliary hypotheses concerning implementation. The response to Jensen's charge that compensatory education has failed has been that it was never tried.

Another consideration concerns the importance of replications in policy research. We are, of course, accustomed to paying lip-service to the necessity to replicate a research finding. In fact, however, we seldom do so. In the case of our doctoral students, we virtually bar them from replicating others' work as their dissertation research. Only in the case of a study whose findings stunningly violate common knowledge—for example, *Equality of Educational Opportunity*—is replication diligently sought. Replication, as used here, refers not to the exact reproduction of an earlier work, but rather, to its reproduction in different settings, under somewhat different implementation conditions, and utilizing alternative data analysis strategies. The variation in implementations of a given policy provides an excellent opportunity for exactly this sort of replication. The model implies the importance of replication and redundancy of information. For if policies are to be altered when expected results are not forthcoming, an alteration should be based on many attempts at implementation in different sites with differing targets. Certainly a policy-maker might be ill-advised to drop a promising strategy in his own jurisdiction on the basis of negative findings in another, or even, for that matter, on the basis of one negative finding in his own. Rather, rational policy change is based on a steady accumulation of research results, all of which bear on the policy rather than a single finding.[22]

In addition to replication, the model requires that policy researchers develop methods of aggregating the findings of diverse studies conducted in numerous settings using varying methods. That is, the model requires that the results of R_a, R_b ... R_n somehow be validly merged to provide reliable information regarding the efficacy of P_1. Such a merging cannot be reasonably accomplished by merely counting each separate study as a "vote" regarding the policy's efficacy. In fact, such a voting procedure will often yield an erroneous conclusion. A methodology for accumulating results is still in its infancy, but promising techniques are available and will need to be utilized.[23]

Two further comments are in order in regard to this point. First, statistical significance carries less weight in policy research than in basic research. Being very certain that a result is not due to chance in one locale is little guarantee that the result may be expected in another. Rather, a policy-maker's confidence in predicting a result is greater when that result has been shown to occur over time in many different situations. That is, the policy is found to be robust. Conversely, a no-significant-difference finding carries greater weight when the policy in question has been repeatedly tried and has repeatedly failed to produce the expected results.

Second, it might be objected that replication is too costly of research manpower. That is, the opportunity cost of replicating previous work is the time to pursue new and potentially fruitful lines of inquiry. This is, of course, correct in a system where resources are scarce. We are not convinced, however, that research manpower is in scarce supply in educational administration. If one is willing to count doctoral theses in this field as research (and we are), then a conservative estimate of research manpower expended in 1975, was on the order of two thousand man-years! Educational administration as a field may well receive more research attention than any other academic specialty, with the possible exception of chemistry.

Generally, then, our model suggests that being rational in policy-making consists in modifying current policy in light of our fundamental objectives and in light of our current success. We thus need to know not just whether something works, but also why it works, when and where it works, and whether it can be made to work. Replication of the sort indicated seems a key part of generating such information.

Finally, the model, in indicating that policies are intended to realize more basic values, implies that we need to develop a measure of what Popham has called "practical significance" in addition to our usual measures of statistical significance.[24] That is, policy-makers need some assessment of the magnitude or import of a policy's effects, in addition to an assessment of the probability that those effects are due to chance. As we are all aware, statistical significance is heavily dependent on sample size. Consequently, with a large enough N, we may be very certain that an effect is real, but nevertheless quite in the dark about whether or not the effect is of any practical import. Two possibilities come to mind in this regard, neither of them satisfactory. One, suggested by Popham, is ω^2 essentially an estimate of the proportion of variance explained, relative to the total variance. A second is some variant of cost-effectiveness analysis. Both of these, however, have serious shortcomings for educational policy research.

Finally, let us close with a somewhat pessimistic comment on methodology in policy research. It is tempting to believe that well-developed methods will provide more definitive answers to policy questions and hence reduce substantive disagreements over what the facts are. Instead, the reverse seems to occur. When the policy implications of a study are in dispute, further and more methodologically sophisticated studies are unlikely to resolve the dispute; they merely move the argument from a public setting to an academic one. Cohen and Garet, in discussing the school effects literature, note:

> ... it seems plain that applied research on the effects of schooling is more complex and difficult to interpret now than it was a decade ago. Improving applied research has produced paradoxical results: knowledge which is better by any scientific standard, no more authoritative by any political standard and often more mystifying by any reasonable public standard. Methodological conflict, then, accompanied by growing technical complexity, is one important reason applied research has failed to produce much authoritative knowledge for decisions.[25]

It is possible, however, to place another interpretation on the growing technical complexity associated with the school effects literature. The increasingly dubious ransacking of data in search of school effects may provide one more criterion of a degenerating research program. Policy-makers at least seem to think so.

Notes

1. David K. Cohen and Michael S. Garet, "Reforming Educational Policy with Applied Research," *Harvard Educational Review* 45, no. 1 (February 1975):17-43.

2. A. Cahn, "Jurisprudence," *New York University Law Review* 30 (1955):150-169.

3. Mark Yudof, "Equal Educational Opportunity and the Courts," *Texas Law Review* 51, no. 3 (March 1973):411-504.

4. Imre Lakatos, "Falsification and the Methodology of Scientific Research Programs," in I. Lakatos and A. Musgrave, eds., *Criticism and the Growth of Knowledge* (Cambridge, England: Cambridge University Press, 1970).

5. Kenneth A. Strike, "An Epistemology of Practical Research," *Educational Researcher* 8 (January 1979):10-16.

6. Lee J. Cronbach and Patrick Suppes, eds., *Research for Tomorrow's Schools* (New York: Macmillan Company, 1969).

7. See for example, James S. Coleman, "Policy Research in the Social Sciences" (Washington, D.C.: General Learning Corporation, 1972); Daniel Stufflebeam et al., *Evaluation and Decision Making* (Itasca, Ill.: F.E. Peacock, 1971); and Donald Campbell, "Methods for the Experimenting Society" (Paper presented at the American Psychological Association Meeting, Washington, D.C., September, 1971).

8. Karl Popper, *The Logic of Scientific Discovery* (New York: Science Editions, 1961).

9. Daniel E. Griffiths, "The Nature and Meaning of Theory," in D. Griffiths, ed., *Behavioral Science and Educational Administration*, NSSE Yearbook (Chicago: University of Chicago Press, 1964), pp. 95-118.

10. Thomas Kuhn, *The Structure of Scientific Revolution*, 2d ed. (Chicago: University of Chicago Press, 1970).

11. Lakatos, "Falsification and Methodology."

12. Strike, "Epistemology of Practical Research."

13. Charles O. Jones, *An Introduction to the Study of Public Policy* (Belmont, Calif.: Duxbury Press, 1970).

14. David Braybrooke and Charles E. Lindblom, *A Strategy of Decision* (New York: The Free Press, 1963).

15. Edwin M. Bridges, Wayne J. Doyle, and David J. Mahan, "Effects of Hierarchical Differentiation on Group Productivity, Efficiency and Risk Taking," *Administrative Science Quarterly* 13, no. 2 (September 1968):305-319.

16. See Emil J. Haller, "Further Notes on the Poverty of Educational Administration" (Paper presented at the National Convention of the American Educational Research Association, Chicago, Illinois, 1972).

17. Emil J. Haller, "Cost Analysis for Educational Program Evaluation," in W. James Popham, ed., *Educational Evaluation: Current Application* (Berkeley, Calif.: McCutchan, 1974).

18. Jean Hills, "The Preparation of Administrators: Some Observations from the Firing Line," *Educational Administration Quarterly* 11, no. 2 (Autumn 1975):1-20. See also, William D. Greenfield, "Complimentary Theories of Practice: Five Principals' Perspectives" (Paper presented at the Northeast Educational Research Association meeting, October, 1975).

19. M. Kent Jennings and Richard G. Niemi, "Patterns of Political Learning," *Harvard Educational Review* 38, no. 3 (Summer 1968):443-467.

20. W.W. Charters, Jr. and John E. Jones, "On Neglect of the Independent Variables in Program Evaluation," in J.V. Baldridge and T.E. Deal, eds., *Managing Change in Educational Organizations* (Berkeley, Calif.: McCutchan, 1975).

21. Coleman, "Policy Research in Social Sciences."

22. Ibid.

23. Richard J. Light and Paul V. Smith, "Accumulating Evidence: Procedures for Resolving Contradictions among Different Research Studies," *Harvard Educational Review* 41, no. 4 (November 1971):429-471.

24. W. James Popham, *Educational Evaluation* (Englewood Cliffs, N.J.: Prentice-Hall, 1975).

25. Cohen and Garet, "Reforming Educational Policy," p. 33. Copyright © 1975 by President and Fellows of Harvard College. Reprinted with permission.

12 Variables Affecting Research in Educational Administration

Glenn L. Immegart and
Howard S. Bretsch

A wide variety of variables condition or affect inquiry in a field, regardless of its professional or disciplinary nature. Some of these variables have already been treated in one or more of the preceding chapters. For example, the research-practice relationship, the state of knowledge in the field, the quality and heuristic value of concepts and theory, inquiry approaches and methodologies, data collection instrumentation, procedures of analysis, and, of course, the quality of the research question or problem have all received explicit attention. However, as a result of the focus of these chapters, some other variables, such as the institutional setting, funding or fiscal support of research, the training and development of researchers, avenues and opportunities for colleagueship, and, indeed, the characteristics of researchers themselves have not been treated.

Obviously, some of these other variables are quite important to research in any field. Yet there has been relatively little research on research, although the sociology of knowledge is experiencing increasing popularity. Actually, the farther away from the process and focus of inquiry these variables are, the less attention they generally have been accorded. There is, however, a very modest but growing concern about several categories of these variables. In particular—and in addition to the mounting concern for the sociology of knowledge—the institutional setting, attributes of researchers themselves, and funding or grant-getting seem to loom, at least experientially, as important conditioners of research. Although grant-getting or research funding was not explored in the seminar giving rise to this book,[1] the two other categories of variables affecting inquiry were. Accordingly, this chapter includes two sections, one on researchers in educational administration and the other on institutional variables affecting research.

In the first section of this chapter Professor Glenn L. Immegart considers the researchers in educational administration. Drawing on available data and experience, Immegart explores what is known about educational administration researchers and raises questions about their current existence and future. Dean Howard S. Bretsch in the second section uses his experience as a professor in four universities and dean of graduate studies in two universities to examine institutional variables affecting research in educational administration. The institutional variables cited by Bretsch are supported by the findings of a number of studies.[2] His analysis is, however, based on his observations as a professor, researcher, and administrator in several different higher education settings.

Researchers in Educational Administration— An Endangered Species?

Glenn L. Immegart

In the course of time mutations are inevitable. In the mid-fifties a rather remarkable one occurred in the professional field of educational administration. As a result, a rare and valuable species emerged—the researcher of educational administration. So unique and distinctive was this addition to the fold that others nurtured the new species, protected it, and provided it with an honored position in the kingdom of educational administration. Spurred by this hallowed existence, and further fed by the funding from outside agencies that saw a wide variety of social and behavioral science research as a panacea, the species grew in numbers and began to do different and wonderful things to the delight of the kingdom. Central to the mounting theory-research emphasis, the researcher not only studied administration but also was an important element in revitalized preparation programs and the analysis of problems and issues in the practice of educational administration. The field looked to the researchers for answers and direction. Even the members of the elite species in other kingdoms who did similar things took note of this species, and together they on occasion attacked that elusive and elevated goal of truth or knowledge about the administration of education.

But what do we know of this species and its members? How is it faring today? What are its prospects in the future? Certainly its effect on inquiry in educational administration is paramount.

Interestingly, we know relatively little about the researchers in educational administration. Most can name some, and, of course, opinions about researchers abound. Despite a growing number of assessments of research, less concern has been expressed for studying researchers themselves. We all speak as if we know educational administration researchers well, but, in fact, we know little beyond our personal impressions and generalized conclusions, usually based on a few cases and not very extensive observation or analysis.

Much of what is known about researchers in educational administration is a by-product of research directed toward other purposes. From a variety of studies, such as those by Campbell and Newell[3] and the Ladd-Lipsett surveys,[4] we know researchers are a distinct subgroup. That is, not all professors (or, of course, practitioners) are researchers. Further, it is obvious that researchers are rare—they are neither numerous nor like those in other subgroups. In addition, those in this subgroup are not "pure." That is, researchers do other things as well as research, although those in other subgroups who do other things do not always do research. And, researchers, like some other valued species—home-run hitters, quarterbacks, and chess players—"wear out" or seem to get less productive over time and eventually find other activities of greater interest. But these are generalizations and are all too familiar to everyone in the field. Do we know more?

A reanalysis of the Campbell and Newell study data on professors of educational administration shows that there is surprisingly little that distinguishes the researchers per se.[5] Using a Chi Square analysis for comparing researchers and nonresearchers in University Council for Educational Administration (UCEA) institutions on all decodable variables in the study, the only statistically significant characteristics of the researchers were: (1) they obtain more funding than nonresearchers and (2) they report more outside salary than nonresearchers. Otherwise, researchers and nonresearchers in UCEA universities are an amazingly homogeneous lot in terms of the Campbell and Newell data. For the total sample of UCEA and non-UCEA professors, however, researchers also consult more and enter the professorship earlier. A number of other interesting tendencies surfaced from the reanalysis. Researchers tend to receive doctorates from eastern or Canadian universities, and assistant professors report doing more research and full professors less. Those with economics backgrounds seem to research more, and those with psychology and public administration backgrounds research the least. In sum, however, there are not many leads from these data for improving our understanding of the species.

From another assessment of research in educational administration, covering the period of 1954-1974,[6] and more recent analysis of these data, a few additional insights emerge. First, professors of educational administration who are researchers display methodological biases or preoccupations, and new methodologies are largely the result of new members entering the professorship. Researchers of educational administration are, nonetheless, prone to shift what they study, and dissertation research clearly reflects, with some time lag, the changing concerns of the professoriate. There is, in fact, a faddish quality to the pursuits of researchers. Not only are researchers in educational administration provincial, evincing regional and institutional biases, but they also appear to operate within definable specializations or subareas of the field, although these are often of an interdisciplinary character.

In terms of quantity of research, educational administration researchers are probably not prolific. There are, however, few ways or standards by which to establish their productivity. In any event, the yearly number of studies is far less than what might be expected from the number of persons who say they spend 20 percent or more of their time researching. Moreover, some of the studies, and frequently some of the most important, are done by outsiders to the field.

Indeed, professors of educational administration contribute but a modest percentage of the published studies of educational administration. Some researchers in educational administration continue to define research rather loosely, and consequently the quality of their efforts varies greatly. Researchers in the field seem to interact surprisingly little in substantive ways—that is, in replicating studies, critically analyzing studies, or carrying on intellectual debates. Nevertheless, research in the field has come a long way since the mid-fifties—from textbook-writing and status studies to inquiry consonant with that in other social and behavioral science fields.

Actually, this last matter looms more important the longer one thinks about it. The mere fact that the prevailing conception of research in the field has changed so dramatically in the course of twenty years, in terms of both range and rigor, may well be enough to expect for that period of time. But this effect of their efforts contributes little to what we know about the researchers.

Readers of the Ladd-Lipsett surveys reported in *The Chronicle of Higher Education* will, however, note that the researcher of educational administration does not differ dramatically in a general sense from counterparts in other disciplines or fields with respect to percentage of the kingdom, doing its unique thing less frequently with advancing age and rank, and in terms of economic rewards, to name but the most obvious.[7] Still, this is again not too helpful in understanding the species.

Experience, on the other hand, does provide some valuable information about the educational administration researcher. For example, researchers do tend to move on to other things. Some seem to find other activities and interests once they become full professors, but there are also other things that happen. Some are attracted to administrative or other positions and appear to exit for good. Researchers of educational administration are lost to deanships, chairmanships, and a variety of university, agency, and association administrative posts. On a continuing basis, this talent drain tends to subsume almost a "who's who" list for the prior decade of inquiry. The member of this species that commits a full and productive career to research appears to be the rarest of the rare.

Evidence now reveals that research flourished most in the first decade of the new species. Despite the rhetoric and continued ceremonial chants about research and researchers, the second decade (mid-sixties to the present) has not been quite so favorable. Research production, in fact, has failed to keep pace with the growing numbers in the professoriate at large. Other forces such as the decline in grant monies, changes in the field of administration, the growing importance of developmental activities, and fragmentation within the species itself have also impacted on the researchers.

This current fragmentation or balkanization of educational administration researchers is of considerable import.[8] Increasingly the researcher is a member of a small subgroup representing a more or less well-defined specialization or special interest within the field. That is, there are educational finance researchers, higher education administration researchers, personnel administration researchers, politics of education researchers, decision-making researchers, and so on. Further, identity more and more lodges with the splinter group rather than the field at large, and "bridging" or dialogue across interest groups is infrequent. Witness only what happens at the annual meetings of the American Educational Research Association and in terms of conferences, publications, and colleagueship generally—as well as the novelty of a seminar such as the one producing this book. There is little collating or pulling together in the larger field, and communications are increasingly fragmented. Even the UCEA network gives evidence of the pervasive balkanization—higher education administration, special education administration, organizational theory, inservice programs, and numerous other interest group networks functioning independently.

Bridging, then, is clearly a problem. From time to time a bridging concept emerges (such as policy analysis now, or organization theory or administrative behavior some time ago), but the propensity toward segmentation is such that today's bridge is another specialization (or two) tomorrow.

The consequences of balkanization go beyond one hand not knowing what the other is doing. It as well affects theory-research linkages, the all-important research-practice linkage, and it gets in the way of consolidating, refining, and extending knowledge about the field. There is also some experiential evidence that this phenomenon may even produce such fragmentation as to lead to the demise or separation of parts of the field.

We further know from experience that researchers are both constrained and aided by institutions, the state of knowledge, the state of the development of the field of educational administration (and this is different and distinct from the state of knowledge), availability of resources, governmental regulations, and by characteristics of the researchers themselves. Like any group, members of this species also exhibit preferences and biases and are affected by their own halos and ego inflation. Unfortunately, we do not know a lot about how such things impinge on researchers and precisely what their effect is on the researcher's work. Systematic inquiry into the origin and nature of the species is needed as well as research on the development, nurture, and protection of it. Without this we can do little to alleviate the growing problems of production (and reproduction) of the species and maintenance of the productive life of its members.

What does this mean, and how does all of this affect research in educational administration? Adding up what we know, sketchy as it is, the research professor of educational administration is at least a species threatened and possibly an endangered species. Researchers are increasingly isolated into splinter and special interest groups. Also they wear out or move on to other things and find other challenges as they grow older or are promoted. There is as well a tight market as a result of declining enrollments and retrenchment, which currently limits the influx of new members. All this in combination with the foregoing does not bode well.

In addition, with the decline in funding and support of the researcher, resources are a growing problem. There have also been shifts in both preparation and the field at large away from research. Because of the larger educational administration job market, preparation has shifted to a focus on practice, and, because of the complexity and tenuous nature of administering, administrators seem to be unable to wait for answers or guidance from researchers. "Leads" or insights from dialogue and "war stories" are better than nothing, particularly when answers are so long in coming as well as so few and far between. Finally, over the past two decades we have done little to improve and strengthen the species or extend its productive life.

In sum, researchers in educational administration are not generally nurtured or faring as well as they once were. Too many assume all is well as other mutations or developments are currently being strengthened, while the one of such import a decade or two ago is left to fend for itself.

Clearly something must be done to counter the threats to the addition of the fifties. It really is not possible for educational administration to rely so heavily on dissertations and outsiders in the quest for knowledge about the administration of education. Not wishing to disparage dissertation researchers, we still must remember that dissertations usually are first efforts, are program requirements, and are additionally restricted by time, budget, and feasibility constraints that tend to minimize or compromise rather than maximize the effort. Programmatic approaches in dissertation inquiry pose further formidable problems. Outsiders have contributed greatly to the study of educational administration, and many such researchers in time have even become insiders. This is, however, a small pool, and many outsiders have their own interests at the forefront and may lack sufficient understanding of education or educational administration to maximize their efforts in our domain. Communications are not always easy with colleagues across fields and disciplines. Interestingly, although this holds for fields and disciplines, communication is frequently easy from a subarea of one field or discipline to a subarea of another. The net effect, nonetheless, remains of a communication problem in the larger sense, because of balkanization or fragmentation within educational administration.

In this age of ferment and change, will the researcher of educational administration, like the dinosaur and passenger pigeon, disappear? Probably not. However, it is time to look at researchers to better understand them and to deal with the problems that threaten their existence and productivity. Without researchers in educational administration and a healthy climate for inquiry, the negative effect on knowledge development in the field should be obvious. What it is that contributes to the distinctiveness of this species and what can be done in order to develop and strengthen the species ought to be priority concerns. The species is not robust and flourishing, nor is it holding its own under the threats of recent developments.

Institutional Variables Affecting Research
in Educational Administration

Howard S. Bretsch

Perhaps the institutional variable affecting research that first comes to mind, or is cited most frequently, is an institution's reward system for its faculty members.[9] Important as this is, attention to other variables may help to place this one in better perspective.[10]

In looking at the other variables, many of which are interrelated but for purposes of identification and emphasis can be treated separately, some may seem obvious and even commonplace. Nevertheless, the meaning given to them by the institution and the profession at large makes a significant difference in the nature and quality of research produced.

The broad goals of the institution and the academic unit (for example, the school or college of education) establish the basic conditions under which research is, or is not, apt to flourish. In those institutions where research as a goal is taken seriously, its implementation: (1) tends to result in an academic climate favorable to research, (2) influences in large measure the quality of research produced, and (3) becomes a bench mark for the employment of faculty members. To achieve these results, it is important that the research goal is stated with a precision that is clear to all concerned and that among those concerned there is general understanding and agreement as to the extent and intensity of the commitment to research. All of us are aware that institutions typically claim that instruction, service, and research are their three main goals. But we also know that efforts to fulfill these goals with equal fervor are sometimes not realized. In fact, research seems to be neglected most often. Obviously in such cases, the goal statements per se are only secondary to the performance of the governing board, the administration, and the faculty of the institution.

As an institutional goal, research must not be interpreted narrowly. For example, the interpretation of what is research must accommodate the efforts of a faculty member for whom some single question results in a lifetime of study. The interpretation of the research goal should not, however, discourage the beginning researcher (faculty member or student) from studying a wide variety of problems in somewhat less depth. Furthermore, the goals for research should not exclude group endeavors, be regarded as discovery only, or exclude the use of research as an instructional medium. In short, the broad goal of research for an institution should take on the attributes of inclusiveness not exclusiveness. If the institution is serious about its commitment to research and support for research is demonstrated, a favorable climate for research will be felt, and a community of scholars is apt to develop where personnel converse about inquiry, study, and discovery. Hence, where the conditions implied are met, the vitality and contributions of research efforts tend to set up self-renewal and self-reinforcing mechanisms—much the result of the institution's goals and commitment to research.

A second variable affecting research at an institution of higher education is its leadership. Notwithstanding the posture of the central administration concerning research, this variable is especially relevant for many colleges or schools of education where major research endeavor has not been its first priority. Presumably, at most institutions, the college or school dean and faculty have considerable latitude in charting the course of the unit. Obviously, some appropriate compatibility with the institution's broader goals must be found, but within reason many colleges of education may determine the unit's primary mission, its curriculum, its faculty, its admission standards, and a variety of other things. Where exceptions to such freedoms are found, forces external to the unit, often embedded in tradition, governance, or legal restraints, create very real road-blocks for the dean. Assuming that all these limitations do not face a dean at once, efforts made in a variety of ways determine whether or not research will flourish. Later reference will be made to the deployment of material resources and the utilization of material incentives, which often have an impact on the behavior of the faculty to engage in research. For now, the leadership capacity of the dean, which tends to affect research production, is the primary consideration.

From my observation, the dean who has engaged in research, uses research findings, and demonstrates that he or she knows what research is all about, sets implicitly or explicitly a clear notion of the research goals for the college or school. The dean, however, cannot stop with rhetoric or demonstration but must incorporate this research orientation into a definition of the mission of the college. The dean must be sensitive to, and tolerant of, divergent views on the matter of research; yet the dean must try to create a climate and an identity for the school that the faculty views as reasonable expectations for inquiry and research. Not to do so may result in superficial dialogue, little commitment, and a pseudo-inquiry or a faking of research endeavor. Beyond making clear the expectations for the faculty to engage in research, the dean must undergird or reinforce the avowed mission of research through a variety of actions and decisions. These range all the way from listening briefly to the researcher who has a new "hot idea," or granting some minor perquisite, to implementing as equitably and effectively as possible the institution's reward system for the researcher. In brief, the college faculty whose dean is only mildly interested in research and who does not, in many tangible and intangible ways, support research will find it easy to divert the faculty's energies to other things. Some of these diversions may be appropriate and fruitful; they may even facilitate efforts of the researcher. On the other hand, their very attractiveness, often with their more immediate rewards, may make it doubly important that the dean decisively and consistently supports and reinforces the research mission. Administrative leadership is imperative to the furtherance of research activity in the school or college of education.

A third variable affecting research in educational administration must be put in a historical and professional perspective. As such, it may be regarded as an institutional variable because of its two-dimensional pervasiveness among faculties in educational administration over the years. This variable is the perception that faculty members in educational administration have of both the kind and place of research efforts in the academic and professional worlds as well as in their college's program for preparing educational administrators.

Except for a very few scholars at a dozen or so institutions, programmatic research as one dimension has never been a first priority of faculty members in educational administration. This is, at least, indicative of a low commitment to research and incremental knowledge development. Surveys in the thirties were popular, but too frequently their purposes and results were appropriately restricted to a particular locale. Then in the fifties and sixties with an infusion of federal and foundation funds, the pace of research effort increased considerably. But, even during that period, it seems safe to say, there was not a large number of faculty members who devoted as much as 50 or even 25 percent of their academic time to research, and programmatic efforts were not more conspicuously present. Many reasons may be advanced for this condition, including increased teaching loads, lags in research skills, attractiveness of other professionally related activities, or whatever. And, whereas surveys and other forms of "housekeeping" research have their place, often they are one-time efforts and along with other more sophisticated one-time efforts do not contribute a great deal toward providing insights or solutions to fundamental and persistent problems. Furthermore, such research efforts, when accompanied by a lack of adequate theory, often stand alone as descriptions of conditions that neither bear replication nor serve as cornerstones on which future research can be built. The fact remains, there continues to be a dearth of significantly programmatic research on the persistent problems in education that relate to educational administration.

There is another dimension to the relationship of research and practice in educational administration. Whereas much of the earlier research in educational administration lacked a theoretical base and was conducted by practitioner-oriented faculty, more recently some faculty members who are long on theory but short on practice have been dealing with problems in a pure or basic research sense. A bit more attention to practical problems and the real world (the use of theory having been satisfied), the better may be the results of such research efforts. Prescribing the right balance between theory and practice in research is not the goal here, but the situations, as described, may be considered institutional variables affecting research, since they relate very closely to faculty recruitment practices. One step in the right direction might be to develop among both the practice-oriented researchers and the more theory-oriented researchers a colleagueship that would draw on the strengths of both.

If, in the future, professors of educational administration are to tackle the kinds of problems referred to here and in the foregoing chapters of this book, it would seem that they must: (1) abandon the pervasive notion that educational administration is only practitioner oriented, (2) behave as though theory-based research were a highly important aspect of their work and profession, (3) insist that their institution's program in educational administration provides instruction and experience in research, and (4) become sufficiently aware of the practical dimensions of administration to render their research of genuine value in solving important problems.

A fourth, but perhaps second-most-important institutional variable (after administrative leadership) that affects research production, is the way in which an institution's reward system works for faculty members. This variable breaks down into two levels of emphasis. The matters of salary, promotion, and tenure in the reward system appear to have long-term impact on the performance of the faculty member. Other matters tend to encourage or discourage research productivity in lesser or "hygienic" ways.

Presumably, the implementation of the reward system should reflect the goals of the institution. Such is not always the case, and herein may lie considerable frustration for the faculty member. For example, in an institution where instruction has high priority, a faculty member may hear that good teaching is rewarded, only to discover that one faculty member out of a thousand gets a yearly "distinguished teaching award," and that being a good (not average) teacher gets him or her the same or nearly the same percentage salary increase as almost all his or her colleagues—be they good, not so good, or indifferent teachers. What does this have to do with research? Nothing, except to suggest that in too many institutions where research is held as a primary goal, the researcher faces this same kind of anomaly unless steps are taken to implement review procedures that realistically examine the relationship between goals and rewards. No system is perfect, but if research within the institution is a top priority, the reward system should be clearly annunciated and fairly implemented. Further, the rewards of the system should follow performance. It is important not to say one thing about research and do another if the avowed basic reward system is to have an impact on what institutions become and the contributions that faculty members make. Also, goals for research ought not be undermined by other unrealistic demands of all kinds on faculty members, and expectations that research be done in "off hours" are unrealistic. The detrimental aspect of the "publish-or-perish" syndrome, where each ersatz attempts as pounds of unrelated, "blurb type," inconsequential, and housekeeping research efforts are substituted for important research, only confound the system further. Recently a U.S. senator from Minnesota said, ". . . there has been more 'didly research' in education than in any other field."[11] Regardless of whether one agrees with this or not, it does represent a common view of educational research; more statements of this kind are no more needed than are the kinds of research that prompt such statements.

Other matters that relate to the institutional reward system, defined here as "satisfiers or dissatisfiers" or "hygienic" factors, also have a bearing on research production in a lesser, but sometimes continuous, sense. We are all aware that few schools or colleges of education can afford the luxury of having very many of their faculties whose entire work-load consists solely of research activities. Nor are there many institutions whose budgets permit the distribution of large grants of funds for research. Furthermore, for the good of the organization, and in the spirit of a strong institutional commitment to research, it does not seem wise to dichotomize the faculty into researchers and nonresearchers. But, with all these restrictions, there remain numerous incentives to encourage research activity by faculty members. Without going into detail, these include reductions in teaching loads, committee assignments, and student advisement duties. Other such incentives include providing summer research grants; student assistance; professional leaves of absence for researchers; freer use of telephone, computer, and library search technologies; travel funds for the presentation of research papers and for collaboration with colleagues at other institutions; adequate secretarial service as well as research supplies and equipment; assistance in the preparation of research proposals; and favorable treatment on university overhead requirements and salary administration related to a grant. In sum, favorable work considerations and the deployment of such material resources on a regular and planned basis convey to the beginner or veteran researcher that the institution really seriously holds research as a number one priority.

Finally, the extent to which an institution is generally known to be a research institution can be a powerful variable affecting future research endeavor. At least two basic developments support this view. First, the work of the researchers at research institutions becomes part of important state and national conferences, and their findings are reported in classrooms, journals, and dissertations. This seems to be as true for educational administration as for other areas. Secondly, the success of some institutions in receiving large grants, year after year, from governmental and foundation sources is well documented. Unfortunately, departments of educational administration on the whole have not benefited too well from the largess of government and foundations.

Being known as a research institution and of having the reputation of attracting research funds has a highly significant impact on faculty recruitment, which reinforces, in kind, the research reputation of the institution. Such a reputation also has considerable bearing on programs of instruction, opportunities for participation of faculty members in a wide variety of scholarly and professional activities, attracting capable and research-oriented graduate students, and the placement of graduates in research positions in both the public and private sectors.

To summarize, from my experience, the major institutional variables affecting research in education and educational administration are: (1) the goals of the institution and its units; (2) the leadership provided by central administration and, more particularly, the dean of the college or school; (3) the extent to which the reward system encourages members of the faculty to engage continuously in research; (4) the assistance provided the researcher through a system of incentives and material resources; (5) the extent to which the profession as a whole views research as a bona fide activity of faculty members in educational administration; and (6) the reputation of the institution as a research institution.

The variables cited obviously do not have equal bearing at all times on the amount, nature, and quality of research produced. Yet it is fair to say that each faculty member who is regarded as a researcher and who attempts to make a contribution to knowledge or practice through research will, at some time during his or her career, feel the impact of these forces.

Notes

1. The study of research funding or grant-getting, when pushed beyond status or survey reports, poses unique problems and is particularly sensitive. Interest in digging deeper into this matter seems to be greater than either the willingness or feasibility of doing so. Growing concern over the political and paternalistic aspects of grant-getting should prompt some investigation of this process, which clearly affects research activity. One recent study on this general topic is Roland J. Liebert, "Research-Grant Getting and Productivity among Scholars," *Journal of Higher Education* 48, no. 2 (March-April 1977):164.

2. Empirical support is contained in the following sources: James Thompson et al., "Truth Strategies and University Organizations," *Educational Administration Quarterly* 5, no. 2 (Spring 1967):4; William F. Glueck and Carey D. Thorp, "The Role of the Academic Administrator in Research Satisfaction and Productivity," *Educational Administration Quarterly* 10, no. 1 (Winter 1974):71; *Critical Requirements for Effective Performance as a Research Administrator*, American Institutes for Research (New York: Carnegie Corporation of New York, 1965); Frank M. Andrews and Donald C. Pelz, *Scientists in Organizations: Productive Climates for Research and Development* (Ann Arbor, Mich.: Institute for Social Research, University of Michigan, 1976); and Dianna M. Crane, *The Environment of Discovery: A Study of Research Interests in Their Setting* (New York: Columbia University Press, 1964).

3. Roald F. Campbell and L. Jackson Newell, *A Study of Professors of Educational Administration* (Columbus, Ohio: University Council for Educational Administration, 1973).

4. As reported periodically by Everett C. Ladd, Jr. and Seymour M. Lipsett in *The Chronicle of Higher Education*.

5. This reanalysis of the original data from Campbell and Newell, *A Study of Professors*, was facilitated by the availability of computer data cards from the University Council for Educational Administration. The assistance of Mr. Colin Hunter and Mr. Frederick Dembowski, graduate students at the University of Rochester, in this reanalysis was appreciated.

6. Glenn L. Immegart, "The Study of Educational Administration 1954-74," in L. Cunningham, W. Hack, and R. Nystrand, eds., *Educational Administration: The Developing Decades* (Berkeley, Calif.: McCutchan, 1977) and subsequent further analysis of the study data on researchers.

7. From data reported by Everett C. Ladd, Jr. and Seymour M. Lipsett in issues of *The Chronicle of Higher Education*, 1977.

8. Appreciation is extended to Dean James I. Doi, of the University of Rochester's Graduate School of Education and Human Development, for his helpful sharing of insights on the phenomenon of balkanization.

9. Institutions as used here are the colleges or schools of education and the universities.

10. The author also wishes to present a disclaimer—this is not a research paper in the sense of formulating hypotheses and amassing a large amount of data, and a long questionnaire was not used to solicit data about conditions for research at a group of institutions. This is a research paper only in the sense that it is a distillation of observations the author has made at the four institutions where he has been a faculty member. To most, these comments have probably been the subject of conversation in many of the offices and corridors with which they are familiar.

11. *Report on Educational Research* (Published by Education News Service, Division of Capital Publications, Inc.) 8, no. 23 (17 November 1976).

**Part V
Synthesis and Implications**

Problem setting . . . is an integral part of the work of the scientist, perhaps the most crucial part, but it has traditionally been the least well codified aspect of research in the canons of methodology and "normal science." There is, in fact, no orderly and prescribed way of problem setting.

—Martin Rein and Sheldon White, "Can Policy Research Help Policy?," *The Public Interest* 49 (Fall 1977): 130-31.

13 Currents in Collective Analysis: Concluding Views on the Research Seminar

Daniel E. Griffiths
Charles E. Bidwell, and
Arthur S. Goldberg

From the outset of the planning for the Rochester seminar on research in educational administration, there was agreement that the objectives of the conference made it imperative to provide for a mechanism for collective analysis and assessment. Consequently, three seminar participants—two who prepared papers and one who participated in all the seminar discussions—were asked to assume the role of critic and synthesizer, and to present their conclusions at the final session of the conference. Their task was to assess both the content of the seminar papers—which comprise the first twelve chapters of this book—and the seminar discussions prompted by the papers.

Their conclusions in part reflect their own views about the individual papers and in part reflect the tenor of the seminar deliberations. Their views are critically evaluative and preserve both converging and diverging themes from the seminar discussions. These three statements thus go beyond the preceding chapters and provide additional leads for inquiry. They also provide an efficient and cogent overview of the seminar and convey some of the flavor of the informal as well as formal seminar discussions. The statements are not, however, verbatim reproductions of the informal concluding comments presented at the seminar. Rather, each of the critics refined their concluding views after the seminar in the light of additional reflection.

The concluding statements are presented here in the same order as at the seminar. Dean Daniel E. Griffiths, of New York University, whose critique appears first, has been a major figure in the theory-research movement in educational administration from its inception. He also has been an active and penetrating critic of the field over that period of time. Professor Charles E. Bidwell, whose commentary follows, is an authority on formal organizations and the sociology of education. He has maintained close ties with educational administration throughout his productive career at the University of Chicago, where he now serves as chairman of the Department of Education. Dean Arthur S. Goldberg, whose remarks conclude the chapter, is the associate dean for graduate studies of the College of Arts and Sciences at the University of Rochester, and is a member of the University's faculty in political science. As both an academic administrator and an insightful social scientist, he provides a relevant external perspective on the seminar and on the field of educational administration.

Seminar Critique

Daniel E. Griffiths

This career development seminar was devoted to a difficult cause: the improvement of questions to be researched. As set forth in the program, the focus was suggested by a statement written by Einstein and Infeld:

> The formulation of a problem is often more essential than its solution, which may be merely a matter of mathematical or experimental skill. To raise new questions, new possibilities, to regard old questions from a new angle, requires creative imagination and marks real advance in science.[1]

Although the majority of the presenters spoke to the topic, it cannot be said that the desired thrust was fully achieved. At most, old problems were reviewed in ways that differed by degrees, not really in new ways.

Given the format of the program, one speaker to a topic, there was little opportunity for consensus. However, there were some points of agreement which arose as various speakers addressed their subjects and during the discussions. Speakers generally concurred on the need for field and/or case studies, the desirability of vastly improved theory, and the low quality of articles appearing in the *Educational Administration Quarterly*. On other than these points there appeared to be little in common among the speakers. This does not mean the seminar was of little consequence, but rather, that there was no spontaneous support for an idea or concept. It might be that, since financial support for research in educational administration has been minimal, researchers are studying their own interests, and they are varied. Since there is so little external support, and there is not likely to be more in the near future, this idiosyncratic approach to research is apt to continue. Just what the results will be is most difficult to predict.

In attempting to critique the seminar I shall impose an organizing scheme on the papers presented and discuss each of the elements of the scheme. No support for the scheme is offered; it is merely a convenient way of reviewing what happened, and others might well have a different organizing pattern in mind as they think about the seminar.

Not What Was Expected

The seminar turned out to be not what was expected at all. One could have reasonably assumed, given the invited speakers and the tenor of the literature on organizations, that the speakers would have been highly critical of the commonly accepted theories. Only Gibson, Greenfield, and Griffiths expressed concern for the paradigm now being used. Getzels, Bidwell, Willower, Guthrie, and Wirt, all seemingly accepted and supported present-day theories, although Wirt continually called attention to their weaknesses. McNamara was highly critical of statistical procedures used in educational administration, but he did not discuss basic theories.

The so-called Greenfield-Griffiths debate was not resumed, possibly because neither the audience nor participants thought it the time or place, but more possibly because of Willower's devastating analysis of phenomenology as a method of research. The subject of the debate, the appropriate methodology for the development of the theory, should receive further intensive attention. The arena of the debate, however, should be broadened, since it started with a disagreement on the usefulness of phenomenology as a basis for research in educational administration. The debate would be more appropriate if it concerned issues in the total field of organizations, which is seething with criticisms of the paradigm used in the past thirty years.[2]

Administrators: Who, What, Where?

As one listened to the presentations and discussions, there emerged the feeling that those at the seminar had an inaccurate and inadequate perception of educational administrators. Who they are, what they do, where they work, and what they feel and think are questions that did not seem to be considered by those participating in the seminar. Instead, there seemed to be the feeling that administrators are still the students of the professors who were present. These administrators need more tutoring, they need to read more research and theory, and they need to come to more meetings conducted by the professors. It appears to me, however, that such an attitude will lead to research and theory that is increasingly abstract and will widen the gap that now exists between professors and practitioners.

Several speakers (Bidwell, Greenfield, Griffiths, Willower, and Wirt) did call for case and/or field studies. If this call is heeded, it might lead to a much better understanding of educational administration as it is practiced today and a closer relationship to administrators. Willower emphasized this relationship when he reminded us of Iannaccone's argument that the content of field studies should have special relevance for practitioners, since that content arises from descriptions of life within school organizations.

Think, Don't Act

Greenfield, Gibson and Griffiths spoke directly to the need for a new paradigm to guide research and theory development in educational administration. Gibson's recommendation for the near future received little attention at the seminar, yet in retrospect it deserves a kinder fate. He urged that, ". . . we relax for a time our empirical bias, if we have it, and engage in some speculation about approaches to the ways in which our ideas about educational administration and, consequently, its study, have been changing during the present century."

Greenfield, in previous papers, has urged that educational administration adopt a phenomenological approach to research and in this seminar alluded to this approach again.

Griffiths argued that the present paradigm has little power and that it is badly in need of new and more potent concepts. Although still positivist in orientation, he believes that when, as it appears, organizations are staffed with people who have a strong phenomenological orientation, the substance of what is theorized about in educational administration must change. He commented, for instance, that none of the presently used theories acknowledge the existence of unions and that there are many elements of educational organizations that cannot be explained by the current paradigm.

Gibson believes that at present we are led to be suspicious not only of our generalizations, but also of our direct experiences. This he calls "critical consciousness." He summarized the paradigm shift in educational administration in the twentieth century as a ". . . movement from a paradigm that emphasized naive particularistic observation to one that gave greater importance to the theoretical base of the paradigm and is now moving to another that reflects greater critical consciousness." It may well be that Gibson is correct in the sense that we have moved, rather suddenly, from a period in which we thought we had a very useful paradigm to a period in which we are questioning most of what we thought we knew.

Time For Action

Willower, in a thoughtful, well-written paper, took a position somewhat at odds with Gibson. He presented a case in which he was quite comfortable with the present paradigm, although stating that new theories and concepts could well replace some of the old. Willower appears to be committed to what Kuhn has called "normal science," that is, research on what is considered to be the accepted paradigm. Willower presented the argument that theories now in use have resulted in much that is useful and that a great deal more research on these theories remains to be done, a very reasonable and acceptable point.

Even though Willower did make the case for normal science he laments the lack of a relationship between inquiry and practice in the administration of school organizations. One is led to believe that Willower feels the proper approach here is more field research, and more research overall, that would explain what is happening in school organizations.

Gibson and Willower appear to be in opposition, yet it would appear that the goals each espouse are worthy. One could agree with Gibson that new conceptualizations are needed, while also agreeing with Willower that educational administration should proceed full-speed ahead in the pursuit of "normal science."

Numbers, More Numbers

Whereas several spoke to the need for case studies, Bidwell discussed in detail his present work with Kasarda in Michigan and Colorado. The research has two phases: first, general surveys in which large quantities of numbers are collected and analyzed, and second, the study of particular cases identified in the first phase. The number-gathering brings back memories of Paul Mort and his associates at Teachers College.[3] It also makes one wonder about the value of this approach, in that Mort was so definitely unsuccessful in his efforts.

Guthrie made reference to Mort in his paper and erroneously contended that, "These studies [Mort's] directly linked school expenditures with student achievement." Mort did not attempt to link school expenditures with student achievement, since he felt there was no relationship. He was strongly influenced by Grimm in his thinking about student achievement. Grimm found that a relationship existed between cost of education and achievement when comparing low-cost with middle-cost, but not when comparing middle- with high-cost schools.[4] This finding, plus a distrust of testing, strongly biased Mort against the use of student achievement in his studies, since he worked almost exclusively with high-expenditure districts.

It would seem that if Bidwell restricted the collection of numbers to that necessary to locate sources for case studies, he would produce more useful research. Indeed, this is probably what he has in mind, because he stressed the need for careful, baseline descriptions of the organizational structure of schools; yet it is disturbing to read such statements as, "As segmentation of instruction increases, adding to the number of schools, the number of school principals and the number of clerks also increase." Fascination with such obvious conclusions was the trap Mort fell into, and he was never able to extricate himself from his fatal case of data fixation.

Confusions

Both Guthrie and Wirt urged educational administration to emphasize policy studies. Wirt talked about this in terms of description, explanation, criticism, and forecast. One detects a positivist orientation running through his paper and would expect that should his suggestions be adopted a thoroughly scientific research agenda would result.

One is not quite as certain of what would result should Guthrie be followed, because it is difficult to detect just where he stands. Guthrie moved back and forth between the study and practice of administration. He appeared at times to assume that present practices are the result of theories or models held by researchers—theories that then resulted in school practices. At other times, he discussed such movements as school consolidation as being explained more parsimoniously as a manifestation of an American ideological bias toward bigness and efficiency than as a product of educational research. At these times he agreed with Bidwell's argument; the schools are more open systems than had been earlier assumed, and school practices are reflections of the values and mores of the total society.

Guthrie's chapter also illustrates the difficulties that result when one attempts to build a research program on certain values to the exclusion of others. He chooses equality, efficiency, and liberty as values that should significantly influence public policy about education, claiming that these are strongly held in the American culture. (It is unfortunate that in discussing progress toward achieving these values his references are so old.) If Guthrie had chosen other values, say for instance, professionalism, then the same facts would lead to opposite conclusions. If one placed high value on educational decisions made by professional educators, then the dilution of representativeness that accompanies the reduction of school districts and, therefore, the reduction of elected school board members would be seen as a blessing rather than a disaster.

It is clear that one cannot follow both Wirt and Guthrie. Wirt's values are in his methodology, Guthrie's in his conclusions. Wirt's advice could lead educational administration toward policy research; Guthrie's advice leads toward ideological conclusions in the guise of policy decisions.

It's No Good

The *Educational Administration Quarterly* came in for a lambasting from many speakers. The poor quality of its articles was reflected in adverse comments concerning research methodology and substance. McNamara, in particular, was highly critical of the tests of significance used, noting that a more rigorous test would result in virtually no findings of significance. Griffiths criticized the research in the *Quarterly* when he reported a small study that showed that the concepts employed were of a very low level of power.

It must be pointed out, however, that the *Quarterly* is only a symptom of the low level of research in educational administration. Only 11 percent of the articles received are published, and then only after arduous labor by the associate editors and the Board of Editors. If high standards were used, the journal would not be the only quarterly published three times a year; it would be the only quarterly published once a year.

A professional journal reflects the level of research and theory its field has achieved. It cannot be better than the people it represents. In order to improve, the field must first raise its academic standards. There must be a commitment to research and theory, an upgrading of educational administration's scholarly stance. There is not much evidence that this is happening, even though Willower maintains there is evidence of slow, but tangible progress. If that is a realistic appraisal, then we must wait many years for the *Quarterly* to demonstrate substantial improvement.

Conclusion

It can be seen that this was a seminar that was more interesting in retrospect than in its experiencing. Its value lies in the differences it produced rather than in consensus, and differences are far more stimulating than similarities. Although educational administration has been subjected to systematic examination for eighty years it can still be said, as Willower did say, "It is plain there is no lack of interesting problems."

Concluding Comments

Charles E. Bidwell

Joseph Ben-David once remarked that there is no proper distinction in the social sciences between pure and applied research. Research problems and theories in social science, he argued, arise willy-nilly from the problems of social life. Whatever the social scientist's intention, his work is closely tied to the practical—from which he draws intellectual (and, increasingly, material) sustenance and to which he contributes ideas, ways of thinking, and modes of analysis.

Educational research generally, and the study of educational administration in particular, often are held up as prototypical fields of applied social science. The sessions of this conference consistently have showed the aptness of Ben-David's observation.

The debate over the merits of hermeneutic and positive analysis, widespread now among the social sciences, ran through several of our discussions. The depiction of organizations as dynamic and as small polities of microeconomies, rather than simply as hierarchical orders of rational decision-makers; awareness of the permeability and instability of organizational boundaries and of the ephemeral quality of organizations' efforts at adaptation; and finally concern for institutional factors in the ordering of organizational environment exchange—all these were themes running, explicitly or implicitly, through the conference.

These themes also are currently important in the analysis of organizations more generally. That social scientists and organizational theorists now center on these themes reflects the increasing pervasiveness of formal organizations as a means for conducting social life, the formalization of social control itself through organizational means, and the comparative view of the problems and means of organizing diverse kinds of activities that has been forced on social scientists by the pervasiveness of formal organization.

If, therefore, the study of educational organizations is to contribute with any effectiveness to the practice of education and to the conduct of educational administration, I think its contribution will be made by seizing the opportunities that the inextricability of organizational theory and practice provides for researchers and practitioners alike—through good theory, replicable findings, and common sense—to see what is truly problematic in the day-to-day practice of administration. I do not think we will be well served by stressing the theoretical or practical uniqueness of educational organizations. They are in certain senses different from other organizations, but surely we need to know more about common structural and dynamic properties of organizations, about comparative forms and processes, and about the ways in which what is common is constrained or conditioned by what is distinctive.

As formal organization has become more pervasive, and as limits on economic and population growth in American society and in the world system of which it is a part have become increasingly evident, students of organization have begun to shift their attention in dynamic analysis from processes of growth to processes of stabilization and decline, selective organizational survival, and demographic, economic, and legal-governmental constraints on organizational expansion and functioning. The effectiveness of organizations and conditions of organizational efficiency call increasingly for study.

This example of the close connection between theory, research, and practice is nowhere more evident than in education. Problems engendered by declining enrollments, legal limits to school district revenues, and governmental and popular demands for accountability, especially, force on educational administrators and policy-makers, and on students of school administration and educational policy, the urgent need to know more about processes of organizational change, about the connections between educational organization and productivity, and about the interplay between forces in the environing and internal polities of educational organizations.

If my remarks so far have any merit, they indicate that we will pursue these questions inevitably. I think in any event that we should, for they hold great promise of increased understanding. They point toward unresolved but very important questions, both substantive and methodological, that we must address. Let me outline them very briefly. Their elaboration is in part contained in the chapters here and the discussion that we have heard.

1. How do decisions get made in educational organizations? To what extent are they the loosely coupled structures that March and others suggest they are? How is decision-making affected by organizational structure, and vice-versa? How does public policy and its implementation influence decisions of actors inside educational organizations, the structures that are formed through their actions, and the ability of educational organizations to change deliberately as environing conditions change?

2. How do actors in educational organizations and members of their constituencies and regulatory bodies assess the effectiveness of their actions and, more globally, of their organizations? How are students of these organizations to define output, productivity, effectiveness, and efficiency and fix on measures of these terms in the absence of obvious units of valuation?

3. Educational organizations, at least public ones, exist in partially protected environments. What are the consequences of this fact for the foregoing phenomena? How alike or different in these respects are educational and other public-sector organizations? What are the central differences between these organizations and those that operate in market-structured environments? Is the market-nonmarket dichotomy useful, or must it be elaborated or replaced?

4. If we are to understand how organizational form and change and administrative behavior in education affect academic outputs or productivity, surely we must understand how these variables affect the instructional processes that take place in the classrooms, curricular tracks, and other work-places of schools. The same questions arise when we ask about the bearing of public policy, governmental regulation, or popular demand and mobilization on the instructional work of schools. Nevertheless, as Barbara Heyns has argued acutely, and as I have myself observed over several years as I have tried to teach a sociologist's course on the social psychology of education, we know very little about instruction or about the relationships between instruction and learning. Many of us have characterized education as technologically deprived, and it may be that, in the absence of strong technology, instruction is especially vulnerable to effects of a school's or school district's decisions about the allocation of pupils, teachers, and materials, or to whatever incentives arise from variation of organizational structure, political process, or policy implementation.

Still, before we can address such questions and try to trace the dynamic connections between such variables, the work of teachers and students, and value added to students' learning (to say nothing of their postschool lives), we must understand how this work is conducted and to what effect. Therefore, understanding of organizational effectiveness or productivity in education demands not only good organizational theory but also a good theory of instruction—no small task. We must, however, move on both fronts before we can understand the connections among these phenomena. We also must consider how, methodologically, to best move on these fronts. The question here especially is of the relative costs and benefits of case studies and large sample studies.

As I say, these are no small tasks. I view them, however, as the most central of the many urgent and potentially rewarding tasks before the student of educational administration and organization.

Concluding Remarks

Arthur S. Goldberg

The position of clean-up batter on a panel of this sort, where one is preceded by commentators of the calibre of Dean Griffiths and Professor Bidwell, is not an enviable position. Indeed, I have spent most of this conference in the position of critic. Yet no sooner has a point of criticism occurred to me, than I have observed it to be quite effectively addressed by one or another of the conference participants.

Nevertheless, there are some parting thoughts that I would like to share. I offer these primarily from the perspective of a political scientist—but a political scientist with a long-standing interest in epistemology.

Let me begin by noting that the conference has left me with the distinct impression that the inquiry into educational administration is a vibrant one, which is in good hands. Time constraints preclude paper-by-paper comments, so I offer only two examples of the evidence on which my impression is based.

The first is both technical and subtle, but is perhaps the more important for being so. James McNamara, after presenting a very interesting paper which made extensive use of correlational measures such as ω^2, was asked why in a particular instance he had not used the standardized regression coefficient β as his measure of strength of association. His reply was to the effect that he did not believe that the operational definitions of the variable had a sufficiently good fit with their conceptual meanings to warrant the use of so precise a measure. This is the sort of thinking in operations research that provides a solid bridge between P.W. Bridgman and Karl R. Popper, and that suggests that things truly are in good hands.

For my second bit of evidence, I direct your attention to the process of inquiry reflected in Charles Bidwell's paper. Therein, one finds field study, informed conjecture, tentative identification of macrolevel and microlevel parameters, modeling, hard data analysis, and an appreciation of institutional structure as the link between macrolevel variables and microlevel performance. For me, this was a refreshing forging together into a mutually supportive process of what are too often seen as disjointed elements.

Those are but two examples and, therefore, a very limited sample. Yet, they were by no means isolated instances. Rather, I see them as representative of much of the discourse that I attended.

Let me now turn to what has troubled me about this conference, and that is the view of politics in relation to educational administration, which I have heard voiced from time to time. Politics seems to be viewed too often as either extrinsic or intrusive. It seems to be viewed either as relating to some necessary evil—usually one from which monies must be elicited (the board of education, the state, the taxpayer)—or as relating to some unnecessary but inescapable intruder into the "normal" operation of the school—usually some minority group seeking to affect both the curriculum and the management of the school system. For such phenomena, politics seems to be viewed as an appropriate, if somewhat unclean, response. Politics, however, does not seem to be viewed as intrinsic to the operation of the school itself. That perspective seems faulty to me. I am not certain whether it is my prejudice as a political scientist, or my experience as an administrator, that leads me to conclude that politics is pervasive in organized societies in any form, but I do so conclude.

It seems to me that wherever one has issues that require decisions impacting on a group so that all do not perceive themselves as equitably advantaged, coercion (implicit or explicit) is involved. Any system for such decision-making will necessitate processes of coalition formation, maintenance, and dissolution—the core process of politics. Neither the most formidable of tyrants nor the most amicable of school board superintendents survives without a supportive coalition, nor are any immune from the formation of opposition coalitions.

I noted reference to the building of a supportive coalition in Professor Getzels' keynote address. Therein, he alluded to a principal who was confronted by a new faculty member, who, in turn, asserted that he (the faculty member) required a high stool on which to sit in order to lecture comfortably. That principal, apparently sensing that there was more at issue, went to some pains to insure that such a stool was available at the appropriate times in each of the rooms in which this new person was to lecture. Professor Getzels noted that this faculty member was a staunch supporter of that principal in all issues that arose thereafter. I submit that the principal in this instance was not unaware of that possibility, and, most particularly, I submit that he was well aware that there would be issues.

Were I to be offered the opportunity to teach a group of would-be researchers into educational administration, or a group of would-be educational administrators, about politics, I would feel comfortable spending several weeks on two books: Machiavelli's *The Prince* and Neustadt's *Presidential Power*. The thrust of my argument in such an exercise would be that the two books say the same thing, within the institutional parameters for which they were written.

I would like to suggest further that the study of politics is more than the reroasting of old chestnuts. Professor Wirt made reference to some of the internecine warfare within the discipline of political science. He spoke of two sides in that confrontation—the institutionalists and the behavioralists. I would add another, namely the positivists. (Perhaps the foremost practitioners of the positivist school are at the University of Rochester, led by the man who is probably the preeminent practitioner of the field, William H. Riker.) This latter group has built on the foundations of utility theory, and their notion of man as a rational decision-maker, coupled with hard data analysis, has helped move forward inquiries into both coalition formation and voting behavior.

If one takes an approach to political behavior that is avowedly rooted in the perspectives of Machiavelli, Hobbes, and Bentham, one is readily labeled a misanthrope, and cast aside. However, here the genius in the REMM (resourceful, evaluative, maximizing man) concept (from utility theory) proposed by William H. Meckling truly comes into its own. Instead of using the words of any of these *realpolitik* types, simply postulate that people are resourceful, evaluative, maximizers of whatever it is they themselves cherish. These prove to be much more palatable concepts. I want to suggest that they are not a bad beginning from which to analyze individual decision-making.

Let me propose, then, that those seeking to do analysis in educational administration take as their dependent variable, decision foci. Then ask: "Who decides?" Assume that these decision-makers fit the REMM pattern. Ask what informs their preferences, what constrains them, and what are the institution's structural incentives and obstacles to the several options before them.

The answers to these questions will not be readily apparent. Indeed, it will take many iterations of the process before there are reliable data on which to base inferences about preferences, perceived probabilities and risks, and institutional impacts. Nevertheless, by focusing on these variables within the paradigm suggested, and by careful operationalization of variables with due sensitivity to their limits, and finally by recognizing and exploring the interplay between micro- and macrolevel phenomena, I believe powerful explanatory theories can be developed in this very large and important area of social decision-making.

As noted earlier, I believe such work is well under way. I would urge only that the political be recognized and addressed not as an anomaly, but as an integral, indeed vital, part of phenomena of concern.

Notes

1. Albert Einstein and Leopold Infeld, *The Evolution of Physics* (New York: Simon and Schuster, 1938), p. 92.

2. Three volumes illustrate the nature of the present criticisms: Charles Perrow, *Complex Organizations: A Critical Essay*, 2d ed. (Glenview, Ill.: Scott Foresman, 1978); J. Kenneth Benson, ed., *Organizational Analysis: Critique and Innovation* (Beverly Hills, Calif.: Sage Publications, Inc., 1977); and David Dunkerly and Stewart Clegg, *Critical Issues in Organizations* (London: Routledge & Kegan Paul, 1977).

3. Donald H. Ross, ed., *Administration for Adaptability* (New York: Metropolitan School Study Council, 1958).

4. Lester R. Grimm, *Our Children's Opportunities in Relation to School Costs* (Springfield, Ill.: Department of Research, Illinois Education Association, 1938).

14 Education's Turbulent Environment and Problem-Finding: Lines of Convergence

William Lowe Boyd and
Glenn L. Immegart

The art of [policy] analysis consists in finding problems—relating resources and objectives—worth solving at the level of action where they occur, within the time frame available, using instruments that interested organizations can control.
—Aaron Wildavsky[1]

Wildavsky's observation sums up some hard-learned lessons for public education. Since the mid-sixties, public education in the United States has been buffeted by a turbulent, changing environment. A host of new problems worth solving have emerged. But the adequate formulation, let alone solution, of these problems has been impeded by formidable difficulties—previously unrecognized—in the coordination and control of the level of action (especially schools and classrooms) and the instruments involved (for example, teachers and curricular materials). The discovery of these difficulties, indeed, has given rise to a whole new literature on such matters as site or service delivery levels, implementation problems, and loosely coupled organizations plagued with ambiguous ends and means.[2]

If some of these discoveries seem obvious with the benefit of "twenty-twenty" hindsight, they were scarcely so evident in the heady days of the early sixties, when education was seen as very nearly a panacea for all that ailed society. This vision, however, was dashed by the meager results of the innovative educational programs of the Great Society and the war on poverty. In the face of pressing problems poorly served by prevailing paradigms, school administrators and educational researchers began a hectic search for promising new approaches. In the flux and fragmentation that followed, new specializations and subfields of research emerged, and communication across the field of educational administration as a whole became increasingly difficult.

Our reading of the chapters in this book suggests that we now can begin to see the outlines of an emerging synthesis in the field. As the seventies come to a close, something approximating a paradigm shift seems to be taking place. Thus, in this concluding chapter we want to direct attention to what we see as the lines of convergence suggested in this volume.[3] Contrary to the climate of despair reflected in assessments of the state of the field a few years ago, there now is an air of excitement stimulated by new approaches and related intellectual controversies.[4]

The Search for New Paradigms

From a benign environment of growth and widely shared, or at least largely unquestioned, values and beliefs in the fifties and early sixties, education moved rapidly into a turbulent environment characterized by conflicting demands and unmet needs, a crisis of authority, and, most recently, declining enrollments and resources. This sudden turnabout quickly called into question the internally oriented models of organizations and administration prevalent in educational administration. These "closed-system" or otherwise inappropriate models largely or entirely ignored the importance of the environment and other related dynamics and placed unrealistic expectations on the leadership and mediating ability of educational administrators. As Charles Bidwell observes in his chapter,

> Closed-system theories have approached organizations as if they were machines. The organization-as-machine is a system that remains undisturbed by events outside its boundary unless "a prime mover" of some kind—most often in these theories either an entrepreneur or top-level administrator—intervenes to change parts of the system or change the ways existing parts act on one another . . . This Newtonian version of organizational theory sets aside problems of dynamics and environments. The prime mover's intervention accounts for both, but as an unanalyzed given.

The defects of such models might have remained largely hidden or of small consequence without the dramatic change in the environment. For, as David Harvey argues, in critiquing Kuhn's theory of scientific revolutions,[5] it is not just *any* anomalies that begin to call into question prevalent paradigms, but anomalies of practical relevance:

> For example, it was known for many years that the orbit of Mercury did not fit Newton's calculations, yet this anomaly was insignificant because it had no relevance to the use of the Newtonian system in an everyday context . . . Therefore, the Newtonian paradigm remained satisfactory and unchallenged until something of practical importance and relevance could *not* be accomplished using the Newtonian system.[6]

Of course, scientific breakthroughs are scarcely restricted to those prompted by practical necessity. As Jacob Getzels notes, problem-finding often:

> is not undertaken to overcome obstacles that must be overcome because they are a threat to personal well-being; on the contrary, the

problems are sought out often at the risk of personal well-being and sometimes of life itself. Galileo raised questions about the accepted cosmology despite the threat of being burnt at the stake for it . . .

However, for the general intellectual climate to be conducive to a paradigm shift, it appears that Harvey's condition of practical relevance needs to be rather widely perceived, not just by an isolated genius like Galileo.[7]

This theme of practical relevance deserves to be underscored. It not only appears central to the dynamics of paradigm shift in our field currently, but it also is at the heart of the synthesis we can begin to see emerging. This synthesis appears to be occurring around a commitment to critically reassess the conventional wisdom of the field and an attempt—through the use of multiple methodologies and the pursuit of conceptual models isomorphic with educational organizations—to come to terms with the distinctive realities and consequences of organizational behavior and administrative practice in educational organizations. What educational administrators actually do and what difference it makes for organizational effectiveness are central concerns. At present, no single new paradigm or approach captures with precision the full range of concerns in the emerging synthesis. Of several promising approaches, however, the research approach that appears most conducive to the new thrust is that of educational policy analysis, that is, the study of the causes and consequences of policy differences at all levels of the educational infrastructure.[8] Although a new paradigm or approach may appear that will better serve the emerging synthesis, the educational policy analysis approach seems peculiarly appropriate for an applied and interdisciplinary field such as educational administration. This is so because, with its focus on the consequences of policies, on what makes a difference at the level of educational implementation, educational policy analysis helps to bind together theory and practice and provides a unifying nexus for research from different disciplines and fields of study.[9]

The onset of environmental turbulence and the expanded gulf it created between theory and practice dramatized the need for ways to draw the two together. Researchers, as well as practitioners, began to complain about this problem, a complaint that persists down to today, as shown in Thomas Greenfield's concern in this book about the disparity between the technical sophistication of research and the validity of the concepts guiding it. Indeed, Greenfield's chapter and several others in this book exemplify the new commitment to a critical reassessment of the field, to what Oliver Gibson, in his discussion of paradigm shift in this volume, calls the mood of "critical consciousness." Both Greenfield, and Emil Haller and Kenneth Strike in their chapter, call attention to the ability of theories and models to live on beyond their time as a result of "theory-saving" exercises by those caught within their spell. They thus challenge the traditional notion of research based on falsifiable hypotheses. And Greenfield is joined by others in this book in questioning the utility of the administrative theory of the past. "What do educational adminis-trators really do," they ask, and "what effects do their actions really have on other parts of their organizations and on organizational productivity?"

Griffiths' summary of the mood is that the paradigm used in educational administration in the past, and by some yet today, is:

> neither useful nor appropriate because it is no longer fruitful in generating powerful concepts and hypotheses; it does not allow us to describe either modern organizations or the people in them; and, as a result, it is not helpful to administrators . . .

> The paradigm consists largely of . . . [theories that] assume that organi-zations have goals which the members strive to attain; that there are roles, sets of expectations for the members that are agreed on (the nomothetic dimension); that behavior is more or less governed by a set of rules (bureaucratic structure); that decision-making is a systematic process; that only legitimate power is employed; and that merit is superior to politics. Administration, organizations, and organizational behavior are viewed as essentially orderly and rational. Organizations function regardless of the individuals within them.

As Griffiths' summary suggests, there are many problems with the amorphous paradigm of the past. It is at best a somewhat opportunistic combination of heterogeneous components, largely borrowed from work on industrial and business organizations. Because of the vague relationship of its elements, the restricted scope and power of its theories for educational organizations fre-quently have been further circumscribed by piecemeal use and application.

In the mood of critical consciousness, revisionist thinking is the order of the day. Naturally, this revisionism generates much divergent thinking as well as the lines of convergence we emphasize here. For example, Greenfield raises the perplexing question of the multiple faces of reality in organizations and challenges the usefulness of many of the quantitative approaches to organiza-tional research. He contends that the hard data such approaches use may just be "cheap data," that is, easily available data. The so-called soft data of qualitative approaches, on the other hand, may come closer, he thinks, to capturing something useful about the realities of educational organizations. Toward this end, Greenfield provides an evocative discussion of alternative ways of viewing schools as organizations; and he is able to point to recent thinking, such as that by James March, which challenges traditional notions or reconceptualizes matters so as to resonate with his critique.

On the other hand, James McNamara and William Meckling argue con-vincingly for the power of investigative rigor and quantification. McNamara's observations on the relationship of quantitative approaches to advances in science and knowledge development should not be overlooked. However, both Meckling and McNamara point out that the key is not only the use of rigorous quantitative approaches but also the quality of the theory involved and appropriate attention to the real world as it is. Weak theory and vague conjecture about practice and its context cannot be overcome by quantitative sophistication.

If there thus is divergence, there nonetheless is general agreement among our authors that a variety of methodologies and approaches should be explored in pursuit of the multiple realities and dimensions of educational organizations and the phenomena relating to them. Amidst this variety, a unifying theme in the critical reassessment of the field is a widespread conviction that we need to take a hard new look at the unique characteristics of educational organizations and their administration. In his chapter on paradigm shift in our field, Gibson traces movement from a naive particularism, emphasizing the personality of the leader, prior to 1950, to the much more conceptual "theory movement," from 1950 to 1970, and, finally, to the present period of "critical consciousness." Underlying this evolution, he sees a continuous movement, as a function of modernization, from a particularistic to a universalistic orientation. And there is no doubt that during the theory movement the thrust of organizational research—by social scientists as well as researchers in educational administration—emphasized the search for commonalities, drew on the broad utility of prevailing but disparate models for organizational analysis, and even, at one time, harbored the possibility of a general theory of organizations and administration. But the search for commonalities now has given way to the realization of the peculiar significance of the unique difficulties of educational organizations mentioned at the opening of this chapter. Thus, at first glance it may appear, paradoxically, that our field is moving back toward a sort of particularism. Yet, as Gibson shows, the new mood of critical consciousness represents a further maturation of the field, a stage reflective of the closer scrutiny of organizational phenomena brought on, as Bidwell notes, by "the increasing pervasiveness of formal organization as a means for conducting social life." This increasing pervasiveness, in turn, is a development consistent with modernization and greater universalism.

The Uniqueness of Public Educational Organizations

There is increasing agreement that public education has suffered from too much indiscriminate borrowing and uncritical application of techniques, theories, and models from other sectors. Although there always has been some recognition of the unique characteristics of public educational organizations,[10] it is easy to see in retrospect that these characteristics and their implications have received insufficient attention. Of course, an important theme in the history of American public education has been the vulnerability of the institution to societal pressures for the adoption of efficiency techniques from the world of business and industry.[11] Yet, despite criticism of the cult of efficiency and the distortions introduced by likening the school to a factory, the propensity to engage in this kind of activity persists. Thus, as James Guthrie observes in his chapter, it is very doubtful that either the technical-industrial model of schooling and accountability or the private sector model of collective bargaining is appropriate for public education. But very few scholars have considered the goodness-of-fit and policy implications of these models for education. Indeed, as Griffiths notes, there has been little effort even to try to establish some criteria or guidelines for testing the transferability of findings or models from other sectors.

The moral that emerges from this is that educational researchers had better attend systematically to these goodness-of-fit problems, because if they do not it is unlikely that anyone else will. If public educational organizations are significantly different from most other kinds of organizations, and if few of the prevailing or existing models of organizations are truly applicable to them, then this argues for a distinctive field of study focusing on educational organizations and educational policy analysis.[12] However, we share Bidwell's concern that an emphasis on the uniqueness of educational organizations could lead to an unproductive narrowness of scholarship. To appreciate the uniqueness of public educational organizations, and to place it into a meaningful perspective, one must systematically compare them with other kinds of organizations, in both the public and private sectors. It increasingly appears that most modern organizations are more loosely coupled and political in their decision-making than the traditional bureaucratic model suggested. Thus, it could be, as some are suggesting, that public educational organizations are not so different from other kinds of organizations after all.[13] Or it may be, as Meckling and others contend, that they are. The final verdict on this is not in yet, but the list of significant differences is now quite impressive.

A useful way to approach these differences, and to summarize some of the themes in this book, is through a fourfold typology of organizations (figure 14-1) that varies on one dimension according to the ambiguity of ends and means (goals and technologies to achieve them) and on the other dimension according to location in the public or private sectors. This typology highlights the intersection of sets of organizational variables that have been of special interest to sociologists and economists. On one hand, sociologists have displayed particular interest in the organizational consequences of varying degrees of ambiguity about ends and means. On the other hand, economists, although mindful of the problems ambiguous ends and means create for the specification of a production function, have emphasized the importance of differences between public and private sector organizations in terms of the structure of incentives and related control and evaluation mechanisms. We suggest that it is the distinctive combination, in public educational organizations, of sets of variables from both of these dimensions that provides much of the basis for the peculiar problems of the species.

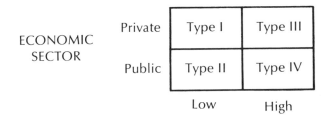

ECONOMIC
SECTOR

	Low	High
Private	Type I	Type III
Public	Type II	Type IV

AMBIGUITY OF ENDS AND MEANS

Figure 14-1. A Typology of Organizations.

Consider, for a moment, the contrasts between the various kinds of organizations in the typology. Type I organizations, such as automobile manufacturers, have relatively precise goals and technologies and respond to the profit incentives of the marketplace. Lacking a profit motive, Type II organizations, such as public sanitation departments, are inclined—sometimes notoriously so—to behave inefficiently, even though they share with Type I organizations the advantages of clear ends and means. Although both Types III and IV are plagued by ambiguous ends and means, private schools and elite psychiatric agencies—as compared to public schools and public mental health agencies—are disciplined by the marketplace. The discipline for Type II and IV organizations, on the other hand, must come about through a largely political process, and variation in ambiguity about ends and means affects this process.

Educational goals are ambiguous in several respects. The schools—and especially the *public* schools, because of their heterogeneous and largely captive clientele—are asked to pursue multiple, diverse, and sometimes conflicting goals. Moreover, there seldom is any consensus about the relative importance (preference ranking) of these goals—beyond goals of a very general nature—or the extent to which, and means by which, these (generally limitless) goals are to be pursued. In the absence of a science of pedagogy, the technology for achieving the ends of education remains something of a mystery. It is far from clear how the inputs into the educational process combine to produce educational outcomes.

The ambiguity of educational ends and means has a number of significant consequences. First, this ambiguity tends to require the use of highly trained employees, that is, professionals, for the delivery of educational services,[14] thereby creating the basis for tensions between professional and rank authority within the quasi-bureaucratic structure of the schools, and between professional prerogatives and client preferences. Second, the ambiguity of educational ends and means contributes to the peculiar loose coupling of educational organizations, which James March and Johan Olsen have characterized—some would say caricatured—as "organized anarchies." By "loosely coupled" organizations, scholars such as March and Olsen, and Karl Weick,[15] mean organizations in which, as John Meyer and Brian Rowan put it succinctly, "structure is disconnected from technical (work) activity, and activity is disconnected from its effects."[16] In this volume, Bidwell reports on research on Michigan school districts supporting loose coupling, but in the more precise terms of Herbert Simon's concept of "nearly-decomposable hierarchies." For example, "In contrast to repeated findings for economic organizations and for certain other kinds of organizations in the public sector . . . variation in the division of production labor . . . has no appreciable effect on either the relative size or the specialization of administration." In addition, Bidwell later notes that,

> Given the postulated near-decomposability of school districts, unless administrative growth is accompanied by proportionate increases in revenues, there will be less money to spend on production staff or materials. Kasarda and I have interpreted in just such terms our finding, first in Colorado and now in Michigan, of negative returns from administrative growth to school effectiveness.

Another consequence of the ambiguity of educational ends and means, and one highly significant in the context of the theme of this book, is that it impedes problem formulation, rational decision-making, planning, and evaluation. Thus, as a first step toward the analysis of school effectiveness, Bidwell calls for "work toward [a] more adequate conceptualization of technology by the naturalistic observation of schools and classrooms at work." The ambiguity of ends and means is functional, however, insofar as it facilitates compromise and the avoidance of the ethnocultural value conflicts that always lurk in the background of public education in a heterogeneous society such as ours. At the same time, this ambiguity often is exploited by contending interest groups as they pursue their own ends. In this regard, the ambiguity of ends and means makes "disjointed incrementalism" in decision and policy-making especially likely in education,[17] in part since groups that cannot agree on ends frequently find that they can agree on means.

To sum up our analysis, the case for the uniqueness of public educational organizations revolves in large part around the high degree of ambiguity surrounding both educational ends and means, and the particular framework within which educational services are delivered, that is, by professionals within public bureaucracies overseen, in the case of public schools, by (usually) nonpartisan elected local school boards.[18] Within this framework, the question of whose interest should be served, and how this should be determined, is, in fact, less clear than would be suggested by an organizational chart of a public school district, with the school board at its apex. Indeed, a central dilemma of public school government arises from "the dual but overlapping responsibility of school officers to a clientele and to a public constituency."[19] This dual responsibility problem makes the public schools essentially hybrid organizations in terms of the organizational typology suggested by Peter Blau and Richard Scott.[20] That is, the schools are partly commonweal organizations—whose chief beneficiary is the public at large—and partly service organizations, whose chief beneficiaries are the clients to whom they directly provide professional services. This hybrid characteristic of the public schools produces a certain ambivalence about their governance, which some have viewed as "schizophrenic."[21] Thus, on a wide array of policy decisions involving what are perceived to be routine and technical matters, the public and school boards generally tend to defer to the professional expertise and advice of educators. Yet, at the same time, the public and school boards profess to believe in lay control of education.

In the final analysis, then, there is a murkiness about the way in which the supply of public educational services is linked to public demands for these services. Here, the perspective of political economists further illuminates the largely sociological analysis above. William Niskanen's economic theory of bureaucracy and representative government suggests that legislatures (for example, school boards) will be unable to oversee or control bureaus (such as public school districts) in such a way as to prevent overspending, oversupply of services, and inefficiency.[22] In public education the problem of legislative oversight is compounded by the ambiguity of educational ends and means, the loose coupling of educational organizations that this ambiguity fosters, and the difficulty of balancing professional versus lay determinations of what needs to be done. Seen in the light of Niskanen's theory, school districts begin to correspond to a third category of Blau and Scott's typology, the mutual benefit organization, whose chief beneficiary is the membership or employees themselves. So, if the public schools, as hybrid organizations, appear schizophrenic, there may be a method in their madness.

Further insight into this "method" may be gained by asking—consistent with the methodology so succinctly, but suggestively outlined by Arthur Goldberg—how public school administrators and teachers are likely to behave given an incentive structure, or reward system, where, as Meckling notes, the organization (1) is tax financed, so there are no residual profits (property rights) and thus little reason for innovation; (2) lacks a survival mechanism, enjoys a largely captive clientele; (3) never has its output objectively evaluated because no one ever buys it; (4) employs a lock-step, seniority-based career ladder, which prevents any significant differential reward of employees for merit; and (5) is government operated, politically controlled, and regulated like a controlled economy. To the extent that individuals behave, as Meckling proposes, as resourceful evaluating maximizers of their utility, one cannot expect that such a perverse reward system will foster creative and efficient organizational behavior.[23] Indeed, given such an incentive structure, it is surprising that the public schools perform as well as they do.

When one recognizes these considerations, it is not surprising that the implementation of educational policy becomes an exceedingly political process within the organization, with substantial alterations of policy occurring during the process. Public school administrators, as Meckling observes, are constrained, caught in the middle between those above and below them, restrained in the alternatives they can pursue. They thus tend to be somewhat the captives of their "context-soaked situations"[24] and, to succeed, must engage in a high degree of political bargaining and coalition-building, although this often takes place in quite subtle ways, as Goldberg suggests in his remarks. Thus, a theme running throughout this book, and especially salient in the contributions by Griffiths, Bidwell, Wirt, and Goldberg, is that there must be more systematic study of the internal politics of schools, but, unlike much of the present politics of education literature, with special attention to variables that can be manipulated and to the consequences of alternative political patterns and policies.

The Promise and Challenge of Educational Policy Analysis

We began this book with Robert Lynd's observation that "the controlling factor in any science is the way it views and states its problems."[25] The contents of this volume show that the field of research in educational administration is experiencing a significant change in this respect. With the stimulus of an extraordinary degree of environmental turbulence, we have entered a period of critical consciousness and revisionist thinking. In the search for new paradigms that have practical relevance for the distinctive problems of educational organizations, the educational policy analysis approach provides a useful point of convergence for the multiple currents of our interdisciplinary field. Among several possible approaches to the concerns of the emerging synthesis, educational policy analysis has two key advantages. First, it can furnish a unifying umbrella for our diverse field and the multiple methodologies our contributors advocate. Second, it can help bridge the gap between theory and practice, because it makes theory and research answer the "so what" question—that is, of what use is this work in the real world? What difference could it make? What consequences for whom?

That the controlling factor in our field is changing is also indicated by the fact that researchers in educational administration are not only taking these questions much more seriously, but are beginning to ask them in a different way, particularly the question, *what* consequences for *whom*? Thus, in pondering the status of research in educational administration, Donald Erickson asks why the field of educational administration has been so preoccupied with organizational effects on administrators and teachers and, at the same time, so inattentive to research concerned with instruction and student outcomes.[26] Why, indeed, when the main purpose of the public schools is supposedly the production of valued student outcomes?

One answer may be that researchers of the past held "heroic" assumptions that whatever was beneficial for teachers and administrators would somehow eventuate in benefits for students. But another answer, in line with our analysis and Meckling's conclusions, is that the incentive system of public education, abetted by the ambiguity of educational ends and means, provides a setting that is not oriented toward student outcomes. Instead, the situation is nearly the opposite, for, as Jacob Michaelsen observes, "with the assurance of a budget independent of satisfied consumers" the final result is that "the needs of teachers and principals for control over their jobs most often take precedence over the needs of individual children and their families."[27] To put the point somewhat differently, since, as Jay Chambers argues, the costs of inefficient behavior in public schools (in terms of student outcomes or consumer satisfaction) are low, this in effect creates a "demand for inefficient behavior."[28] Thus, rather like regulatory agencies that are the captives (consciously or unconsciously) of the industries they are supposed to regulate, researchers in educational administration, in their selection of topics, may have assisted practitioners in responding to an incentive system that could scarcely be better designed to produce goal-displacement.

The task before us, then, is to redirect research and practice in educational administration toward a primary (but obviously not exclusive) concern for student outcomes. This would seem to be an obvious step, but the first challenge for a viable policy analysis approach will be to bring it off. The most expeditious way to shift to a concern for student outcomes—if not the most likely way, because of political obstacles—would be to change the incentive system of public education.[29] But, failing this, the task is not as insurmountable as our stark portrait of the unique context of public schools may at first suggest. The picture we have sketched out in broad strokes, under the strong influence of economic analyses of school decision-making, probably exaggerates the difficulties in front of us. First, at the microlevel—especially the classroom level—one can select, pursue, and evaluate educational ends and means that are not hopelessly ambiguous, as McNamara shows with his example drawn from the Murnane report. This example also shows that such inquiry can be linked to organizational decision-making and operations. Second, the professionalism of educators is not just a canopy for self-interest; it also accounts for much of the good that is done in spite of the perversities of the existing reward structure. The trick, to paraphrase Wildavsky, is to find organizational problems affecting student outcomes that can be solved at the level of action where they occur, within the time frame available, using instruments that can be controlled in public schools. To accomplish this fully, we ultimately shall have to link a more sophisticated organizational theory with a now practically nonexistent theory of instruction. This, as Bidwell notes, is no small task. But we do not have to build Rome in a day. There are leads in the literature now for how to proceed—incrementally but productively—if we will only look for them.[30]

For those who embark on this path, there are further challenges. The bulk of the most substantial and most rigorous work in educational policy analysis, the so-called school effects studies, has been done by sophisticated methodologists—economists and sociologists—who are not primarily identified with the field of educational administration. To fully understand this work, not to mention to do work at this level of sophistication, most researchers in educational administration will have to significantly upgrade their methodological skills.[31] At the same time, those pursuing the sophisticated school-effects studies, which typically have been done at the macrolevel, will need to increase their understanding of important microlevel considerations and to incorporate these considerations into their models in an effort to comprehend more fully the relationship between macrolevel variables and microlevel performance.

Another hurdle to be overcome, if the full promise of the educational policy analysis approach is to be realized, is the problem of communication. Researchers trained in the various applicable disciplines and fields—economics, sociology, psychology, political science, management, and educational administration—tend to approach educational policy and organizational questions in rather different ways and to use different jargons. Communication among these groups, and the blending of these approaches, although often laborious and never easy, is clearly worth the effort; we already can see the more sophisticated conceptions that emerge when the various facets the alternative approaches reveal are juxtaposed and reconciled.[32] When, at last, these and other related challenges are met, we can benefit from the full development of a sophisticated new approach to our field of study, one enabling scholars from the various disciplines to join together in improving the functioning of educational organizations—which by then will be much better understood. If this book helps to move us in this direction, we shall have been well served.[33]

Notes

1. Aaron Wildavsky, "Policy Analysis Is What Information Systems Are Not," *New York Affairs*, 4, no. 2 (Spring 1977):10-23.

2. See, for example, Michael Lipsky, "Toward a Theory of Street-Level Bureaucracy," in Willis Hawley et al., *Theoretical Perspectives on Urban Politics* (Englewood Cliffs, N.J.: Prentice-Hall, 1976), pp. 196-213; Dale Mann, ed., *Making Change Happen?* (New York: Teachers College Press, 1978); Paul Berman and Milbrey W. McLaughlin, *Federal Programs Supporting Educational Change*, vol. 4, *The Findings in Review* (Santa Monica, Calif.: Rand Corporation, R-1589/4-HEW, April 1975); James G. March and Johan Olsen, *Ambiguity and Choice in Organizations* (Bergen, Norway: Universitetsforlaget, 1976); and William Lowe Boyd, "The Politics of Curriculum Policy-Making for American Schools," *Review of Educational Research* 48, no. 4 (Fall 1978):577-628.

3. Clearly, the extent to which the proceedings of this seminar suggest an

emerging synthesis will be a matter of debate and personal interpretation. We acknowledge, as Daniel Griffiths emphasizes in his critique of the seminar, that there was much divergent thinking in evidence. But, in line with Charles Bidwell's concluding commentary, we also see significant lines of convergence on which our field can build and, indeed, already is building.

4. As Dean Griffiths remarked, in the presentation of his critique of the seminar, "the mood of the participants was much better" than at some of the recent conferences assessing aspects of educational administration.

5. Thomas S. Kuhn, *The Structure of Scientific Revolutions* (Chicago: University of Chicago Press, 1962).

6. David Harvey, *Social Justice and the City* (Baltimore, Md.: The Johns Hopkins University Press, 1973).

7. For an interesting discussion of the complexities of the intellectual climate for paradigm shift, see chapter 9 by Thomas Greenfield.

8. On the importance of the policy analysis approach, see especially the chapters by Haller and Strike, Bidwell, Guthrie, and Wirt.

9. For a discussion of some of the controversies surrounding the policy analysis approach, including the contention that it is "just a fad," see William Lowe Boyd, "The Study of Educational Policy and Politics: Much Ado about Nothing?," *Teachers College Record* 80, no. 2 (December 1978):249-271.

10. See especially Roald F. Campbell, "What Peculiarities in Educational Administration Make It a Special Case," in Andrew Halpin, ed., *Administrative Theory in Education* (New York: Macmillan, 1958); Richard O. Carlson, "Environmental Constraints and Organizational Consequences," in Daniel E. Griffiths, ed., *Behavioral Science and Educational Administration*, 63rd Yearbook of the National Society for the Study of Education, part 2 (Chicago: University of Chicago Press, 1964), pp. 262-276; and Matthew B. Miles, "Planned Change and Organizational Health," in *Change Processes in the Public Schools* (Eugene, Ore.: Center for the Advanced Study of Educational Administration, University of Oregon, 1965), pp. 11-34.

11. Raymond E. Callahan, *Education and the Cult of Efficiency* (Chicago: University of Chicago Press, 1962).

12. For an elaboration of the argument for a distinctive field of educational policy analysis, see Boyd, "The Study of Educational Policy and Politics."

13. See the rather ambivalent commentaries on this matter in Marshall W. Meyer and associates, *Environments and Organizations* (San Francisco: Jossey-Bass, 1978). For a recent review of the literature on the differences between public and private sector organizations, see Hal G. Rainey, Robert W. Backoff, and Charles H. Levine, "Comparing Public and Private Organizations," *Public Administration Review* (March/April 1976):233-244.

14. See, for example, J. Victor Baldridge et al., "Alternative Models of Governance in Higher Education," in Gary L. Riley and J. Victor Baldridge, eds., *Governing Academic Organizations* (Berkeley, Calif.: McCutchan, 1977), p. 4.

15. Karl E. Weick, "Educational Organizations as Loosely Coupled Systems," *Administrative Science Quarterly* 21 (March 1976):1-19.

16. John W. Meyer and Brian Rowan, "The Structure of Educational Organizations," in Meyer and associates, *Environments and Organizations*, p. 79. The loose coupling of public schools has seemed so striking to some researchers recently that they have felt that "there was reason to doubt whether they were studying organizations at all." Since public schools are obviously some *kind* of organization, this comment serves as a further example of the limitations of the bureaucratic conception that has so deeply influenced thinking about what organizations "look like." For this comment, see John H. Freeman, "The Unit of Analysis in Organizational Research," in Meyer and associates, *Environments and Organizations*, p. 335.

17. On this and other points in this paragraph, see Rachel Elboim-Dror, "Some Characteristics of the Education Policy Formation System," *Policy Sciences* 1, no. 2 (Summer 1970):231-253.

18. This summation is drawn from Boyd, "The Study of Educational Policy and Politics."

19. Charles Bidwell, "The School as a Formal Organization," in James G. March, ed., *Handbook of Organizations* (Chicago: Rand McNally, 1965), p. 1012.

20. Peter Blau and W. Richard Scott, *Formal Organizations* (San Francisco: Chandler, 1962).

21. L. Harmon Zeigler, "School Board Research: The Problems and the Prospects," in Peter J. Cistone, ed., *Understanding School Boards* (Lexington, Mass.: Lexington Books, D.C. Heath and Company, 1975), p. 8.

22. Both Niskanen and Michaelsen suggest that the distinctive features of this process, as it occurs in different areas of activity (such as school districts), may require separate modeling. See William A. Niskanen, *Bureaucracy and Representative Government* (Chicago: Aldine, 1971); Niskanen, "Bureaucrats and Politicians," *The Journal of Law and Economics* 18 (December 1976):617-643; and Jacob B. Michaelsen, "Revision, Bureaucracy, and School Reform," *School Review* 85, no. 2 (February 1977):229-246.

23. See the similar analyses by Michaelsen, "Revision, Bureaucracy, and School Reform"; and Jay G. Chambers, "An Economic Analysis of Decision-Making in Public School Districts" (unpublished paper, University of Rochester, 1975).

24. This evocative phrase is drawn from Dale Mann, "What Peculiarities in Educational Administration Make It Difficult to Profess," *Journal of Educational Administration* 13, no. 1 (May 1975):140.

25. Robert Lynd, as quoted in Ira Katznelson, "The Crisis of the Capitalist City," in Willis D. Hawley et al., *Theoretical Perspectives on Urban Politics* (Englewood Cliffs, N.J.: Prentice-Hall, 1976), p. 216.

26. Donald A. Erickson, "Research on Educational Administration: The-State-of-the-Art," *Educational Researcher* 8 (March 1979):9-14.

27. Michaelsen, "Revision, Bureaucracy, and School Reform," pp. 236, 240.

28. Chambers, "Decision-Making in Public School Districts." For a lucid and provocative exposition of this kind of analysis, applied to a diverse range of matters, such as the "demand for reckless driving," see Richard B. McKenzie and Gordon Tullock, *The New World of Economics* (Homewood, Ill.: Richard D. Irwin, Inc., 1975).

29. Proposals for the adoption of some sort of "voucher plan" are perhaps the best known alternative for changing the incentive system of public education. For a penetrating discussion of the legal and political obstacles to voucher plans, see Tyll van Geel, "Parental Preferences and the Politics of Spending Public Educational Funds," *Teachers College Record* 79, no. 3 (February 1978):339-363.

30. See the leads provided in the chapters by Guthrie, and by Haller and Strike, and those found in Erickson, "Research on Educational Administration"; and Erickson, *Educational Organization and Administration* (Berkeley, Calif.: McCutchan, 1977).

31. Fortunately, as a practical matter it appears that useful work can be done without necessarily invoking the full armamentarium of the school-effects researchers. See especially the suggestions in Erickson, "Research on Educational Administration."

32. In this respect, see, for example, the papers prepared for the National Invitational Conference on School Organization and Effects (San Diego, Calif., January 27-29, 1978) sponsored by the National Institute of Education (NIE). Interdisciplinary work has received a much needed, and very beneficial, boost from the NIE-supported centers and conferences on school productivity and organization.

33. It should be noted, finally, that although we believe that the educational policy analysis approach has compelling advantages—it is interdisciplinary, it embraces a variety of methodological approaches, and it has the potential to forge a stronger link between research and practice—it is but one of several avenues toward the concerns of the emerging synthesis in the field. It is not a panacea or the only approach. For example, there are also sound arguments in support of the "normal science" approach, as advocated by Willower (as distinct from Kuhn's use of the concept), and for the use of more powerful theory (new paradigms) in the study of organizational decision-making, as espoused by Griffiths, Goldberg, Meckling, and Gibson. Indeed, none of these avenues are mutually exclusive. In the end, it will probably be the avenue that is most inclusive of the concerns in a period of critical consciousness that takes inquiry and practice the farthest.

Index

Subject Index

Academic research: difference from operational research, 191; value of, 191-192
Administrative component: factors affecting size of, 118-119
Administrative technologies: list of, 217
Administrators: what they do, 43, 45-47, 77
Administrators as individuals: need for research on, 43, 45, 77
Analysis of variance: use of, 192-193

Career Development Seminar: reasons for, xiv; focus of, xiv; points of agreement at, 263
Cheap data: defined, 168, 278; contrasted with hard data, 168
CIPP model of evaluation: eleven criteria for, 215-217
Closed systems: models, 276; theory, iii
Coleman Report, 95
Collective bargaining in school districts, 99, 101-102
Consistency principle, 176
Consolidation of school districts, 98, 100-101; motives for, 98
Controlling factor, xiii
Cost-quality studies, 94-95
Created problem situation, 8, 19-20
Creativity, 10-11
Critical consciousness, 28, 33, 264, 279

Data: nature of, 168, 171, 172
Dilemmas: defined, 5-6, 15, 19
Disciplinary matrix, 52-53
Discovered problem situation, 7, 11, 19-20
Dynamic theory of educational production: development of, 115-116

Ecological analysis of organizational change, 123, 124-125, 128-129
Educational administration: constraints on, 162; objectives of, 162-163; political nature of, 140-141; political turbulence in, 141; and politics, 271-272
Educational goals: ambiguity of, 281-282
Efficiency in schools, 90-91, 94-95, 101-102, 103
Enlarged metaphor: defined, 136; uses of, 136
Equality of educational opportunity, 90-92, 103
Error variance: failure to consider in research, 171-172

Field studies: advantages of, 64, 66, 68; disadvantages, 67; need for, 263; similarities to multivariate approach, 69-70
Formulation of problems, 5, 9, 18-19, 20

Garbage Can Model of decision making, xv, 50, 55
Great Man Theory, 52, 57

Hard data: comparison with soft data, 168; defined, 168; in quantitative studies, 278-279
Hypothesis: falsification of, 164, 229-230

Idée fixe, 56, 58
Idiographic leadership, 11, 19, 57-58
Inquiry and practice: alliance of, 77-78, 79
Institutional effects on research, 251-256

Legal reform strategies, 90-94
Liberty in schools, 90-91, 97-98, 102-103
Loosely coupled structures, 55, 269, 275, 280; defined, 282; schools as, 117, 119, 120-121, 124, 128

Management techniques: defined, 159
Managers: constraints on educational, 161-162; evaluation of and rewards for educational, 162-163; responsibilities of, 158-159; techniques used by, 159-160; types of knowledge useful to, 157-158
Mathematical models: application of, 211-212
Methodology: defined, 159
Michigan school study, 117-123
Model of man, 158-159
Modernization: process of, 26-27, 33, 279-280
Multivariate methods of research: problems of, 69-70

Nomothetic leadership, 11, 19, 57
Normal science, 57, 66-68, 264-265

Omega squared, 270; advantages of, 199; as criticism of *EAQ* articles, 200-202; defined, 194-195; formula for, 195; mathematical calculations of, 194-198; to measure practical significance, 200-202, 241; in policy research, 241; size of scores with, 202, 203; suggested use in research, 203-205; use of, 193-198

295

About the Contributors

Charles E. Bidwell is professor of education and sociology and chairman of the Department of Education at the University of Chicago. He specializes in the sociology of education and currently is studying the relationships between organizational form and productivity in education.

Howard S. Bretsch, professor emeritus of education, University of Rochester, specializes in personnel and school district administration and the administration of higher education.

Jacob W. Getzels is the R. Wendell Harrison Distinguished Service Professor in the Departments of Education and Behavioral Sciences and the College at the University of Chicago. His research interests include the study of higher cognitive processes, values, and organizational theory.

R. Oliver Gibson is professor of education at the State University of New York at Buffalo. His research interests include personnel administration and intellectual history, especially related to educational administration.

Arthur S. Goldberg is the associate dean for graduate studies in the College of Arts and Sciences at the University of Rochester. His specialties include the philosophy of science, research methods, and evaluation design.

Thomas B. Greenfield is professor of education at the Ontario Institute for Studies in Education. His work currently centers on a reinterpretation and critique of organizational theory in educational administration.

Daniel E. Griffiths is the dean of the School of Education, Health, Nursing, and Arts Professions at New York University. He is a specialist in organizational theory and has engaged in extensive research on administration and decision making.

James W. Guthrie, professor of education, University of California, Berkeley, is a specialist on school finance and school governance. In this area, he recently has written on problems of accountability and the promise of the school site-management approach.

Emil J. Haller is associate professor of education at Cornell University. His research interests concern social class and schooling, policy research, and socialization processes in graduate schools.

James F. McNamara is professor of interdisciplinary education and educational administration at Texas A & M University. He is a specialist in management science, the use of quantitative methods, and educational policy research.

William H. Meckling is dean and professor of economics of the Graduate School of Management at the University of Rochester. He has done extensive research on the role of property rights and contracts in our society as they relate to human rights and freedom.

Robert L. Sproull is the president of the University of Rochester. Following an academic career as a physicist, his interests and activities have centered around the administration of higher education.

Kenneth A. Strike is associate professor in the philosophy of education at Cornell University. His interests include educational policy and philosophy of science with a particular interest in research policy.

Donald J. Willower is professor of education at the Pennsylvania State University. His main interests are schools as organizations and the theory-practice relationship in administration.

Frederick M. Wirt is professor of political science at the University of Illinois. His specialties include urban and educational politics. He currently is engaged in a comparative study of the role of the states in school policymaking in Australia and the United States.

About the Editors

Glenn L. Immegart is professor of education and chairman of the Center for the Study of Educational Administration, Graduate School of Education and Human Development, University of Rochester, Rochester, New York. His specializations are organizational behavior, decision-making, and leadership in education. He has done research on administrative behavior and ethics, decision-making, and systems approaches. He has also assessed research on leadership and educational administration and has developed case studies and simulated materials for the training of educational administrators. Immegart is coauthor of *An Introduction to Systems for the Educational Administrator* (1973) and coeditor of *Ethics and the School Administrator* (1969). Beginning in September 1979, he will be editor of the *Educational Administration Quarterly*.

William Lowe Boyd is associate professor of education in the Center for the Study of Educational Administration, Graduate School of Education and Human Development, University of Rochester, Rochester, New York. His specializations are educational policy and politics, the governance of higher and lower education, and organizational behavior. He has studied and written about curriculum policy-making, urban and suburban school politics, school board-administrative staff relationships, community control and decentralization, and school district governance under conditions of declining enrollments and retrenchment. He also has served as editor of the *Politics of Education Bulletin*, associate editor of *Educational Administration Abstracts*, and guest editor of special issues of *Education and Urban Society*. Beginning in September 1979, he will be an associate editor of the *Educational Administration Quarterly*.